speakout 2ND EDITION

Starter
Teacher's Book

with Resource and Assessment Disc

Jane Comyns Carr with Gabby Maguire

contents

TEACHER'S BOOK

Introduction

Teacher's notes

Resource bank

TEACHER'S RESOURCE AND ASSESSMENT DISC

Extra resources

- Class audio scripts
- Class video scripts
- BBC interviews
- Worksheets for BBC interviews

Tests

- Unit tests
- Achievement tests
- Mid-course test
- End of course test
- Test audio
- Test audio scripts
- Test answer key

STUDENTS' BOOK CONTENTS

DVD-ROM: **BBC** DVD CLIPS AND SCRIPTS　　�»)) BBC INTERVIEWS AND SCRIPTS　　▶ CLASS AUDIO AND SCRIPTS

LISTENING/DVD	SPEAKING	WRITING
listen to people say *hello*	introduce yourself	learn to use capital letters
	ask questions about people	
listen to people give personal information	give personal information	
BBC Around the World: watch a BBC programme about people around the world	speak about yourself and your country	write a personal introduction
listen to someone talk about photos	talk about photos of family and friends	learn to use contractions
listen to people talk about their daily routines	check information about people	
listen to people making suggestions	suggest things to do	
BBC The Royal Wedding: Willliam and Catherine: watch a BBC programme about a royal wedding	talk about five people in your life	write a description of five people in your life
listen to conversations between students	ask about objects	
	talk about possessions	use linkers *and, but*
listen to people in a café	order food and drink	
BBC Francesco's Mediterranean Voyage: watch a BBC programme about a famous market	buy things in a market	write about a market
listen to people talk about life in the USA	find things in common	use linkers
	find differences in pictures	
listen to people tell the time	tell the time	
BBC Amish: a secret life: watch a BBC programme about an unusual family	do a class survey	write a short report about lifestyles
listen to people talk about what drives them crazy	discuss bad habits	
	talk about what you eat	use to linkers to sequence
listen to a tourist asking questions	ask for tourist information	
BBC How to feed your kids: watch a BBC programme about children and food	discuss what food and drink to take to a desert island	write a forum entry

STUDENTS' BOOK CONTENTS

LISTENING/DVD	SPEAKING	WRITING
listen to a man stuck at a station	talk about places in towns; find differences between places	start and end emails
	ask and answer questions about transport	
listen to someone buy a bus ticket	buy a ticket for travel	
BBC **Visions of India: Rush Hour**: watch a BBC programme about rush hour in India	talk about travel in your country	write a travel forum entry
listen to people talk about New Year 2000	find out where people were in the past	improve your punctuation
	talk about the past	
listen to people give opinions	give your opinion	
BBC **The Chilean Miners' Rescue**: watch a BBC documentary about the Chilean miners	do a quiz	write a history quiz
	talk about first meetings	use linkers *so* and *because*
listen to a radio programme about holidays	ask and answer questions about a good holiday	
listen to someone asking for directions in a supermarket	give directions in a supermarket	
BBC **Little Britain Abroad**: watch a BBC comedy about tourists in Spain	tell a bad holiday story	write a travel review
listen to a radio programme about shopping mistakes	talk about how you spend money	write photo captions
listen to someone shopping	find the right gift	
listen to a woman talk about her problems getting to work	ask people to do things	write a story using linkers
BBC **Leila, the 'borrowing shop'**: watch a BBC programme about a borrowing shop	describe a favourite possession	write about a useful possession
listen to job interviews	discuss the best job for you	
listen to street interviews about people's goals	talk about plans	check your writing
listen to people start and end conversations	start and end conversations	
BBC **Miranda**: watch a BBC comedy programme about someone who wants to change their life	talk about when you tried to learn something new	write an interview

COMMUNICATION BANK page 148   AUDIO SCRIPTS page 154

Our first priority in writing *Speakout Second Edition* was to find out what people liked about the first edition and what could be improved. To that end, we asked teachers and learners around the world for feedback on every level of the course. What did they like? What worked well in class? What changes would they like to see?

We then took a fresh look at every single exercise in the series and improved or updated it based on the feedback we'd received. We revised the grammar, vocabulary and skills syllabuses in line with the *Global Scale of English*, we ensured that there was more recycling and practice of key language, and we included a wealth of up-to-date new material:

- **New BBC video clips** – The BBC video clips which accompany each unit are one of the most original features of the course. We've retained the most popular clips and included some wonderful new material from the BBC archive to engage and motivate learners.

- **New reading/listening texts** – Teachers really appreciated the range of authentic texts in the first edition. We've broadened the range of genres in the second edition to reflect the types of texts learners read outside the classroom. Listening texts are also more authentic and we've included a wider variety of international accents.

- **New pronunciation sections** – We've developed a stronger pronunciation syllabus. Teachers wanted more support in this area, so we now have a wider range of pronunciation features in the three input lessons in each unit. Further pronunciation practice can also be found in *Speakout Extra*.

- **New images and clearer design** – The overall design is lighter, less cluttered and easier to navigate. We've refreshed the photos and illustrations completely, and selected dramatic images to introduce each new unit. Great images motivate learners, and provide excellent prompts for language activities.

- **New supplementary material** – One thing teachers always ask for is 'more'. More grammar, more vocabulary, more pronunciation. There's only so much we can fit into the Students' Books but, for those who want more practice in specific areas, *Speakout Extra* provides a bank of additional exercises that can be accessed via the *Speakout* website. *Speakout Extra* includes grammar, vocabulary, pronunciation and skills practice as well as ideas and activities for exploiting the BBC clips and interviews. *Speakout Extra* will be updated regularly so don't forget to check it out.

We really appreciate the feedback you've given us and hope you find *Speakout Second Edition* even more stimulating and user-friendly than the first edition.

From left to right: Steve Oakes, Antonia Clare, JJ Wilson and Frances Eales

OVERVIEW OF THE COMPONENTS

STUDENTS' BOOK WITH DVD-ROM

- Ten units with 90 to 120 hours of teaching material
- Comprehensive *Language bank* with detailed explanations and extra practice
- *Photo bank* to expand vocabulary
- Audio material for use in class
- DVD content (BBC clips and interviews)
- Audio and video scripts

CLASS AUDIO CDs

- Audio material for use in class

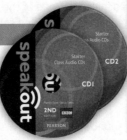
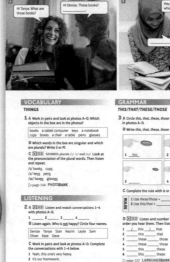
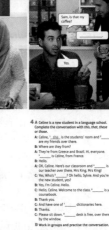

WORKBOOK

- Additional grammar, vocabulary and pronunciation exercises to complement material in the Students' Book
- Additional functional language practice exercises
- Additional reading, listening and writing practice
- Regular review sections
- With- and without-key versions

WORKBOOK AUDIO

- Audio material to practise listening, pronunciation and functional language
- Visit www.english.com/speakout to download the audio

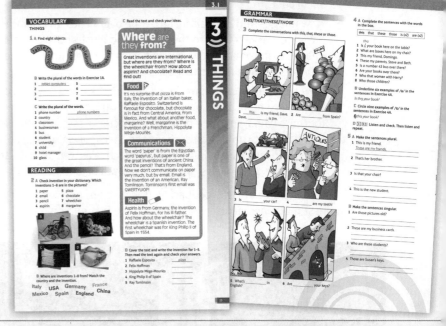

MYENGLISHLAB

Learning Management System that provides:

- Interactive Workbook with instant feedback
- Extra practice in grammar, vocabulary and skills
- Unit and achievement tests
- Mid- and end of course tests
- BBC interviews and interactive exercises

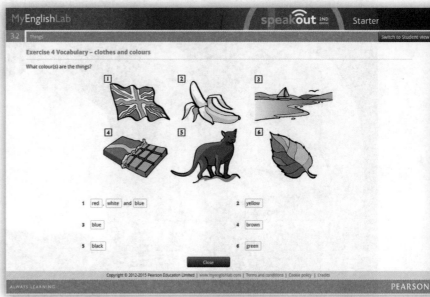

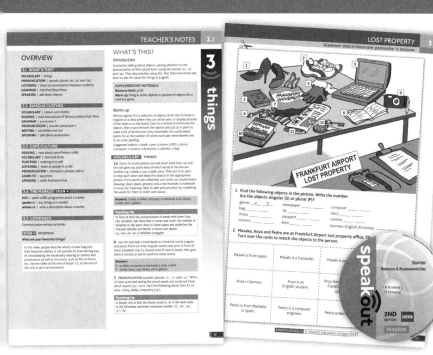

TEACHER'S BOOK WITH RESOURCE AND ASSESSMENT DISC

- Teacher's notes for every unit with warmers, fillers, alternative suggestions, culture notes and answer keys
- Generic teaching tips on useful areas such as grammar, lexis, pronunciation, using video, etc.
- Photocopiable grammar, vocabulary, and functional language worksheets for every unit
- Class audio and video scripts
- BBC interviews, worksheets and scripts
- Unit and achievement tests
- Mid- and end of course tests
- Test audio, audio scripts and answer keys

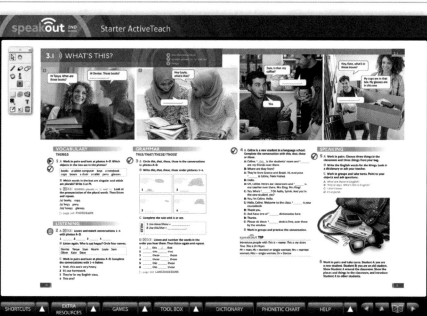

ACTIVETEACH

Software for classroom use to help teachers get the most out of the course:

- Integrated audio and video content
- Answer-reveal feature
- Large extra resources section
- Grammar and vocabulary review games
- BBC interviews and worksheets
- Assessment package containing all the course tests
- A host of useful classroom tools

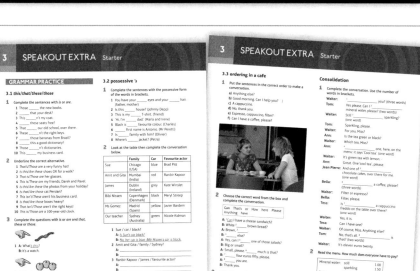

WEBSITE AND SPEAKOUT EXTRA

- Information about the course
- Sample materials
- Placement test
- Teaching tips and ideas
- Free downloadable worksheets provide additional grammar, vocabulary, pronunciation and skills practice (Speakout Extra)
- Extra video-exploitation activities to help learners get the most out of the course (Speakout Extra)

Speakout Extra and other teacher's resources available at:

www.pearsonelt.com/speakout

A UNIT OF THE STUDENTS' BOOK

Speakout Second Edition Students' Book is clearly designed and easy to use. Each unit follows the same pattern with an introductory page, two main input lessons covering grammar, vocabulary, pronunciation and skills work, a functional lesson and a skills-consolidation lesson based on a clip from a BBC programme. The unit culminates with a page of *Lookback* exercises and there is a detailed *Language bank*, *Photo bank* and *Communication bank* at the back of the book.

1. Striking images provoke interest in the topic
2. Language focus and outcomes clearly stated at the start of each lesson
3. BBC interviews provide 'models' of authentic language
4. Grammar presented in context with clear explanations and plenty of practice
5. Learners referred to Language bank at the back of the book for further practice
6. Key lexis introduced in context and expanded in Photo bank at the back of the book
7. Special pronunciation sections in each lesson
8. Focus on reading and/or listening in every spread
9. Writing sections focus on different genres and sub-skills
10. Focus on useful functional language
11. *Learn to* sections develop listening/speaking skills
12. Useful learning tips in each unit

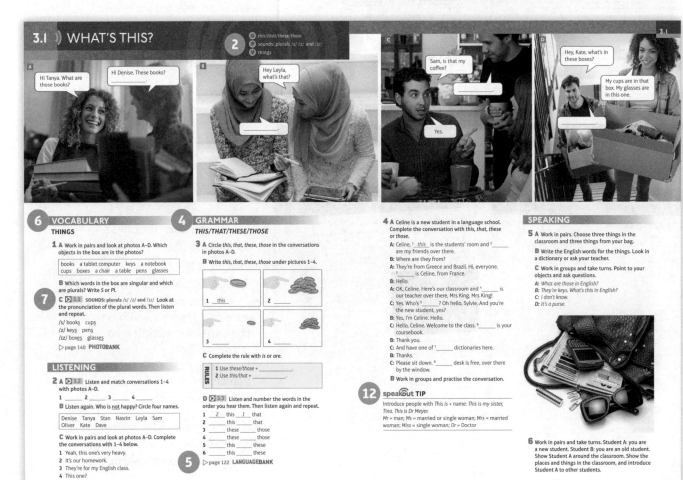

possessive 's
sounds: possessive 's
colours and clothes

6

VOCABULARY

COLOURS AND CLOTHES

1 A Write the colours and clothes from the boxes under the pictures below.

colours

| black white ~~brown~~ green |
| red blue |

clothes

| a hat jeans a shirt a jacket |
| a sweater shoes |

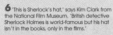

1 brown shoes   2 _____

3 _____   4 _____

5 _____   6 _____

B ▶ 3.4 Listen and check. Then listen again and repeat.

C Work in pairs and sit back to back. Take turns to describe your partner's clothes.

A: *Your shoes are brown.*
B: *No they aren't, they're white.*
▷ page 141 PHOTOBANK

2 A Complete the conversation in two different ways with words from the box.

| ring shoes great Spain |
| good on you my girlfriend |

A: Nice ¹_____ ²_____!
B: Thanks. It's/They're from ³_____ /_____
A: It's/They're ⁵_____ /⁶_____
B: Thanks.

B Work with other students and practise the conversation about their clothes or other possessions.

A: *Nice ring!*
B: *Thanks. It's …*

READING

8

3 A Look at the photos of films 1–6. Who are the film characters?

B Match the clothes a)–f) to the film characters 1–6.

C Read the article and check your ideas.

D Read the article again and find:

one nationality   two red things
one city   two jobs
two names of films   five names of people in films

4 A Work in pairs. Write two famous things or clothes from films.

B Work in groups. What are the best things or clothes for the exhibition?

A: *A black umbrella from Mary Poppins.*
B: *That's a good idea.*
C: *I don't know that film.*

IN THE FILMS

'In the Films' is a great new exhibition for cinema fans – an exhibition of famous clothes from films. So, what are the top six?

6 'This is Sherlock's hat,' says Kim Clark from the National Film Museum. 'British detective Sherlock Holmes is world-famous but his hat isn't in the books, only in the films.'

5 'Dorothy's shoes from *The Wizard of Oz*. They're a beautiful red colour,' says Kim. 'I really love red.'

4 'These are Mr Bean's brown jacket and red tie,' says Kim. 'His YouTube video from the London Olympics is famous around the world.'

3 'Harry Potter's glasses from the famous children's films. The boy wizard's glasses are in all eight films.'

2 'Is this James Bond's jacket?' I ask. 'Yes, it's James Bond's evening jacket,' Kim says. 'But in this photo of actor Daniel Craig as James Bond, his dinner jacket is black.'

SO WHAT'S NUMBER ONE?

'It's this gold ring' says Kim. 'Frodo's ring from *The Lord of the Rings*. It's the most famous ring in the world.'

a)
b)
c)
d)
e)
f)

GRAMMAR

POSSESSIVE 'S

5 A Add 's in the correct place in each sentence. Use the text to help.

1 This is Sherlock hat.
2 'These are Mr Bean brown jacket and red tie.'
3 'Is this James Bond jacket?' I ask.
4 At number five are Dorothy shoes from *The Wizard of Oz.*

B Complete the rule.

RULES | Use a name + _____ for the possessive.

6 A Add words to make the questions and answers.

1 these / Nico / books? Yes / they.
Are these Nico's books? Yes, they are.
2 that / Yasmin / bag? Yes / it.
3 those / James / books? No / they.
4 this / Kate / phone? No / it.

B ▶ 3.5 SOUNDS: possessive 's
Listen and check. Then listen again and match the names in 1–4 with the sounds.

/s/
/z/ Nico's
/ɪz/

C Change questions 1–4 to make questions about students and things in your classroom.

1 Are those Julio's books?

D Work in pairs and take turns. Ask and answer the questions.
▷ page 122 LANGUAGEBANK

WRITING

9

LINKERS *AND*, *BUT*

7 A Complete the sentences with *and* or *but*.

1 My favourite colour is blue _____ I really love this red T-shirt.
2 My favourite colour is blue _____ my favourite film is *The Lord of the Rings.*

B Choose the correct endings of the sentences.

1 It's a big gold ring with writing around it but
   a) it's the most famous ring in the world.
   b) the writing isn't in English.
2 Sherlock's hat is in all the films and
   a) it isn't in the books.
   b) it's a traditional hat from the countryside.
3 In the exhibition the jacket's white but
   a) in the photo it's black.
   b) it's from an old James Bond film.
4 One pair of these shoes is in a Hollywood museum and
   a) their price is two to three million dollars.
   b) Dorothy's dress is not in the museum.

C Add *and* (x3) and *but* (x3) to the information.

but
My name's Yves. It's a French name I'm not French, I'm Canadian. My parents are teachers I'm not a teacher. I'm a hotel manager my wife's the chef in our hotel. She's from Argentina her name's Natalia. She's a great chef at home I'm the cook! Our son's name is Tomas he's nine years old.

D Write about yourself and your family. Use *and* and *but*. Write 50–70 words.

SPEAKING

8 Work in pairs. Student A: turn to page 149. Student B: turn to page 151.

---

ordering in a café
intonation: phrases with *or*
food and drink

A global café

The first American-style Hard Rock Cafe (now forty-five years old) is in the centre of London. There are Hard Rock Cafes and Hotels in fifty-nine countries around the world: from Hong Kong, China to Buenos Aires, Argentina and Istanbul, Turkey. The cafés all have rock and roll memorabilia: guitars, photos and even a Cadillac from the 1950s. And clothes – for example, Michael Jackson's famous red jacket is in the Hard Rock Cafe in Washington D.C. These words are on the walls of all Hard Rock Cafes: LOVE ALL, SERVE ALL.

VOCABULARY

FOOD AND DRINK

1 A Look at the photo. Is there a Hard Rock Cafe in your town? What other countries is it in?

B Read the information. Are the sentences true (T) or false (F)?

1 The first Hard Rock Cafe is in the USA.
2 Hard Rock Cafes are in a lot of different countries.
3 The cafés all have rock and roll singers.
4 The jacket in one Hard Rock Cafe is Michael Jackson's.
5 Hard Rock Cafes all have one thing in common.

C Work in pairs and answer the questions.

1 What's your favourite type of café or restaurant, e.g. Chinese, Indian, pizza?
2 What cafés or restaurants are good near you?
3 What's your favourite food and drink in a café?

2 A Match phrases 1–6 with pictures A–F.

1 A sandwich and a coffee
2 A tea and a cake
3 A mineral water and a sandwich
4 A cola and a cake
5 A tea and a mineral water
6 A coffee and a cola

A
B
C
D
E
F

B Work in pairs and check your answers.

C Work in pairs and cover the words in 1–6 above. Take turns to order the food and drink.

A: *Can I help you?*
B: *A sandwich and a coffee, please.*
A: *OK, here you are.*

FUNCTION

10

ORDERING IN A CAFÉ

3 A ▶ 3.6 Listen to the conversations and correct the customers' orders.

1 one white coffee with sugar
2 two espresso coffees and one cappuccino
3 one egg sandwich (white bread), one chocolate cake, one cola
4 one sparkling mineral water, one sandwich

B Who says the sentences? Write C (customer) or W (waiter).

a) How much is that? C
b) Anything else?
c) Still or sparkling?
d) Can I have a mineral water, please?
e) No, thank you.
f) That's three euros.
g) Sparkling, please.

C ▶ 3.7 Number sentences a)–g) in order. Then listen and check.

4 A Complete the table.

	I have	a two	mineral water, please? coffees, _____?
Still Espresso		_____	sparkling? cappuccino?
			Sparkling, please. Espresso, please.

7

B ▶ 3.8 INTONATION: phrases with *or* Listen and tick the intonation you hear. Then listen again and repeat.

1 Still or sparkling?   2 Still or sparkling?

C Work in pairs and take turns. Ask and answer using the words in the box.

| Coffee / tea?   Espresso / cappuccino?   Still / sparkling? |

A: *Coffee or tea?*
B: *Can I have a tea, please?*

5 A Work in pairs. Add words to make a conversation.

Student A

| have / coffee, please? |
| Can I have a coffee, please? |

Student B
| espresso / cappuccino? |
| *Espresso or cappuccino?* |

| cappuccino |

| Anything else? |

| have / mineral water, please? |

| still / sparkling? |

| sparkling |

| OK / five euros |

B Work in pairs and take turns. Practise the conversation.
▷ page 122 LANGUAGEBANK

LEARN TO

11

SAY PRICES

6 A ▶ 3.9 Listen and number the prices in order.

| 3.00   2.50   10   1.50 J   5.20   12.75 |

B Listen again and repeat.

C ▶ 3.10 Listen to the conversations and write the prices.

speakout TIP

Say prices with the name (e.g. euros) or with no name: 3.99 = *three euros ninety-nine* OR *three ninety-nine.*

D Write four things and four prices.

newspaper – 1.25

E Work in pairs and take turns. Student A: read the things and the prices. Student B: write the things and the prices.

SPEAKING

7 Work in pairs. Student A: turn to page 148. Student B: turn to page 153. Then change roles.

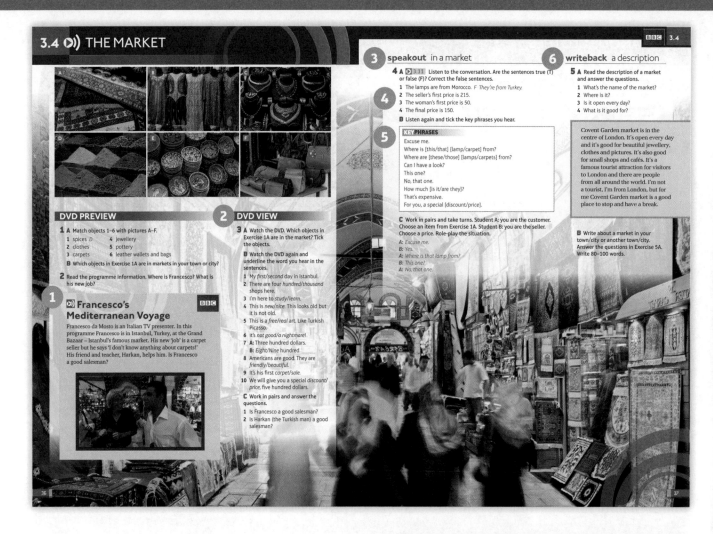

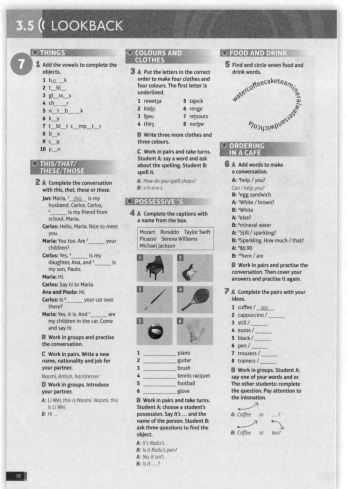

Speakout Second Edition Students' Book has a motivating DVD spread at the end of every unit. Based on authentic clips from the BBC's rich archive, these lessons are designed to consolidate language and act as a springboard for further speaking and writing tasks.

The *Lookback* page provides a review of key language covered in the unit with exercises that can be done altogether at the end of the unit or individually as and when appropriate. *Speakout Second Edition* also has a detailed *Language bank*, a *Photo bank* and *Communication bank*.

1 Learners read about the DVD clip in preparation for viewing

2 Different viewing tasks help learners understand and appreciate the DVD clip

3 *Speakout* tasks consolidate language and build learners' confidence

4 'Models' are provided to help learners perform the task

5 Key phrases give learners the language they need to perform the task

6 *Writeback* tasks provide further communicative practice

7 *Lookback* exercises are an enjoyable 'test' of language covered in unit

8 *Language bank* provides detailed explanations and further practice

9 *Photo bank* extends key lexical sets

10 *Communication bank* provides further opportunities to practise key language

8 GRAMMAR

3.1 this/that/these/those

	here ↓	there →
singular	this key	that key
plural	these keys	those keys

With *this/that*, use *is*:
*This **is** my book.*   *That's your book.*
With *these/those*, use *are*:
*These **are** my DVDs.*   *Those **are** your DVDs.*

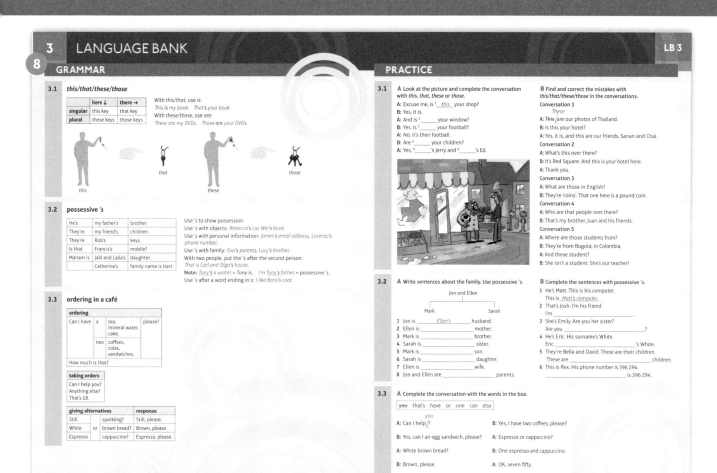

this   *that*   *these*   *those*

3.2 possessive 's

He's	my father's	brother.
They're	my friend's	children.
They're	Rob's	keys.
Is that	Francis's	mobile?
Mariam is	Jalil and Laila's	daughter.
	Catherine's	family name is Hart.

Use *'s* to show possession.
Use *'s* with objects: *Rebecca's car, Wei's book*
Use *'s* with personal information: *James's email address, Lorenzo's phone number.*
Use *'s* with family: *Eva's parents, Lucy's brother*
With two people, put the *'s* after the second person:
That is Carl and Olga's house.
Note: *Tony's a waiter. = Tony is.*   *I'm Tony's father. = possessive 's.*
Use *'s* after a word ending in s: *I like Boris's coat.*

3.3 ordering in a café

ordering

Can I have	a	tea, mineral water, cake,	please?
	two	coffees, colas, sandwiches,	
How much is that?			

taking orders

Can I help you?
Anything else?
That's £8.

giving alternatives		response
Still		sparkling?	Still, please.
White	or	brown bread?	Brown, please.
Espresso		cappuccino?	Espresso, please.

PRACTICE

3.1

A Look at the picture and complete the conversation with *this, that, these* or *those.*
A: Excuse me, is ¹ _this_ your shop?
B: Yes, it is.
A: And is ² _____ your window?
B: Is ³ _____ your football?
A: No, it's their football.
B: Are ⁴ _____ your children?
A: Yes, ⁵ _____'s Jerry and ⁶ _____'s Ed.

B Find and correct the mistakes with *this/that/these/those* in the conversations.
Conversation 1
    These
A: ~~This~~ /are our photos of Thailand.
B: Is this your hotel?
A: Yes, it is, and this are our friends, Sanan and Chai.
Conversation 2
A: What's this over there?
B: It's Red Square. And this is your hotel here.
A: Thank you.
Conversation 3
A: What are those in English?
B: They're 'coins'. That one here is a pound coin.
Conversation 4
A: Who are that people over there?
B: That's my brother, Juan and his friends.
Conversation 5
A: Where are those students from?
B: They're from Bogotá, in Colombia.
A: And those student?
B: She isn't a student. She's our teacher!

3.2

A Write sentences about the family. Use possessive *'s.*

Jon and Ellen
Mark   Sarah

1 Jon is _____ _Ellen's_ _____ husband.
2 Ellen is _____ mother.
3 Mark is _____ brother.
4 Sarah is _____ sister.
5 Mark is _____ son.
6 Sarah is _____ daughter.
7 Ellen is _____ wife.
8 Jon and Ellen are _____ parents.

B Complete the sentences with possessive *'s.*
1 He's Matt. This is his computer.
This is _Matt's computer._
2 That's Josh. I'm his friend.
I'm _____
3 She's Emily. Are you her sister?
Are you _____?
4 He's Eric. His surname's White.
Eric _____'s White.
5 They're Bella and David. These are their children.
These are _____ children.
6 This is Rex. His phone number is 396 294.
_____ is 396 294.

3.3

A Complete the conversation with the words in the box.

you   that's   have   or   one   can   else

    you
A: Can I help /↓   B: Yes, I have two coffees, please?
B: Yes, can I an egg sandwich, please?   A: Espresso or cappuccino?
A: White brown bread?   B: One espresso and cappuccino.
B: Brown, please.   A: OK, seven fifty.
A: Anything?

PHOTO BANK

9

1 A Match the adjectives with photos A–H.
1 angry   5 scared/afraid
2 happy   6 surprised
3 ill   7 unhappy
4 interested   8 well/fine

B Are the adjectives good (+) or bad (−)? Complete the table.

+	−
happy	

C Cover Exercises A and B and practice alone or with another student. Point to a picture and say the sentence.
He's angry.   She's ill.

Lesson 3.1 OBJECTS

1 A Match the names of the objects with the photos A–J.
1 a bag   6 a business card
2 a credit card   7 a newspaper
3 a picture   8 a clock
4 a dictionary   9 a pencil
5 a glass   10 a watch

B Work in pairs. Which objects are in the classroom?

2 A Write the plurals of the words in Exercise 1A in the correct place.

most words	+ -s	key – keys	pens
after -x, -ss, -sh, -ch	+ -es	box – boxes	
after consonant + -y	y + -ies	city – cities	

B Write the words in the box under the photos.

a boy   a man   children   girls boys   a woman   a girl   men a child   women

a boy

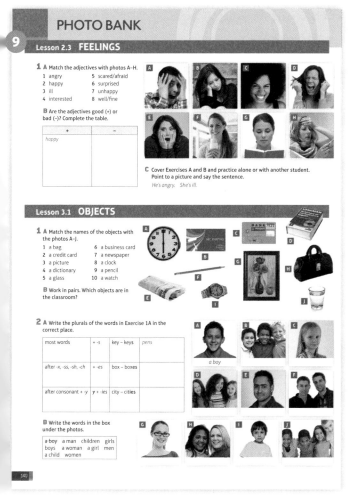

COMMUNICATION BANK

10

Lesson 1.2

6 A Student A: write two *yes/no* questions about each photo A–C. Ask about jobs and places.
Photo A: Is she a singer? Is she from the USA?   *Photo C: Is it in Russia?*

Kenji is from Japan. He's an actor.
Fatima is an engineer from Libya.
It's the city of Florence, in Italy.

B Ask Student B your questions about photos A–C.

C Listen to Student B and answer questions about photos D–F.

Lesson 1.3

2 A Student A: read the letters below to Student B. Listen to Student B and write the letters.

BBC   USA   VIP   FAQ   OK

Lesson 2.1

7 A Student A: look at the photos of your friends. Complete the notes below.

1
Name:
Nationality:
Job:
Where is he now?

2
Names:
Nationalities:
Jobs:
Where are they now?

B Work with other students. Cover your notes and talk about the photos.

Lesson 2.2

8 A Student A: look at the information below. Write questions to find the missing information.
1 *How old is Jakub Tomassi?*
2 *What's his …?*

Jakub Tomassi, ¹ _____ (age), and Julia Tomassi, 35, are husband and wife. Jakub is ² _____ (nationality) and Julia is from Canada. Their business is in ³ _____ (city), and they're taxi drivers. Their company name is ⁴ _____ (name) and their special taxi-bus is good for families and big groups.

Jon and Liz ⁵ _____ (surname) are brother and sister, and their Moroccan restaurant, *Rocco*, is in ⁶ _____ (country). They're not from Morocco, they're from England, but their restaurant is very good for Moroccan food.

B Work in pairs and take turns. Ask and answer the questions.
A: *How old is Jakub Tomassi?*
B: *He's 38. How old is Julia Tomassi?*
A: *She's 35.*

Lesson 3.3

7 Student A: you are the waiter. Take the customer's order.

MENU
€2.60   €2.40
€2.50   €1.75
€3.25   €3.90

WORKBOOK

Speakout Second Edition Workbook contains a wide variety of review and practice exercises and covers all of the language areas in the corresponding Students' Book unit. It also contains regular review sections to help learners consolidate what they have learned.

1 Extensive practice of vocabulary and grammar covered in the Students' Book

2 Additional practice of pronunciation points covered in the Students' Book

3 Reading and listening texts develop learners' skills

4 Writing exercises focus on useful sub-skills

Speakout Second Edition Workbook Audio is available online. Visit www.english.com/speakout to download audio material to accompany the pronunciation, listening and functional practice exercises.

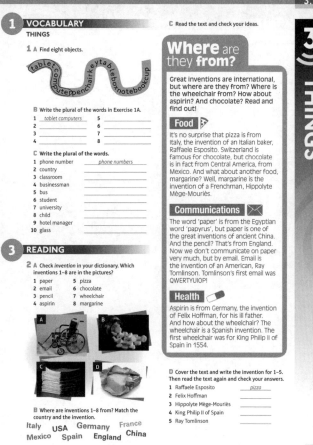

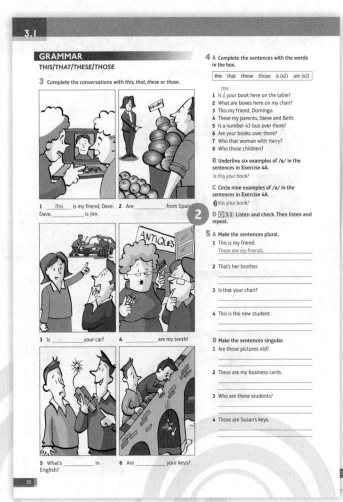

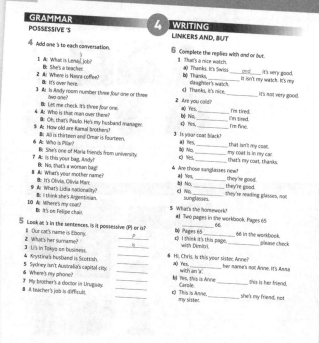

MYENGLISHLAB

MyEnglishLab provides a fully blended and personalised learning environment that benefits both teachers and learners. It offers:

- An interactive Workbook with instant feedback and automatic grade book
- A common error report that highlights mistakes learners are making
- Tips and feedback that direct learners to reference materials and encourage them to work out answers themselves
- Unit and achievement tests
- Mid- and end of course tests
- BBC interviews and interactive exercises

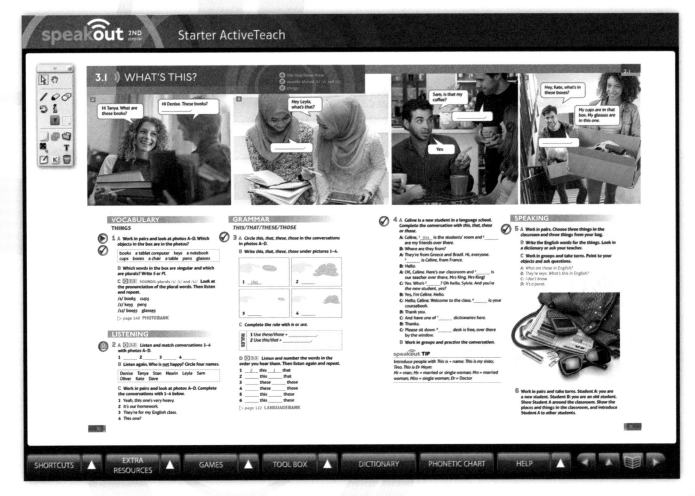

ACTIVETEACH

Speakout Second Edition ActiveTeach contains everything you need to make the course come alive. It includes integrated whiteboard software that allows you to add notes, embed files, save your work and reduce preparation time.

- Answers to exercises are revealed a the touch of a button
- Audio and video content fully integrated with time-coded scripting
- Shortcuts to the relevant pages of the *Language bank* and *Vocabulary bank* make navigation easy

- Extra resources section includes editable scripts, photocopiable worksheets, tests and BBC interviews for every unit with accompanying worksheets
- Grammar and vocabulary review games
- Assessment package containing all the course tests
- Useful tools include a regular keyboard, a phonetic keyboard, a stopwatch and scoreboard.

WEBSITE

Speakout Second Edition's website provides a wealth of information to support the course including:

- Information about the course, components and authors
- Introductory videos by the authors of the course
- Sample materials and free downloadable worksheets
- Teaching tips
- Placement test
- Editable audio and video scripts
- Global Scale of English mapping documents

Visit www.pearsonelt.com/speakout to check out the range of material available.

SPEAKOUT EXTRA

Speakout Extra provides a bank of additional downloadable exercises that can be accessed via the companion website:

- Downloadable grammar, vocabulary, pronunciation and skills worksheets
- BBC interviews and accompanying worksheets
- Additional worksheets to accompany DVD clips in the Students' Books
- Updated regularly with new material

Visit www.pearsonelt.com/speakout to check out the range of material available.

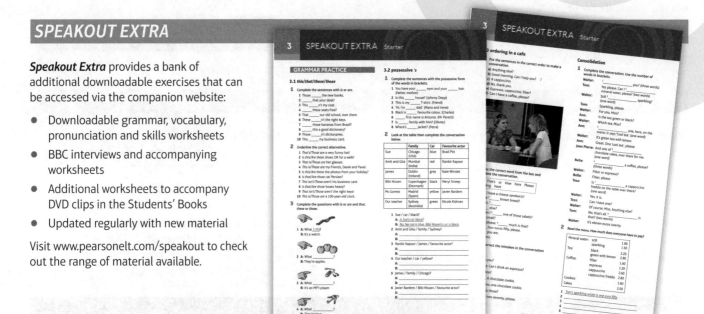

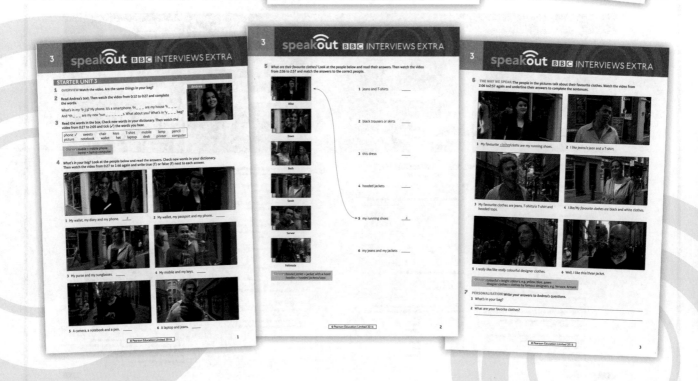

The thinking behind
Speakout Second Edition

Speakout Second Edition has been significantly updated and refreshed following feedback from students and teachers from around the world. It offers engaging topics with authentic BBC material to really bring them to life. At the same time it offers a robust and comprehensive focus on grammar, vocabulary, functions and pronunciation. As the name of the course might suggest, speaking activities are prominent, but that is not at the expense of the other core skills of reading, writing and listening, which are developed systematically throughout.

With this balanced approach to topics, language development and skills work, our aim has been to create a course book full of 'lessons that really work' in practice. Below we will briefly explain our approach in each of these areas.

TOPICS AND CONTENT

In *Speakout Second Edition* we have chosen topics that are relevant to students' lives and are global in nature. Where a topic area is covered in other ELT courses we have endeavoured to find a fresh angle on it. It is clear to us that authenticity is important to learners, and many texts come from the BBC's rich resources (audio, visual and print) as well as other real-world sources. At lower levels, we have sometimes adapted materials by adjusting the language to make it more manageable for students while trying to keep the tone as authentic as possible. We have also attempted to match the authentic feel of a text with an authentic interaction. Every unit contains a variety of rich and authentic input material including BBC interviews (filmed on location in London, England) and DVD material, featuring some of the best drama, documentary and light entertainment programmes that the BBC has to offer.

GRAMMAR

Knowing how to recognise and use grammatical structures is central to our ability to communicate with each other. Although at first students can often get by with words and phrases, they increasingly need grammar to make themselves understood. Students also need to understand sentence formation when reading and listening, and to be able to produce accurate grammar in professional and exam situations. We share students' belief that learning grammar is a core feature of learning a language and believe that a guided discovery approach, where students are challenged to notice new forms, works best. At the same time, learning is scaffolded so that students are supported at all times in a systematic way. Clear grammar presentations are followed by written and oral practice.

In *Speakout Second Edition* you will find:

- **Grammar in context** – We want to be sure that the grammar focus is clear and memorable for students. Grammar is almost always taken from the listening or reading texts, so that learners can see the language in action, and understand how and when it is used.

- **Focus on noticing** – We involve students in the discovery of language patterns by asking them to identify aspects of meaning and form, and complete rules or tables.

- **Cross-references to *Language bank*** – As well as a summary of rules within the unit, there are also cross-references to the *Language bank* at the back of the book which provides further explanation of the grammar point in focus as well as additional practice.

- **Plentiful and varied practice** – We ensure that there is plenty of practice, both form- and meaning-based, in the *Language bank* to give students confidence in manipulating the new language. Additional form-based grammar practice is also provided in the Workbook and in *Speakout Extra*. On the main input page we include personalised practice, which is designed to be genuinely communicative, and to offer students the opportunity to say something about themselves or the topic. There is also regular recycling of new language in the *Lookback* pages. Again, the focus here is on moving learners towards communicative use of the language.

VOCABULARY

Developing a wide range of vocabulary is key to increasing communicative effectiveness; developing a knowledge of high-frequency collocations and fixed and semi-fixed phrases is key to increasing spoken fluency. An extensive understanding of words and phrases helps learners become more confident when reading and listening, and developing a range of vocabulary is important for effective writing. Equally vital is learner-training, equipping students with the skills to record, memorise and recall vocabulary for use.

There is a prominent focus on vocabulary in *Speakout Second Edition*. We include vocabulary in almost all lessons, whether in a lexical set linked to a particular topic, as preparation for a speaking activity, or to aid comprehension of a DVD clip or a listening or reading text. Where we want students to use the language actively, we encourage them to use the vocabulary to talk about their own lives or opinions. At lower levels, the *Photo bank* also extends the vocabulary taught in the lessons, using memorable photographs and graphics to support students' understanding. Vocabulary items have been selected according to their usefulness with a strong focus on the following:

- **Vocabulary 'chunks'** – As well as lexical sets, we also regularly focus on how words fit together with other words, often getting students to notice how words are used in a text and to focus on high-frequency 'chunks' such as verb-noun collocations or whole phrases.

- **Vocabulary systems** – We give regular attention to word-building skills, a valuable tool in expanding vocabulary. At higher levels, the *Vocabulary plus* sections deal with systems such as affixation, multi-word verbs and compound words in greater depth.

- **Recycling** – Practice exercises ensure that vocabulary is encountered on a number of occasions: within the lessons, on the *Lookback* page, in subsequent lessons and in the *Photo bank/Vocabulary bank* at the back of the book. Additional vocabulary practice is also provided in the Workbook and in *Speakout Extra*.

- **Learner training** – One of the main focuses of the *Speakout* tips – which look at all areas of language learning – is to highlight vocabulary-learning strategies, aiming to build good study skills that will enable students to gain and retain new language.

FUNCTIONAL LANGUAGE

One thing that both teachers and learners appreciate is the need to manage communication in a wide variety of encounters, and to know what's appropriate to say in given situations. These can be transactional exchanges, where the main focus is on getting something done (buying something in a shop or phoning to make an enquiry), or interactional exchanges, where the main focus is on socialising with others (talking about the weekend, or responding appropriately to good news). As one learner commented to us, 'Grammar rules aren't enough – I need to know what to say.' Although it is possible to categorise 'functions' under 'lexical phrases', we believe it is useful for learners to focus on functional phrases separately from vocabulary or grammar.

The third lesson in every unit of *Speakout Second Edition* looks at one such situation, and focuses on the functional language needed. Learners hear or see the language used in context and then practise it in mini-situations, in both a written and a spoken context. Each of these lessons also includes a *Learn to* section, which highlights and practises a useful strategy for dealing with both transactional and interactional exchanges, for example, asking for clarification, showing interest, etc. Learners will find themselves not just more confident users of the language, but also more active listeners.

SPEAKING

The dynamism of most lessons depends on the success of the speaking tasks, whether the task is a short oral practice of new language, a discussion comparing information or opinions, a personal response to a reading text, or a presentation where a student might speak uninterrupted for a minute or more. Students develop fluency when they are motivated to speak. For this to happen, engaging topics and tasks are essential, as is the sequencing of stages and task design. For longer tasks, students often need to prepare their ideas and language in a structured way. This all-important rehearsal time leads to more motivation and confidence as well as greater accuracy, fluency and complexity. Also, where appropriate, students need to hear a model before they speak, in order to have a realistic goal.

In *Speakout Second Edition* there is a strong focus on:

- **Communicative practice** – After introducing any new language (vocabulary, grammar or function) there are many opportunities for students to use it in a variety of activities which focus on communication as well as accuracy. These include personalised exchanges, dialogues, flow-charts and role-plays.

- **Fluency development** – Opportunities are included in every unit for students to respond spontaneously. They might be asked to respond to a series of questions, to comment on a BBC DVD clip, interview or text, or to take part in conversations, discussions and role-plays. These activities involve a variety of interaction patterns such as pairs and groups.

- **Speaking strategies and sub-skills** – In the third lesson of each unit, students are encouraged to notice in a systematic way features which will help them improve their speaking. These include, for example, ways to manage a phone conversation, the use of mirror questions to ask for clarification, sentence starters to introduce an opinion and intonation to correct mistakes.

- **Extended speaking tasks** – In the *Speakout Second Edition* BBC DVD lesson, as well as in other speaking tasks throughout the course, students are encouraged to attempt more adventurous and extended use of language in tasks such as problem solving, developing a project or telling a story. These tasks go beyond discussion; they include rehearsal time, useful language and a concrete outcome.

LISTENING

For most users of English, listening is the most frequently used skill. A learner who can speak well but not understand at least as well is unlikely to be a competent communicator or user of the language. We feel that listening can be developed effectively through well-structured materials. As with speaking, the choice of interesting topics and texts works hand in hand with carefully considered sequencing and task design. At the same time, listening texts can act as a springboard to stimulate discussion in class.

The listening strands in *Speakout Second Edition* focus on:

- **Authentic material** – In *Speakout Second Edition*, we believe that it is motivating for all levels of learner to try to access and cope with authentic material. Each unit includes a DVD extract from a BBC documentary, drama or light entertainment programme as well as a BBC Interview filmed on location with real people giving their opinions. At the higher levels you will also find unscripted audio texts and BBC radio extracts. All are invaluable in the way they expose learners to real language in use as well as different varieties of English. Where recordings, particularly at lower levels, are scripted, they aim to reflect the patterns of natural speech.

- **Sub-skills and strategies** – Tasks across the recordings in each unit are designed with a number of sub-skills and strategies in mind. These include: listening for global meaning and more detail; scanning for specific information; becoming sensitised to possible misunderstandings; and noticing nuances of intonation and expression. We also help learners to listen actively by using strategies such as asking for repetition and paraphrasing.

- **Texts as a context for new language** – We see listening as a key mode of input and *Speakout Second Edition* includes many listening texts which contain target grammar, vocabulary or functions in their natural contexts. Learners are encouraged to notice this new language and how and where it occurs, often by using the audio scripts as a resource.

- **Texts as a model for speaking** – In the third and fourth lessons of each unit the recordings serve as models for speaking tasks. These models reveal the ways in which speakers use specific language to structure their discourse, for example, with regard to turn-taking, hesitating and checking for understanding. These recordings also serve as a goal for the learners' speaking.

READING

Reading is a priority for many students, whether it's for study, work or pleasure, and can be practised alone, anywhere and at any time. Learners who read regularly tend to have a richer, more varied vocabulary, and are often better writers, which in turn supports their oral communication skills. Nowadays, the internet has given students access to an extraordinary range of English language reading material, and the availability of English language newspapers, books and magazines is greater than ever before. The language learner who develops skill and confidence in reading in the classroom will be more motivated to read outside the classroom. Within the classroom, reading texts can also introduce stimulating topics and act as springboards for class discussion.

The reading strands in *Speakout Second Edition* focus on:

- **Authentic texts** – As with *Speakout Second Edition* listening materials, there is an emphasis on authenticity, and this is reflected in a number of ways. Many of the reading texts in *Speakout Second Edition* are sourced from the BBC. Where texts have been adapted or graded, there is an attempt to maintain authenticity by remaining faithful to the text type in terms of content and style. We have chosen up-to-date, relevant texts to stimulate interest and motivate learners to read. The texts represent a variety of genres that correspond to the text types that learners will probably encounter in their everyday lives.

- **Sub-skills and strategies** – In *Speakout Second Edition* we strive to maintain authenticity in the way the readers interact with a text. We always give students a reason to read, and provide tasks which bring about or simulate authentic reading, including real-life tasks such as summarising, extracting specific information, reacting to an opinion or following an anecdote. We also focus on strategies for decoding texts, such as guessing the meaning of unknown vocabulary, understanding pronoun referencing and following discourse markers.

- **Noticing new language** – Noticing language in use is a key step towards the development of a rich vocabulary and greater all-round proficiency in a language, and this is most easily achieved through reading. In *Speakout Second Edition*, reading texts often serve as valuable contexts for introducing grammar and vocabulary as well as discourse features.

- **Texts as a model for writing** – In the writing sections, as well as the *Writeback* sections of the DVD spreads, the readings serve as models for students to refer to when they are writing, in terms of overall organisation as well as style and language content.

WRITING

In recent years the growth of email and the internet has led to a shift in the nature of the writing our students need to do. Email has also led to an increased informality in written English. However, many students need to develop their formal writing for professional and exam-taking purposes. It is therefore important to focus on a range of genres, from formal text types such as essays, letters and reports to informal genres such as blog entries and personal messages.

There are four strands to writing in *Speakout Second Edition* which focus on:

- **Genres** – In every unit at the four higher levels there is a section that focuses on a genre of writing, emails, for example. We provide a model to show the conventions of the genre and, where appropriate, we highlight fixed phrases associated with it. We usually then ask the students to produce their own piece of writing. While there is always a written product, we also focus on the process of writing, including the relevant stages such as brainstorming, planning, and checking. At Starter and Elementary,

we focus on more basic writing skills, including basic written sentence patterns, linking, punctuation and text organisation, in some cases linking this focus to a specific genre.

- **Sub-skills and strategies** – While dealing with the genres, we include a section which focuses on a sub-skill or strategy that is generally applicable to all writing. Sub-skills include paragraphing, organising content and using linking words and pronouns, while strategies include activities like writing a first draft quickly, keeping your reader in mind and self-editing. We present the sub-skill by asking the students to notice the feature. We then provide an opportunity for the students to practise it.

- **Development of fluency** – At the end of every unit, following the DVD and final speaking task, we include a *Writeback* task. The idea behind these tasks is to develop fluency in their writing. While we always provide a model, the task is not tied to any particular grammatical structure. Instead the emphasis is on using writing to generate ideas and personal responses.

- **Writing as a classroom activity** – We believe that writing can be very usefully employed as an aid to speaking and as a reflective technique for responding to texts – akin to the practice of writing notes in the margins of books. It also provides a change of pace and focus in lessons. Activities such as short dictations, note-taking, brainstorming on paper and group story writing are all included in *Speakout Second Edition* and additional writing practice is provided in *Speakout Extra*.

PRONUNCIATION

In recent years, attitudes towards pronunciation in many English language classrooms have moved towards a focus on intelligibility: if students' spoken language is understandable, then the pronunciation is good enough. We are aware, however, that many learners and teachers place great importance on developing pronunciation that is more than 'good enough', and that systematic attention to pronunciation in a lesson, however brief, can have a significant impact on developing learners' speech.

In *Speakout Second Edition*, we have taken a practical, integrated approach to developing students' pronunciation, highlighting features that often cause problems in conjunction with a given area of grammar, particular vocabulary items and functional language. Where relevant to the level, a grammatical or functional language focus is followed by a focus on a feature of pronunciation, for example, the weak forms of auxiliary verbs or connected speech in certain functional exponents. Students are given the opportunity to listen to models of the pronunciation, notice the key feature and then practise it.

Each input lesson looks at a specific feature of pronunciation and the following strands are covered:

- **Sentence stress** – We help learners to identify which words are stressed in a sentence. This is particularly important for helping learners to understand rapid spoken English where the important information is highlighted by the speaker.

- **Word stress** – When dealing with new vocabulary, we emphasise the importance of using the correct word stress patterns. This helps listeners to identify the word being used and helps the speaker to use the correct vowel sounds.

- **Intonation** – We look at how intonation and the way we deliver a sentence can influence its meaning, or how the sentence is received.

- **Connected speech** – We help learners to understand rapid spoken English by looking at how the sounds change in fast speech. To encourage fluency we also help learners to produce rapid speech.

- **Individual sounds** – Sometimes specific individual sounds can cause problems for learners. We help learners to identify and produce specific sounds where they are important.

Additional pronunciation practice is provided in the Workbook and in *Speakout Extra*.

TEACHING STARTER LEARNERS

Starter can be the most rewarding level to teach; every lesson brings learners tangible advances in knowledge and skills, as they leave the lesson able to do or say something that an hour or two before was completely unknown to them. The particular challenges a teacher faces with starters require less in terms of knowledge of the language and more in terms of technique, in particular the ability to convey meaning of new language and instructions to people who may have heard little or no English in their lives.

It's sometimes said that there are no true starters in English among adult learners, because of the omnipresence of the language, but of course there are many who are beginning their study of English with no more than a handful of words and phrases and perhaps very little experience learning a language in a classroom. This point is perhaps one of the most important to keep in mind – that your starter students may find the context and routines of your classroom completely alien. Their expectations will be informed by their previous learning experiences, and may include a view of the teacher's role as authoritarian and directive. Routines and formats we take for granted, like checking an exercise in pairs, completing communicative activities with more attention to meaning than form, and working out grammar rules and meanings of words from context, may be new and even shocking to the starter learner. For this reason, considerable attention needs to be given to orienting starters to what's expected of them, to how to complete basic procedures, and most of all to taking initiative in indicating when they don't understand something. The nodding, smiling face of a starter may be hiding an utterly confused individual too afraid to show their disorientation, and it's vital that the teacher establishes a clear communication with students from the start, so that minutes and lessons don't pass where one or more students don't know what's going on.

Here are our top tips to help at this level:

- When planning your lessons, think through in detail how you will set up activities. It can be useful for starters to hear instructions in English and become familiar with some basic expressions, and that should be part of your routine. It's also important to invest time in demonstrating to students how an activity is supposed to be done. This is essentially learner training –training students how to function in a modern language classroom.

- Be realistic in your expectations of what starters can produce; while some starters can comfortably carry out speaking tasks in the Students' Book, some will be very reticent about saying anything at all. Aside from providing encouragement and support, often there is little you can do to hurry the pace of their learning.

- Review of vocabulary is important at any level, but at starter it is crucial. In part, because the sound system of English is new, starters find retention of vocabulary extremely difficult. Try to work vocabulary review games and activities into your warmers, fillers and coolers.

- Whenever learners do written tasks, whether they're copying from the whiteboard or completing a task in their books, closely monitor what they write in their notebooks. It's common for starters to have serious difficulties with English spelling, and important that the record they go home with is accurate.

- If you have a monolingual group and speak the learners' mother tongue, consider doing so very selectively. It's useful for learners to hear English as much as possible, and careful planning of instructions can make them valuable listening practice. And the more you rely on their L1 to communicate, the more they will – and the greater difficulty they'll have becoming functional in English.

- If you have a multilingual group, consider providing extra support and/or homework for learners who are not able to rely on having similar words or grammar in their language or who have particular skills needs such as coping with a different script.

- If you're the kind of teacher who likes to adapt the Students' Book, consider limiting the extent to which you do this at starter. A first English course can be daunting for beginners, and the Students' Book can serve as a kind of anchor for them; and if they found a lesson completely overwhelming, it's much easier for them to go home and review the lesson if it came directly from the Students' Book.

- Be consistent about giving and checking homework, such as exercises in the workbook. A large proportion of learning – particularly retention – happens during self-study rather than during formal lessons.

- Finally, keep in mind that a language lesson may be an emotional and stressful experience for starters, more than at any other level. For this reason, things that make each individual feel recognised and 'human' – encouragement, praise, the use of students' names, even a well-placed smile or eye contact (where culturally appropriate) – can go a long way towards students leaving a lesson feeling positive and motivated, and looking forward to the next one.

Antonia Clare, Frances Eales, Steve Oakes and JJ Wilson

The Global Scale of English

The Global Scale of English (GSE) is a standardised, granular scale that measures English language proficiency. The scale is part of a wider GSE ecosystem that includes Learning Objectives or 'can do' statements that describe exactly what a learner can do at each point on the scale, teaching and learning materials in a variety of media, and low- and high-stakes tests – all aligned to the Global Scale of English. Using the Global Scale of English students and teachers can now answer three questions accurately: Exactly how good is my English? What progress have I made towards my learning goal? What do I need to do next if I want to improve?

Unlike some other frameworks that measure English proficiency in broad bands, the Global Scale of English identifies what a learner can do at each point on a scale from 10–90, across each of the four skills: listening, reading, speaking and writing. This allows learners and teachers to understand a learner's exact level of proficiency, what progress they've made and what they need to learn next.

The Global Scale of English is designed to motivate learners by making it easier to demonstrate granular progress in their language ability. Teachers can use their knowledge of their students' Global Scale of English levels to choose course materials that are precisely matched to ability and learning goals. The Global Scale of English serves as a standard against which English language courses and assessments worldwide can be benchmarked, offering a truly global and shared understanding of language proficiency levels.

Visit English.com/gse for more information about the Global Scale of English.

SPEAKOUT SECOND EDITION AND THE GSE

The authors and editorial team were informed by the GSE Learning Objectives for Adult Learners during the writing and development of *Speakout Second Edition*. Revisions to the grammar, vocabulary and skills syllabuses were influenced by these GSE Learning Objectives, and they helped to ensure that the outcomes of each lesson are clear, meaningful and relevant to learners. The spread below shows how the GSE Learning Objectives for Adult learners are reflected in the skills content of a typical lesson of Speakout *Starter Second Edition*:

1. Can identify basic factual information in very simple texts. (Reading GSE 36)
2. Can follow speech which is very slow and carefully articulated, with long pauses. (Listening GSE 36)
3. Can use brief, everyday expressions to describe wants and needs, and request information. (Speaking GSE 37)
4. Can write simple sentences about things that they and other people have. (Writing GSE 37)

Visit www.pearsonelt.com/speakout for the full list of GSE Learning Objectives for Adult Learners covered in each level of *Speakout Second Edition*.

LEAD-IN

The activities on the Lead-in page are designed for you and your Ss to check what English they already know. Use the activities to help build Ss' confidence and encourage good classroom habits such as working in pairs to share ideas, check answers and practise speaking.

> **SUPPLEMENTARY MATERIALS**
> **Speakout tip:** bring in a small notebook to show Ss how to start a phrasebook.

NUMBERS 1–10

1A Start by demonstrating the activity: write *0 _____ 1 _____ 2 _____* on the board and ask Ss to call out the numbers. Write *two zero one* underneath, point at *0 _____* and gesture for Ss to call out the word, then write *zero* in the gap. Direct Ss to the activity and allow time for them to complete the gaps.

B Gesture to show Ss that you want them to listen and check their answers, then play the recording. Play the word *zero* again and pause the recording: gesture to invite the whole class to repeat together. Then play the rest of the recording, stopping if necessary to make sure Ss have time to repeat.

> **Answers: 1** one **2** two **3** three **4** four **5** five **6** six **7** seven **8** eight **9** nine **10** ten

> **Lead-in** Recording 1
>
> zero   one   two   three   four   five   six   seven   eight   nine   ten

C Demonstrate the activity by playing the first number on the recording and gesturing for Ss to write it down. Ask Ss to tell you the number (*seven*) and write it on the board. Play the rest of the recording, then give Ss time to compare their answers in pairs.

> **Lead-in** Recording 2
>
> seven   two   five   three   ten   nine   four   one   zero   eight   six

> **Optional extra activity**
>
> Tell Ss to write a list of five numbers (from 0–10) in any order. Put Ss in pairs and tell them to take turns to dictate their numbers to their partner. They then check each other's lists.

D Demonstrate this yourself with a **stronger student**, then put Ss in pairs. You could extend the activity by asking Student B to say the previous number instead of the next number.

INTERNATIONAL ENGLISH

2A Direct Ss to the photos and ask them to call out the names of the items. Then direct them to the word box and ask them to write the words next to the correct photos.

B Play the recording for Ss to check their answers. Play the recording again and encourage Ss to repeat the words in chorus.

> **Answers: 1** DVD **2** chocolate **3** hotel **4** phone **5** bus **6** football

> **Lead-in** Recording 3
>
> **1** DVD **2** chocolate **3** hotel **4** phone **5** bus **6** football

C Before putting Ss into pairs, use the photos and mime to elicit one or two further examples of international words, e.g. *sport, computer, radio*. To make the activity more competitive, you could give the pairs a time limit of ninety seconds to think of more international words. Then invite pairs to share their answers with the class.

> ▷ **PHOTOBANK** p138
>
> In Ex 1A, Ss match the words with the photos, then compare answers in pairs. In Ex 1B, Ss work in pairs and tick ✓ the words which are the same in their language, then count them and compare their totals with the rest of the class.
>
> **Answers:**
> **1A 1** B **2** C **3** J **4** H **5** L **6** G **7** N **8** I **9** K **10** M **11** E **12** A **13** D **14** F

CLASSROOM LANGUAGE

3A Tell Ss to cover the conversations (e.g. with their notebooks). Write on the board: a) in a taxi, b) in a supermarket, c) in a classroom, then gesture for Ss to listen and tell them to decide where the people are. Play the recording (Answer: c) in a classroom).

Teaching tip

It is important to make sure that students understand the context of a recording (where it takes place, who is speaking, etc.), e.g. by giving them a 'gist' question to answer, before they look at the details of the language used.

Direct Ss to the conversations in their books and focus on the underlined example. Establish that 'What's *libro* in English?' is correct (e.g. with a ✓ on the board). Direct Ss to the next line and ask if *I not know* or *I don't know* is correct. Put Ss in pairs to continue. Play the recording again for them to check their answers.

Answers: 2 don't **3** write **4** don't **5** page **6** repeat

B You could start by asking a ***stronger student*** to take the B role and practise each of the conversations with you in front of the class, then put Ss in pairs to practise. You could extend the activity by asking them to substitute different English words in Conversation 1 and different page numbers in Conversation 2. Monitor the practice and ask pairs who did well to perform their conversations for the class.

Lead-in Recording 4

Conversation 1
A: OK, Antonio. What's 'libro' in English?
B: Sorry, I don't know.
A: It's 'book'.
B: Can you write it, please?
A: Yes …

Conversation 2
A: OK. Open your books, please.
B: Sorry, I don't understand.
A: Open, like this.
B: Which page?
A: Page eight.
B: Can you repeat that, please?
A: Yes, page eight.
B: Thank you.

▷ PHOTOBANK p138

Ss match the words with the photos, then compare answers in pairs.

Answers:
2 D **3** F **4** C **5** K **6** J **7** A **8** B **9** G **10** L **11** I **12** E

Optional extra activity

Put Ss in pairs and tell Student A to cover the list of classroom language verbs, Photobank p138. Student B reads out a verb from the list and Student A acts it out.

speakout TIP

Show Ss the notebook you brought in and write *phrasebook* on the board. Tell Ss to bring a notebook like this to their English lessons and direct them to the examples (*Hello, Hi*, etc.). Ask the class what classroom language phrases they could write in the book (*Can you write it, please?* etc.).

OVERVIEW

1.1 WHERE ARE YOU FROM?

LISTENING | listen to people say hello
GRAMMAR | *be: I/you*
PRONUNCIATION | sentence stress
VOCABULARY | countries
PRONUNCIATION | word stress
WRITING | learn to use capital letters
SPEAKING | introduce yourself

1.2 ARRIVALS

VOCABULARY | jobs
PRONUNCIATION | word stress
READING | read descriptions of people arriving at an airport
GRAMMAR | *be: he/she/it*
SPEAKING | ask questions about people

1.3 HOW DO YOU SPELL ...?

VOCABULARY | the alphabet
PRONUNCIATION | the alphabet
FUNCTION | giving personal information
PRONUNCIATION | sentence stress
LISTENING | listen to people give personal information
LEARN TO | check spelling
SPEAKING | give personal information

1.4 AROUND THE WORLD B B C))) DVD

DVD | watch a BBC documentary about people from around the world
speakout | speak about you and your country
writeback | write a personal introduction

1.5 LOOKBACK

Communicative revision activities

B B C))) INTERVIEWS

Where are you from?

In this video people introduce themselves, say where they are from and what their job is. It can provide a fun introduction to the unit, but it is also valuable as a revision tool at the end of the unit, consolidating Ss' knowledge of the verb *be* as well as vocabulary related to introducing yourself and jobs.

WHERE ARE YOU FROM?

Introduction

Ss practise introducing themselves, using *be* and the names of countries and towns/cities. They also practise listening, and learn to use sentence and word stress in speaking, and capital letters in writing.

> **SUPPLEMENTARY MATERIALS**
> **Resource bank:** p141
> **Warm up:** have a map of the world available in the classroom, e.g. on a poster, a globe or on the internet.
> **Ex 6A:** prepare slips of paper for Ss to write chat messages.

Warm up

Use the world map to brainstorm the names of countries. Ask Ss to call out any countries whose names they know in English, and point to the relevant countries on the map as they are called out. Don't worry too much about correcting pronunciation at this stage, as this will be dealt with in the lesson. Alternatively, invite Ss to take turns coming to the map and pointing to countries for their classmates to name.

LISTENING

1A Direct Ss to one of the photos (A–C) and encourage them to predict where the people could be from, by pointing to each one and asking *England? Spain?* etc. Establish that there are many possibilities. Gesture to show that Ss are going to listen to a recording, then write the numbers 1–3 on the board. Point to the three photos and demonstrate that you want Ss to write the letter A, B or C next to each number. Explain Ss should listen to the background noise to establish where the conversations are by using 'restaurant' as an example: people talking and laughing, background music, the sounds of glasses, plates, cutlery, etc. Play the recording and give Ss time to compare their answers before eliciting them.

Answers: 1 C   2 B   3 A

> **Teaching tip**
>
> Put Ss in pairs to compare their answers to a listening task. This helps to build their confidence before sharing their answers with the class, and encourages a cooperative, non-competitive atmosphere in the classroom. As you monitor this pairwork, you can also see whether Ss are struggling with some of the answers, and identify whether you need to give more guidance on what to listen for and play the recording again.

B Before playing the recording again, spend a few minutes helping Ss to familiarise themselves with the names in the table (by writing or displaying a copy of it on the board). Point out/Elicit that Steve is male and Carmen and Katie are female. Read out the names of the countries and cities, so that Ss recognise them when they hear them on the recording. Demonstrate that Ss need to match the names, countries and cities by drawing arrows between them, as in the example. Play the recording, then give Ss time to compare answers. Replay the recording if necessary. Then check the answers with the class.

Answers: 2 Katie–Ireland–Dublin   3 Steve–Australia–Melbourne

Teaching tip

When checking answers with the whole class, call on individual Ss to give their answer, then ask the rest of the class if they agree, rather than allowing several Ss to call out their answers at once. This gives you more control over the feedback and makes the process clearer for the Ss.

Unit 1 Recording 1

Conversation 1
A: Hello, I'm Diana.
B: Hi, I'm Carmen.
A: Nice to meet you.
B: You too.
A: Where are you from?
B: I'm from Spain.
A: Oh, where in Spain?
B: From Madrid.

Conversation 2
A: Hi, I'm Tom.
B: Hi, I'm Katie.
A: Nice to meet you.
B: You too.
A: Are you from Ireland?
B: Yes, I am.
A: Oh, where in Ireland?
B: From Dublin.

Conversation 3
A: Hi, I'm James.
B: Hello, I'm Steve.
A: Nice to meet you.
B: You too.
A: Where are you from?
B: I'm from Australia
A: Oh. Are you from Sydney?
B: No, I'm not. I'm from Melbourne.

GRAMMAR *BE: I/YOU*

2A You may want to write or display copies of these tables on the board. Demonstrate *complete* by pointing to the first gap and eliciting from Ss that *are* is missing, then write it in. Also point out that *I'm* is short for *I am*, but that people always use *I'm* in conversation. Give Ss a minute or two to complete the tables: you could encourage them to consult the audio script if they wish.

Answers: Where *are* you from?/*Are* you from Sydney? No, I'm *not*. (NB: Remind Ss that the capital *A* is necessary because *are* is at the beginning of the question. You could also point out that the first question could have many answers, whereas the second has the answers *Yes* or *No*.)

B PRONUNCIATION sentence stress Write the answers on the board (without the underlining) and give Ss time to copy them into their notebooks. Before playing the recording, say *I'm Carmen* in two ways: *I'm Carmen* and *I'm Carmen* (you will need to exaggerate the stress to make sure that Ss hear the difference) and point out/ elicit that the first way sounds more natural because the stress is on the important information, i.e. the person's name. Demonstrate underlining the stressed word in the sentence, then play the recording.

Answers:
I'm Carmen. I'm from Spain.
Where are you from?
Are you from Sydney?
Yes, I am.
No, I'm not.

C Pause the recording after each sentence and gesture for Ss to repeat in chorus. You could then also ask a few individual Ss to repeat, taking the opportunity to correct any problems with word stress.

▷ LANGUAGEBANK 1.1 p118–119

Give Ss a minute or two to look at the tables and point out the inversion of the subject and *be* in the question form. Ss could do Ex 1.1A in class, then practise the complete conversation in pairs. They could do Ex 1.1B in class or for homework.

Answers:
A 2 I   3 Are   4 Am   5 not   6 aren't   7 I'm   8 're   9 'm
   10 you're   11 you   12 I'm
B 2 Where are you from?   3 I'm from Italy.
   4 Are you from Rome?   5 No, I'm not.   6 I'm from Venice.
   7 Are you from Rome?   8 No, I'm not from Italy.
   9 I'm from Ankara, in Turkey.

3A Go through the example with the class. You could also complete the second gap with the class as another example. Ss can then complete the conversations individually or work in pairs. If Ss ask about the meaning of *meet*, you could demonstrate this by acting out meeting a student for the first time. Point out that *You too* is a short way to say *Nice to meet you* when you reply.

Teaching tip

There are many phrases such as *Nice to meet you* and *You too* which are easier to deal with as a 'fixed' phrase, i.e. what we say when we meet someone new. Remind Ss to add these to their phrasebooks.

B Play the recording for Ss to check their answers. You may want to write or display the conversations on the board in order to go through the answers with the class.

Answers:
2 'm   3 are   4 'm   5 'm   6 'm   7 are   8 'm   9 Are

C Put Ss in pairs to practise the conversations. Monitor and listen for examples of good use of the verb *be* and give the class praise for these in feedback.

D Start by demonstrating this yourself with a **strong student**, or ask two **stronger Ss** to demonstrate. Then put Ss in pairs to practise. You could extend this by asking Ss to stand up and walk around, introducing themselves to the rest of the class. Demonstrate this by walking up to a student and introducing yourself, then gesture for everyone to stand up and do the same.

VOCABULARY COUNTRIES

4A Direct the class to the country outlines and ask them to call out the names of the countries. Don't worry about correcting pronunciation: this will be covered in the next two stages. Put Ss in pairs to write the names of the countries in the box next to the capital cities.

B Play the recording for Ss to check their answers.

Answers: 1 Russia   2 China   3 the UK   4 Brazil   5 the USA
6 Germany   7 Turkey   8 Italy

C PRONUNCIATION word stress Demonstrate underlining the stressed syllable in *Russia* on the board, pointing out that Ss need to underline the vowel – *a, e, i, o* or *u*. Before Ss listen again, they should write out the countries in the order that they appear on the recording in their notebooks, to make the underlining task more manageable.

> **Answers:** 2 China 3 the UK 4 Brazil 5 the USA 6 Germany
> 7 Turkey 8 Italy

When you play the recording again for Ss to repeat in chorus, pause on the more difficult countries and invite individuals to repeat. This will give you a chance to correct pronunciation.

D Demonstrate this yourself two or three times with **stronger Ss** and point out that the answers start *It's in …* (Ss are likely to say *Is in …*). Then put Ss into pairs to practise. You could extend this activity by telling Student A to say a country and Student B to reply with the name of its capital city.

speakout TIP

You may want to suggest that Ss keep new vocabulary in their phrasebook, and perhaps have pages for different topics, e.g. countries and cities. You could also show them how to keep a record of the stress pattern next to the word, using large and small circles, e.g. Russia Oo.

> ▷ **PHOTOBANK** p139
>
> Ss match the countries with the flags, then in pairs complete the table with the correct countries.
>
> **Answers:**
> A 1 A 2 E 3 G 4 H 5 D 6 C 7 F 8 B
> B 1 the USA 2 Argentina 3 Colombia 4 Germany 5 Italy
>   6 Chile 7 Mexico 8 Russia 9 China 10 Japan 11 the UK
>   12 Poland 13 Spain 14 Turkey

WRITING CAPITAL LETTERS

5A To check that Ss understand *capital letter*, write *a b C d* on the board and ask *Where is the capital letter?* Then go through the example and give Ss a few minutes to do the rest of the exercise. They can compare their answers with a partner before class feedback.

> **Answers:** b) Hi, I'm Tony Ferrari. c) Are you from Italy?
> d) No, I'm American. I'm from Washington D.C.
> e) Are you a student? f) Yes, I am.

B Go through the example with the class, checking the names in sentences a and b. Then give Ss a few minutes to match the rules. For **stronger classes**, ask Ss to cover the rules first, and give them a minute or two in pairs to think about and tell you why the capital letters are used in sentences a–f.

> **Answers:** 2 c), d) 3 d) 4 a), b), d), f) 5 a)–f) 6 d)

Depending on your teaching context, you may want to point out that pronouns like *you, he, she,* etc. and normal nouns (e.g. *student, teacher*) only have a capital if they are at the beginning of a sentence.

C Start by asking two Ss to read out the messages and establish that there are no capital letters. Ask Ss to write out the messages in their notebooks with capitals where necessary. For feedback, you could invite different Ss to write the corrected messages on the board, and check that the others agree.

> **Answers:**
> 1 Hi, I'm Bao, and I'm a teacher in China.
> 2 Hi, I'm Sylvia. I'm Russian. Are you from Beijing?
> 3 No, I'm from Shanghai. Are you from Moscow?
> 4 Yes, I am. I'm a student.

6A Give each student four slips of paper to write on. Ask them to write a message to their partner like the model in messages 1 and 2 in Ex 5C.

B Ss answer their partner's message and pass the answer back. They can then continue the chat, following the model.

SPEAKING

7A Demonstrate that Ss should write the country and city in their notebooks and keep them secret. Circulate and help with spelling and pronunciation as necessary. To extend the practice Ss could write more than one country and city.

B Start by demonstrating the activity with the class: show Ss that you have written the name of a country and city on a folded slip of paper, then prompt them to ask *Where are you from?* then *Are you from …?* until they guess the city. Put Ss into groups of 4–6 to take turns. Monitor and listen for examples of good pronunciation and give the class praise for these in feedback.

> **Homework ideas**
> * Ss exchange email addresses with someone they didn't work with during the lesson, then email messages to each other like the ones in Ex 5C.
> * Ss find (e.g. three) small pictures of famous people to bring to the next lesson and write the countries the people are from on the front of the pictures.
> * **Workbook:** Ex 1–5, p6–7

ARRIVALS

Introduction

Ss practise reading and talking about jobs, using the verb *be* and jobs vocabulary. They also learn to use word stress on jobs vocabulary.

SUPPLEMENTARY MATERIALS

Resource bank: p142

Ex 6 (optional extra activity): bring in a selection of photos of famous people, with their country of origin written on the picture (Ss should also bring in photos, as in the homework idea in lesson 1.1).

Project: bring in a large poster map of the world and small sticky labels for Ss to stick onto it.

Warm up

Elicit the word *teacher* by saying to Ss: *You're students. I'm a …?* Write *teacher* on the board and the heading *Jobs* above it. Ask Ss for another example of a job in English and write it under the heading. Then tell Ss they have thirty seconds in pairs to think of any other jobs they know. After thirty seconds invite the pairs to share their ideas, and if they are correct, add them to the list on the board. Ss can later compare this list with the names of jobs they study in the lesson.

VOCABULARY JOBS

1A Ask the class for the name of the first job, then give Ss a few minutes to write the rest. They can work in pairs, or work individually and compare answers with a partner. If Ss ask about the use of *a/an* in front of the job names, reassure them that they will study this in the next part of the lesson.

B Play the recording for Ss to check their answers.

Answers: 1 a teacher **2** a waiter **3** a doctor **4** a singer
5 an engineer **6** a businessman/businesswoman **7** a taxi driver
8 an actor

C PRONUNCIATION word stress Ask Ss where the stress is on *teacher* and write <u>tea</u>cher on the board. Play the recording again for Ss to underline the stressed syllable in each job. Point out that all the jobs apart from *engineer* have the stress on the first syllable, and that the *-er* and *-or* endings are 'weak' (you may want to show Ss the /ə/ sound at this point) and the 'r' sound is not pronounced. Then play the recording one more time for Ss to repeat in chorus, or simply say the names of the jobs yourself as the model.

Answers: 1 a <u>tea</u>cher **2** a <u>wai</u>ter **3** a <u>doc</u>tor **4** a <u>sing</u>er
5 en<u>gi</u>neer **6** a <u>bus</u>inessman/<u>bus</u>inesswoman **7** a <u>ta</u>xi driver
8 an <u>ac</u>tor

Watch out!

Ss may have trouble pronouncing *businessman/businesswoman*: demonstrate that *business* only has two syllables: /ˈbɪznɪs/ and ask Ss to repeat this separately first. They may also need extra practice with *engineer* because of the unusual stress pattern, with the stress on the last syllable. You could use stress circles to help: ooO.

2A Ask two pairs of Ss to read out the conversation, and ask the class when they think we use *a* and when we use *an*. Then direct Ss to the rules and give them a minute or two to underline the alternatives. They can work in pairs or individually.

Answers: 1 an **2** a

B Check that Ss understand that the rule about *a/an* applies to nationalities: focus Ss on *an English student* in the conversation in Ex 2A and ask which other nationalities start with a vowel (e.g. *American, Argentinian, Italian*). Write *singer, American* and *actor, German* on the board (as in the example) and ask Ss if you should write *a* or *an* in front of them. Demonstrate the activity yourself with a **strong student**, then put Ss in pairs to practise. You could extend the practice by asking Ss to include any other jobs from the list they made in the Warm up.

C Demonstrate by miming a job first, for Ss to ask questions. Put Ss in pairs or small groups to practise. Monitor the activity and listen for good examples of *a/an* and pronunciation of jobs and praise the class for these in feedback, as well as dealing with any confusion or pronunciation problems.

▷ **PHOTOBANK** p139

Ss match the jobs with the photos, then in pairs complete the table.

Answers:

A 2 I **3** D **4** B **5** A **6** H **7** C **8** E **9** J **10** G
B man: actor, waiter, businessman
woman: businesswoman, waitress, actress, sportswoman

READING

3A Start by teaching *tourist, on holiday* and *happy*. You could do this by acting out a scenario where you are on holiday, sitting smiling and relaxing in a café with a cold drink, walking round taking photos and admiring the city, etc. Check that Ss understand *conference*, e.g. with a simple definition such as 'a big meeting for two or three days'. Then focus Ss on the photos (tell them not to read the texts yet) and establish that the people are in an airport: ask Ss the name of important airports in their country/countries. Give Ss a minute or two to look at the people and decide who is a tourist. Conduct brief feedback to see which person most Ss chose.

B Write *Who is a tourist?* on the board and tell Ss to read and answer the question.

Answer: Wei Zhang

C Direct Ss to the table (you may want to write or display a copy of it on the board) and make sure they understand the four types of information they need to find in the text, including *first time in New York*. Do an example with the class, then give Ss about five minutes to complete the table and compare their answers with a partner.

Answers:

Name	Sonia Conti	Wei Zhang	Maria Silva	Jack Brown
Job	business student	computer engineer	English teacher	actor/ waiter
Country	Italy	China	Brazil	Australia
First time in New York?	no	yes	yes	no

(NB: For Sonia and Jack it is not their first time in New York because they study or work there.)

Culture note

Columbia University is in New York City. Many famous people have studied there, including Barack Obama, Franklin D. Roosevelt, Amelia Earhart, Jake and Maggie Gyllenhaal.

GRAMMAR   *BE: HE/SHE/IT*

4A Start by reminding Ss of the *I* and *you* forms of *be*, which they have studied already. Indicate a male and female student to establish that *he* is for male subjects and *she* is for female subjects, then point to a window, book, bag, etc. to establish that *it* is for things. Write the four sentences on the board and give Ss a minute or two to identify the verb *be*, then underline the examples on the board.

> **Answers:**
> 2 She's an English teacher. (point out that *is* becomes *'s*)
> 3 It *isn't* my first time in England. (point out that *not* becomes *n't*)
> 4 *Is* it a good university? Yes, it *is*. (point out that in a *yes/no* question and an affirmative short answer we don't contract *is*)

B Give Ss a minute or two working individually to complete the tables. Monitor and check their accuracy.

> **Answers:** Is   isn't   's (the question begins with a *Wh-* word, so it's possible to contract *is* to *'s*)

C Tell Ss to write the numbers 1–6 in their notebooks and explain that they need to write each sentence as they hear it. (NB: Each sentence is said twice, the second time at normal speed.) Play the first example, pausing the recording to write the sentence on the board. For **weaker classes**, you may want to continue playing one sentence at a time and writing up the answer with the whole class; otherwise, play the rest of the sentences then give Ss time to compare what they've written with a partner.

> **Answers:** 1 He's an actor.   2 She's a student.   3 Is he from India?
> 4 Is it your first time here?   5 Yes, it is.   6 Where's she from?

Play the recording again. Each sentence is said slowly first, for Ss to hear how the words are linked together, then at natural speed, for Ss to repeat. You could ask Ss to repeat the sentence in chorus, then pause the recording and ask individuals to repeat. Help Ss to link words, e.g.
He's‿an‿actor,
She's‿a, Is‿he (NB: the *h* in *he* is not pronounced)
Is‿it, it‿is.
Where's‿she …

> ▷ **LANGUAGEBANK 1.2** p118–119
>
> Give Ss time to read through the summary. If you want to give Ss some extra practice in class, you could give half the class Ex 1.2A and the other half Ex 1.2B and provide keys for Ss to check their answers when they've finished. Then pair up Ss who have done different exercises and tell them to exchange answers.
>
> **Answers:**
> A 2 It's in Libya.   3 She's from Colombia.   4 Yes, she is.
>   5 No, it isn't. It's from Japan.   6 It's in Turkey.
>   7 No, she isn't. She's from the UK.   8 No, it isn't. It's in Argentina.
> B 2 Where's, from   3 Is, in   4 Where's   5 Is he a   6 Is she a
>   7 Is it   8 Where's

5A Look at the example with the class. Ss can then work in pairs or individually to add *'s* in nine more places. You could run this as a race with Ss working in pairs to finish the exercise first. They can then read out their answers for the rest of the class to confirm or correct.
For **stronger classes**, you could point out that we say we're *in* a place *for* a conference (also *for work, for a meeting, for a wedding*) but *on holiday* or *on business*.

> **Answers:**
> 1 Ellie Turner's from Liverpool in the UK. She's a teacher at UCL. It's a big university in London. She's in New York for a conference.
> 2 Yong-Joon's from Korea. He's a taxi driver in Seoul, the capital. He's in New York on holiday. He's happy to be here.
> 3 Monika's a businesswoman from Ottawa in Canada. She's in New York on business.

> **Optional extra activity**
> Tell Ss to imagine that they are at JFK airport and to think of a reason why they are in New York. Put them in pairs and ask them to tell their partner why they are in New York. Then tell them to write two or three sentences about their partner, like the examples in Ex 5A.

B Go through the example with the class, and remind Ss to think about where to add words like *a/an, in, from, on*, as well as *is/Is*. Ask Ss to write the questions in their notebooks, so they can use the prompts in their Students' Book for speaking practice later.

> **Answers:** 2 Is she a doctor?   3 Is UCL in New York?
> 4 Is Yong-Joon from Japan?   5 Is he in New York on holiday?
> 6 Is Ottawa in Canada?

C Tell Ss to pay attention to the pronouns *he/she/it* as they match these questions and answers.

> **Answers:** a) 3   b) 5   d) 4   e) 6   f) 2

D Before you put Ss in pairs to practise, you could say the questions for Ss to repeat in chorus, to give them a good model of the pronunciation. Tell Ss to cover the answers and use the prompts in Ex 5B to ask the questions. You could then extend the practice by asking Ss to write one more question about each person in Ex 5A to ask each other (e.g. *Is Ellie in New York on holiday? Is Yong-Joon happy to be in New York? Is Monika a tourist?*).

SPEAKING

6 Put Ss in pairs and direct A and B to the correct page, telling them not to show each other their information. Demonstrate what Ss have to do by drawing a simple sketch of a person's head and shoulders on the board, and eliciting some possible questions from Ss. Give Ss a few minutes to write their questions and circulate to help. Then tell them to ask their questions, starting with Student A. Monitor the activity and note down any examples of good use of the verb *be*, and any problem areas, so you can praise Ss and deal with any problems after the activity has finished.

> **Optional extra activity**
> Hold up a picture of a famous person so that Ss can't see it, tell them it's someone famous and guide them to ask you questions to guess who it is, e.g. *Is it a man or woman? Where's he/she from? Is he/she (a singer)? Is he/she (a politician)?* Once you have done two or three examples, put Ss in groups to continue the activity using their own photos of famous people.

> **Homework/Project ideas**
> • **Project:** if your Ss are from different countries, they write their names on sticky labels and stick them onto the correct part of the country on the world map poster. If your Ss are from the same country, they write the names of famous people on the sticky labels, and stick them onto the appropriate part of the world map. They can then add to the poster as the course goes on.
> • **Workbook:** Ex 1–5, p8–9

HOW DO YOU SPELL ...?

Introduction

Ss practise using the alphabet and learn to check spelling. They practise using sentence stress in questions. They also practise listening to and giving personal information.

> **SUPPLEMENTARY MATERIALS**
> **Resource bank:** p143 and p144
> **Warm up:** a ball or soft object to throw.
> **Ex 1C (optional extra activity):** prepare a set of cards with the letters of the alphabet, large enough for the whole class to see when you hold them up, and small sets of alphabet cards for Ss to use in groups of 4–6.

Warm up

Use either of these warm up ideas if you think your Ss have some knowledge of the English alphabet. Don't worry about correcting Ss' pronunciation of the letters at this stage.

Stand with Ss in a circle, say *A* and throw a ball or soft object to a **strong student**, who says *B*, throws the ball to another student, who says *C*, and so on until you reach the end of the alphabet. If a student doesn't know a letter, encourage the rest of the class to help, so that Ss pool their knowledge.

Alternatively, draw a line down the middle of the board and divide the class into two groups. Invite a student from each group to come and start the alphabet on the board, saying the first letter out loud as they write it, then tell them to run back to their group and pass the pen to a student who knows how to say and write the next letter, and so on. The aim is to be the first group to finish writing the alphabet on the board.

VOCABULARY THE ALPHABET

1A Before playing the recording, you could put Ss in pairs and give them time to go through the alphabet, putting a small tick ✓ by any letters they think they can pronounce, and a question mark *?* by any that they're not sure of. Play the recording once through for Ss to hear the pronunciation, then play it again for them to repeat in chorus.

B PRONUNCIATION sounds: the alphabet You could demonstrate that the activity is about the sounds of the letters by reading out the first group and asking Ss for the missing letter. Encourage Ss to work in pairs and help each other with this.

> **Answers:** 1 A H J K   2 B C D E G P T V   3 F L M N S X   4 I Y   5 O   6 Q U W   7 R

C Play the recording twice for Ss to check their answers and repeat the groups of letters. Ss could then 'test' each other in pairs: Student A says the number of a group of letters from Ex 1B, Student B says the letters in that group, e.g. Student A: *3* Student B: *F L M N S X*.

Optional extra activity

Using a large set of alphabet cards, hold up letters one at a time that spell a word (e.g. a job or the name of a country). The class calls out each letter as you hold it up, then the first person to work out the word you've spelled wins a point, and so on. You could then put Ss into groups of 4–6 with sets of small alphabet cards, to continue the activity. Or Ss could hold up letters that spell the name of another student in the group, then, once someone has worked out the name, the cards are passed to that student to spell another name, etc.

2A Start by demonstrating the activity: tell Ss to listen and write the letters you say, then say *H–I* and *B–Y–E*. Ask a **strong student** to dictate back what they wrote down, then to spell a short word for you to write on the board. Then put Ss in pairs and direct them to their activities.

B Tell Student B to read out their letters for Student A to write. Then tell them to check each other's writing.

FUNCTION GIVING PERSONAL INFORMATION

3A Focus Ss on the photos and elicit some ideas about where the places are, e.g. A school, B conference (centre), C gym. You could also elicit some ideas about what the people in each of the photos are saying (e.g. *Good morning, What's your name? Where are you from?*). Play the first conversation and pause to check that Ss understand which photo it matches, before playing the other two conversations.

> **Answers:** 1 C   2 B   3 A

B Direct Ss to the table and check that they understand what to listen for in each column: use one or two Ss' names to demonstrate *first name* and *surname*. Play the recording again, and give Ss time to compare answers with a partner before checking with the whole class.

> **Answers:**
>
> | | First name | Surname | Room number |
> |---|------------|---------|-------------|
> | 1 | Mike | Thompson | 10 |
> | 2 | Allen | Byrne | 379 |
> | 3 | Anabella | Almeida | 124 |

Unit 1 Recording 9

Conversation 1
A: OK, what's your surname?
B: Thompson, T-H-O-M-P-S-O-N.
A: Ah-huh. And what's your first name?
B: Michael.
A: How do you spell that?
B: M-I-C-H-A-E-L.
A: Ah yes, for the fitness class in room 10.
B: That's right.
A: What's your phone number?
B: Er ... it's oh five three two, four one nine.
A: And what's your email address?
B: It's mike at bmail dot com.
A: OK, thank you.

Conversation 2
A: Good morning. Can I help you?
B: Yes. My name's Byrne. Allen Byrne.
A: How do you spell that?
B: B-Y-R-N-E.
A: B-Y-R-N-E.
B: Yes.
A: And your first name?
B: It's Allen.
A: A-L-L ... is it a-n?
B: No, e. E as in England. A-L-L-E-N.
A: Thanks. OK, here's your visitor's name badge. The conference is in room 379.
B: Thank you.
A: You're welcome.

Conversation 3
A: Can I help you?
B: Yes, I'm a student, a new student.
A: Welcome to the school. What's your surname?
B: Almeida.
A: How do you spell Almeida?
B: A-L-M-E-I-D-A.
A: And what's your first name?
B: Anabella.
A: OK, Anabella. Here's your student card.

B: Thank you. Oh, my first name's wrong.
A: Oh, sorry. How do you spell it?
B: It's Anabella, A-N-A-B-E-L-L-A.
A: A-N-A-B-E-L-L-A.
B: That's right.
A: OK, Anabella. You're in room 124.
B: 124?
A: Yes.

4A Establish with Ss that this is an example of the type of form they might complete to join a club, a library, a class, etc. Then give Ss a minute or two to complete the form.

Answers: Surname   Nationality   Phone number   Email address

Optional extra activity

Use the Riverside gym form from Ex 4A to prepare Ss for the language work in Ex 4B. Put Ss in pairs to practise spelling the names and nationality, and reading out the phone number and email address.

B Look at the example with the class, then Ss can work individually or in pairs to choose the correct alternatives.

C Play the recording again for Ss to check their answers.

Answers: **2** spell   **3** oh   **4** at, dot
(NB: *Oh* is used in British and American English. *Zero* is also possible, particularly in American English.)

D PRONUNCIATION sentence stress Before playing the recording, write the two questions on the board and ask Ss which is the most important word in each question (*phone* and *email*, the 'information' words). Play the recording, then underline the stressed words on the board. Play the recording again for Ss to repeat in chorus.

Answers:
1 <u>What's</u> your <u>phone</u> <u>number</u>?   **2** <u>What's</u> your <u>email</u> <u>address</u>?

Teaching tip

To help Ss with the stress patterns on questions, build the questions up from one word, asking Ss to repeat after you each time, e.g:
phone? – phone number? – what's phone number? – what's your phone number?
email? – email address? – what's email address? – what's your email address?
This helps Ss to see that *your* is 'squashed' between the other words, because it isn't stressed.

▷ LANGUAGEBANK 1.3 p118–119

The Language bank has a summary of the questions and answers covered in Exs 3 and 4. Ss can do Ex 1.3 in class or for homework: if they do it in class, you could ask one or two pairs to act out the corrected conversation.

Answers:
A: What's your first name?
B: Ana.
A: And what's your surname?
B: *It's* Fernandez.
A: And what's *your* nationality?
B: I'm Italian.
A: And your *phone number*?
B: It's 0372 952 594.
A: What's *your* email address?
B: It's anastella247@hotmail.com.
A: How *do* you spell 'anastella'? With one 'n'?
B: Yes, one 'n' and two 'l's.

5A Ss either write their own phone number and email address or invent them. To extend the practice, ask Ss to write two or three phone numbers and email addresses. Tell Ss not to show their partner what they've written, so they have to listen carefully for the information.

B You could ask two **stronger Ss** to demonstrate this first. (NB: Choose two Ss who are not sitting near each other, so they have to speak up and everyone can hear.) Tell Ss to practise asking and answering, and to write down the information so their partners can check that it's accurate afterwards.

LEARN TO **CHECK SPELLING**

6A Give Ss a moment to familiarise themselves with the four lines of conversation and establish that they need to underline the individual letters that are stressed, not the words. You could demonstrate this by spelling the name of one of your Ss, stressing one or two of the letters, and asking the class which letter(s) were stressed.

Answers:
A: A-l-l … is it <u>a</u>-n?
B: No, <u>e</u>. <u>E</u> as in England. A-l-l-<u>e</u>-n.

speakout TIP

Before Ss look at the tip, give them one or two more examples of how to use *as in* and a word, e.g. *b as in book, d as in doctor*. You could elicit some ideas for *Y* and *J*, then let Ss compare with the ideas in the tip. Give them a moment or two to think of words for *G, I* and *E* (e.g. *good, Italy, email*).

B Demonstrate the example with a **strong student**. Then give Ss time to prepare for the activity by going through the pairs of names and underlining the letter that needs correcting.

SPEAKING

7 Give Ss a minute or two to look through the table and remind them that the question for *Nationality* is *Where are you from?* Ss can sit in groups of four to complete the table, if possible with Ss they don't usually sit next to. Alternatively, they could stand up and walk round the room, finding three different Ss to talk to. Monitor the activity closely and note down examples of good language use and any problems with grammar, pronunciation, etc. to deal with in feedback.

Teaching tip

When monitoring a speaking activity, try to stand or sit near enough to the Ss to hear them, without making them feel self-conscious. Have a small notebook and pen handy so that you can write down examples of language from the lesson that a student uses well, as well as examples of mistakes. In feedback, write the good examples on the board and praise the Ss, then (without mentioning individual Ss) write the mistakes on the board and encourage the class to correct them. Feedback like this helps Ss to see the benefit of this type of speaking activity. In smaller classes, make sure that it isn't possible to identify who said the examples, e.g. by varying the examples slightly while retaining the aspects you want to highlight.

Homework ideas

- Ss exchange phone numbers with two or three classmates that they didn't speak to in the lesson, and practise asking for and giving personal information on the phone.
- Ss make a list of 6–10 international words (as in the lead-in lesson) and practise spelling them aloud.
- **Workbook:** Ex 1–4, p10

AROUND THE WORLD

Introduction

Ss watch an extract from the BBC programme *Around the World* where people talk about their country, city or village, their job and the importance of English for them. Ss then learn and practise how to give a personal introduction in spoken and written form.

> **SUPPLEMENTARY MATERIALS**
> **Warm up:** a map of the world, e.g. on a globe, a poster or on the internet.

Warm up

Using the world map, demonstrate that *around the world* means *in many places/parts of the world*. Divide the class into groups of 3–4 and play 'around the world': say the name of a country that begins with the letter *A*, then choose a group to say a country beginning with the letter *B*; they then choose the next group, who say a country beginning with the letter *C*, and so on. Groups get a point every time they can think of an appropriate country; if they can't, they have to say *Pass*. The winning group is the one with the most points.

DVD PREVIEW

1A Lead in via a brief discussion with the class about what they can see in the photos, including the larger background photo. This should give you an idea of how much of the vocabulary in Ex 1 is familiar to at least some of the Ss. Direct Ss to the word box and find examples of *a city* in the photos with the class, e.g. Santiago. Put Ss in pairs to match the rest of the words. In feedback, check the pronunciation of: *countryside*, *mountain*, *village* and *building*.

mountain village building
/ɪ/   /ɪ//ɪ/   /ɪ//ɪ/

> **Suggested answers:**
> A Santiago, Chile: a city, a building
> B Finland: the countryside, a mountain
> C Oman: a village, a mountain
> D Kuala Lumpur, Malaysia: a city, a building
> E Malasyia: a beach, the sea
> F Canada: a mountain, a river, the countryside
> Background photo: a beach, the sea/a river, a mountain

B You could use *old* as an example, e.g. point to the buildings in the photo of Oman, and ask Ss for the opposite, pointing at the buildings in the photo of Santiago. Then put Ss in pairs to find two more pairs, and to decide which word does not have an opposite (*beautiful*). Check that Ss understand *beautiful* by pointing to the photo of Malaysia, and also by asking them to name a beautiful place in their city/country.

> **Answers:** old – new small – big cold – hot

C You could demonstrate this with the class first, giving an example for one of the photos for Ss to guess. Then put Ss in pairs to practise.

> **Suggested answers:**
> a beautiful/big mountain – Canada/Finland
> a cold/beautiful river – Canada/Finland
> an old/beautiful building – Kuala Lumpur, Malaysia
> a new/big building – Santiago, Chile
> a big/beautiful/hot beach/sea – Malaysia
> a small/hot/old/beautiful village – Oman

2 Explain that Ss are going to watch some people talking from different countries around the world. Ss could predict which countries by looking at the photos, then read the text to check.

> **Answers:** Finland, Oman, Chile, Malaysia, Canada

DVD VIEW

3A Demonstrate that Ss need to write a number from 1–5 next to each country when they see or hear about it on the DVD. You could also tell Ss to note down any of the things from Ex 1A that they see on the DVD. Play the DVD.

> **Answers: a)** 2 **b)** 1 **c)** 4 **d)** 5 **e)** 3

B Put Ss in pairs to discuss which of the things from Ex 1A they saw on the DVD, and which of the words from Ex 1B they heard.

C Play the DVD again. Give Ss time to compare answers in pairs and help each other before checking with the whole class.

> **Answers:**
> Canada: rivers, mountains, beautiful
> Oman: beautiful city, big buildings, small village, countryside, hot
> Finland: city, cold, countryside, beautiful
> Malaysia: big city, new buildings, countryside, beautiful, beaches, sea, rivers, hot

D Before putting Ss in pairs, teach *winter/summer sport* (e.g. mime skiing and playing golf) and *shop/office assistant* (mime someone on a till and someone doing filing). Give Ss 1–2 minutes to compare answers, then play the DVD again.

> **Answers: 2** cold **3** waiter **4** student **5** village **6** winter
> **7** new **8** shop

E Teach *favourite*, e.g. by telling Ss about your favourite colour/food/singer/actor, etc. Then put Ss in small groups to tell each other their favourite country from the DVD. Encourage them to give a reason, e.g. *X is my favourite because the buildings are beautiful.*

> **Optional extra activity**
> Personalise the topic by putting the following prompts on the board for Ss to complete about their country or a country they know:
> (X) … *is a beautiful beach in* … (Y)
> … *is a new building in* …
> … *is an old city in* …
> … *is a small village in* …
> … *is a big river/mountain in* …
> Ss compare their sentences in pairs or small groups.

> **DVD 1** Around the World
>
> **Pablo:** Hello, or, ah, 'Hola' from Chile. My name is Pablo and I'm from Santiago. Santiago is a mix of old buildings and new buildings. My job? – I'm a bus driver in Santiago. In my job I speak Spanish and English. The mountains in Chile are very beautiful. It's very cold, but I love it.
>
> **Eric:** Hello, my name's Eric and I'm from British Columbia in Canada. I'm a waiter in a restaurant, a restaurant on a train. It's a good job; people are very nice, very friendly. I speak English and French in my job. Canada is beautiful – the rivers, the mountains – really beautiful. I love it here.
>
> **Mizna:** 'Assalamu alaikum', that's hello in my country, Oman. My name is Mizna and I'm a student at university in Muscat. I speak English and Arabic at university. Muscat is a beautiful city with many big buildings, for example, the Grand Mosque. But I am not from Muscat. I am from a small village in the countryside. It's very hot in my village, but I love it.

Kustaa: Hello, or 'Hei' from Finland. My name's Kustaa and I'm from Helsinki, the capital city of Finland. I'm a businessman in Helsinki. I speak English and Finnish in my work, and yes it's very, very cold here. The countryside around Helsinki is beautiful, and it's very good for sports – winter sports. I really love it here.

Aisha: Hi from Malaysia. I'm Aisha and I'm from Kuala Lumpur. KL is a big city with a lot of new buildings. I'm a shop assistant in a tourist shop. I speak English and Malay in my job. The countryside in Malaysia is beautiful – the beaches and the sea and the rivers. It's very hot here. I love it.

speakout you and your country

4A Start by teaching the words *very* (e.g. by comparing something in the classroom that's small with something very small), and *centre* (e.g. ask for the name of a building/shop in the centre of the city where they're studying). Also demonstrate the difference between *I like it* and *I love it*, e.g. by using stress and intonation to show that *I love it* is stronger. Then tell Ss they're going to listen to a woman called Catarina answering questions 1–7 and give them time to read through the questions, so they know what information they're listening for. Establish that they only need to write short answers, e.g. two or three words, as in the example, not full sentences. Play the recording, then give Ss a few minutes in pairs to check their answers. Check the spelling of *hotel receptionist* and that Ss understand the job (someone who answers the phone and helps guests when they arrive).

> **Answers:** 2 no   3 yes   4 hotel receptionist   5 centre of Dublin
> 6 yes   7 the countryside is beautiful, the villages are old and beautiful

B Give Ss a few moments to look at the key phrases. Check that Ss understand *town* (between a village and a city in terms of size). You may want to pause the recording after every couple of sentences, to give Ss time to tick the phrases.

> **Optional extra activity**
>
> To help Ss with the pronunciation of the key phrases, elicit some different combinations from the options given and ask Ss to repeat them both in chorus and individually, e.g.
>
> *It's an Irish name.*
> *I'm a teacher at the university.*
> *I'm an engineer at (name of company).*
> *Dublin is a city in Ireland.*
> *It's very small.*
> *It isn't very big.*
> *The countryside here is beautiful.*
> *I really love it here.*

> **Answers:**
> It's a(n) [Irish/Italian ✓/...] name.
> I'm a/an [teacher/hotel receptionist ✓/engineer/...] at ...
> [Dublin/Positano/It] is [a city/a town/a village] in ...
> It's/It isn't very [small ✓/big/beautiful/hot/...].
> The countryside [here ✓/in Ireland/in ...] is very beautiful.
> I really love it here. ✓

Unit 1 Recording 12

A: So, your name's Catherine?
B: No, it's Catarina.
A: Catarina?
B: Yes, it's an Italian name. I'm from Italy.
A: Yeah? Where in Italy?
B: I'm from Positano.
A: Positano! I don't know it. Is it big?
B: No, it isn't. It's very small. Very small and very old. Look. Here's a photo.
A: Oh, it's beautiful!

B: Yes ... I love it.
A: And ... what's your job?
B: In Dublin?
A: Yes, here in Dublin.
B: I'm a hotel receptionist here in the centre of the city.
A: Oh really? So English is important for you.
B: Yes, of course. In my job I speak English, and I also speak German and Italian of course. Italian people visit Dublin a lot. They love it.
A: And you? Do you like Dublin?
B: Oh, yes. I really love it here.
A: Why? What's good about it?
B: Well, the countryside here is very beautiful, with mountains, rivers and the sea. And the villages are old and beautiful. I really love it here. And you ... are you Irish?
A: Yes, but not from Dublin. I'm from a small town in County Wexford.

5A Tell Ss to write the numbers 1–7 in their notebooks, and to write full sentences for their answers. If your Ss are all from the same country, encourage them to comment on different parts of the country when talking about the countryside. Circulate and help, reminding Ss to use the key phrases. You could also encourage them to practise saying the answers, so they don't need to read them aloud from their notebooks.

B Before putting Ss in pairs you could give the whole class some practice in asking the seven questions, repeating in chorus and individually after your model. This will give you the opportunity to help Ss with pronunciation. Ss then practise asking and answering, trying to refer to their books as little as possible. When Ss seem confident, you could invite several pairs to ask and answer their questions in front of the class. Finally, give Ss feedback on their use of language, both with praise for good examples and correction of common mistakes.

writeback a personal introduction

6A Introduce the idea of a class blog and ask Ss what information they think will be in it. Direct Ss to the blog and the list of information 1–8. Give Ss time to read the blog and tick the information, then ask the class which information is not in the blog (email address and *Goodbye*). Focus on the use of *with* in the text: ask Ss to underline the examples of *with* (three in total) and elicit/ demonstrate how they are used, i.e. when you say the name of your company (*I'm a businesswoman **with** Volkswagen*), for adding information about your city (*Berlin is a city **with** ...*) and for adding information about what makes the countryside beautiful (*the countryside is beautiful, **with** mountains and ...*).

> **Answers:** 2, 4, 5, 6, 8

B Encourage Ss to write some notes first, using the list of information in Ex 6A to help, and also the key phrases and the audio script, if they wish. Circulate and help with grammar, provide vocabulary that Ss need, etc. Once Ss have written their introduction, they can swap and read each other's work, perhaps suggesting additions and/or improvements.

> **Homework ideas**
> * Ss write a final version of their personal introduction.
> * **Workbook:** Ex 5, p10

LOOKBACK

SUPPLEMENTARY MATERIALS

Ex 3B: prepare a list of jobs from the unit, including some from the Photo bank, if your Ss have studied them.

Ex 4B: prepare a list of facts about famous people and places to give to Ss who run out of ideas.

Ex 6A: blank pieces of paper/card about the size of a business card (enough for all the Ss in the class).

BE: I/YOU

1A Point out that the questions and answers are referring to sentences 1–6 in Ex 1B below. Go through the example, then give Ss 1–2 minutes to complete the sentences, working alone.

Answers: 2 'm 3 you 4 am 5 in 6 not 7 five 8 I

B Either go through the example or demonstrate the activity with the class: tell Ss you're thinking of one of sentences 1–6 and invite them to ask you questions until they guess the right one. Put Ss in pairs to continue.

COUNTRIES

2A Show Ss the example and point out that they have the first letter of each country to help them. Put Ss in pairs to write the countries. Once you've checked the answers, Ss could take turns to 'test' each other: Student A closes their book, Student B says names of cities and Student A responds with the correct countries, then Student B says names of countries and Student A responds with the correct cities.

Answers: 2 Germany 3 Russia 4 Italy 5 China 6 Turkey

B Ss work alone to write five more countries and a city from each. Circulate and help with spelling as necessary.

C Demonstrate the example with the class taking the role of Student A, and you responding as Student B. You could do one or two more examples like this, then put Ss into pairs. Monitor the activity to check Ss' pronunciation of the countries and deal with any problems in feedback.

JOBS

3A Ss could work in pairs and do this as a race, i.e. the first pair to finish wins five points, then further points are awarded to pairs around the class for correct spelling and pronunciation. Alternatively, this could be done as a competition in teams: write the gapped words on the board one at a time (Ss have books closed) and the first team to 'buzz' and answer correctly wins a point.

Answers: 1 waiter 2 taxi driver 3 engineer 4 doctor 5 actor 6 teacher 7 singer 8 businesswoman

B Demonstrate this first with you taking the role of Student A and the Ss asking questions to guess the job. Point out that you can only answer *Yes* or *No*. Ss could choose any job from 1–8 or anywhere in the unit (including the Photo bank if they have studied it).

Alternative approach

Prepare a list of jobs, including ones from the Photo bank if appropriate. Divide the class into groups, then one member from each group comes to you and looks at the first job on the list. They run back to their group and draw or mime the job. When the group has worked out the job, another member comes to you, tells you their answer, then looks at the next job on the list, and so on.

BE: HE/SHE/IT

4A Say the first sentence from the exercise and see if Ss can correct it before they look at the example. Then give Ss time to correct the sentences, working alone or with a partner. Alternatively, you could run this as a competition (Ss have books closed), writing the sentences on the board (or for more of a challenge, simply reading out the sentences) for teams to 'buzz' and correct.

Answers: 2 Russia 3 Turkey 4 Germany 5 China 6 Japan 7 Spain 8 India 9 the USA 10 the UK

B Give Ss a few minutes to do this in pairs, and circulate to provide help with grammar, spelling, etc. You may want to have some facts about famous people and places available to give to Ss who run out of ideas. Both Ss in the pair should write down the three sentences in case they are separated in the next stage of the activity.

C For this stage, you could put three pairs of Ss together into groups of six, or separate the pairs and put the Ss into new groups of 4–6. Monitor the activity and check that Ss are using *he*, *she* and *it* correctly, so you can provide feedback and correction afterwards.

Project idea

If your Ss started a world map project in lesson 1.2, sticking their names and/or the names of famous people onto a world map poster, they could add the people and places from Ex 4 to it, using small sticky labels.

THE ALPHABET

5A Ss work alone to correct the spelling of the words. They could also practise saying the spelling of the words to themselves.

Answers: 2 television 3 camera 4 university 5 restaurant 6 email 7 football 8 chocolate 9 information 10 internet

B Choose two *stronger Ss* to demonstrate the activity, then put Ss in pairs and suggest that they ask about the spelling of words at random, rather than working through the words in numerical order. Monitor and be prepared to deal with any problems with the pronunciation of letters in feedback.

GIVING PERSONAL INFORMATION

6A Go through the example with the class, then give Ss time to write the other questions alone or with a partner.

Answers: 2 What's your surname? 3 Where are you from? 4 What's your phone number? 5 What's your email address?

B Ss work alone to make three changes to the information.

C Demonstrate the activity with a *stronger student*, showing that Ss circle the three things on the card that their partner changes.

Homework ideas

Ss need to find two photos of their friends and family to bring to the next lesson. They should also find a photo of themselves when they were a baby/teenager.

BBC interviews and worksheet

Where are you from?

In this video people introduce themselves, say where they are from and what their job is. The material consolidates Ss' knowledge of the verb *be*, as well as vocabulary related to introducing yourself and jobs.

OVERVIEW

2.1 FAMILY PHOTOS

VOCABULARY | family
PRONUNCIATION | sounds /ʌ/
LISTENING | listen to someone talk about photos
GRAMMAR | be: you/we/they
PRONUNCIATION | contractions
WRITING | learn to use contractions
SPEAKING | talk about photos of family and friends

2.2 A FAMILY BUSINESS

VOCABULARY | numbers 11–100
PRONUNCIATION | word stress: numbers
READING | read about family businesses
GRAMMAR | possessive adjectives
SPEAKING | check information about people

2.3 LET'S HAVE A BREAK

VOCABULARY | feelings
FUNCTION | making suggestions
LISTENING | listen to people make suggestions
LEARN TO | resond to suggestions
PRONUNCIATION | intonation: showing interest
SPEAKING | suggest things to do

2.4 ROYAL WEDDING BBC ◄)) DVD

DVD | watch a BBC programme about the Royal Wedding
speakout | talk about five people in your life
writeback | describe five people in your life

2.5 LOOKBACK

Communicative revision activities

BBC ◄)) INTERVIEWS

Who is in your family?

In this video people talk about their families and friends. The authentic material recaps and consolidates key vocabulary and grammatical structures with the verb *be* that Ss can use for talking about important people in their lives. Use the video after lesson 2.2, at the end of the unit or set it as homework.

FAMILY PHOTOS

Introduction

Students practise talking about their families, using *be* and family vocabulary. They also practise the sound /ʌ/, and learn to pronounce and write contractions.

> **SUPPLEMENTARY MATERIALS**
> **Resource bank:** p146
> **Warm up:** bring in photos of yourself and two/three friends when you were younger, e.g. as a teenager.
> **Ex 1A:** be prepared to draw a simple version of your family tree on the board.
> **Ex 6B:** bring in two photos of your family and/or friends and be prepared to talk about them.

Warm up

Show Ss the photos of yourself and two/three friends when you were younger, but don't say which one is you. Put the photos on the board, number them 1, 2 and 3 and ask Ss *Which photo is me?* Get Ss to vote for the photo they think by putting their hands up, then finally reveal which one is you. If Ss have brought photos of themselves as babies/teenagers, collect them in so that they're anonymous, then mix them up and display them on the board or around the classroom. Ss work in pairs and guess who the photos belong to, saying *I think this is (Jorge)*, etc. Finally, Ss can reveal their identities, e.g. *No, it's not Jorge, it's me!*

VOCABULARY FAMILY

1A Illustrate the idea of *family* by drawing a very simple version of your family tree on the board, with your name somewhere on it. Point to it and say *My family* (leave it on the board for reference in Ex 1C). Then direct Ss to the family photos and elicit some ideas for which people are in photo A. Put Ss in pairs to help each other match the other photos to family members. Check answers with the whole class.

> **Answers:** 1 C 2 A 3 B 4 D 5 C

> **Teaching tip**
> Putting Ss in pairs for a vocabulary matching activity encourages them to use their passive knowledge and help each other with unfamiliar words. Try to ensure that two *weaker Ss* are not paired together for this: put them with a *stronger student* to make a group of three, if necessary.

B PRONUNCIATION sounds /ʌ/ Model the /ʌ/ sound, as in *but* and *cup*, for Ss to familiarise themselves with before they listen to the recording. Demonstrate that Ss need to underline the sound when they hear it by writing *bus* on the board. Play the recording, then give Ss time to compare answers in pairs.

> **Answers:** husband, brother, son, mother
> (NB: You may want to elicit/point out that the letters 'o' and 'u' often have this sound.)

Play the recording again, pausing after each pair of words for Ss to repeat in chorus.

> **Teaching tip**
> The ending *-er*, e.g. *brother*, is unstressed and pronounced /ə/. You could ask Ss how many other family words in Ex 1A end like this (*mother, father, sister, daughter*), then say them yourself for Ss to repeat. The ending *-er* is also often found in jobs vocabulary, e.g. *teacher, waiter, driver*.

C Remind Ss about your family tree, then focus them on the one in Ex 1C. Tell Ss to find *Emma* and *Suzy*, then look at the example. You could also tell Ss to find *Tom* and *Julia* and complete number 6 as another example with the class. Then put Ss in pairs to complete the rest of the sentences. As you go through the answers with the class, correct pronunciation of the family vocabulary as necessary. Also check that Ss have put an *-s* on *daughters* and remind Ss of the plurals *brothers, sisters, sons, parents*. If Ss ask about *children*, explain that this is an irregular plural.

> **Answers:** 2 brother   3 father   4 mother   5 parents   6 wife
> 7 daughters   8 son   9 children

D Demonstrate the activity with a student, then put Ss in pairs. They could also 'reverse' the prompts, so B says the names, and A responds with who they are. Monitor and deal with any pronunciation problems in feedback.

> **Optional extra activity**
>
> Ask Ss to draw a simple version of their own family tree, then put them in pairs to show each other their family tree and explain who the people are, e.g. *(name) … is my …*

LISTENING

2A Tell Ss they're going to listen to two people talking about three of the photos. They need to write A, B, C or D next to the numbers 1–3. Play the recording, then give Ss a moment or two to compare their answers with a partner.

> **Answers:** 1 C   2 A   3 B

B Direct Ss to the first sentence and demonstrate on the board that they need to listen and underline the number they hear for each person. Give them a moment or two to look at the other sentences, and if necessary check *musician* by miming playing some musical instruments, and *football team* by naming one or two famous football teams. Play the recording again, then put Ss in pairs to check their answers.

> **Answers:** 1 3, 6, 10   2 Jennifer   3 Amy's   4 Tim   5 Lucy   6 He's

Unit 2   Recording 2

Conversation 1
B: Hi, Lucy. Coffee?
A: No, thanks.
B: Hey, photos. Let's see …
A: Yes, from the weekend.
B: Is this your family?
A: Yes, me, my husband, my son Johnny and my daughter Amy.
B: How old are they?
A: Erm, Johnny's three and Amy's six.
B: Where are you?
A: We're in the park.
B: Great photo. Lovely family.
A: Thanks. It's Johnny's first time on a bike …

Conversation 2
A: … and this is a photo of the children.
B: Oh, it's a great picture.
A: Yeah.
B: Let's see. This is, erm, Amy?
A: Yes, that's right.
B: And Johnny and …
A: Yes …
B: … and in the middle? Your other daughter?
A: Yes. Jennifer. She's ten now.
B: Oh. And Jennifer and Amy, are they at the same school?
A: No, they aren't. Jennifer's at a special music school. Violin, piano …
B: Really? Wow, a real musician.

A: Well, she's only ten, so …
B: But that's great. And the other children?
A: Amy's on the football team.

Conversation 3
A: This is Tim …
B: Your husband.
A: Yeah. And Johnny.
B: Is Tim British?
A: Oh yes, he's from Cambridge.
B: And you, you aren't British. You're from China, right?
A: No, I'm from the US.
B: Oh …
A: My father's Chinese and my mother's American.
B: I see. Interesting. Erm, is your husband a businessman?
A: Yes, he's in the hotel and restaurant business.
B: Oh. What's his job?
A: He's a hotel manager.
B: Oh, what's the name of the hotel …?

> **Optional extra activity**
>
> For practice of *yes/no* questions with *he/she*, ask Ss to work alone and write 4–6 questions (with the answer *Yes* or *No*) about the information in the recording (they can consult the audio script). Give them one or two of these examples:
> *Is Johnny three?*
> *Is Amy a musician?*
> *Is Tim from Cambridge?*
> *Is Tim a teacher?*
> *Is Lucy from China?*
> Once Ss have written their questions, they work in pairs: Student A closes his/her book and answers Student B's questions, and vice versa (if the answer is *No*, they should give the correct information, e.g. *No, he isn't. He's a businessman.*).

GRAMMAR   BE: YOU/WE/THEY

3A Write the example on the board and remind Ss of the verb *be* in the *I/you/he/she/it* forms. While Ss are underlining the other verbs, write/display the sentences on the board so that Ss can come up and underline the verbs in feedback.

> **Answers:**
> 1 **A:** Where <u>are</u> you?   **B:** We're in the park.
> 2 **A:** <u>Are</u> they at the same school?   **B:** No, they <u>aren't</u>.
> 3 **A:** You <u>aren't</u> British.   **B:** No, <u>I'm</u> from the US.

B Before asking Ss to complete the tables, make sure that they understand *you* (plural), *we* and *they*. You could go through the tables with the whole class, or give Ss a moment or two to work on them alone.

> **Answers:** aren't   Are   are   are

C **PRONUNCIATION contractions** Play the recording through once for Ss to familiarise themselves with the sound of the contractions, i.e. they sound like one word. When you play the recording again, encourage Ss to repeat all three examples of *you're, we're* and *they're* in each sentence.

D Tell Ss to write the numbers 1–6 in their notebooks and to write the six sentences they hear. You may need to repeat the recording if Ss seem to have difficulty with any of the sentences. When Ss have checked the answers, tell them to close their books (so they don't read aloud) and play the recording again for them to repeat the sentences.

> **Answers:** 1 We're from England.   2 They're actors.
> 3 We're in Japan.   4 You're right.   5 We're in class.   6 They're here.

▷ **LANGUAGEBANK 2.1** p120–121

The Language bank reminds Ss that *you* can be used for one person or more than one. If you feel Ss need more consolidation of the difference between *we/you/they*, they could do Ex 2.1A in class.

Answers:
A **2** We're from France. **3** You're in the wrong room.
4 Are they Brazilian? **5** They're Louise and Kerri.
6 We're married. **7** They aren't in class.
8 A: Where are you? **B:** We're in class.
B **A:** Hi, where are you from?
B: We're from California.
A: Are you from Los Angeles?
B: No, we aren't. We're from San Francisco.
A: Are you Kathy and Chris?
B: No, they're in Room 205!

4A Start by setting the context here: demonstrate that Student A is showing Student B two photos, and Student B is asking questions about them. Go through number 1 with the class as an example, then give Ss a few minutes to complete the exercise.

Answers: **2** we aren't **3** We're **4** Are they **5** aren't **6** they
7 aren't **8** They're **9** Is **10** are

B Tell Ss to check their answers, then play the recording.

C Ss practise the conversation. Monitor and listen for good use of contractions or any problems, so you can give Ss praise and deal with the problems in feedback.

WRITING **CONTRACTIONS**

5A Write the example (*They are my parents.*) on the board, then rub out the *a* in *are* and write in the apostrophe, showing how the two words 'close up' together and look like one. Give Ss a few moments to write the other contractions.

Answers: **2** She's my daughter. **3** We aren't sisters.
4 Tom's my brother.

B You could go through the rules with the class, eliciting their ideas, or give Ss time to think about the rules and compare ideas with a partner.

Answers: **1** Use **2** Use
(NB: You could point out that it's only in more formal writing that Ss shouldn't use contractions.)

C Focus Ss on the example and give them a few minutes to rewrite the text messages, working alone.

Answers:
1 *I'm* at the airport but your brother *isn't* here. *What's* his mobile number? It *isn't* in my phone.
2 Hi, Tom. *I'm* sorry, I don't know. We're in an English class now.
3 Hi, Marianna. It's OK. Luca's here now. See you soon.

D Ss take turns to be Marianna or Tom, and read out their messages.

Optional extra activity

Write the following words/phrases from the messages on the board and ask Ss to substitute different words/phrases: *airport, brother, mobile number, an English class, Luca.* Ss work in pairs to think of alternatives then read out the 'new' sequence of text messages to the class.

SPEAKING

6A If any Ss haven't found photos to show, they could draw rough sketches/silhouettes of the people. Give Ss time to write notes, reminding them that they can refer to the audio script for the listening in Ex 2 and previous lessons for jobs and nationalities. Circulate and help Ss with any language they need. Also suggest that they practise talking about the photos alone, using their notes, before the next stage where they talk to other Ss.

B If you've brought in some family photos, you could demonstrate what you want Ss to do, showing them that you are not referring to your notes and encouraging them to ask you questions at the end. Either put Ss in small groups to talk about the photos, or ask them to walk around the class and talk to different people. To finish, you could ask three or four Ss to hold up their photos and ask the rest of the class what information anyone remembers about them, e.g. *That's Suzanne. She's from France. She's a singer in the theatre.*

Teaching tip

For speaking activities where Ss have to give a talk/present information, encouraging them to practise their talk alone (e.g. by whispering or mumbling what they are going to say: you may need to demonstrate this) before talking in front of other Ss can help to build confidence, as well as making them sound more natural because they don't need to keep referring to their notes.

7 For this activity, Ss invent the information about the people in the photos. You may want to ask them to choose just one of the two photos to write notes about. Direct Ss A and B to the appropriate pages and give them time to prepare their notes. When Ss have finished talking about the photos you could ask a few As and Bs to talk in front of the class, and ask the other Ss to find similarities and differences in the information that, for example, two As prepared for the same photos.

Homework ideas

- Ss exchange mobile numbers with two other Ss and arrange a time to have a 'text conversation', e.g. *I'm in/at … Where are you? I'm in/at … with … Are you OK? Yes, I am.*, etc.
- Ss write two short paragraphs about the photos they presented in Ex 6.
- **Workbook:** Ex 1–4, p11–12

A FAMILY BUSINESS

Introduction

Ss practise reading and talking about family businesses, using possessive adjectives and numbers. Ss also practise recognising and using word stress on numbers.

> **SUPPLEMENTARY MATERIALS**
> **Resource bank:** p145
> **Ex 3B:** bring in a slip of paper with the names and ages of four of your family members or friends, and be prepared to tell Ss about them.

Warm up

Review the alphabet, family and jobs vocabulary. Ask the class *How do you spell 'mother'?* and write the word on the board as Ss call out the letters. Do the same with *manager*, then put Ss in pairs and tell them to take turns asking their partners how to spell words related to jobs and family. You may want to give Ss time to prepare their list of words first, referring to pages 10–11 and 18–19 of their Students' Book, and the Photo bank p139.

VOCABULARY   NUMBERS 11–100

1A Write the number *1* on the board and gesture to Ss to tell you the next number, and so on until you reach 10. Then ask Ss what comes next, and if they start to call out *11, 12,* direct them to the example and tell them to choose the correct numbers to write next to the words.

> **Answers:** twelve 12   sixteen 16   nineteen 19   fifteen 15
> eighteen 18   twenty 20   fourteen 14   seventeen 17   thirteen 13

B Play the recording for Ss to repeat the numbers, in chorus and individually.

C Demonstrate this by writing a number on the board and asking a student to say it. Then put Ss in pairs to continue, writing the numbers on a page of their notebooks.

2A Read through the first four numbers and tell Ss that the three missing numbers end in *-ty*. Give them a minute to write the numbers and check in pairs.

> **Answers:** 70 seventy   80 eighty   90 ninety

B Play the recording once for Ss to check their answers, then again for them to repeat.

C PRONUNCIATION word stress: numbers Demonstrate the activity by writing *forty* on the board and asking Ss what you should underline: *for-* or *-ty*. Then do the same with *fourteen*. Leave the words on the board to use for demonstrating Ex 2D. Play the recording. Then play the recording again for Ss to repeat in chorus.

> **Teaching tip**
> Using large and small circles on the board to highlight stressed syllables (e.g. Oo oO ooO) can help Ss to see that the stressed syllable is 'bigger', i.e. slightly longer and slightly louder. Encourage Ss to use this method of recording stress in their notebooks, too.

D You could demonstrate this by asking a **stronger student** to come to the board and point to *forty* or *fourteen* as you say it. Put Ss in pairs to practise. Monitor and deal with any difficulties with the word stress in feedback.

E Tell Ss to write the numbers 1–8 in their notebooks and to listen and write eight numbers. Give Ss time to check their answers in pairs before checking with the class (or playing the recording again if they had difficulties).

> **Answers:** 2 82   3 12   4 57   5 93   6 39   7 28   8 11

Optional extra activity

In pairs, Ss take turns to dictate eight numbers to their partner, then check each other's answers to see if they're written correctly.

3A Tell Ss to write the names and ages but not to show their information to other Ss.

B Demonstrate the activity yourself first. Write four names and ages on the board, tell Ss about one of the people and prompt them to ask you how old he/she is and how to spell his/her name. Then put Ss in pairs to ask and answer about their four people.

READING

4A Focus Ss on the first photo and say *Are they brothers or friends? What do you think?* Elicit one or two ideas from the class, then put Ss in pairs to talk about the other two photos.

B Tell Ss to read the text quickly, just to find the answers to Ex 4A. Reassure them that they will have time to read the text again afterwards.

> **Teaching tip**
> Set a time limit when you want Ss to read a text quickly to find the answers to a prediction activity or to get a general idea of the text. This helps to prevent Ss from thinking they need to read every word and getting 'stuck' on unfamiliar language in the text. The time limit should be at least twice as long as it takes you to read and find the answers yourself.

> **Answers:**
> 1 a father, two sons and a friend
> 2 a woman and her father, son and daughter
> 3 a wife and a husband

C Before Ss read the text again, you could check the following vocabulary: *downtown* (in the business part of the city – mainly used in the USA), *friendly* (demonstrate someone being friendly), *great* (very good), *perfect* ('number 1'), *chef* (someone who cooks in a restaurant), *the best* (good → very good → best). Direct Ss to the table and the examples. Elicit where number 1 is (Washington, D.C.), then give Ss a few minutes to complete the table. Ss can work alone on the activity then compare answers, or work on the activity in pairs. Check answers with the class. You could then put Ss in pairs and ask them to rank the businesses from 1–3, starting with the one they like best. Then ask a few pairs to tell the class what they decided, and compare rankings.

> **Answers:**
>
> | Business | Where? | Good things |
> |---|---|---|
> | restaurant | Washington, D.C. | small, friendly, the food is great |
> | fish shop | Sydney, Australia | the fish is the best in the city |
> | supermarket | Bath, England | it's open 24/7 |

GRAMMAR POSSESSIVE ADJECTIVES

5A Start by telling Ss to cover the reading text. Then say *My name's …* and elicit the question *What's your name?* Write *my* and *your* on the board and above them the title *possessive adjectives*. Direct Ss to the sentences and the example, and give them a few minutes to complete the sentences, working alone or in pairs. They can then uncover the text and check their answers.

Answers: 1 their 2 your 3 My 4 Her 5 its (point out that *its doors* means *the doors of the supermarket*) 6 Our

B Focus Ss on the table and check that they understand the difference between *I* and *my*, e.g. *I'm a teacher. It's my job.* You may want to go through the table with the class, or give Ss a minute or two to complete it alone, then check their answers in Language bank 2.2.

Answers:

subject pronoun	possessive adjective
I	my
you	your
he	his
she	her
it	its
we	our
they	their

▷ LANGUAGEBANK 2.2 p120–121

Use the Language bank to highlight the difference between *its* and *it's*. Remind Ss that you don't add an *-s* to possessive adjectives for plural nouns, e.g. *your books*, not *yours books*.

If Ss need extra practice of possessive adjectives before Ex 6, give Ex 2.2A to half the class and Ex 2.2B to the other half. Give each half an answer key to check their answers, then have pairs from one half read out the correct conversations, so the Ss from the other half can complete those conversations, and vice versa.

Answers:
A 1 A: Hi, *my* name's Gina. What's *your* name?
  B: Hi, I'm Brad.
 2 A: Who's she?
  B: Oh, *her* name's Julia.
  A: And who's the man with Julia?
  B: I don't know *his* name.
 3 A: It's an American sport.
  B: What's *its* name?
  A: American football!
 4 A: Mr and Mrs Black, what's *your* phone number?
  B: *Our* phone number's 2048 306 8420473.
 5 A: This is a photo of *our* children.
  B: What are *their* names?
  A: Jake and Patsy.
B Conversation 1: 1 your 2 it 3 My 4 you 5 I
 Conversation 2: 6 She 7 her
 Conversation 3: 8 you 9 we 10 our 11 I

6A Tell Ss that the sentences in this exercise are about a business (like the ones in the texts they read), and to think about what the business is while they choose the correct answers.

Answers: 2 Her 3 his 4 Their 5 Its 6 your 7 Our 8 my

B Ss tell each other what they think the business is and why. They could also speculate about why David isn't happy in his job (perhaps because he works very long hours as the receptionist and the chef).

Answers: It's a hotel. (receptionist, rooms)

7 Before Ss look at the text, direct them to the picture and ask them where they think Mama's Salsa comes from. Then tell Ss to read the text quickly to find out if they were right (it's from South America). Ss then complete the sentences, working alone or with a partner.

Answers: 2 its 3 Her 4 their 5 his 6 our

SPEAKING

8A Tell Ss that they're going to look at information about two more family businesses, but their information isn't complete. Put Ss into pairs of AA and BB (or groups of As and Bs) and direct Ss to their incomplete texts. Tell them to prepare questions to find the missing information in each gap, e.g. *Lucia is from _____.* Question: *Where's Lucia from?*
Monitor while Ss write their questions.

Answers:
Student A:
1 How old is Jakub Tomassi?
2 What's his nationality?/Where's he from?
3 Where's their business?
4 What's their company name?
5 What's their surname?
6 Where's their restaurant?
Student B:
1 How old is Julia Tomassi?
2 Where's she from?
3 What are their jobs?
4 What's the name of their restaurant?
5 Where are they from?

B Pair up Students A and B, and tell them to ask and answer their questions, and write the missing information in their texts. Remind them to ask about spelling if they're unsure. Monitor while they do this and make notes of any good use of question forms, possessive adjectives, etc. as well as any problem areas, to use for praise and correction in feedback.

Optional extra activity

Put Ss in pairs and tell them to invent a family business and be prepared to answer the following questions:
1 What's your business?
2 Where is it?
3 How old is it?
4 Who's the manager?
5 What family members are in it? What are their jobs?
6 What are the good things about it?
Circulate and help while Ss prepare the answers to the questions. Then put pairs of Ss into groups of four and tell them to ask and answer the questions about the business. They should also make a note of the other pair's answers, as they will need the information later. In feedback, ask Ss to report to the class about another pair's business, e.g. *It's a flower shop in London. It's two years old. The manager is Chantal and her mother is a shop assistant and her sister is the driver. The good things are: it's open on Sunday, and the flowers are the best in London.*

Homework ideas

• Ss write a short text about a family business, using one or more of the texts on p20–21 as a model. You may want to go through one of the texts in class and show Ss where and how they can change the information to make it about their invented business.
• **Workbook:** Ex 1–5, p13–14

LET'S HAVE A BREAK

Introduction

Ss practise making and responding to suggestions, using vocabulary related to feelings. They also practise listening, and learn to recognise and use intonation to show interest.

> **SUPPLEMENTARY MATERIALS**
> **Resource bank:** p147 and p148
> **Warm up:** bring in a selection of pictures or short extracts of music to elicit 'happy' or 'sad'.

Warm up

Use music or pictures to introduce the idea of feelings: ask Ss *Are you OK? Are you happy?* then *What's the opposite of happy?* You could draw a happy and a sad face on the board. Then put Ss in pairs or small groups and pass round some pictures (e.g. of beautiful scenery, a cold winter's day) and/or play some short extracts of music (upbeat or slow and sombre) and ask them to tell each other how they feel (happy or sad) after each one.

VOCABULARY FEELINGS

1A Look at the example with the class, then Ss can work alone or with a partner to match the rest of the adjectives.

B Play the recording for Ss to check their answers. Play it again for them to repeat in chorus.

> **Answers:** A hot B hungry C tired D cold E thirsty F bored

In feedback, make sure Ss understand the difference between *tired* (wanting to sleep) and *bored* (having nothing to do). Also, check the pronunciation of <u>hungry</u>, <u>thirsty</u>, *tired* and *bored* (the last two are pronounced as one syllable, not *tir-ed* or *bor-ed*).

C You could demonstrate this first, pointing to a picture, asking a student *What's the problem?* and prompting them to answer *He's/She's …* Then give Ss a minute or two to practise in pairs. You could also demonstrate that Ss can act out the feeling as they give their answer.

D Ask two **stronger Ss** to demonstrate the example. To show Ss *things in common*, write the following on the board:
Jon: cold, thirsty, tired, hungry
Luigi: hot, tired, bored, hungry
Tell Ss that Jon and Luigi have two things in common: they are both tired and hungry. Then put Ss in pairs and tell them to find three things in common. In feedback to the class, encourage Ss to say *We're both …, … and …*

> ▷ **PHOTOBANK** p140
>
> If Ss are confident with the adjectives in Ex 1, direct them to Ex 1A–C on p140. Ss work alone or in pairs on Ex 1A and B, then use the pictures to 'test' each other on the adjectives in Ex 1C. Check the number of syllables in *interested* Ooo, *scared* O and *surprised* oO.
>
> **Answers:**
> A 1 D 2 C 3 H 4 G 5 A 6 E 7 B 8 F
>
> | B + | − |
> |---|---|
> | happy
interested
well/fine | angry
ill
scared/afraid
unhappy |
>
> *surprised* is fairly neutral

Optional extra activity

For extra practice of the feeling adjectives, including the ones from the Photo bank if Ss have studied them:
Put Ss in pairs. Student A mimes a feeling, Student B asks *Are you …?* Student A either replies *Yes, I am.* or *No, I'm not.* and Student B guesses again.
Listen to Ss' pronunciation of the adjectives during the practice and deal with any problems in feedback.

FUNCTION MAKING SUGGESTIONS

2A Focus Ss on the photos and ask *Who are they?* and *Where are they?* to help Ss to predict the three situations in the recording. Then direct Ss to the verbs in the box and establish that *have a break* is in all the photos (a break from running, a break from studying, a break from work) then let Ss find the other verbs in pairs.

> **Answers:** A stop, have a drink B go, have a coffee, have a break C sit down, have a coffee

Optional extra activity

To check that Ss understand the verbs (and to provide a little light relief), tell Ss to follow your instructions, but only if you start with *Please*. As an example, say to Ss, *Please stand up* (Ss stand), then *Sit down* (Ss should stay standing, because you didn't start the instruction with *Please*). Then continue the activity, using the verbs from the box, e.g. *Please sit down. Please have a coffee/go/eat. Please eat a pizza.* etc.

B Tell Ss to listen and write a letter (A–C) next to numbers 1–3. Play the recording, then give Ss time to compare answers in pairs before checking with the class.

> **Answers:** 1 B 2 C 3 A

C Give Ss a few moments to read through the sentences. Play the first part of the recording for Ss to hear that the example (1a) is true, then play the rest of the recording.

> **Answers:** 1 b) F 2 a) F 2 b) F 3 a) T 3 b) F

D You could correct these sentences with the whole class, or do Ex 1b as an example, then give Ss time to do the other three alone or in pairs.

> **Answers:** 1 b) Café Lugo is an Italian café. 2 a) It's their first meeting. 2 b) His first name's Ken. 3 b) They aren't hungry.

Unit 2 Recording 11

Conversation 1
A: Good class.
B: Yes, very good.
A: I'm hungry.
B: Yeah, me too. Let's eat something.
A: OK. Where?
B: Erm … that Italian café? What's its name?
A: Lugo?
B: Yeah, that's right. Let's go to Café Lugo.
A: OK, good idea.

Conversation 2
A: Hello, are you Mr Tajima?
B: Yes.
A: I'm Lena Smith.
B: Oh, hello. Nice to meet you, Ms Smith.
A: And you. Please call me Lena.
B: OK, Lena. And I'm Ken.
A: Let's sit down. Coffee?
B: Erm … Yes, please.

Conversation 3
A: Let's have a break.
B: Good idea. I'm tired
A: Me too.
B: … and hot.
A: Yeah. Let's stop.
B: Yeah, OK. Let's have a drink.
A: OK.

3A Look at the example with the class and give Ss a few moments to read through the conversations before playing the recording.

> **Answers: 2 B:** Let's *sit down*.   **3 A:** Let's *have a break*.
> **4 A:** Let's *stop*. **B:** Yeah, OK. Let's *have a drink*.

B Complete the rule with the class. You may want to clarify that *let's* means *it's a good idea for you and me* (i.e. not just for *you*, as in the suggestion *Why don't you …?*).

C Establish that Ss are only listening for the stressed words in the suggestions: *Let's …* Ss may wish to copy the five suggestions into their notebooks. In feedback, elicit/point out that the stress is on the information words in the sentence, not on *Let's*. Play the recording again for Ss to repeat in chorus.

> **Answers: 2** Let's <u>sit down</u>.   **3** Let's have a <u>break</u>.   **4** Let's <u>stop</u>.
> **5** Let's have a <u>drink</u>.

> ▷ **LANGUAGEBANK 2.3** p120–121
>
> The Language bank introduces the negative form, i.e. *Let's not …* which you may want to point out to **stronger classes**.
>
> > **Answers:**
> > **1 A:** I'm very tired.   **2 A:** I'm hungry.
> >   **B:** OK, *let's* stop now.   **B:** *Me* too.
> >   **A:** That's a good idea.   **A:** *Let's* eat at the pizzeria.
> >   **B:** And let's *have* a coffee.   **B:** Good idea.
> >   **A:** No, thanks. I'm not thirsty.

4A Look at the example with the class, then Ss can complete the conversations in pairs or alone.

> **Answers: 2** too   **3** Let   **4** problem (or *matter*)   **5** 's   **6** break
> **7** Me   **8** a

B Ss can start by reading the conversations aloud with their partners. Then they could choose one conversation to practise without reading from the book: tell them to write one-word prompts in their notebooks to help them remember the lines, e.g. *bored – stop*. Monitor the practice and, in feedback, ask two or three pairs who did well to act out their conversation for the class.

LEARN TO   RESPOND TO SUGGESTIONS

5A PRONUNCIATION intonation: showing interest Before playing the recording, demonstrate saying *Good idea* with interest and without interest. Play the first part of the recording for Ss to hear the example, then play conversations 2–6.

> **Answers: 2** –   **3** –   **4** +   **5** –   **6** +

Unit 2 Recording 13

1
A: Let's have a break.
B: Good idea.

2
A: Let's sit down.
B: OK.

3
C: Let's have a coffee.
D: OK.

4
C: Let's eat something.
D: OK.

5
E: Let's go.
F: Great.

6
E: Let's stop.
F: Yes, let's.

speakout TIP

Put the intonation arrow on the board and say *OK* in an interested way two or three times for Ss to repeat. Then do the same with *Good idea*, showing Ss that the stress is on *idea* and that the intonation falls after that.

B Draw the two circles with + and – on the board, and do an example with one or two **strong Ss**. They say *Great, OK* or *Good idea*, either in an interested way or not, and you point to the appropriate symbol.

SPEAKING

6A Put Ss in pairs to complete the conversation. Tell them to write the conversations in their notebooks, rather than filling in the gaps in their Students' Books, so they leave just the prompts for practice later.

> **Answers:**
> Let's eat. (OK. Where?)   Let's go to … (Good idea.)

B Ss could read the conversation aloud from their notebooks the first time, then close their notebooks and use the prompts in Ex 6A for support.

C You could ask Ss to close their books to act out the conversation so they sound more natural and spontaneous. Encourage them to repeat the conversation, making any changes they wish. Monitor and make a note of good use of grammar and intonation for praise in feedback, as well as any problems for correction.

7 Before Ss start their conversations they may need a few minutes to think of places to suggest for each adjective. Then change the pairs so that everyone has a new partner, or ask Ss to walk around and talk to at least two other Ss in the class.

> **Optional extra activity**
>
> To provide **stronger classes** with more language for Ex 7, give them a list of adjectives and activities to match, e.g.
>
> | A | B |
> |---|---|
> | bored | sit down |
> | tired | go to the cinema |
> | hungry | have a coffee or tea |
> | hot | go inside |
> | thirsty | eat |
> | cold | get a taxi |
> | | play tennis |
> | | have a sandwich |
> | | go to the park/the beach |
> | | have a cold drink |
> | | have a rest |

> **Homework ideas**
>
> **Workbook:** Ex 1–3, p15

ROYAL WEDDING

Introduction

Ss watch a BBC programme about the wedding of Prince William and Kate Middleton, with a focus on the people who attended the wedding. Ss then learn and practise how to speak and write about important people in their lives.

Warm up

Tell Ss to close their books. Teach *royal family* using a simple board picture of a king and queen wearing crowns and two children. Ask Ss to think of countries that have a royal family. Then teach *wedding* (a special day when a man and woman are husband and wife) and ask Ss to think of examples of royal weddings. If they mention William and Kate's wedding, ask them what they know about the British royal family, the names of some guests at the wedding, etc.

DVD PREVIEW

1A Check that Ss know who Kate and William are, using their photos to help. Go through the example, then put Ss in pairs to discuss the rest. (NB: You may want to teach *grandparents* using a simple family tree on the board.)

Answers:
Prince Charles is his father.
Queen Elizabeth and Prince Philip are his grandparents.
Pippa Middleton is her sister.
David and Victoria Beckham are his friends.
Elton John is his friend.

Culture notes

Prince William (born in 1982) and **Prince Harry** (born in 1984) are the sons of Prince Charles and Diana, Princess of Wales (died in 1997).

Elton John (born in 1947) is an English singer-songwriter. He was a close friend of Diana, Princess of Wales.

David Beckham (born in 1975) is an English footballer.
Victoria Beckham (born in 1974) is an English singer and fashion designer.

B Direct Ss to the two questions and give them a minute or two to find the answers in the text. Vocabulary to check: *thousands, billions* (both used to emphasise the large numbers of people watching the wedding).

Answers: Family and friends of William and Kate are at the royal wedding. It's at Westminster Abbey.

Culture note

Westminster Abbey is in the City of Westminster, in London. There have been sixteen royal weddings there. The funeral of Diana, Princess of Wales was also there.

DVD VIEW

2A Tell Ss to watch and write the number next to the correct photo.

Answers: **2** Elton John   **3** Kate Middleton   **4** Pippa Middleton
5 Prince William   **6** Prince Harry
7 Queen Elizabeth and Prince Philip   **8** Prince Charles

B Tell Ss to read through 1–6 and a)–f) and then match the sentences to the people.

Answers: **2** f)   **3** b)   **4** a)   **5** e)   **6** d)

C Play the DVD for Ss to check their answers.

D Give Ss a minute or two to read through the sentences. They may already be able to find some of the mistakes. Check that Ss understand *ring* (point to an example in the class).

Answers:
2 Victoria and David Beckham, friends of Prince William, are ~~hungry~~.   here
3 The rich and famous are here including the ~~actor~~, Elton John …   singer
4 Her sister, Pippa Middleton, arrives with children of friends and ~~fathers~~.   family
5 The big moment … and a ~~woman~~ with the ring.   problem
6 The end of a big ~~holiday~~ for Kate and William.   day

DVD 2   Royal Wedding

It's London 2011. Today is the wedding of Prince William and Kate Middleton. Two billion people around the world watch it on TV. Thousands of people are in the streets of London. Victoria and David Beckham, friends of Prince William, are here.

Prime Minister David Cameron and his wife Samantha arrive at Westminster Abbey. The rich and famous are here including the singer Elton John, a great friend of Princess Diana.

Kate and her father go to Westminster Abbey. Her sister, Pippa Middleton, arrives with children of friends and family. The Royal family arrive, first Prince William and his brother Harry.

Then their grandmother the Queen and grandfather Prince Philip. And their father Prince Charles and his wife Camilla. Kate arrives at the Abbey. Her sister Pippa meets her.

The big moment … and a problem with the ring. Kate and William are now husband and wife. Thousands of people in the streets celebrate the Royal Wedding.

The end of a big day for Kate and William.

Optional extra activity

Ss imagine what some of the people at the wedding are saying to each other. Pause the DVD just as each of the following people speak and either elicit from Ss or ask them to discuss with a partner and write down what the people say:

David Beckham to a friend as he arrives
David Cameron to his wife Samantha
Kate to her father in the car
William to the clergyman as they walk up the aisle
Camilla to the Queen
Pippa to Kate when she meets her at the car
William to Kate in the carriage
William to Kate on the balcony

Ss could also act out some of their ideas for the class.

speakout five people in your life

3A Focus Ss on the title and elicit some ideas about who those people could be, e.g. a friend, a husband/mother/sister, a person at work, etc. Tell Ss to write the names of five people in their lives for later in the lesson. Direct Ss to Jo and the five names around her, and to the people 1–5, including the example, *Duncan*. Check which people are male and which female (Duncan and Mark are male). Tell Ss to listen and match names with people 2–5.

> **Answers:** 2 Wendy 3 Sarah 4 Rosa 5 Mark

B Give Ss a few moments to look at the key phrases. You may want to check *together* (demonstrate: *We're together in this classroom*). Then play the recording again for Ss to tick the phrases. (NB: Demonstrate with an example on the board that Ss may only need to tick part of a phrase, or they may need to tick two alternatives within the same phrase.)

> **Answers:**
> OK, five people in my life. The first is … ✓
> Duncan's [my brother ✓/a very good friend/my manager/…].
> Who is [she ✓/he/Mark ✓/…]?
> [She/He's ✓] very nice, very friendly.
> Wendy is [my sister/a student/…].
> We're in a Spanish class together. ✓
> We're friends.

Unit 2 Recording 14

A: OK, five people in my life.
B: Yeah, who's first?
A: The first is Duncan. Duncan's my brother.
B: How old is he?
A: He's thirty-one, and he's a businessman.
B: And Sarah … Who is she?
A: Sarah's a very good friend, my best friend really.
B: Where's she from?
A: She's from Scotland and she's a teacher.
B: Uh-huh …
A: We're on the phone a lot! She's great.
B: Nice. And Mark? Who is Mark?
A: Mark is from work. I'm an office worker and Mark's my manager.
B: Is he friendly?
A: Yes, he's very nice, very friendly.
B: Um, and Wendy?
A: Wendy is in my class. We are in a Spanish class together.
B: Who's your teacher?
A: Her name's Rosa. She's from Madrid in Spain. Wendy and I sit together in the class and now we're friends.
B: Is your class good?
A: Yes, the *class* is good … but our Spanish isn't very good!

C Tell Ss to draw a diagram like the one in Ex 3A in their notebooks, so they can write the names of five people. Ask Ss to write notes about each of the five people, i.e. who they are, where they're from, their job, something about their personality, etc. on another page in their notebooks using the key phrases to help. Circulate and help with ideas, as well as words and phrases that Ss need, and check that everyone has written notes about five people. As Ss finish writing their notes, encourage them to practise talking (quietly, to themselves) about the people to help build confidence.

D Put Ss in pairs and tell them to show each other their diagrams and ask/answer about the five people. For **stronger classes**, you could put Ss in small groups, so they have a bigger 'audience' to speak to. You could also tell the people listening to make notes about their classmates' five people and ask them to report back afterwards about some they found interesting, e.g. *Her best friend is her husband, but he's in the USA on business. They're on the phone a lot!*

writeback a description

4A Focus Ss on the three questions (check *best friend = number 1 friend*) and give them a minute or two to find the answers in the text.

> **Answers:** 1 Emir, her brother and Ali, her mother 2 Pasqualo 3 Talya

B Encourage Ss to use the text about Melis as their model, with the following framework:
My name is _____. I'm (age). I'm (nationality) and I'm (job).
There are five important people in my life:
(Name) is _____.
For each person they should mention some of the following: friend/family relation, age, job, where she/he is, his/her personality (e.g. *nice*, *friendly*, *funny*, *kind*).
Circulate and help while Ss write their descriptions. You could then put Ss in pairs or small groups to read out their descriptions to each other.

Optional extra activity

Collect in all the Ss' descriptions, then redistribute them and ask Ss to read out the description they have been given to the class, without the first part which identifies the person (i.e. they just read about the five people). The other Ss try to guess who wrote the description.

Homework ideas

Ss write the text *Five people in my life* from the point of view of Kate Middleton or another famous person they know about.

LOOKBACK

> **SUPPLEMENTARY MATERIALS**
> **Ex 1A:** be prepared to draw your family tree and ask Ss questions about it.

FAMILY

1A Start by checking that Ss understand how the family tree works. Point to Sam and ask Ss *Who is Anne?* (his wife), then point to Billy and ask Ss *Who is Tina?* (his sister). Look at the example with the class, then Ss can work in pairs or alone to write the other names.

> **Answers:** 2 Jim   3 Billy   4 Sue   5 Nas   6 Anne

B Demonstrate to Ss that it's possible to write more than one sentence about the same person, e.g. for Al: *My wife is Nas and my mother is Anne.* Circulate and help as Ss work alone on their sentences.

C Ask two **stronger Ss** to demonstrate this for the class, then put Ss in pairs to continue.

> **Optional extra activity**
> Ss draw their own family tree and write four sentences like the ones in Ex 1A. Then they swap notebooks with a partner. Their partner writes the names of the people next to the sentences.

BE: YOU/WE/THEY

2A Tell Ss that A and B are looking at a photo of two people and talking about them. Ss complete the conversation alone, then check their answers in pairs. (NB: Remind Ss that if any of the missing words are at the beginning of a sentence, they must have a capital letter.) Ask two Ss to read out the conversation for the class to check their answers.

> **Answers:** 2 They   3 are   4 they   5 They   6 're   7 Are   8 we
> 9 Are   10 is   11 is

B Tell Ss to write two names and to think about where the people are from, how they know them (school/university/work/gym), if they're married or not, where they are now, etc.

C Demonstrate the activity by writing the names of two of your friends on the board and inviting Ss to ask you questions about them. As they do this, write up some prompts, to help them remember the questions without having to refer to their Students' Books: *Where … from?   … friends from …?   … married?   Where … now?* Put Ss in pairs and give them a few minutes to ask and answer. In feedback, you could ask one or two Ss to report back about their partner's friends, e.g. *His/Her friends are … and …, they're from …,* etc.

NUMBERS 11–100

3A Go through the example with the class. Check the pronunciation of *plus* and *minus* (and *equals,* if you decide to teach it, otherwise Ss can just say *is*). Ss write the other numbers, then read out their answers to the class.

> **Answers:** 2 eighty-eight   3 ninety-seven   4 twenty-seven

B Give Ss a minute or two to write in the numbers and to think of how to say the answer to the sum in each case.

C Demonstrate number 1 with an example of your own, e.g.
T: What's 62 minus 20?
Ss: 42
T: That's correct!
Put Ss in pairs to continue.

POSSESSIVE ADJECTIVES

4A Tell Ss there is one mistake in each sentence. They can work alone or in pairs to correct the mistakes. Alternatively, run this as a competition. Tell Ss to close their Students' Books and put them in small groups/teams. Write or display the first sentence on the board: the first group to correct the sentence wins a point. Continue for the rest of the sentences.

> **Answers:**
> 1 I'm Chinese and *my* name's Jun.
> 2 You're in Room 108 and Mr Watts is *your* teacher.
> 3 He's John. *His* surname's Wayford.
> 4 *Her* name's Vera and she's a singer.
> 5 We're students and *our* class is Room 10.
> 6 *Their* names are Ahmed and Ali and they're from Egypt.

B Before Ss start the activity, you may want to give them the opportunity to check the spelling of each others' names and/or family names: encourage them to ask each other across the class, so other Ss can hear and make a note, e.g. *Excuse me, Pia, how do you spell your family name?* Focus Ss on the examples and tell them to try to use different content from the sentences in Ex 4A, as long as it fits the pattern. Also make sure that Ss understand the idea of the false sentence by giving two examples about yourself, one true and one false, and asking Ss which one is false, e.g. *My name's … and I'm from …* Give Ss a few minutes to write their sentences, while you circulate and help as necessary.

C Focus Ss on the example and point out that Student B should wait until Student A has read out all their sentences before deciding which one is false. Monitor the pairwork and note down any good examples of language use as well as any problems for feedback.

FEELINGS

5A Start by eliciting the five vowels (*a, e, i, o, u*) from the class and writing them on the board. Check that Ss can pronounce the vowels accurately by pointing to them at random for Ss to call out. Give Ss a minute or two to add the vowels to the words, then in feedback, ask Ss to tell you just the missing vowel(s) for each feeling.

> **Answers:** 2 hungry   3 tired   4 cold   5 thirsty   6 bored

B If Ss have studied the feelings from the Photo bank p140, they could include some of these in the mime activity.

MAKING SUGGESTIONS

6A Go through the example with the class, then tell Ss to write out the lines of the conversation in their notebooks.

> **Answers:**
> B: No, I'm tired. Let's sit down.
> A: OK, let's stop and have a break.
> B: Are you thirsty?
> A: Yes, I am.
> B: Let's go to a café.
> A: Good idea.

B Ss choose any key word that will help them remember the line. You could give them slips of paper to write the key words on, so they don't refer to their notebooks.

C Monitor the pairwork and in feedback be prepared to give Ss praise for good language use and to deal with any problems.

CONSOLIDATION I: UNITS 1-2

Introduction

The aim of the consolidation units is for Ss to revise and practise the grammar, vocabulary and pronunciation from the previous two units in a different context. The context for this consolidation unit is a music festival.

READING AND GRAMMAR

1A Direct Ss to the pictures and ask them one or two questions, e.g. *Who's she? Who's he? Where are they?* then put them in pairs to talk about their ideas. In feedback, establish that the people are at a *music festival* and that *a fan* is someone who likes music a lot. You could elicit examples of other types of festivals, e.g. film/food/wine/comedy festival and ask Ss which of these they have in their city/country, and when/where they are. (NB: Keep this brief, as Ss have time to discuss music festivals in Ex 1D.)

Culture notes

Attending music festivals is a popular summer weekend activity in many countries. The larger festivals last for several days and feature famous and less well-known bands playing at different times during the day. The festivals often take place in large open spaces, where there is room for people to camp, and there are food and drink stalls available on the site. Probably the best known festival in England is the Glastonbury festival, which takes place for five days in June.

B Focus Ss on the three messages and establish that they are written by people at a festival, e.g. messages on social media, text messages, messages on notice boards. Tell Ss to read quickly, just to find the names. Reassure Ss that they will read the messages in detail later. You may want to check the following words, or deal with them in Ex 1D: *a mix of* (e.g. a city that is a mix of old and new buildings), *traditional and modern* (opposites, give examples of traditional and modern music), *concert* (where you go to listen to live music).

Answers: **A** Katja   **B** Lukas   **C** Azra   **D** Fifi   **E** Bruno

C Show Ss how to find the information about the example, i.e. scan the texts looking only for numbers until they find the correct one. They could work in pairs to help each other with the rest.

Answers: 217 room, Katja and Lukas   4439089442 phone, Jasmine   24 age, Azra   1 age, Fifi

D Put some prompts on the board and either spend a few minutes discussing them as a class, or put Ss in small groups to talk about them:
• names of music festivals – where?
• types of music – traditional/modern/rock/jazz/opera, etc?
• are they good?
• who's a music fan in the class?

Optional extra activity

Broaden the discussion activity to include all types of festivals: music, food, wine, film, art, comedy. Put Ss in groups and the following prompts on the board:
• names of festivals – where?
• when?
• type of (music/food/wine/film/art/comedy)?
• good?
• which is the best?
Ask people from different groups to report back to the class so they can compare their ideas and opinions.

2A Look at the example and elicit/point out that the questions are about the messages in Ex 1. Remind Ss that they need a capital letter if a word is at the beginning of a question. Give Ss a few minutes to complete the questions working alone.

Answers: **2** Is   **3** his   **4** is/'s   **5** her   **6** Are   **7** they   **8** How
(*it* is not used)

B To help Ss with pronunciation, you could start by saying the questions yourself for Ss to repeat in chorus and individually. Then put Ss in pairs to ask and answer. Monitor and listen for good pronunciation and language use, as well as problems, so you can give praise and deal with problems in feedback.

Answers:
2 No, he isn't. He's an office worker.
3 Yes, she is.
4 She's from Bogotá, Colombia.
5 It's tonight at 8p.m.
6 No, they're not. They're dogs.
7 Yes, they are.
8 He's four.

3 Establish that these messages are from different people who are also at the music festival.

Answers: **2** 're   **3** is   **4** isn't   **5** are   **6** Are   **7** are   **8** are

Optional extra activity

Write the following questions on the board for Ss to answer:
Is the group of students from Russia?
Is it their first time at the festival?
Is their hotel nice?
Are Jeff and Robin in room 112?
Is Arturo at the HJ Hotel? (NB: the answer here is *I don't know.*)
Put Ss in pairs to ask and answer the questions.
For **stronger classes** you could just write the following prompts:
the group of students / Russia?
they at the festival / the first time?
their hotel nice?
Jeff and Robin / room 112?
Arturo / the hotel?

LISTENING

4A Focus Ss on the name *Morelli* and ask them *Where's Morelli from?* Elicit the phrase *I think Morelli's from (Italy)* or *I think Morelli's (Italian)*, then put Ss in pairs to say what they think about the other names. Have a brief discussion with the whole class.

B Tell Ss to listen and write the nationality adjective next to each name. For **weaker classes** you could write the adjectives on the board in random order, so Ss just need to choose and copy the correct one as they listen: *English, Colombian, Japanese, Australian, American, Canadian*. Play the recording, then give Ss time to compare their answers in pairs.

Answers: Morelli – American   Haru – Japanese   Fatimah – English   Takahashi – American   Churchill – Australian   Gonzales – Colombian

C Check that Ss know they only need to write the letter, not the whole word. Play the recording again and give Ss time to compare answers.

Answers: **1** M   **2** F   **3** D

D Put Ss in pairs to decide on the missing words, then play the recording again for them to check their answers.

Answers: 1 good   2 first   3 eat   4 US, sorry

Optional extra activity

Ss invent a new identity for themselves (first name, surname, nationality, city). Direct Ss to the audio script on p155 and tell them to choose one of the conversations, then act it out, substituting their new identity information in the appropriate places. Monitor and ask one or two pairs who did well to act out their conversation for the class.

Consolidation 1 Recording 1

Conversation 1
A: Hello, I'm Tony Morelli.
B: Hi, I'm Haru Nakamuru.
A: Nice to meet you.
B: You too. Is Morelli an Italian name?
A: Yes, it is, but I'm American.
B: I see.
A: And are you from China?
B: No, Haru is a Japanese name. My parents are from Japan. It's good music, yeah?
A: Yeah, it's good. The singer is my friend …

Conversation 2
A: Hi, I'm Fatimah.
B: Hello, my name's Terry. Terry Gonzales.
A: Nice to meet you.
B: You too. Is Fatimah your surname or your first name?
A: It's my first name. It's an Arabic name.
B: Oh. Where are you from?
A: My father's from Egypt, but I'm English. And you? Is Gonzales a Spanish name?
B: Yes, it is, but I'm not from Spain, I'm from Colombia.
A: Oh, where in Colombia?
B: Bogotá.
A: Hey, I'm hungry.
B: Me too. Let's go and eat something.
A: Good idea. So, what …?

Conversation 3
A: Brad Churchill, nice to meet you.
B: Sue Takahashi. Nice to meet you, too.
A: Your English is very good!
B: Thanks, but I'm from the US.
A: Oh, I'm sorry. But Takahashi is a Japanese name.
B: Yes, my family is from Japan, but I'm American.
A: Ah. Yes, my name's Churchill, very English! But I'm Australian, from Sydney.
B: Oh, I know Sydney.
A: Really? Hey, let's go and have a coffee.
B: OK, yeah I …

SPEAKING

5 Give Students A time to find their table and tell Ss not to show their partner the information. Establish that they should ask questions to get the information they need to complete the table and give them a few minutes to think about the questions. Circulate and help (you may need to check the meaning and pronunciation of *nurse* with As, so they can explain it to Bs when the time comes). Tell the pairs to start asking and writing down the information, and monitor and make a note of anything you need to deal with in feedback.

6A Focus Ss on the example and tell them to complete five circles with information about three people, writing the information in random order. Point out that the information (ages, jobs, etc.) should be mixed up, so that partners will need to ask questions to find out which information refers to each person.

While Ss are writing their notes, draw five circles on the board and write the information about three members of your family in random order.

B Start by demonstrating the activity with the class, inviting different Ss to ask you questions about your circles and answering *Yes …* or *No …* Ss could do the activity in pairs or small groups. In feedback, you could ask a few Ss to tell the class something interesting they found out about their partner/someone else in the group.

SOUNDS: /æ/ AND /ə/

7A Direct Ss to the pictures and point out that the symbols represent the sounds. Play the recording for Ss to listen to the sounds and the words. You may also want to show Ss how the shape of the mouth is different for the two sounds: open, like a big smile for /æ/, and relaxed, nearly closed for /ə/. Play the recording again for Ss to repeat.

B Point out that Ss need to look at the underlined syllable when they decide which group to put the words in. Pause the recording if necessary to give Ss time to write.

Answers:
/æ/ taxi, actor, nationality, understand, happy
/ə/ teacher, doctor, England, computer, daughter (NB: *actor* and *understand* could also be in this group)

8A/B Put Ss in groups of 3–4 to help each other with these words. Tell them to practise saying the words aloud to each other, so they can hear which syllable has the sound in it.

Answers:
/ə/ children, seven, internet, television, India
/æ/ family, actress, bank, capitals, manager

Optional extra activity

To give Ss more practice in distinguishing between the sounds /æ/ and /ə/, write the following words from the consolidation unit on the board, and ask Ss to divide them into two groups.
Scotland fan festival cats Jasmine concert black brother

Answers:
/ə/ Scotland, festival, concert, brother
/æ/ fan, cats, Jasmine, black

Homework ideas
Workbook: Ex 1–6, p16–17

BBC interviews and worksheet
Who's in your family?
In this video people talk about their families and friends. The authentic material recaps and consolidates key vocabulary and grammatical structures with the verb *be* that Ss can use for talking about important people in their lives.

OVERVIEW

3.1 WHAT'S THIS?

VOCABULARY | things
PRONUNCIATION | sounds: plurals /s/, /z/ and /ɪz/
LISTENING | listen to conversations between students
GRAMMAR | *this/that/these/those*
SPEAKING | ask about objects

3.2 FAMOUS CLOTHES

VOCABULARY | colours and clothes
READING | read descriptions of famous clothes from films
GRAMMAR | possessive *'s*
PRONUNCIATION | sounds: possessive *'s*
WRITING | use linkers *and*, *but*
SPEAKING | talk about possessions

3.3 CAFÉ CULTURE

READING | read about some famous cafés
VOCABULARY | food and drink
FUNCTION | ordering in a café
LISTENING | listen to people in a café
PRONUNCIATION | intonation: phrases with *or*
LEARN TO | say prices
SPEAKING | order food and drink

3.4 THE MARKET BBC DVD

DVD | watch a BBC programme about a market
speakout | buy things in a market
writeback | write a description about a market

3.5 LOOKBACK

Communicative revision activities

BBC INTERVIEWS
What are your favourite things?

In this video people describe what's in their bag and their favourite clothes. It can provide an entertaining way of consolidating the vocabulary relating to clothes and possessions, as well as structures such as *This is/That is*, etc. Use the video at the end of lesson 3.2, at the end of the unit or set it as homework.

WHAT'S THIS?

Introduction

Ss practise talking about objects, paying attention to the pronunciation of their plural form, using the sounds /s/, /z/ and /ɪz/. They also practise using *this*, *that*, *these* and *those* and learn to ask the name for things in English.

> **SUPPLEMENTARY MATERIALS**
> **Resource bank:** p150
> **Warm up:** bring in some objects or pictures of objects for a memory game.

Warm up

Memory game: Put a selection of objects (6–8) that Ss know in English on a desk where they can all be seen, or display pictures of the objects on the board. Give Ss a minute to memorise the objects, then cover/remove the objects and put Ss in pairs to make a list of all the ones they remember. You could award points for a) the number of words each pair remembered and b) accurate spelling.
Suggested objects: *a book, a pen, a phone, a DVD, a photo, a passport, a camera, a dictionary, a calendar, a bag.*

VOCABULARY THINGS

1A Direct Ss to the photos and ask them what they can see: this will give you some idea of which words in the box are familiar, e.g. *a book, a cup, a table, pens.* Then put Ss in pairs to help each other and label the objects in the appropriate photos. If any words are unfamiliar, you could use simple board drawings (*keys, boxes, glasses*) and a real example (*a notebook*) to show the meaning. Help Ss with pronunciation by modelling the words for them to listen and repeat.

> **Answers:** books, a tablet computer, a notebook, cups, boxes, a table, pens, glasses

> **Teaching tip**
> To help Ss with the pronunciation of words with more than two syllables, ask them first to listen and count the number of syllables in the word, then to listen again and underline the stressed syllable and finally to listen and repeat, e.g. *com–pu–ter (3 syllables) computer.*

B Use the example *a book/books* to check the words *singular* and *plural*. Point out that singular words have *a/an* in front of them. Establish that Ss should write *Pl* next to *books*, then give them a minute or two to mark the other words.

> **Answers:**
> S – a tablet computer, a notebook, a chair, a table
> P – books, keys, cups, boxes, pens, glasses

C PRONUNCIATION sounds: plurals /s/, /z/ and /ɪz/ When Ss have practised saying the plural words, you could ask them which sound (/s/, /z/or /ɪz/) the following words from Ex 1A have: *chairs, tables, computers* (/z/).

> **Teaching tip**
> A simple rule is that the plural sound is /s/ if the word ends in the following unvoiced consonant sounds: /f/, /k/, /p/, /t/, /θ/.

49

▷ **PHOTOBANK** p140

Ss could work on these exercises in class or for homework. Ex 1 introduces ten more 'everyday' objects and Ex 2 deals with the spelling of plurals and irregular plurals. Bear in mind that the speaking practice in Ex 5 (p31) involves Ss asking each other for the names of common objects in English, which would provide an opportunity for Ss to review some of these words.

Answers:
1A 1H 2C 3G 4D 5J 6B 7E 8A 9F 10I
2A + -s: bags, credit cards, pictures, business cards, newspapers, clocks, pencils
+ -es: glasses, watches
+ -ies: dictionaries
2B **B** boys **C** a girl **D** girls **E** a man **F** men **G** a woman **H** women **I** a child **J** children

LISTENING

2A Direct Ss back to photos A–D and tell them to match conversations 1–4 to the photos as they listen to the conversations. Demonstrate on the board that we often use *one* (e.g. in *This one?*) when we don't want to use a noun too many times: *What's in these boxes? My cups are in that box. My glasses are in this ~~box~~ one.*

Answers: 1 B 2 A 3 D 4 C

B Before Ss listen to the recording again, check the pronunciation of all the names. Elicit/point out that if someone is not happy, other people often say *Sorry* to them. You could demonstrate by 'accidentally' bumping into a student's desk and saying *Sorry*.

Answers: Stan Nasrin Oliver Kate

C Give Ss a few minutes to complete the conversations and check their answers.

Answers: 1 D 2 B 3 A 4 C

Unit 3 Recording 2

Conversation 1
A: Hi, Nasrin.
B: Hi, Leyla. How are you?
A: Fine, thanks. You?
B: Yeah, good.
A: Sit down.
B: Hey, Leyla, what's that?
A: It's our homework.
B: For this lesson?
A: Yes, Nasrin.
B: Oh no!

Conversation 2
A: Hi, Tanya. What are those books?
B: Hi, Denise. These books? They're for my English class.
A: Wow! They're big!
C: Shhh!
B: Sorry, Stan! Oh, they're not so big. They're really good!
A: Who's your teacher?
B: Mr White.
A: Ah. He's good.
C: Shhh! This is a library! Please be quiet!
A/B: Sorry, Stan!

Conversation 3
A: Hey, Kate, what's in these two boxes?
B: My cups are in that box. My glasses are in this one.
A: Yeah, this one's very heavy.
B: Yeah it's … Oh, be careful!
A: Oh, no. Sorry.
B: Oh, Dave …
A: Really, I'm sorry.

Conversation 4
A: Wait a minute!
B: What's the problem?
A: Sam, is that my coffee?
B: This one?
A: Yes.
B: Oh, yes it is. Sorry, Oliver.
A: And this is *your* coffee.
B: Oh. Let's get new cups.
A: Good idea.

GRAMMAR THIS/THAT/THESE/THOSE

3A Look at photo A with the class and elicit the examples: *those books, these books*. Give Ss a minute or two to circle the other examples of *this/that/these/those* in the photos and compare their answers with a partner.

Answers:
Photo A: What are <u>those</u> books? / <u>These</u> books?
Photo B: Hey. What's <u>that</u>?
Photo C: Is <u>that</u> my coffee? / <u>This</u> one?
Photo D: Hey, Kate, what's in <u>these</u> two boxes? / My cups are in <u>that</u> box. My glasses are in <u>this</u> one. / Yeah, <u>this</u> one's very heavy.

B/C You could look at the rules with the whole class, or give Ss a minute or two to complete the exercise in pairs first.

Answers:
B 2 these 3 that 4 those
C these/those + are this/that + is

D This exercise focuses on the difference between the short /ɪ/ sound in *this* and the longer /iː/ sound in *these*. You could start by demonstrating the two sounds, exaggerating the longer sound so that Ss can hear the difference. Write the first pair of words on the board and pause the recording for Ss to look at the example. You could go through number 2 with the whole class, then play the rest of the pairs (3–6) for Ss to number 1 or 2. If necessary, play the recording again for Ss to check their answers, then play it again for them to repeat in chorus.

Answers: 2 this, that 3 those, these 4 these, those 5 this, these 6 these, this

Optional extra activity

Put Ss in pairs and tell them to write *this, that, these* and *those* in their notebooks. As an example, write *this, that, these* and *those* on the board, and ask a stronger student to call out one of the words for you to point to. Ss continue in pairs: A says a word, B points to the word she/he hears.

▷ LANGUAGEBANK 3.1 p122–123

If you feel Ss need more practice of *this/that/these/those*, give half the class Ex 3.1A and the other half Ex 3.1B. Give them each an answer key, then they can pair up with a student from the other half of the class and talk each other through the answers to the exercises.

Answers:
A 2 that 3 this 4 those 5 that 6 that
B Conversation 1
  A: *These* are our photos of Thailand.
  B: Is this your hotel?
  A: Yes, it is, and *these* are our friends, Sanan and Chai.
Conversation 2
  A: What's *that* over there?
  B: It's Red Square. And this is your hotel here.
  A: Thank you.
Conversation 3
  A: What are *these* in English?
  B: They're 'coins'. *This* one here is a pound coin.
Conversation 4
  A: Who are *those* people over there?
  B: That's my brother, Juan, and his friends.
Conversation 5
  A: Where are those students from?
  B: They're from Bogotá, in Colombia.
  A: And *that* student?
  B: She isn't a student. She's our teacher!

4A Start by setting the context here: demonstrate that A is showing Celine around the school, first taking her to the students' room, then the classroom. Ss can complete the conversations in pairs or working alone. Remind them to use a capital letter if *this/that/these/those* is at the beginning of a sentence.

Answers: 2 those 3 This 4 that 5 that 6 This 7 these 8 That

B Put Ss in groups of three to practise the conversation.

Teaching tip

Encourage Ss to be less reliant on the written word when practising a conversation:
• Ss read the conversation aloud once.
• Ss read a line aloud and do an action to go with it (pointing to friends 'over there', etc.).
• Ss look at a line, then look up and say it, still doing the action.
• Ss try to practise the conversation without looking and without worrying about being totally accurate.

speakout TIP

You could act out introducing 'Tina' and 'Dr Meyer' to each other, using two Ss. Then Ss could practise introducing the people sitting on their left and right to each other. Alternatively, they could walk round the class in pairs, introducing their partners to other Ss (they may also want to invent new identities for this).

SPEAKING

5A Put Ss in pairs and check they understand that they should choose six things in total. Ss could also refer to the Photo bank, p140 to find words.

B Circulate and help, checking that Ss can pronounce the words they find. You could give them a minute or two to practise saying the words aloud to each other, before moving on to the next stage.

C Before putting Ss in groups, model the four questions below for them to listen to and repeat. Elicit/Point out that the stress is on *this/that/these/those* and that the intonation falls at the end of the question:
What's this/that in English? ↘
What are these/those in English? ↘
Give Ss a minute or two to decide whether they need to use *this/these* or *that/those* to ask about their things, depending on how near they are. You could also encourage Ss to extend the conversations by asking for repetition and about spelling:
Sorry, can you repeat that, please?
OK, how do you spell that?
Put two pairs of Ss together to make groups of four and give them time to ask and answer about all the objects. In feedback, you could ask two or three Ss what new words they learnt in the activity.

6 Remind Ss about the conversation they practised in Ex 4, and the Speakout tip about introducing people with *This is …* Give Ss a few minutes to think about what to say when they show their partner round the classroom. Put Ss in pairs and encourage them to stand up and walk round the classroom to make the practice more realistic. Monitor and make a note of good use of *this/that/these/those* and vocabulary so you can give praise in feedback, as well as any problem areas to deal with.

Homework ideas
• Set up the following as a way for Ss to learn the names of objects at home: Tell Ss to write the names of objects (e.g. *table, chair, clock, picture*) on sticky notes and to stick them on the objects at home. Every time they see the label, they should practise saying the word. When they think they've learnt the word, they can remove the label and write a new one for another object, and so on.
• **Workbook:** Ex 1–5, p19–20

FAMOUS CLOTHES

Introduction

Ss practise reading about famous film characters' possessions and practise talking about clothes and colours, using the possessive 's. Ss also learn to use the linkers *and/but* in writing.

> **SUPPLEMENTARY MATERIALS**
> **Resource bank:** p149 and p151
> **Warm up:** a box to put objects in.

Warm up

Revise names of objects, *this, these* and *your*. Collect an object from each student, e.g. a phone, a pen, a set of keys, etc. Put all the objects in a box, including something of yours, then redistribute the objects so all Ss have something belonging to someone else. Demonstrate that Ss should walk round asking *Is this/Are these your …(s)?* and answering *Yes, it is/they are* or *No, it isn't/they aren't.* The activity ends when all the objects have been handed back to their owners.

VOCABULARY   COLOURS AND CLOTHES

1A You could start by eliciting the names and colours of the items of clothing you're wearing to see how much Ss already know. Then direct them to the words and the pictures. Ss can work in pairs.

B Play the recording for Ss to check their answers. As you go through the answers, point out that *jeans* are always plural, so we don't say *a jeans*, and that we don't add an *-s* to an adjective when the noun is plural. Play the recording again for Ss to repeat in chorus and individually. Check that Ss are pronouncing the vowel sounds in *sweater* and *shirt* correctly.

> **Answers:** 2 a green jacket   3 a black hat   4 a red sweater
> 5 a white shirt   6 blue jeans

C (NB: For **stronger classes**, you may want Ss to do the exercises in the Photo bank, p141 before setting up this practice so they can incorporate some extra clothes items and colours into the activity.) You could demonstrate this with a **stronger student**, making sure that Ss understand they need to sit back to back and take turns. Point out that when a student remembers any clothes correctly, their partner can say *That's right!*

> ▷ **PHOTOBANK** p141
>
> If Ss do Ex 1 in class, in feedback point out that *trousers* and *glasses* only exist in the plural, like *jeans*. Also check the pronunciation of *gloves*, and *skirt* versus *shirt*.
> If Ss do Ex 2 in class, you could teach them the question *What's your favourite colour?* and get them to ask and answer around the class.
>
> **Answers:**
> 1 1G 2D 3B 4F 5J 6I 7C 8A 9E 10H
> 2 A orange B brown C red D white E green F purple
>   G pink H yellow I black J blue

2A You could demonstrate that the conversation is about paying a compliment by going up to a student and saying *Nice (watch)!* which should prompt the student to say *Thank you.* Put Ss in pairs to complete the conversation. Check their answers, pointing out that *good on you* is only for things you wear.

> **Answers:** 2 shoes   3 Spain   4 my girlfriend   5 great
> 6 good on you

B Help Ss with pronunciation by modelling the lines of the conversation for Ss to repeat, paying attention to the intonation, which should sound friendly and positive. Either put Ss in groups to practise giving compliments about clothes and possessions, or ask them to stand up and walk around the classroom, talking to different people.

READING

3A Tell Ss to cover the text with their notebooks and direct them to the photos of the famous film characters (point out that *famous* means *many people know them*). Discuss with the class who the characters are.

> **Answers:** 1 Mr Bean   2 Frodo   3 Harry Potter   4 Dorothy
> 5 James Bond   6 Sherlock Holmes

B Direct Ss to the photos of clothes and put them in pairs to match the clothes to the people.

Culture notes

Sherlock Holmes is a fictional detective created by Scottish author Sir Arthur Conan Doyle. Most of the stories about him (four novels and fifty-six short stories) are narrated by his friend Dr Watson. Two of the most famous are *The Hound of the Baskervilles* and *The Sign of Four*.

Harry Potter is a boy wizard and the main character in a series of novels by British author JK Rowling. It is the best-selling book series in history and has been translated into seventy-three languages. The link between all the novels is Harry's battle with the Dark Wizard, Lord Voldemort.

Mr Bean is a television character ('a child in a man's body') whose comic adventures rely on physical humour, since the character himself rarely speaks. The series was influenced by performers such as Jacques Tati and comic actors from silent films.

James Bond is a British secret agent (007) created by writer Ian Fleming. In the twenty-three film adaptations, Bond has been played by many actors including Sean Connery, Pierce Brosnan, Roger Moore and most recently, Daniel Craig.

Dorothy, a young girl, is the main character of the 1939 American musical fantasy film *The Wizard of Oz*. She was played by Judy Garland. The film won an Academy Award for the song *Over the Rainbow*.

Frodo is a hobbit (a small, fictional, human-like race), and the main character of JRR Tolkien's *The Lord of the Rings*. He inherits the *One Ring* and goes on a journey to destroy it in the fire at Mount Doom.

C Introduce the article and explain that it's about an *exhibition* (an event where people can go and see things, e.g. paintings by famous artists) of famous clothes from films. Tell Ss to read the article quickly to see if their matches between famous film characters and their clothes were correct.

> **Answers:** 1 c)   2 f)   3 d)   4 b)   5 e)   6 a)

Teaching tip

It's important for Ss to realise that they can read a simple text and find key pieces of information or understand the general idea of the text without needing to understand every word in it. When Ss have a simple task to do, such as the one in Ex 3B, discourage them from looking up unfamiliar vocabulary in their dictionaries. It should also help to build confidence when they see that they can complete the task in spite of the unfamiliar vocabulary.

D Focus Ss on the task and suggest that they circle the things when they find them in the text. Give Ss a few minutes to complete the task and compare answers in pairs.

Answers:
One nationality – British
One city – London
Two names of films – *The Wizard of Oz*, *The Lord of the Rings*
Two red things – Dorothy's shoes, Mr Bean's tie
Two jobs – detective, actor
Five names of people in films – Sherlock Holmes, Dorothy, Mr Bean, Harry Potter, James Bond

4A Put Ss in pairs and give them a few minutes to think of some things/clothes. Circulate and help with vocabulary as necessary. Possible film series to suggest for ideas: *Pirates of the Caribbean*; *Jurassic Park*; *Star Trek*; *Star Wars*; *Spiderman*; *The Twilight Saga*.

B Before you put Ss into groups, you could teach them some phrases for discussing which item to choose, e.g. *That's a good idea; I think (XX) is the best idea; What do you think? That's not really famous; Maybe; Yes, great*. Put pairs together into groups of four or six to discuss their ideas and choose one thing/clothes item for the exhibition. Ask a student from each group to tell the class their decision.

GRAMMAR POSSESSIVE 'S

5A Focus Ss on the position of 's in the example and give them a minute or two to add the apostrophes to the other sentences.

Answers:
2 'These are Mr Bean's brown jacket and red tie.'
3 'Is this James Bond's jacket?' I ask.
4 At number five are Dorothy's shoes from *The Wizard of Oz*.

B You could go through this on the board with the class.

Answers: 's

6A Go through the example with the class, reminding Ss that *Is* and *Are* need a capital letter, then give them a minute or two to complete the other questions and answers.

B PRONUNCIATION sounds: possessive 's Play the recording for Ss to check their answers to Ex 6A. Then demonstrate the three sounds /s/, /z/ and /ɪz/ and tell Ss to listen again and match the possessive 's on the names with the sounds. Play the recording again.

Answers:
A 2 Is that Yasmin's bag? Yes, it is.
  3 Are those James's books? No, they aren't.
  4 Is this Kate's phone? No, it isn't.
B /s/ Kate's
  /z/ Nico's, Yasmin's
  /ɪz/ James's (elicit/point out that this is the pronunciation of 's when the name ends in -s)

C Use one or two Ss' names to demonstrate how the questions can be changed to make them about people and things in their own classroom.

D Ss could point to the relevant items in the room, or the pairs could walk round the classroom as they ask and answer.

Alternative approach

Put Ss in groups of 5–6. Ask one student in the group to close their eyes or turn their back while the others each put something of their own on the table in front of them. The student then opens their eyes and tries to guess who owns each thing: *Is this (X's) bag/pen/watch/phone/book?* Then another student closes their eyes and the others put different things on the table, etc.

Optional extra activity

Ss write three or four sentences about the colours of other Ss' clothes or things, e.g. *(X's) jeans are black. (Y's) phone is white.* One of the sentences should be false. Put Ss in pairs to read out their sentences and say which of their partner's sentences is false.

▷ LANGUAGEBANK 3.2 p122–123

Use the Language bank to highlight the difference between 's for possession and 's for the contracted form of *is*. Point out where the 's goes if the object belongs to two people. Ex 3.2A also reviews family vocabulary.

Answers:
A 2 Ellen is Mark and Sarah's (Sarah and Mark's) mother.
  3 Mark is Sarah's brother.
  4 Sarah is Mark's sister.
  5 Mark is Jon and Ellen's (Ellen and Jon's) son.
  6 Sarah is Jon and Ellen's (Ellen and Jon's) daughter.
  7 Ellen is Jon's wife.
  8 Jon and Ellen are Mark and Sarah's (Sarah and Mark's) parents.
B 2 I'm Josh's friend.
  3 Are you Emily's sister?
  4 Eric's surname's White.
  5 These are Bella and David's children.
  6 Rex's phone number is 396 294.

WRITING LINKERS AND, BUT

7A You could write the two sentences on the board and go through them with the class, establishing that *but* is used to join two pieces of information where the second one tells us something different, that we didn't expect.

Answers: 1 but 2 and

B Tell Ss that the four sentences are about the famous film clothes in the exhibition. You may want to check the meaning of *gold* (point to something made of gold), *writing* (point to something with writing on it), *traditional* (give an example of a traditional clothing item in the Ss' country), *countryside* (not in the town), *pair* (point to a pair of shoes/gloves/socks), *museum* (give an example of a local museum). Give Ss a few minutes to choose the correct ending and compare their answers in pairs.

Answers: 1 b) 2 b) 3 a) 4 a)

C Go through the example with the class, then Ss can work on the rest of the text alone or in pairs.

Answers: My name's Yves. It's a French name *but* I'm not French, I'm Canadian. My parents are teachers *but* I'm not a teacher. I'm a hotel manager *and* my wife's the chef in our hotel. She's from Argentina *and* her name's Natalia. She's a great chef *but* at home I'm the cook! Our son's name is Tomas *and* he's nine years old.

D While Ss write their short text, circulate and help with any language they need. When they have finished, Ss can read and comment on their partner's text.

Optional extra activity

For practice of *and/but* on the topic of favourite things, write the following sentence patterns on the board for Ss to complete about themselves:

My favourite colour is … but …
My favourite shoes are … and …
My favourite jeans are … but …
My favourite film is … and …
My favourite film character is … but …

Ss then compare their sentences in groups of three and see how much they have in common.

SPEAKING

8 Direct Ss to their pictures and tell them not to show each other. Establish that they both have a picture of the same people at a party but there are six differences between the clothes in the pictures. Take the part of Student A and use a **stronger** Student B to demonstrate the activity. Then monitor as Ss do the activity and note examples of good language use and any problems for praise and correction in feedback.

Homework ideas

- Ss research and write a short text, like the one in Ex 7C, from the point of view of a famous film character.
- **Workbook:** Ex 1–6, p21–22

CAFÉ CULTURE

Introduction

Ss practise ordering in a café, using food and drink vocabulary. They learn to identify the intonation used to offer a choice. They also practise listening and learn to say prices.

SUPPLEMENTARY MATERIALS
Resource bank: p152
Warm up: bring in pictures of food and drink to check items which may come up in the brainstorming activity and may be unfamiliar to some Ss, e.g. *chocolate, cake, sandwich, biscuit.*
Ex 5B (optional extra activity): bring in a set of eight blank slips of paper or card for each pair of Ss.

Warm up

Brainstorm food and drink vocabulary: tell Ss they are in a café or restaurant and put the headings *food* and *drink* on the board. Put Ss in pairs and give them one minute to write down all the names of food and drink they can think of. Then compile two lists on the board of their ideas, using pictures, board drawings or examples to check that Ss understand each other's ideas. Possible words: *coffee, tea, beer, chocolate, cake, biscuit, pizza, pasta, salad, burger, sandwich, fish and chips.*

VOCABULARY   FOOD AND DRINK

1A Tell Ss to cover the text with their notebooks and focus them on the photo. Elicit some ideas from the class about which countries the Hard Rock Cafe is in.

Alternative approaches

1 With the text covered, focus Ss on the photo and put them in pairs to write two things they know about the Hard Rock Café, and two things they would like to know, i.e. two questions. They then read the text to check their ideas and answer their questions.

2 Use the true/false sentences in Ex 1B as a prediction activity: Ss cover the text and, in pairs, try to answer the true/false sentences, then read the text to see if they were correct.

B Give Ss time to read through the true/false sentences before they read the text, and check that they understand them. Give Ss a time limit to read the text and find the answers, then check in pairs.

Answers:
1 F (it's in London)
2 T (in 59 countries)
3 F (rock and roll memorabilia, not singers)
4 T (in Washington D.C.)
5 F (they have two or more things in common: rock and roll memorabilia and a sign with the words 'Love all, serve all')

C Ss could work in pairs or small groups to discuss the questions. Ask a few Ss from different pairs or groups to report back to the class on favourite cafés/restaurants and food/drink that they have in common. You could finish with a vote to find out the most popular type of café and food in the class.

Culture notes

The **Hard Rock Cafe** was founded by two Americans and opened in London in 1971. The collection of rock and roll memorabilia started in 1979, with the gift of Eric Clapton's guitar. In total there are more than 70,000 items. The largest Hard Rock Cafe is in Orlando, Florida, where there is a pink Cadillac that belonged to Elvis. The Cafes are best known for their burgers, but also serve steaks, ribs, sandwiches and salads.

2A Tell Ss that the pictures are of food and drink that people order in a café, and give them a few minutes to match the phrases.

Answers: 1 D 2 F 3 C 4 A 5 B 6 E

B Tell Ss to check by asking each other *What's (B)? A tea and a mineral water*, etc. To help Ss say the orders naturally, you could model them at natural speed for Ss to repeat, showing them that items of food and drink are stressed and the other words are 'squashed' in between them, e.g. *a sandwich and a coffee*.

C You could start by setting the scene in a café (e.g. write the name of a local café on the board), then demonstrate that you are a waiter and invite a **stronger student** to come and be a customer. Ask Ss what the waiter says to elicit *Can I help you?* then indicate that the customer should order something from Ex 2A. As you mime handing over the order, elicit or give *Here you are.* Tell Ss to look at their pictures in Ex 2A but cover the words. Put them in pairs to practise the conversation. Ss take turns to be the waiter/waitress or the customer.

FUNCTION ORDERING IN A CAFÉ

3A Before you play the recording, give Ss time to read through the orders and check any unfamiliar vocabulary, e.g. *white coffee* (with milk: elicit that the opposite is *black coffee*), *sugar* (mime putting a spoonful of sugar in a cup of coffee and stirring it), *espresso* and *cappuccino* (mime using a coffee machine), *egg* (draw a picture), *white bread* (a picture, elicit/teach that the opposite of *white* here is *brown*), *sparkling* (a picture showing the bubbles in the water, a glass of *still water* to show the opposite). Tell Ss to cross out any words that are wrong and write the correct ones above them. Play the recording. Give Ss time to compare their answers and play the recording again if necessary.

Answers:
1 one *black* coffee with sugar
2 two espresso coffees
3 one egg sandwich (*brown* bread), one chocolate cake, one *mineral water*
4 one sparkling mineral water

B Look at the example with the class, then give Ss a minute or two to go through the rest of the conversation.

Answers: b) W c) W d) C e) C f) W g) C

C You could find the first line (d) with the class, then put the Ss in pairs to put the rest in order. Play the recording for Ss to check.

Answers: 1 d) 2 c) 3 g) 4 b) 5 e) 6 a) 7 f)

Conversation 1
A: Can I have a coffee, please?
B: With milk?
A: No, thanks. Black.
B: Sugar?
A: Yes, please. One.
B: One black coffee with sugar! That's four euros.

Conversation 2
A: Can I have two coffees, please?
B: Espresso or cappuccino?
A: Oh, espresso, please.
B: Anything else?
A: No, thanks. How much is that?
B: That's five euros fifty.

Conversation 3
A: Hi.
B: Hi. Can I have an egg sandwich, please?
A: White or brown bread?
B: Oh, brown bread, please.
A: Anything else?
B: Yeah, can I have one of those cakes?
A: These ones?
B: No, the chocolate ones.
A: Anything to drink?
B: Yes, a mineral water, please. How much is that?
A: That's four euros for the sandwich, three for the cake and two for the mineral water. That's nine euros.
B: Here you are.

Conversation 4
A: Can I have a mineral water, please?
B: Still or sparkling?
A: Sparkling, please.
B: Anything else?
A: No, thank you. How much is that?
B: That's three euros.

4A Give Ss time to read through the table, then elicit the missing words from the class.

Answers:

Can I have	a two	mineral water, please? coffees, *please*?
Still Espresso	or	sparkling? cappuccino?

B **PRONUNCIATION intonation: phrases with *or*** Remind Ss that the arrows show if the voice is going up or down. Play the recording several times if necessary, for Ss to hear the pattern and repeat.

Answers: 2

Teaching tip

A rising intonation pattern, as on *still* here, often shows that the speaker hasn't finished (in this case because they are going to offer another choice). In contrast, a falling intonation suggests the speaker has finished.

C Demonstrate this with one or two Ss first, prompting them to ask you the question. For **stronger classes** you could ask Ss to suggest other choices, e.g. *black/white (coffee or tea), small/large (cola), white/brown (bread)*.

5A Tell Ss to write the completed conversation in their notebooks so they can refer back to the prompts in their Students' Book for speaking practice later. Ss can work in pairs, or work alone and compare answers with a partner.

Answers:
A: Can I have a coffee, please?
B: Espresso or cappuccino?
A: Cappuccino, please.
B: Anything else?
A: Yes, can I have a mineral water, please?
B: Still or sparkling?
A: Sparkling, please.
B: OK, that's five euros.

B Before you put Ss in pairs, help them with pronunciation of the conversation by saying each line at natural speed for them to repeat in chorus. In the first line focus on the weak form of *Can* /kən/ and the linking between *Can* and *I*. Give Ss time to practise the conversation twice, so they say both the customer's and the waiter's lines. For **stronger classes**, encourage Ss to change three or four words in the prompts, e.g. *cappuccino, still, six*. Monitor and note down common problem areas, so you can decide whether to do extra practice from the Language bank in class.

Optional extra activity

To help Ss to move away from the prompts and gain confidence, give each pair a set of eight blank slips of paper or card, and ask them to write the prompt for a line of the conversation on each of them. Ss then put the prompts in front of them in the correct order as they practise the conversation.

▷ **LANGUAGEBANK 3.3** p122–123

Ss could do Ex 3.3 in class if they are making mistakes with the word order, etc. or phrases in the conversation.

Answers:
A: Can I help *you*?
B: Yes, can I *have* an egg sandwich, please?
A: White *or* brown bread?
B: Brown, please.
A: Anything *else*?
B: Yes, *can* I have two coffees, please?
A: Espresso or cappuccino?
B: One espresso and *one* cappuccino.
A: OK, *that's* seven fifty.

LEARN TO   SAY PRICES

6A Give Ss a minute or two to read through the prices and think about how to say them. Then play the recording, pausing after the example to check that Ss are on task.

Answers: 2 3.00   3 2.50   4 12.75   5 5.20   6 10

B Play the recording for Ss to listen and repeat. Then put Ss in pairs. Tell them to take turns pointing to a price and saying it.

C Tell Ss to write the numbers 1–5 in their notebooks, with space next to each to write a price. Play the recording for Ss to write the prices, then give them time to compare answers in pairs.

Answers: 1 1.80   2 4.15   3 2.90   4 6.35   5 11.40

speakout TIP

To give Ss more examples of this, write prices on the board, and ask Ss to say them in both ways. They could also practise the same prices with *dollar(s)* and *pound(s)*. (NB: Point out that if the price is a 'round' number, e.g. $2, you do need the name: *two dollars*.)

D Elicit some examples of things that Ss could write, e.g. other food items: *a coffee, a tea, a burger, a pizza, a sandwich, a cola* or other things Ss might have with them, e.g. *a pen, a dictionary, a notebook*. Ss could choose to write their prices with or without the name of the currency.

E Demonstrate this by saying two things and two prices for Ss to write, then check them by asking two Ss to come and write them on the board. Monitor the activity and deal with any language problems afterwards.

SPEAKING

7 You could group all the As and Bs together to prepare this role-play. Circulate and help with vocabulary and pronunciation.

As: The waiters need to think about the choices they can offer the customer for *coffee* or *tea* (e.g. black/white), *cola* (e.g. large/small), *cake* (e.g. chocolate/vanilla), *mineral water* (e.g. still/sparkling), *sandwich* (e.g. egg/cheese). They also need to practise saying the prices.

Bs: The customers need to think about what type of coffee/tea/sandwich/cake they want. They also need to think about what they can get for two people with their money.

Pair up As and Bs and give them time to practise. You could then move Ss around the classroom, so they're working with different partners, and practise the role-play again. Monitor the role-plays and note down examples of good language use for praise in feedback, as well as any problems to deal with. You may also want to ask two or three pairs to act out their role-play for the class.

Homework ideas

- Ss go to their favourite café and make some notes about the food and drink on the menu and the prices. Then they write some sentences about the café.
- **Workbook:** Ex 1–6, p23

THE MARKET

Introduction

Ss watch a BBC extract about a man's first day as a salesman in an Istanbul market. Ss then learn and practise how to buy items in a market, and write a paragraph about a market they know.

SUPPLEMENTARY MATERIALS

Ex 4C: for *stronger classes*, prepare a vocabulary sheet with simple labelled pictures of jewellery and pottery (see notes for suggestions).
Ex 5B: bring in some photos and information (e.g. from the internet) about some famous markets, e.g. Camden or Portobello Road in London.

Warm up

Direct Ss to the main photo and put them in small groups to answer the following questions about it:
What's in the photo?
What country is it?
Is it a good market?
Where is a good market in your country/city?

DVD PREVIEW

1A Look at the example with the class and check the pronunciation of *spices*. Put Ss in pairs to help each other match as many words as they can. As you check the answers, help Ss with the pronunciation of *clothes*, *jewellery* and *leather*.

Answers: 2 B 3 A 4 C 5 E 6 F

B Discuss the question with the class. You could also ask for examples of other things that are in their local markets, e.g. food, drink, toys, pictures, books, old things (antiques), things for your house.

2 Read out the two questions to the class and tell Ss to read quickly and find the answers. Vocabulary to check: *TV presenter* (give an example), *carpet seller* (a person who sells carpets), *a salesman* (a man who sells things).

Answers: He's in Istanbul, at the Grand Bazaar. He's a carpet seller.

DVD VIEW

3A Direct Ss back to the photos in Ex 1A and tell them to look for any of the objects. You may want to play the DVD without sound the first time, so Ss don't get distracted by trying to understand the conversation. Otherwise, reassure Ss that they'll watch the extract again.

Answers: spices, carpets, jewellery, pottery, leather wallets and bags

B Before playing the DVD again, give Ss time to read through the sentences and check the following vocabulary: *thousand*, *old/new*, *silk* (if possible, take in something/a picture of something made of silk), *real* (here used to emphasise how good the carpet is), *a nightmare* (a big problem, e.g. *Traffic/Parking in my city's a nightmare!*), *a sale* (act out selling something), *a special price*, *a discount* (draw a price ticket with $500 crossed out and $350 written above it). Give Ss a few minutes to compare and check answers with a partner.

Answers: 1 second 2 thousand 3 learn 4 new 5 real
6 a nightmare 7 Eight 8 friendly 9 sale 10 discount

C You could also ask Ss if they think it's an easy or difficult job and put some prompts on the board: *opening time? street market cold? no sales? people not friendly?* Don't worry about correcting Ss' mistakes in a discussion like this, it's more important to encourage them to try to say whatever they can.

DVD 3 The Market

F = Francesco da Mosto   H = Harkan Nayveen   M1 = 1st man
M2 = 2nd man   M3 = 3rd man   S = Seller   W = Woman

F: My second day in Istanbul, and it's seven o'clock in the morning – opening time at the Grand Bazaar.
There are four thousand shops here, selling jewellery, pottery, spices, carpets, leather and, of course, Turkish Delight.
Lost!
I'm meeting carpet seller, Harkan Nayveen.
Ciao.
H: Ciao, how are you?
F: Very well.
H: It's good to see you.
F: So, I'm here to learn.
H: Yes.
F: I have to tell you that really I don't know anything about carpets.
H: Yeah, no?
F: I'm totally in your hands.
H: Yeah, no problem, no problem.
This is new. This looks old but it is not old. This is pure silk carpet.
F: Wow.
H: This is a real art. Like Turkish Picasso.
F: Hello, hello, would you like to, to have a look at some carpets, sir?
M1: No, no.
F: Carpets with silk, Turkish silk …
M1: No.
F: No. Er would you like to buy a carpet?
M2: What?
F: Carpet, er, 'tappeto'. It's nice, really, come. Just have a look, you don't have to buy it.
M3: Don't like carpets.
F: You don't like carpets, you have carpets at home?
M3: No.
F: No carpets?
M3: No carpets.
S: It's not that easy, not that easy.
F: Yeah, it's a nightmare, a nightmare.
This is Turkish silk, it's very good, it's big.
W: Three hundred dollars.
F: Er, eight hundred.
W: No. Six …
F: So, six.
W: No, five, five hundred – no, no.
F: Five eighty, five eighty.
H: Francesco, you are doing very good, and are you from America?
W: Yes.
H: Americans are good.
W: Yes, they are.
H: They are friendly. As you see you can stop and talk to Americans.
F: OK five hundred, five hundred, OK, five hundred.
W: All right.
F: OK, so …
H: Let me, let me help. It is his first sale. He is doing very good, so we will give you a special discount, five hundred dollars …
F: And it's good.

speakout in a market

4A Tell Ss they are going to hear a conversation in a market, then direct Ss to the sentences. Give Ss a minute or two to read the sentences through and tell them to correct the false sentences. Play the recording.

Answers:
2 F The seller's first price is 200.
3 T
4 F The final price is 100.

B Give Ss a few moments to look at the key phrases. You may want to check the following vocabulary: *have a look* (= look), *this/that one* (you could demonstrate that *one* replaces *lamp*, so the speaker doesn't keep repeating it, and give one or two more examples, e.g. *How much is that carpet? This one? Yes.*), *expensive* (you could contrast this with *cheap*).

Play the recording again for Ss to tick the phrases. (NB: You may also want to highlight *the (blue) one* from the recording, showing Ss that they can put in a different adjective (e.g. a colour, *big/small*) to help to identify the object.)

Answers:
Excuse me. ✓
Where is [this/that] [lamp/carpet] from?
Where are [these/those ✓] [lamps ✓/carpets] from?
Can I have a look? ✓
This one? ✓
No, that one. ✓
How much [is it ✓/are they]?
That's expensive.✓
For you, a special [discount ✓/price].

Unit 3 Recording 11

A: Excuse me.
B: Yes.
A: Where are those lamps from?
B: They're from Turkey.
A: Can I have a look?
B: Yes. This one?
A: No, that one. The blue one.
B: It's very nice.
A: How much is it?
B: It's two hundred.
A: That's expensive. Hmm. Fifty.
B: One hundred and fifty.
A: Seventy-five.
B: For you, a special discount. Only one hundred.
A: OK. One hundred.
B: It's a very good price.

C Ss should take turns at being the seller and the customer. Give them a minute or two to agree on an item and think about the price they're willing to pay/accept. For **weaker classes** you could suggest that Ss choose an item of clothing for this role-play, so they can review some of the items from lesson 3.2. For **stronger classes**, you could provide a vocabulary sheet with simple labelled pictures of items of jewellery (e.g. *ring, necklace, earrings*) or pottery (e.g. *plate, cup, bowl*) so that Ss are more challenged. Monitor the role-plays and make a note of good language use and problem areas for praise and correction in feedback. You could also ask two or three pairs to perform their role-plays for the class.

writeback a description

5A You could start by asking Ss where they might see this kind of text, e.g. in a guidebook or on a tourist information website. Ask different Ss to read out the questions to the class, then give Ss a few minutes to read and answer the questions.

Answers:
1 Covent Garden market
2 It's in the centre of London.
3 Yes, it is.
4 It's good for jewellery, clothes, pictures, small shops and cafés.

B You could start by giving Ss some alternative ways of answering the questions, e.g.
2 It's in the centre of …/It's near …
3 It's open on weekdays/at weekends.
4 It's a good market for visitors/local people.

You could also take in some photos and information (e.g. from the internet) about famous markets in different countries to give Ss ideas. Circulate and help with vocabulary, etc. as Ss write their information. When Ss have finished writing, you could:
• put their information on the wall so they can walk round and read each other's work.
• put Ss in groups to read out their information to each other.
• (in a smaller class) ask each student to read out their information to the class.

You could finish by asking the class to vote on the most interesting market.

Homework ideas

Ss review all the new vocabulary items they've studied in this lesson and choose five that they think will be most useful to remember. They write a short conversation in a market that includes all five items.

LOOKBACK

THINGS

1 You could run this as a team game (Ss have their books closed). Display one word at a time: team members 'buzz' to answer, then call out just the missing vowels. The team wins a point for each correct vowel in the word, then when the word is complete, an extra point if they can pronounce the word correctly.

> **Answers: 1** book **2** table **3** glasses **4** chair **5** notebook **6** key **7** tablet computer **8** box **9** cup **10** pen

THIS/THAT/THESE/THOSE

2A To familiarise Ss with the content of the conversation before they complete the gaps, give them a minute or two to read through it and answer these questions: *Who's Carlos?* (Jan's husband) *Who's Maria?* (Jan's friend) *Who are Ana and Paolo?* (Jan and Carlos's children). Then put Ss in pairs to complete the conversation.

> **Answers: 2** this **3** these **4** this **5** this **6** that **7** those

B Put Ss in groups of five and tell them to practise the conversation two or three times, changing roles each time. Then you could ask Ss to write one or two key words from each person's line in their notebooks to act as prompts so they can close their books and practise the conversation again.

C You could give Ss slips of paper to write the new information on, then pass the slips to their partner. When they have their new 'identity', give them a few moments alone to practise talking about it, e.g. spelling their name, saying where they're from and what their job is.

D Put Ss in groups of six, and establish that when one person is introducing their partner, the other four should participate and ask questions, e.g.:
A: This is (Soraya).
B: Hello. Nice to meet you.
C: Nice to meet you, too.
D: That's a nice name. How do you spell it? etc.
Monitor the group work and note down examples of good language use and any problem areas for praise and correction.

COLOURS AND CLOTHES

3A You could put the letters for the first word in order as an example with the class. Ss can work in pairs, or work alone and compare answers with a partner. Alternatively, you could run it as a race: Ss work in pairs to put the letters in order as quickly as they can and run to the front of the class with their answers when they've finished. The first pair to finish with all correct answers wins 5 points, then any pair can win 3 points for spelling any of the words aloud correctly.

> **Answers: 1** sweater **2** black **3** blue **4** shirt **5** jacket **6** green **7** trousers **8** brown

B Point out that Ss should not let their partner see the words as they are writing them.

C Demonstrate this with a student, then put Ss in pairs.

POSSESSIVE 'S

4A Go through the objects in pictures 1–6 and check the pronunciation of *guitar oO* and *racquet Oo*. Check that Ss know who the people are.

> **Answers: 1** Mozart's piano **2** Taylor Swift's guitar **3** Picasso's brush **4** Serena Williams's tennis racquet **5** Ronaldo's football **6** Michael Jackson's glove

Culture notes

Wolfgang Amadeus Mozart (1756–1791) was an Austrian classical composer. He started composing at the age of five and composed more than 600 works.

Pablo Picasso (1881–1973) was a Spanish painter and sculptor. He co-founded the Cubist movement.

Cristiano Ronaldo (born 5 February 1985) is a Portuguese professional footballer who plays for the Spanish club Real Madrid and the Portugal national team. He is a forward and serves as the captain for Portugal.

Taylor Swift (born 13 December 1989) is an American singer-songwriter and actress. She is one of the best-selling artists of all time, having sold more than 40 million albums.

Serena Williams (born 26 September 1981) is an American professional tennis player who is ranked number 1 in women's singles tennis. She is widely recognized by many tennis legends and commentators as the greatest women's tennis player of all time.

Michael Jackson (29 August 1958–25 June 2009) was an American singer, songwriter, record producer, dancer and actor. Called the King of Pop, he was a global figure in popular culture for over four decades.

B Demonstrate this first, naming a student in the class as in the example, then invite the other Ss to ask you three questions. Put Ss in pairs to continue.

FOOD AND DRINK

5 You could run this as a team game. Display the wordsnake on the board: team members 'buzz' when they find a word, then they must spell it aloud correctly in order to win a point for their team.

> **Answers:** water   coffee   cake   tea   mineral water   sandwich cola

ORDERING IN A CAFÉ

6A Look at the example with the class, then tell Ss to write out the lines of the conversation in their notebooks.

> **Answers:**
>   **2** Can I have an egg sandwich, please?
>   **3** White or brown bread?
>   **4** White, please.
>   **5** Anything else?
>   **6** Yes, can I have a mineral water?
>   **7** Still or sparkling?
>   **8** Sparkling, please. How much is that?
>   **9** That's $6.90.
>   **10** Here you are.

B Ss practise once by referring to the conversation they've written in their notebooks, then close their notebooks and practise using the prompts in their Students' Books.

Optional extra activity

Ss change four things in the conversation and practise it again. Then they act out their conversations for the rest of the class. The other Ss note down the four things that are different.

7A Ss work on this in pairs. Point out that there may be more than one alternative for some of the pairs.

Answers: 2 espresso   **3** sparkling   **4** dollars/pounds   **5** white
6 pencil   **7** jeans/skirt   **8** shoes

B Demonstrate this by saying *Coffee or …?* and gesturing for the class to finish the question in chorus. Remind Ss about the rising, then falling intonation pattern. Put Ss in small groups to practise.

BBC interviews and worksheet

What are your favourite things?

In this video people describe what's in their bag and their favourite clothes. It can provide an entertaining way of consolidating the vocabulary relating to clothes and possessions, as well as structures such as *This is/That is*, etc.

OVERVIEW

4.1 WHAT'S DIFFERENT?

VOCABULARY | verb phrases
LISTENING | listen to people talk about life in the USA
GRAMMAR | present simple: *I/you/we/they*
PRONUNCIATION | sentence stress
SPEAKING | find things in common
WRITING | use linkers *and, because*

4.2 A GOOD MATCH

READING | read an interview with two people
GRAMMAR | present simple: *he/she/it*
PRONUNCIATION | 3rd person s
SPEAKING | find differences in pictures
VOCABULARY | days; time phrases

4.3 WHAT TIME IS IT?

VOCABULARY | events
FUNCTION | telling the time
LISTENING | listen to people tell the time
LEARN TO | check times
PRONUNCIATION | intonation for checking
SPEAKING | tell the time

4.4 A SECRET LIFE BBC DVD

DVD | watch a BBC programme about an Amish family
speakout | do a group survey
writeback | write a report

4.5 LOOKBACK

Communicative revision activities

BBC INTERVIEWS

What do you do for fun?

In this video people talk about their lifestyles: what they like to do with their friends or on their own. The material provides authentic usage of the present simple which is the focus of lesson 4.1 and lesson 4.2, as well as recycling vocabulary for talking about leisure activities. Use the video after lesson 4.1 or 4.2 or at the end of the unit.

WHAT'S DIFFERENT?

Introduction

Ss practise listening and talking about people's lifestyles, using the present simple and verb phrases. They practise sentence stress in present simple questions. They also learn to use the linkers *and* and *because* in writing.

SUPPLEMENTARY MATERIALS
Resource bank: p154
Warm up: prepare sets of cards for each group of Ss (4–6 Ss per group) with items of vocabulary (see notes below).

Warm up

Vocabulary review in groups.

Prepare sets of cards with the following words: *a phone, a cola, a coffee, a hamburger, homework, a credit card, an office, a house, a shop, a flat, a café, a taxi, university, parents, a brother, sport, clothes, glasses, a week, an evening.*

Divide Ss into groups of 4–6 and place the cards face down in a pile in the centre of each group. Demonstrate that Ss should take turns to pick a card (without showing the rest of the group) and mime, draw or give a very short verbal clue for the word on it. The first student in the group to guess the word gets the card, and picks up the next one. The winner is the student with the most cards when the pile is finished. (NB: If a student doesn't know the word on the card, he/she puts it at the bottom and takes another one. Clarify any words that are left at the end.)

VOCABULARY VERB PHRASES

1A Before Ss start this exercise, you may want to check what a verb is. Say *I'm a teacher. I'm from (country)* and write these on the board. Then mime drinking a coffee and looking contented. Say *I like coffee* and write this on the board. Then ask Ss to identify the verb in each phrase: *Where's the verb?* Focus Ss on the example and say *I like baseball and I like hamburgers and I like coffee* to show that the same verb matches all the nouns. Give Ss a few minutes to complete the word webs and compare answers with a partner.

Answers: **3** in an office **4** a small car **5** English **6** in a flat **7** to a restaurant **8** Exercise 3A

B Put Ss in pairs and direct them to the photos of things from the USA.

Answers: go to a restaurant, like hamburgers, like baseball, do sport, live in a house

C Elicit one or two examples of words/phrases to add to *like* and *have* (e.g. *like chocolate, like Taylor Swift; have two sisters, have a car*) then put Ss in pairs to add words/phrases to the other verbs. Point out that they can look back through their Students' Book for ideas if necessary.

Suggested answers:
work: in a shop, at home, in the mornings
drive: a bus, to work
study: maths, at school, in the evenings
live: in Spain/Japan, with my husband
go: to work, inside, home
do: exercise, my/your work

4 life

D You could demonstrate this with one or two **stronger Ss**, then put Ss in pairs to practise. You could also tell Ss to 'reverse' the activity, i.e. A says the word or phrase, B says the verb:

A: At university
B: Study at university. To work.
A: Go to work. Sport.

E Demonstrate this with a student taking the part of Student A. Ss should be familiar with *Me too*. Tell them that *I don't* is the negative answer, but leave the grammatical analysis of this for later in the lesson. Tell Ss to take turns as A and B, and give them a few minutes to practise.

speak◌ut TIP

Explain that learning verb phrases will help Ss to speak more in English and sound fluent more quickly. You could suggest that Ss keep separate pages in their notebooks (or in separate vocabulary books) for some of the more common verbs, e.g. *have, go, do*, so they can keep adding phrases as the course goes on.
Put Ss in pairs and give them a few minutes to think of five phrases with *be*, then compile a list on the board with the class.

> **Suggested answers:** *be* + feeling adjective (hungry/tired)
> *be* + from city/country (Madrid/Spain)
> *be* + *at* + place (home/work/school) *be* + age (15/21)
> *be* + job (a student/an actor) *be* + adjective (big/small)

▷ PHOTOBANK p142

When Ss have completed the exercises, encourage them to add the verb phrases to their notebooks or vocabulary books.

> **Answers:**
> **A B** read **C** listen **D** play **E** cost **F** watch **G** write
> **H** want
> **B b)** be **c)** listen **d)** read **e)** watch **f)** play **g)** cost
> **h)** write

LISTENING

2A Tell Ss they're going to listen to people talking on a radio programme called the *USA Today*. Give them a moment or two to read the information and answer the question. Check *the same* and *different* by using objects in the classroom, e.g. two Students' Books – *the same*, two notebooks – *different*.

> **Answer:** No, the people are from different countries. (NB: You may want to ask Ss if they think people will say life in the USA is the same or different to their countries, i.e. to predict from their background knowledge.)

B Show Ss that *houses* is number 1, and check that they're listening for three more topics, to be numbered 2–4.

> **Answers:** **2** students **3** cars **4** friends

C Give Ss a minute or two to read the sentences before you play the recording again. Then get Ss to check their answers in pairs.

> **Answers:** **1** houses **2** evenings **3** drive **4** the same

D Ss work in pairs to discuss similarities and differences. Ask a couple of pairs to report back their ideas to the class.

Unit 4   Recording 1

A: Excuse me. Do you have a moment?
B: Yes?
A: You aren't American?
B: No, no, I'm from Japan. I'm on holiday here.
A: OK. So, my question is: what's different for you about life here?
B: Erm … well, here people live in houses … they live in big houses. I'm from Tokyo, and we live in flats, small flats. So that's very different.
A: … and so for you, what's different about life here?
C: Erm … well, I study at university here. And it's very different from my country because here, in the United States, the students have jobs. They work in the evenings, maybe ten hours a week.
A: And you? Do you work?
C: Me? No, I don't. I don't have time. And in my country students don't work, they only study.
D: What's different here? Erm … oh yeah, people drive everywhere. I mean, they drive two hundred metres to the shops.
A: Do you have a car?
D: Yes, I do, but I don't drive to the shops. Not two hundred metres! I walk.
A: And where are you from?
D: I'm from England.
E: I think it's not so different. I'm from Italy and my American friends are not so different from me. Er … we like sport … we like clothes … We, er … we go to the cinema, restaurants, have a coffee …
A: So you like the same things?
E: Yeah, the same … not different.

GRAMMAR   PRESENT SIMPLE: I/YOU/WE/THEY

3A/B Write the sentences on the board and ask Ss to tell you which words to underline. Check that the present simple refers to *all the time*, not just *now*. (NB: If Ss ask why *he/she/it* are missing, tell them they're different and that they'll study them in the next lesson.)

> **Answers:**
> **A 2** work **3** like **4** don't drive
> **B** I/You/We/They *don't* live in a house. (Elicit/Point out that *don't* = *do not* and that we use contractions in speaking.)

4A Go through the example with the class, then give Ss a minute or two to complete the sentences. As you check the answers, write the completed sentences on the board so you can demonstrate the next stage.

> **Answers:** **2** have **3** don't have **4** study **5** don't work
> **6** don't like

B Demonstrate this first by ticking the sentences that are true for you, then making changes to the others to make them true, e.g. 2 I *don't have* two sisters, I have *three brothers*. 3 I *have* a camera. Give Ss time to work on their sentences, then put them in pairs to read out their sentences and find out if any are the same.

5A Give Ss a few minutes to look at the tables and think about the answers, then elicit the complete questions and answers and write them on the board. Demonstrate to Ss that when the question begins with *Do*, the answer is either *Yes* or *No*, and that when *What* or *Where* is added in front of *do*, the question is 'open', i.e. there are many possible answers.

> **Answers:**
>
> | Where | do | you | live? |
> |-------|-----|------|--------|
> | What | | | study? |
> | Do | you | have | a car? |
> | Yes, I do. | | No, I don't. | |

B PRONUNCIATION sentence stress Write *Where do you live?* on the board and play the first line of the recording twice for Ss to hear the stressed words. Then play the rest of the conversation twice. As you check the answers, you could use large/small circles to show the stressed/unstressed syllables, e.g A: OooO? B: oOo. A: ooOooO? B: OoO.oO? A: OoO.oOooO.

> **Answers:**
> **B:** In Lon<u>don</u>.
> **A:** Do you <u>live</u> in a <u>flat</u>?
> **B:** <u>Yes</u>, I <u>do</u>. And <u>you</u>?
> **A:** <u>No</u>, I <u>don't</u>. I <u>live</u> in a <u>house</u>.

C Ss practise the conversation twice, taking turns to say A and B's lines.

> **Teaching tip**
>
> To help Ss with sentence stress when practising a conversation, tell them to just say the stressed words the first time so they get used to the rhythm, e.g.
> A: *Where – live?* B: *London.* A: *live – flat?* B: *Yes – do. You?*
> Then demonstrate that the unstressed words are 'squashed' between the stressed words, so that the rhythm stays the same.

6A Go through the example with the class, then Ss could work alone or in pairs to make questions. When you've checked the answers, ask Ss which questions need a *Yes/No* answer, and which are 'open' questions (1–4 are *Yes/No* questions, 5–6 are open). Then you could ask Ss to repeat the questions, showing them that 1–4 have rising intonation at the end, and 5–6 have falling intonation at the end.

> **Answers: 2** Do you like American films? **3** Do you have a dictionary?
> **4** Do you like cola? **5** What sports do you like?
> **6** Where do you live?

B Remind Ss to answer *Yes, I do./No, I don't. And you?* for each question. When they've asked all the questions, you could tell them to change one word in each question (i.e. *cats, American, dictionary, cola, sports, live*), and ask/answer again.

> ▷ **LANGUAGE**BANK **4.1** p124–125
>
> The Language bank summarises the positive, negative, question and short answer forms. Ex 4.1A practises the positive and negative forms, the other exercises practise question and short answer forms. You may want to give Ss more practice of question forms before doing the Speaking activity in Ex 7A on p41.
>
> **Answers:**
> **A 2** like **3** don't have **4** don't drive **5** write **6** live **7** eat
> **8** don't know
> **B 2** Do you and Jack live together?
>   **3** Do you work in an office?
>   **4** Do you have a black sweater?
>   **5** Do your parents understand Spanish?
>   **6** Do you walk to work?
> **C 2** No, we don't. **3** Yes, I do. **4** No, I don't. **5** Yes, they do.
>   **6** No, I don't.
> **D 2** Where do you work?
>   **3** When do we have a break?
>   **4** How do you spell George?
>   **5** What do they like?

SPEAKING

7A Demonstrate this by writing *I like _____* and *I have _____* on the board and finishing the sentences with something that is true for you. As Ss work alone on their sentences, circulate and help, reminding Ss to put an *-s* on plural nouns after *like/don't like*.

B Demonstrate by going up to a few Ss and asking *Do you like (Chinese food)?* until someone answers *Yes*, then ask them to spell their name and mime writing it in a notebook. Ask Ss to stand up and walk around the classroom, asking their questions until they have five names in column A. Monitor the activity and note down good examples of language use as well as any problems, for praise and correction in feedback.

C Go through the example, reminding Ss that we use *both* when we have the same answer/opinion. Give them a minute or two to choose a sentence from their five to tell the class.

> **Watch out!**
>
> Ss may say *(Lucie) and I both don't like (cola)*. Point out that *both* is only for positive answers, so they should just say *(Lucie) and I don't like (cola)*.

WRITING LINKERS AND, BECAUSE

8A Focus Ss on the question and tell them to read the blog and see how many things are the same for them. Demonstrate that they should put a tick (✓) in the margin when they find something the same. Ss can discuss their answers in pairs or with the whole class.

B Give Ss a minute or two to complete the sentences and check in the text, then write the two sentences on the board and ask Ss for the missing words.

> **Answers: 1** and **2** because

C Write the sentence starting *Because …* on the board and ask Ss if you should underline *why* or *where*.

> **Answers:** why

> **Optional extra activity**
>
> Write the following sentences on the board and ask Ss to write *because* in the correct place in each sentence:
> 1 I drive to the shops they're five kilometres from my house.
> 2 I walk to work I don't have a car.
> Then give Ss a minute or two to check in the blog.

D Ss work alone on the sentences, then compare answers with a partner and check with the class.

> **Answers: 1** and, because **2** and, because **3** because, and

9 You could give Ss some prompts to help them structure the blog entry, e.g.
I'm from …   I live in …   I work for (company)/in (place) …   I study …
I drive/don't drive to … because …   I'm often … because …
For **stronger classes**, simply give them a list of verbs to use in their blog: *live, work, study, like, drive, walk, have, be*. Circulate and help with vocabulary, spelling, etc. while Ss write their entries. Tell Ss to swap their entries with a partner and write *S* or *D* in the margin to indicate what is the same or different for them. In feedback, ask two or three pairs to give an example of what is the same for them, e.g. *We both live with our parents.*

> **Homework ideas**
>
> • Ss imagine that they're living in the USA (or another country) and write a short paragraph about what is the same or different for them.
> • Ss work on the exercises about verb phrases in the Photo bank, p142 and write eight sentences which are true about themselves.
> • **Workbook:** Ex 1–6, p24–25

A GOOD MATCH

Introduction

Ss practise reading about people and their lifestyles, and practise talking about people's lives using the present simple (*he/she/it*), days of the week and time phrases. They also practise the pronunciation of 3rd person present simple verb endings.

> **SUPPLEMENTARY MATERIALS**
> **Resource bank:** p153 and p155
> **Warm up:** prepare a list of 12–15 verb phrases from lesson 4.1 and the Photo bank, p142, e.g. *have a coffee, work in an office, go to a café, go to the gym, do your homework, play the guitar, play tennis, cost a lot, want a new job*, etc.

Warm up

Revise verb phrases: Put Ss into groups of 4–6. One student from each group comes to you and you show them one of the verb phrases on your list. The student runs back to their group and mimes the verb phrase. When another student guesses it, that student runs to you and says the phrase and, if correct, you show them another verb phrase to mime to their group, etc.

Alternativelty, put Ss into two or three teams. Write the second part of a verb phrase on the board (e.g. *an email, a coffee, the guitar, football, to work, a lot, a flat, ten hours a week*) and ask Ss to think of a verb to complete it. The first person to 'buzz' from a team must say the complete verb phrase to win a point for their team, e.g. *cost a lot*. Other teams can win bonus points if they can think of different ways to complete the phrase correctly, e.g. *cost ten dollars*.

> **Answers:** 1 partner 2 meet

READING

1A Direct Ss to the introduction and to the photos. Give Ss a minute or two to read the sentences and choose an alternative. As you discuss the answers with the class, check *meet for/go on a date* (two people go somewhere, e.g. to a film/for a coffee/for a walk because they like each other romantically – you could draw a ♥ on the board to clarify).

> **Answers:** 1 partner 2 meet

B Divide the class in half and tell one half that they're all Student A, and the other half are all Student B. Tell As to read only Ben's answers and Bs to read only Emma's answers. Ss then decide which three things Ben and Emma have in common. Vocabulary to check: *love*, e.g. *I love the beach* (contrast with *like*, e.g. *I like the beach* ✓ *I love the beach* ✓✓✓), *cook (Italian) food* (mime cooking spaghetti), *a holiday* (a long visit to a place away from home, e.g. the beach, a famous city), *good-looking* (beautiful), *important* (number one).

C Direct Ss to the example, then put the As together to discuss their answers as a group (or in several groups if you have a large class), and do the same with the Bs. (As and Bs do not work together until Ex 2C.)

> **Answers:** they both like football/the same type of music/tennis and films, and they both want to go to South America

2A Go through the example, then put Ss in pairs to work on the questions. Check answers with the class.

> **Answers:**
> 2 Do you like football?
> 3 Is family important to you?
> 4 What do you do in the evening?
> 5 What do you do at the weekend?
> 6 Where do you go on holiday?

B Ss could work in the same pairs to read their texts again (As read Ben's interview about Emma, Bs read Emma's interview about Ben) and find the answers to questions 1–6. For example, for Student A, the answer to question 1 about Emma is *work for a bank*. Point out that Ss should make a note of these answers because they will need them in the next activity.

> **Suggested answers:**
> 2 They both like football, but they like different football teams.
> 3 Family isn't important to Emma, but it's important to Ben.
> 4 Ben doesn't go out during the week. He goes out at the weekend. Emma goes to the gym or cooks during the week and plays tennis at the weekend.
> 5 She's good at tennis, he's not.
> 6 She likes beach holidays, he doesn't.

C Tell As that they are Emma, and Bs that they are Ben. Tell Ss to pair up as Emma and Ben and sit together. Then they ask each other questions 1–6 in Ex 2A and find three differences between Emma and Ben. When they've finished, discuss the differences as a class.

GRAMMAR PRESENT SIMPLE: *HE/SHE/IT*

3A Give Ss a minute or two to look at the sentences, then write them on the board and underline the verbs.

> **Answers:** 1 lives/works 2 watches 3 doesn't like

B Give Ss a few minutes to complete the table. They can work alone or with a partner. When you check the answers, elicit/point out that *doesn't* is the contracted form of *does not* and that you use it in speaking. Also highlight that, in the negative form, there is no *-s* on the verb.

> **Answers:**
>
> | | | | |
> |---|---|---|---|
> | + | He
She
It | comes
likes
costs | from a big family.
football.
a lot of money. |
> | – | He | has | two brothers. |
> | | He | *doesn't go* | out in the week. |
> | | She | *doesn't have* | any sisters. |

C Go through the rules on the board with the class.

> **Answers:** 1 -s 2 has 3 -es 4 doesn't

4A PRONUNCIATION 3rd person *s* Tell Ss they will hear eight verbs in the *he/she/it* form. Play the recording, pausing if necessary, for Ss to write each verb.

> **Answers:** lives, works, teaches, goes, talks, watches, costs, does

B Tell Ss to write /s/, /z/ or /ɪz/ next to each verb and play the recording again. Then ask Ss to listen and repeat. (NB: The same rule for the pronunciation of *-s* applies as for plurals, see lesson 3.1.)

> **Answers:**
> /s/ works, talks, costs
> /z/ lives, goes, does
> /ɪz/ teaches, watches

▷ **LANGUAGEBANK 4.2** p124–125

Use the Language bank to highlight the spelling rules for the third person -s. Ss could do Ex 4.2A and 4.2B in two groups: As do Ex A and Bs do Ex B. Give them a key to check their answers, then they pair up with someone from the other group and go through the answers to both exercises.

Answers:
A 2 doesn't email, phones **3** drives, walks
4 works, doesn't like **5** has, doesn't like
6 understands, doesn't speak
B Conversation 1
A: My wife, Kalila, is a teacher.
B: Near here?
A: Yes, she *has* a job at City School. She *teaches* Arabic.
B: Is it a good place to work?
A: Yes, but she *doesn't* like the travel every day.
Conversation 2
A: My son Jaime *studies* engineering at Madrid University.
B: Oh, my daughter *goes* there. She likes it a lot.
A: Yes, Jaime *says* it's good too.

5A Give Ss a few minutes to complete the text and check their answers with a partner.

Answers: 1 have **2** lives **3** work **4** doesn't have **5** has
6 doesn't go **7** costs **8** meet **9** doesn't know **10** says
11 loves **12** doesn't want

B Tell Ss to close their Students' Books and put them in pairs. Tell them to write as many sentences as they can about Alex and Keira, and decide if they are a good match or not, and why. You could then put the pairs together to make groups of four: Ss compare what they remember about Alex and Keira and discuss whether they are a good match.

SPEAKING

6A Put Ss in pairs (As and Bs together) and give them a few minutes to look at their picture and prepare what they will say about Daniel or Yoshi. Point out that they can refer to lesson 4.1 and the Photo bank on p142 for verb phrases they may need.

B Put Ss in new pairs of A and B. Go through the example with the class, then Ss continue in pairs. Tell Ss to write six sentences together: five differences and one thing that is the same. Monitor carefully so that you can give Ss feedback on language use after the activity. Ask a few of the pairs to share their sentences with the class.

Answers:
Daniel is Spanish, Yoshi is Japanese.
Daniel studies Chinese, Yoshi studies English.
Daniel plays golf, Yoshi plays tennis.
Daniel reads newspapers, Yoshi listens to (music) on an MP3 player.
Daniel has/likes dogs, Yoshi likes cats.
They both have a car.

VOCABULARY DAYS; TIME PHRASES

7A Ss could work in pairs to number the days of the week, saying them aloud as they do so.

Answers: 2 Tuesday **3** Wednesday **4** Thursday **5** Friday
6 Saturday **7** Sunday

B Before Ss listen and repeat, you could ask them to choose which of the following stress patterns the days have:
Ooo oO Oo ooO
(Saturday = Ooo, the other days = Oo)

8A Look at the example and check that Ss understand *every* (e.g. *every day* = Monday, Tuesday, Wednesday, etc.). Put Ss in pairs to complete the table. They could use the text in Ex 1 to help.

Answers: 2 at **3** in **4** on

B Give Ss a minute or two to underline the alternatives, then compare answers.

Answers: 1 every **2** in **3** on **4** at **5** every **6** on

C Demonstrate how to change sentence 1 in different ways, e.g.
I have tea every morning.
I have coffee every afternoon.
Give Ss a few minutes to work on the sentences alone, then put Ss in pairs to read out their sentences and compare answers. Tell the class to be prepared to talk about two things that are the same and two things that are different about them and their partner, and show them the example in Ex 8D.

D Either put Ss in groups to tell each other about their partner, or tell them to walk around the class and talk to different people.

Optional extra activity

Tell Ss to think about someone in their life who is a good friend, and to write some notes answering the five questions in the interview texts in Ex 1, i.e. *What do you like about (name)? Do you like the same things?* etc. Give Ss time to write their notes, then put them in pairs to ask and answer about the friend (starting with the question *What's your friend's name?*).

Homework ideas

• Ss write a text like the one in Ex 5 about themselves and someone they know who is very different from them.
• **Workbook:** Ex 1–6, p26–27

WHAT TIME IS IT?

Introduction

Ss practise telling the time, using vocabulary related to events. They also practise listening and learn to check times using appropriate intonation.

> **SUPPLEMENTARY MATERIALS**
> **Resource bank:** p156
> **Ex 3A (optional extra activity):** take in a toy clock with hands that Ss can move (you could make this from cardboard).

Warm up

Review numbers from 1–100 by doing some counting activities. Ss count in multiples of two, e.g. *two*, *four*, *six*, etc. and *one*, *three*, *five*, etc. then in multiples of five, e.g. *five*, *ten*, *fifteen*, etc. They could do this around the class, or in groups of 4–6. Rather than going around in order, give Ss a ball or soft object: the first student says a number, e.g. *two*, then throws the ball to the person they choose to say the next number, and so on.

VOCABULARY EVENTS

1A Direct Ss to the pictures and put them in pairs to match the events from the box to pictures A–F. As you check the answers with the class, elicit verbs associated with the events, e.g. *see a play/film/match*, *go to a party/match/concert*, *have a party*. You could also elicit some activities that people do at the events, e.g. *listen to music*, *dance* (a party, a concert, a festival). Check also the pronunciation and the plural form of the events: *films*, *parties*, *plays*, *concerts*, *matches*, *festivals*.

> **Answers:** **A** a festival **B** a concert **C** a play **D** a party
> **E** a match **F** a film

B Ask two Ss to demonstrate, using the example, then put Ss in pairs to practise. For **stronger classes**, you could encourage Ss to extend the conversations by asking for a reason, e.g.

A: I don't like concerts, but I like plays.
B: Why?
A: Because I like the actors.

FUNCTION TELLING THE TIME

2A Elicit/Give the names of some famous London venues, e.g. the O$_2$ arena, Wembley stadium (a match, a concert), The Old Vic theatre, Shakespeare's Globe theatre (a play), the Odeon Leicester Square (a film), the Oval (a cricket match), Wimbledon (a tennis match) and, outside London, Glastonbury (a festival, see Consolidation 1).

Direct Ss to numbers 1–5 in Ex 2A and tell them to write an event next to each number when they hear the people talk about them. Play the recording, then give Ss time to compare answers in pairs.

> **Answers:** **2** a festival **3** a party **4** a play **5** a match

B Direct Ss to the diary and tell them to write one event in each space as they listen to the recording again. For **weaker classes**, just ask Ss to write the type of event: **stronger classes** can try to write any other information, e.g. the name of the place. Play the recording again and give Ss time to compare their answers in pairs.

> **Answers:**
>
> | | Saturday | Sunday |
> |---|---|---|
> | afternoon | Susie's party | football match |
> | evening | The Shakes concert, A1 arena | *Hamlet* the Round Theatre |

C Give Ss a minute or two to read through the conversations before you play the recording again.

> **Answers:** **1** six **2** six **3** three, o'clock **4** past **5** twelve

Unit 4 Recording 5

Conversation 1
A: Hi, Pete.
B: Hi, Mia. London tomorrow!
A: Yeah! Great! I just want to check the times.
B: OK.
A: Erm. What time's the concert?
B: Let me check. It's at half past six. Yes. The Shakes … concert at the A1 … half past six.
A: Half past six. So do you want to go at six?
B: Erm … Let's go at quarter to six. And erm, Mia, the food festival is in the afternoon. The international food festival.
A: But the afternoon is the party. Susie's party.
B: Oh, yes. Erm … maybe you …
A: No, the invitation is for Mia and Pete. For me and you.
B: OK. What time's the party?
A: From three o'clock to six o'clock. So that's only two hours at the party because of the concert.
B: So the party in the afternoon and the concert in the evening.
A: Yes.
B: OK. See you tomorrow at the station. What time …?

Conversation 2
B: Good concert!
A: Yes, great!
B: Hey, Mia. You like Shakespeare, yes?
A: Yes. Why?
B: I have tickets for *Hamlet*. At the Round Theatre, tomorrow.
A: Really! My favourite play! Afternoon or evening?
B: In the evening.
A: What time in the evening?
B: Half past seven. Seven-thirty.
A: Seven-thirty. That's good.
B: And in the afternoon … the food festival?
A: Ah, but tomorrow is the football. It's the final.
B: Oh yes. I want to watch that. What time is the match?
A: It's at a quarter past two.
B: Sorry, What time?
A: Quarter past two.
B: Quarter past two. OK. Let's watch the match and go to the theatre after that.
A: OK. I'm tired. What time is it?
B: It's quarter past twelve. Let's get a taxi …

▷ **LANGUAGEBANK 4.3** p124–125

Use the Language bank to clarify the difference between *What time is it? It's (two o'clock)* and *What time's the (concert)? It's at (two o'clock)* or *It's at (two)*. Ss could do Ex 4.3 in class or for homework.

Answers:
1 five o'clock   2 quarter past six   3 half past nine
4 quarter to nine   5 quarter to five   6 half past twelve
7 eleven o'clock   8 quarter past seven

3A Focus Ss on the four positions of the hands on the clock (A–D), then play the recording for them to listen and repeat.

Optional extra activity

Take in a large toy clock with moveable hands. Pass the clock to a student who sets the time, then chooses another student and asks *What time is it?* If that student answers correctly, the clock is passed to them to set the time, and so on.

B Demonstrate an example with a student, then put Ss in pairs to practise. Monitor and note any problems with saying the time to deal with in feedback.

▷ **PHOTOBANK** p142

This exercise introduces *five, ten, twenty, twenty-five past/to*. Ss practise writing times to match the photos. You may want to go through these with the class first, then Ss can write the times or ask and answer in pairs, e.g. *What time is it in C?* etc.

Answers:
A five past eight   B ten past ten   C twenty past three
D twenty-five past one   E twenty-five to ten   F twenty to four
G ten to two   H five to twelve

Optional extra activity

For **stronger classes**, use the times in Ex 3B for Ss to practise the difference between *What time is it?* and *What time's the (event)?* Student A points to a time and asks either *What time is it?* or *What time's the (party/film/lesson/match/play/concert/festival)?* Student B answers either *It's (7.30)* or *It's at (7.30)*.

LEARN TO   CHECK TIMES

4A You could write the conversation on the board and point out that B didn't hear the time, so they need to check. Ask Ss which sentences to underline.

Answers: A: Sorry? What time?   A: Quarter past two.

B PRONUNCIATION intonation: checking Ss could look at the arrows and try to predict how to say the two words. Then play the recording, giving Ss a few opportunities to repeat.

Teaching tip

A fall–rise intonation pattern is often used to show uncertainty. It sounds more polite than a rise, which can sound rather abrupt. To help Ss copy the pattern, say each word slowly, exaggerating the high start and the following fall and rise.

C Ask two Ss to demonstrate the example conversation for the class, encouraging them to exaggerate their intonation. Point out that Student B shouldn't look at the exercise while checking and writing the time. Put Ss in pairs to practise.

speakout TIP

You could ask Ss for one or two more examples for *I'm sorry I'm …*, e.g. at the beginning of the lesson: *I'm sorry I don't have my homework*; at someone's house for dinner: *I'm sorry, I don't eat (meat/fish)*. You could also ask Ss to mime one or two situations for *Oh, I'm sorry*, e.g. bumping into someone, knocking something off a desk, etc. Encourage Ss to make a note of these uses of *sorry* in their phrasebooks.

SPEAKING

5A/B Give Student Bs time to find their page and activity, and tell Ss not to look at each other's information. You could elicit *Let's go to a … on …* and *Do you want to go to a … on …?* by saying *I want to go to a festival with (student's name): what can I say?* Then direct the class to the example conversation and act it out with a student, taking the part of B yourself, so you can demonstrate writing the event and time into the correct space in the diary. Tell Ss to ask and answer until all the spaces are complete. Monitor carefully. Note good language use and any problem areas for praise and correction later.

Optional extra activity

Ss invent their own weekend diary, writing two events and times for each day. Encourage them to be creative and write more than one word for each event, e.g. *music/food festival, Lina's party, dancing lesson, tennis match*, etc.
Ss could also refer to real events (e.g. a concert, a film, a match) that are happening locally. Then they either work in groups, or walk round the class, talking to different people and asking them to the events. Remind Ss to note down the name of the student who agrees to go to each event with them. In feedback, Ss can report back on what they've got in their diaries, e.g. *Saturday, 4.30, a jazz concert with Alicia*, etc.

Homework ideas
Workbook: Ex 1–4, p28

A SECRET LIFE

Introduction

Ss watch an extract from a BBC programme about the Amish people and their lifestyle. Ss then learn and practise how to conduct a group survey and write a report on the results of their survey.

Warm up

Write the following words on the board: *a car, a clock, a computer, a phone, a pen, a TV, a credit card, an ATM, a business card, keys*. Tell Ss to think about how much they use these things in their life and write the following options on the board: *every day/week/month/six months/year, never*. Put Ss in small groups to compare their ideas. Ask the groups to share their answers with the class, and find out which things Ss use the most and the least.

DVD PREVIEW

1A Focus Ss on the main photo and ask them where they think it is and if it is from the present or the past. Put Ss in pairs and direct them to the phrases (1–6) and the smaller pictures (A–F). Give them a few minutes to match the pictures and phrases. In feedback, check the pronunciation of *carriage* /ˈkærɪdʒ/.

Answers: 1 F 2 C 3 A 4 D 5 B 6 E

B Give an example about yourself, e.g. *I go to a supermarket every week. I never cut wood*. Point out the position of *every week* at the end of the sentence, and *never* before the verb. Put Ss in pairs to discuss their answers.

2 Before Ss read the information, check *lifestyle* (the way you live, what you do every day, etc.), *electricity* (show Ss something that is plugged into a socket, e.g. a TV or computer cable), *day-to-day* (every day). Give Ss a few minutes to discuss the things the Amish people do/never do. In feedback, also ask the class to suggest what they do in their free time.

Answers: Ss are speculating here: they are likely to choose *cut wood, collect eggs, travel by horse and carriage*, and are unlikely to choose the other three items.

DVD VIEW

3A Tell Ss to watch the programme and see if they were correct. Play the DVD, then give Ss time to discuss their answers in pairs.

Answers: The family does all of the things in Ex 1A.

Culture note

The first group of Amish arrived in Lancaster County in the 1720s or 1730s. Today, the Amish can be found in twenty-three states in the US and in one Canadian province. Because of their large families, the total Amish population has more than doubled since 1960 to over 85,000.

The Amish have very strong religious beliefs. They believe in the literal interpretation and application of Scripture as the Word of God. Their families and their farms are their top priorities, second only to God. They take seriously the Biblical commands to separate themselves from the things of the world. Their lifestyle is a deliberate way of separating from the world and maintaining self-sufficiency.

B Before playing the DVD again, give Ss time to look at and discuss in pairs which things are not in the programme. Play the DVD, then tell Ss to check together whether they were correct.

Answers: a clock, keys, a pen are not in the programme

C Give Ss a few minutes to read through sentences 1–8 before you play the DVD again. Check *youngest* and *oldest* (write four names and ages on the board, e.g. John 11, Sara 15, Julia 6, Sam 9, then write *the oldest* next to Sara, and ask Ss who is the youngest), *together* (in the same place, with each other), *happiest* (give an example about yourself: 'I'm happy when … but I'm happiest when …'). Demonstrate underlining the correct word, then play the DVD again. Ss compare their answers in pairs.

Answers: 1 son 2 visitors 3 daughter 4 electricity 5 horse
6 normal 7 houses 8 family is

D Ss could discuss this in pairs or small groups then share their ideas with the class and see how many people liked the same thing.

DVD 4 The Amish

N = Narrator   L = Lynn   D = Dave   S = Steve   B = Ben
M = Miriam

N: The Amish people live in Lancaster, Pennsylvania, USA. They have a traditional lifestyle, very different from other people in America. In this programme we visit an Amish family and learn about their day to day life.
Our visit takes us to the home of David and Miriam, a young husband and wife, and their five children.
L: Good morning.
D: Good morning.
L: How are we?
D: I'm good. I'm David Lapp.
L: So nice to see you. This is Steve.
D: Hello, Steve.
S: Good morning, David. Good morning.
L: It's a lovely day, isn't it?
D: It is. How are you this morning?
S: Very well.
D: This is my young son, Bennon.
L: Hello. Good morning.
D: Say hi, Ben.
B: Hi.
D: We got visitors.
M: OK! Good morning.
S: Good morning.
L: Good morning. How are you?
M: Fine, how about you?
L: Good, good. It's a lovely day out there, isn't it?
M: Yes, it is.
L: Yes.
M: Hi, Steve.
D: This is Katie. This is our oldest daughter.
M: Katie, Lynn.
L: Actually, it's a little bit dark in here. Could we …?
N: It's dark in the house because the Amish don't use electricity. The Amish don't use modern machines – no television, radio, or internet.
Family is important, and the children help their parents around the house. They cut wood together. They collect eggs.
They travel everywhere by horse and carriage.
M: It takes at least five minutes to get my horse out, and the children. But I like it. I always like to get out with my horse.
N: But they also go into town and go to normal shops. They go to the supermarket. They eat at a fast food restaurant. Miriam goes to the bank and gets money.
Amish people use telephones, but not in the house, so David's phone is two minutes away, in a small building, called a shanty.
D: This is the phone shanty. The traditional Amish in Lancaster County don't have phones in their houses, so they have a phone in a shanty outside somewhere.
N: David has a building business. He works together with non-Amish workers. He loves his work, but at the end of the day, he's happiest when he's at home and his family is all together, enjoying their traditional Amish lifestyle.

speakout a group survey

4A Demonstrate this by giving your own answers to questions 1 and 2 for one of the phrases (a–h) about the Amish lifestyle. Put Ss in pairs and give them time to discuss a)–h). You could also encourage Ss to make a note in their vocabulary books of the useful verb phrases: *work outside/inside, live in the countryside/the city, do the housework, help around the house.*

B Demonstrate the idea of a survey: mime going up to two or three Ss with a clipboard, reading out questions and noting down their answers. Direct Ss back to the topics a)–h) in Ex 4A. Tell Ss to tick the topics the people talk about, and write the number of people who think they're a good thing. Play the recording, then Ss compare answers in pairs.

> **Answers:**
> They talk about a), e) and f).
> One person says a) (no computer or TV) is a good thing.
> One person says e) and f) are a good thing.

C Give Ss a few moments to look at the key phrases. Then play the recording again for them to tick the phrases. As you check the answers, you could ask Ss to repeat the phrases in chorus, including the different options for *I think it's …*

> **Answers:**
> I'll go first ✓/next.
> My question is about [e) and f)/the computer/the man and the woman]. ✓
> Do you think that's a good thing? ✓
> Why? Why not? ✓
> In my family, this is normal. ✓
> I think it's [OK ✓/a good thing ✓/a good idea/a bad thing/ a problem ✓].
> I think you're right. ✓/ I agree with you.
> I don't agree with you.

Unit 4 Recording 8

S = Sam   I = Isabelle   M = Milan

S: I'll go first. My question is about a), the computer and TV. The Amish family doesn't have these things. Do you think that's a good thing? Isabelle?
I: Well, for me it isn't a good thing.
S: Why not?
I: A computer is important for information, from the internet.
S: How about you, Milan?
M: I think it is a good thing. I have a computer, but I think I use it too much.
S: And TV?
M: I don't have a TV.
I: I do, but I don't watch it. How about you, Sam?
S: I have both a computer and a TV and they're important for me. So for me, the Amish lifestyle with no computer or TV is a bad thing.
I: OK, my turn. My question is about e), the woman does the housework and f), the man has a job. A good thing or bad thing? Milan?
M: In my family, this is normal. I think it's OK.
S: Really? I think it's a problem. Maybe the woman wants to work.
M: Well, in this family I think they're all happy. Miriam is happy at home.
S: We don't know that. Isabelle, what do you think?
I: I think you're right, Sam. But … I think housework *is* a job. It's a very *big* job.
M: Hmm … Well, it's hard but it's not a job …

5A Ss work alone to decide on their two topics and think about what they'll say, referring to the key phrases. Then put Ss in groups of 3–5 and tell them to take turns to ask everyone in the group their questions. Remind them to say *I'll go next* when they want to ask their questions, and to make a note of the answers. Monitor as Ss conduct their surveys and note down examples of good language use, particularly of the key phrases, for feedback.

B Direct Ss to the examples and give them a minute or two alone to prepare what they will say about their results. Ss could either tell the class their results, or you could put them in pairs with a person from a different group to tell each other their results.

writeback a report

6A Ss read the report and choose a topic for each heading, then compare answers in pairs.

> **Answers:**
> 1 h) the family is together a lot
> 2 g) the children help around the house

B Tell Ss to use the example in Ex 6A as a model for their reply, e.g.:
In our group _____ people/person think(s) _____ is a good thing because _____.
_____ people/person think(s) it's a problem because _____.
We all think _____ is a good idea because _____.

> **Optional extra activity**
> Ss prepare and conduct surveys on different topics and whether they are a good or a bad thing, e.g.
> *go to the gym every day*
> *watch TV every evening*
> *read a lot of books*
> *study every evening*
> *get up early at weekends*
> *have a big family*
> *live in the countryside*
> *learn another language*

> **Homework ideas**
> • If Ss want to learn more about the Amish, they could do some research on the internet about them.
> • If Ss prepare and conduct surveys on other topics (as in the optional extra activity), they can write reports on the results for homework.

LOOKBACK

> **SUPPLEMENTARY MATERIALS**
> **Ex 4 (optional extra activity):** prepare a 'Find someone who …' handout for each student (see notes).

VERB PHRASES

1A Point out that sometimes a phrase is not correct because there's a small word (like *in* or *to*) missing. Ss can work in pairs and check their answers with the class.

> **Answers:** 2 city 3 university 4 hungry 5 a flat 6 bored
> 7 work 8 tennis

B Direct Ss to the example and point out that they can change what comes after the verbs. Circulate and help as Ss write their sentences.

C Put Ss in pairs and tell them that while Student A reads his/her sentences, Student B should think of a 'follow up' question to ask about Student A and his/her friend, and vice versa.

PRESENT SIMPLE: I/YOU/WE/THEY

2A You could draw the table on the board, and demonstrate how the three columns link together to make the beginning of the example question. Tell Ss to write a minimum of four questions. *Stronger classes* could write eight questions, one for each verb.

B Before you put Ss in pairs, focus on the questions beginning *Do your friends …?* and *Do the other students in the class …?* and establish that Ss may not know the answer. Tell Ss to say *I don't know/I'm not sure/I think so/I don't think so.*
You could follow up by asking different pairs to check their ideas about the other Ss in the class, e.g.
Ss: *We think the other students in the class watch TV every day.*
Ss: *That's true!*
Ss: *That's not true!* etc.

PRESENT SIMPLE: HE/SHE/IT

3A Go through the example and tell Ss to write the sentences in their notebooks.

> **Answers:** 2 She lives in a flat.   3 He doesn't like hamburgers.
> 4 She has a brother.   5 He doesn't like shopping.
> 6 She does sport at the weekend.

B Tell Ss that it doesn't matter if they don't know whether the information is true about the other Ss because they'll have a chance to check later.

C Ss can check the information either by asking across the class or by walking around and asking the relevant Ss.

DAYS; TIME PHRASES

4A You could run this as a spelling game in teams (Ss close their books first). Write the first two letters of a day on the board (go through the days at random, rather than in order), and the first student to 'buzz' spells the rest of the word. If all the letters are correct, they win two points for their team, but they lose points for wrong letters and hesitation.

> **Answers:** Tuesday Wednesday Thursday Friday Saturday
> Sunday

B Look at the example first, then Ss can work alone or in pairs on the rest.

> **Answers:** 2 d) 3 a) 4 f) 5 b) 6 e)

C Check that Ss know they need to write six sentences. Circulate and help with vocabulary while Ss write their sentences.

D You could demonstrate this with an example of your own and encourage the class to guess when you do the activity.

> **Optional extra activity**
> *Find someone who …*
> Prepare the handout below and give one to each student. Ss work in pairs to complete the gaps with their own ideas. Then the pairs separate and walk round the class, asking other Ss *Do you …?* until someone answers *Yes* and they write that person's name next to the question. They continue until they have a name next to each question. Ss then return to their partners and compare the answers they found. Then they can report back to the class, e.g. *Mica and Franca drive to work every day.*
> *Find someone who …*
> drives _____ every _____.
> plays _____ at the weekend.
> listens to _____ in the _____.
> watches _____ every _____.
> wants _____.
> reads _____ in the _____.
> goes _____ at the weekend.
> writes _____ every _____.

EVENTS

5A You could run this as a team game (Ss close their books). Write each gapped word on the board: team members 'buzz' and tell you only the missing vowels. They win a point for each correct vowel.

> **Answers:** 2 concert 3 party 4 play 5 festival 6 match

> **Alternative approach**
> To provide more of a challenge, write blanks for the whole word, e.g. for *concert*: _ _ _ _ _ _ _.
> Ss from the teams 'buzz' and call out any letter they think may be in the word. If the letter is in the word, write it in the correct place and give the team a point; if it isn't in the word, give the team a penalty point. The winning team is the one with the fewest penalty points at the end.

B Go through the example with the Ss and put them in pairs.

TELLING THE TIME

6A Give Ss a few minutes to write the times, working alone.

> **Answers:** 2 half past twelve 3 quarter past seven 4 three o'clock
> 5 quarter to four 6 quarter past eleven

B Demonstrate that Ss should write any times, apart from the ones in Ex 6A. Tell them not to show their partner the times.

C Demonstrate the activity with a student, taking the part of Student A yourself, so that you can show Ss how to stress the incorrect numbers.

CONSOLIDATION 2: UNITS 3–4

Introduction

The aim of the consolidation units is for Ss to revise and practise the grammar, vocabulary and pronunciation from the previous two units in a different context. The context for this consolidation unit is favourites.

SUPPLEMENTARY MATERIALS

Ex 4C: be prepared to talk about your favourite categories.

Ex 5C (optional extra activity): prepare a matching handout to review verb + noun combinations (see notes).

LISTENING AND GRAMMAR

1A Start by checking *favourites*, i.e. the things you like the most, and *bookmarks*, another word for *favourites* on the computer, for saving links to websites. Then check *icon* (a small sign or picture, e.g. on a computer or phone screen) and put Ss in pairs to match the words to the icons A–F. As you check the answers with the class, elicit two or three examples for each icon, e.g. *people* – friend, sister, boss; *clothes* – dress, jacket, shoes; *cafés* – names of local cafés that Ss know, and so on.

Answers: A places B people C websites D clothes E films

B Demonstrate the example with a student, then put Ss in pairs. Tell them to give an example from each icon at least twice.

2A Tell Ss to write the list of icons from Ex 1A in their notebooks and write a number from 1–6 next to each one when they hear them. You could play the first part of the recording and tell Ss to say 'Stop!' when they hear the woman mention the first icon (people). Then play the rest of the recording. Vocabulary to check: *meet* (e.g. *I meet my friends at the café*), *traveller* (someone who travels a lot), *ice cream* (simple board drawing), *love* (e.g. *I love ice cream*).

Answers: 1 people 2 places 3 clothes 4 websites 5 cafés 6 films

B Play the first part of the recording again for Ss to hear the three people mentioned (e.g. Alicia, Keith and Monique), then play the rest of the recording. Give Ss time to compare their answers in pairs before checking with the class.

Answers: Cafés – 1 Clothes – 1 Films – 2 Places – 3 Websites – 1

3A Go through the example with the class, then give Ss a few minutes to complete the sentences, working alone. Then Ss can compare their answers in pairs before checking with the whole class.

Answers:
2 William says Alicia is beautiful.
3 Beth knows Keith from university.
4 Beth and Monique aren't friends.
5 Beth has a red party dress.
6 She likes the BBC website.
7 She goes to the Gelatino Café every day.

B Ss can either check the audio script or you could play the recording again. Ask Ss what the corrected sentence should be.

Answers: Sentence **7** is false. Correct answer: *She doesn't go to the Gelatino Café a lot.*

Consolidation 2 Recording 1

A: So if I press this …
B: Beth, who's that?
A: These are my favourite people.
B: That woman. She's beautiful.
A: William! That's my sister, Alicia. Watch it!
B: Your sister? Oh … who's that then?
A: That's Keith. He's a good friend from university.
B: Do you meet a lot now?
A: No, but we email each other every day.
B: And this?
A: Monique, from work.
B: Are you friends?
A: Not really. But I like her a lot.
B: And if I press this … Oh, look!
A: Yeah, Paris …
B: … Cairo … and the Great Wall of China. Big traveller!
A: Yeah, then here …
B: Hey, nice dress.
A: You know that dress. My black party dress.
B: Yeah, I like that dress. Oh, you like the BBC.
A: Yeah, the website's great for the news.
B: Let's look at … What's this? Ice cream?
A: Yeah, from the Gelatino Café. I love it. But I don't go there a lot.
B: And what's this?
A: Johnny Depp.
B: Is he one of your favourite people?
A: No, but *Pirates of the Caribbean is* one of my favourite films.
B: And here's another film. *Pirates of the Caribbean II.* Johnny Depp again and here's …
A: OK, that's enough …

SPEAKING

4A You could draw the table on the board and demonstrate choosing three categories for yourself, pointing out that Ss need to choose categories where they can think of the names of several things or people to include.

B Tell Ss that for most categories they simply need to write a name, e.g. *Erica, Bar Italia, Prague, Star Wars*, etc. For *music* they could write the name of a band or a type of music, and for *animals* the name of a pet or a type of animal. For *clothes* they need to write the items, e.g. *black jacket*. Tell them that they also need to be able to explain why each thing/person is a favourite.

C Demonstrate this by choosing a student to ask you about your favourites. Ss can then walk around the class and talk to (three or four) different people. Monitor the activity carefully and note down examples of good language use and any problem areas for praise and correction later. In feedback, you could ask Ss if they found anyone who had the same favourite as one of theirs, e.g. *Yes, Monica. We both like Tino's Café because the chocolate cake is very good!*

Alternative approach

Ss write one sentence in their notebooks about each favourite item from the table, but don't write the name. In pairs, Student A shows Student B their favourites and reads one of their sentences. Student B guesses which favourite item the sentence is about, e.g.
A: It has very good Greek food.
B: 'Sofie's'?
A: Yes!

READING AND GRAMMAR

5A You could elicit/remind Ss that Alicia is Beth's sister and Keith is her friend from university. Tell Ss to read the texts quickly, just to find out what their jobs are, what their favourite thing about their job is and what they don't like. Vocabulary to check: *alone* (contrast simple board drawings of person standing in a group and person standing alone), *difficult* (mime trying to do a difficult sum), *a typical day* (usual, like every day), *welcome* (act out welcoming a student), *check* (act out checking someone's name on a list).

> **Answers:** Keith is a taxi driver.   Alicia is a hotel receptionist.
> Favourite things about the job: Keith – the people, Alicia – every day is different.

B Go through the example with the class then give Ss a few minutes to find the answers.

> **Answers:** 2 K   3 A   4 A   5 A   6 K

C Ss could work in pairs to write the questions, or work alone and compare answers in pairs.

> **Answers:**
> 2 Do you work in an office?
> 3 Do you speak on the phone (a lot)?
> 4 Do you use a computer in your job?
> 5 Do you work in the evenings?
> 6 Do you drive a lot in your job?

Optional extra activity

Review some of the verb + noun combinations from the texts, so that Ss can use them in Ex 5D and Ex 6. Prepare the following matching activity on a handout or on sets of cards (one set per pair of Ss):

1 work	4 welcome	a) people	d) people's names
2 answer	5 check	b) alone	e) around the city
3 get	6 drive	c) tired	f) the phone

When Ss have matched the verbs and nouns, they could fold the handout in half or turn over some of the cards so they can only see half of the combination, then try to remember the whole phrase.

> **Answers:** 1 b)   2 f)   3 c)   4 a)   5 d)   6 e)

D/E You could do an example comparing your day to Keith's and Alicia's. If Ss don't work, they could invent a job, or talk about their parents' or friends' jobs, or you could give them a job. When Ss have finished, ask two or three pairs to tell the class their answers.

SPEAKING

6A Put Ss in groups of three or four. Tell them to write their list of jobs on a large piece of paper that everyone in the group can see.

B Elicit/Remind Ss of some of the questions they could ask (only *yes/no* questions), e.g. *Do you work alone/at night/in an office? Do you answer the phone? Do you take people's money? Do you have special clothes? Do you like your job?*
When a student thinks they've guessed the job, they ask *Are you a …?* Monitor the activity carefully so you can give Ss feedback on their use of vocabulary and pronunciation.

SOUNDS: /s/ AND /z/

7A Direct Ss to the pictures and point out that the symbols represent the sounds. Play the recording for Ss to listen to the sounds and the words. You may also want to show Ss that they need to 'use their voice' to make /z/: if they put their hands over their ears and make /z/ they should hear their voice in their heads, whereas with the sound /s/ there is no voice. Play the recording again for Ss to repeat.

B You may want to ask Ss to predict which group the words belong to before they listen.

> **Answers:**
> /s/ sandwich, sport, this
> /z/ has, euros, drives

8A Go through the example with the class, then put Ss in pairs to complete the exercise.

> **Answers:** 2 Tom's   3 trousers   4 it's   5 bags   6 likes

B Pause the recording if necessary while Ss are checking their answers.

C You may want to go through these rules with the whole class or, with **stronger classes**, give Ss the opportunity to work out the rules in pairs.

> **Answers:** 1 /s/   2 /s/   3 /z/

9A You could go through the first sentence with the class, as an example.

> **Answers:**
> 1 My son lives near the sea and the mountains.
> 2 The lamps and the clocks are in the rooms near the beds.
> 3 Can I have six eggs, please?
> 4 Sue emails her parents on Sundays.

B Encourage Ss in pairs to read the sentences aloud to each other, so they can hear how the 's' is pronounced.

> **Answers:**
> 1 My son lives near the sea and the mountains.
>   /s/   /z/   /s/   /z/
> 2 The lamps and the clocks are in the rooms near the beds.
>   /s/   /s/   /z/   /z/
> 3 Can I have six eggs, please?
>   /s/   /z/ /z/
> 4 Sue emails her parents on Sundays.
> /s/   /z/   /s/ /s/ /z/

C You may want to pause the recording for Ss to repeat the sentences in shorter 'chunks'.

Homework ideas

- Ss write two sentences about one favourite from each category in Ex 4, beginning: *One of my favourite (places) is … I like/love it because …*
- **Workbook:** Ex 1–5, p29–30

BBC interviews and worksheet

What do you do for fun?

In this video people talk about their lifestyles: what they like to do with their friends or on their own. The material provides authentic usage of the present simple which is the focus of lesson 4.1 and lesson 4.2, as well as recycling vocabulary for talking about leisure activities.

OVERVIEW

5.1 BAD HABITS

VOCABULARY | daily routines
LISTENING | listen to people say what drives them crazy
GRAMMAR | present simple questions: *he/she/it*
PRONUNCIATION | weak form: *does*
SPEAKING | discuss bad habits

5.2 YOU ARE WHAT YOU EAT

VOCABULARY | food
READING | read about the eating habits of a sportsman and a model
GRAMMAR | adverbs of frequency
PRONUNCIATION | word stress
SPEAKING | talk about what you eat
READING | read about someone's morning routine
WRITING | use linkers to sequence

5.3 WHEN DOES IT OPEN?

VOCABULARY | hotel services
FUNCTION | asking for information
LISTENING | listen to a tourist asking questions
PRONUNCIATION | sentence stress
LEARN TO | use two-part exchanges
SPEAKING | ask for tourist information

5.4 HOW TO FEED YOUR KIDS [BBC] 🔊 DVD

DVD | watch a BBC programme about children and food
speakout | talk about desert island food
writeback | write a forum entry about food you eat

5.5 LOOKBACK

Communicative revision activities

[BBC] 🔊 INTERVIEWS

What do you usually do at the weekend?

In this video people describe their weekend activities: what time they get up and what they do. The material enables Ss to consolidate and extend the vocabulary used for talking about routines and also offers authentic usage of adverbs of frequency (focused on in lesson 5.2). Use the video after lesson 5.2 or at the end of the unit.

BAD HABITS

Introduction

Ss practise listening and talking about daily routines and things that drive them crazy. They use present simple questions, with a focus on the pronunciation of the weak form *does*, and related vocabulary.

> **SUPPLEMENTARY MATERIALS**
> **Resource bank:** p158

Warm up

Review days of the week and verb phrases. Prompt a student to ask you what your favourite day of the week is and why, e.g.
S: What's your favourite day of the week?
T: Thursday.
S: Why?
T: Because I go to my dance class in the evening.
Put Ss in pairs or small groups to ask and answer about their favourite day of the week. Ask a few Ss to report back to the class about their partners, e.g. *Kirsten's favourite day is … because she …*

VOCABULARY DAILY ROUTINES

1A Tell Ss to write the numbers 1–7 in their notebooks. Play the first sound and check that Ss understand *get up* by asking a student to act it out. Then play the rest of the recording: you may want to stop after each sound for Ss to confer in pairs about which verb it matches. When you've checked the answers, Ss could work in pairs, taking turns to say a verb for their partner to act out.

> **Answers:** 2 have breakfast   3 go to work   4 have lunch   5 get home   6 have dinner   7 go to bed

B Direct Ss to the example and point out that all their questions should start *What time do you …?* Put them in pairs to practise asking and answering.

> **Optional extra activity**
>
> Ss imagine that they have a job where the daily routine is different from their own (they could look at the Photo bank p139 lesson 1.2 Jobs for ideas) and answer their partner's questions about their routine. Their partner has to guess the job.

> ▷ **PHOTOBANK** p143
>
> For Ex 1, you may want to clarify go to *work* vs *come home* by acting them out, showing that *come* means move towards a place, when the person speaking is in that place. You could also give more examples: *come here, come to my house.* For Ex 2, give Ss an opportunity to practise 'testing' each other on the phrases in pairs (as in Ex 1B on p52).
>
> **Answers:**
> 1 1D 2B 3C 4A
> 2A 2 go 3 get 4 leave 5 make 6 start/finish

speakout TIP

Give Ss a few minutes to write seven true sentences in their phrasebooks. Point out that they could do this with any items of vocabulary that they want to remember: choose about six items to put into sentences (e.g. about themselves or people they know) and practise repeating them every day. They could do this with some of the verb phrases from the Photo bank.

LISTENING

2A Direct Ss to the photos and ask them which person is angry and why.

> **Suggested answers:**
> The man in photo A because he can't sleep.
> The woman in photo C, because the man doesn't listen to her.

B Before you play the recording, you could put Ss in pairs and tell them to imagine what the people in photos A–C would say to a friend about their situation. Ask one or two stronger pairs to act out their ideas.

> **Answers: 1** B   **2** C   **3** A

C Go through the example with the class and give Ss a few moments to read the sentences, then play the recording again. Give Ss time to correct the sentences and check their answers in pairs.

> **Answers:** Sentence 6 is true.
> **2** Clara gets up at eleven at the weekend.
> **3** Clara doesn't talk to her parents.
> **4** Julio doesn't listen to Paula.
> **5** Paula talks about her problems.
> **7** Wayne's neighbour gets home at half past four.
> **8** Wayne doesn't get up at eight o'clock./Wayne gets up at five o'clock.

D You could start by giving an example of a problem you have, e.g. with a neighbour or friend (show Ss that they don't need to talk about things that are too 'close to home' if they don't want to). Also check *It drives me crazy* (mime being exasperated by something). Then put Ss in pairs to discuss. If appropriate, invite Ss to report back to the class about their partner.

Unit 5 Recording 2

Conversation 1

A: How's the family?
B: Fine. Well, you remember Clara?
A: Clara, your daughter? Yes, how old is she now?
B: She's seventeen.
A: She isn't at school?
B: No.
A: Does she have a job?
B: No, she doesn't. That's the problem.
A: So what does she do all day?
B: Well, she listens to her music and … and she sleeps a lot.
A: What time does she get up?
B: I don't know because I'm at work. At the weekend she gets up at eleven.
A: Does she want a job?
B: I don't know. She doesn't talk much.
A: What do you mean?
B: Well, for example, in the evenings, we have dinner together. But Clara just sits there and listens to her music. Or she answers her phone and talks to her friends, but not to her family. It drives me crazy.
A: Does she …?

Conversation 2

A: Hi, Paula.
B: Hi. What's the problem? You look bad.
A: It's Julio.
B: Julio?
A: Yeah. Well, he doesn't listen to me.
B: What do you mean?
A: Well, I talk about my problems and he just checks his text messages or watches TV.
B: Does he talk to you?
A: Yeah … well, no … he says 'Mmmm'.
B: 'Mmmm'! What does that mean?
A: It means he doesn't really listen.
B: Oh, my boyfriend is exactly the same.

Conversation 3

A: Hey, Wayne. What's up? You look tired.
B: Yeah. No sleep.
A: What's the problem?
B: Neighbours. Problem neighbours. Or just one, the man in the flat upstairs.
A: Why? Does he play loud music? Big parties?
B: No, he doesn't. The problem is he works at night. He goes to work at six in the evening. I get home and I see him go to work every night.
A: What's his job?
B: He sells coffee in a snack bar at the train station.
A: And when does he get home?
B: About half past four. And then he watches television for two or three hours.
A: So when does he go to bed?
B: Oh, about six or seven.
A: And what time do you get up?
B: Huh! Now I get up at five. It's impossible to sleep. So I listen to music, drink coffee, then I go to work around eight.
A: And when do you go to bed?
B: Late. Midnight or 1a.m.
A: Ooh, four hours' sleep. Not good.

GRAMMAR   PRESENT SIMPLE QUESTIONS: HE/SHE/IT

3A Give Ss a minute or two to complete the tables while you copy them onto the board. As you check the answers, you could point out that the questions are the same in form as those for *I/you/we/they*, but with *does/doesn't* instead of *do/don't*.

> **Watch out!**
>
> If Ss want to say *What does it means? What time does she gets up?* etc., point out that the third person -s is on *does*, so it isn't necessary at the end of the verb.

Answers:

What time When	*does*	she he	get up? go to bed?
What		it	mean?

Does	she he	have a job? play loud music?	
Yes, he/she *does*.		No, he/she *doesn't*.	

B PRONUNCIATION weak form: *does* Give Ss time to familiarise themselves with the phonemic script and decide if /dəz/ is stressed or unstressed. Then play the recording at least twice for Ss to listen to the weak forms, before you ask them to repeat the questions.

Teaching tip

To help Ss to see why auxiliary verbs like *do/does* are pronounced like this, write the following on the board:

What / mean?

When / go to bed?

have / job?

Elicit/point out that these words carry the main 'message' of the question, so they are stressed: the other 'helping' words are not stressed, so they become 'squashed' together.

▷ LANGUAGEBANK 5.1 p126–127

You could set Ex 5.1.A, B and C in class. Half the class does Ex 5.1A and the other half does Ex 5.1B (Ss check their answers against a key). Then for Ex 5.1C, Ss match the questions and answers across the class. Ss could do Ex 5.1D for homework or in pairs in class.

Answers:

A **2** Does Stefan speak Chinese?   **3** Does Katia have children?
   4 Does your brother like his job?   **5** Does your cat have a name?
   6 Does this word mean 'very big'?

B **b)** does   **c)** doesn't   **d)** does   **e)** doesn't   **f)** does

C **2** e)   **3** b)   **4** d)   **5** f)   **6** c)

D **2** does he work   **3** does Cristina get home
   4 does she have dinner   **5** does 'late' mean
   6 does the lesson start

4 Go through the example with the class, and remind Ss that *does* is used in short answers as well as questions. Ss can check their answers in pairs and practise reading the conversations, paying attention to the pronunciation of *Does he/she/it …?*

Answers:

Conversation 1

A: What time *does* Mike come home in the evenings?

B: At about eight o'clock.

A: So, *does* he play with the children?

B: No, he doesn't. They go to bed at seven.

A: And *does* he work at the weekends?

B: Yes, he *does*, or he goes out and plays golf!

Conversation 2

A: Ana, *does* your sister phone you on your birthday?

B: No, she doesn't.

A: When *does* she phone you?

B: On her birthday because she wants money!

A: Really! So *does* it drive you crazy?

B: Yes, it *does*.

5A Focus Ss on the example, then give them a few minutes to complete the questions, working in pairs or alone.

Answers: **2** Does she do   **3** Does he have   **4** Does she study
5 Does your teacher read   **6** Do you listen
7 Does your sister watch   **8** Does he go   **9** Does she have
10 Do you go

B Do the first example for the class, using the name of one of the Ss. Encourage Ss to use a different name for each question.

C Demonstrate the example, using a student as A and taking the role of B yourself. Remind Ss to use a rising intonation on their questions and demonstrate this, asking them to repeat a few examples in chorus. Tell Ss to make a note of the answers and give them a few minutes to ask and answer. Choose a few Ss to tell the rest of the class what they found out about different people.

SPEAKING

6A You may want to demonstrate this activity by inviting different Ss to ask you the ten questions. This will also allow you to check vocabulary, e.g. *all the time* (a lot), *for hours* (for a long time), *take selfies* (mime taking a selfie), *loud* (contrast with *quiet*, e.g. shout, then whisper), *fast* (contrast with *slow*, e.g. speak fast, then slowly). When Ss have asked all the questions, they can agree as a class how many of the habits you have. Put Ss in pairs to ask and answer, then ask a few pairs to report back about which of them has more bad habits.

B You could suggest that Ss write a number from 1–10 next to each habit in the quiz, then tell each other their opinions (rather than looking at the numbers their partner has written in their Students' Book), e.g. *I think 'talk in films' is really bad, number 1. Number 2 is 'eat on trains'*, etc. In feedback, ask a few pairs which habits they agreed about, then you could have a class vote on the number one habit that drives people crazy.

C Go through the example with the class, highlighting the question *Does he/she have any other bad habits?* You may want to elicit some ideas of other bad habits from the class (e.g. get up early/come home late and make a lot of noise; leave dirty plates and cups in the kitchen; talk loudly on the phone on the train) before putting Ss in small groups to discuss the habits of friends, family members, people they work with, etc. You could also encourage Ss to listen 'actively' when other people in the group are talking by saying, e.g. *Oh no!/Really?/That's bad./My _____ is exactly the same.*

Homework ideas

- Ss think of two people in their lives (friends, family, neighbours, people at work/school, etc.) and write a few sentences about their daily routines, using vocabulary from the Photo bank as well as Ex 1, e.g. *My brother gets up at _____. He doesn't have breakfast. He leaves home at _____ and goes swimming before work.*
- **Workbook:** Ex 1–4, p32–33

YOU ARE WHAT YOU EAT

Introduction

Ss practise reading and talking about people's eating habits, using food vocabulary and adverbs of frequency. They also practise recognising and using word stress and learn to use linkers in writing.

> **SUPPLEMENTARY MATERIALS**
> **Resource bank:** p157 and p159
> **Ex 5B:** be prepared to demonstrate this activity.

Warm up

Put Ss in pairs (with their books closed). Give the pairs one minute to write a list of as many names of food and drink as they can think of. Then tell the pairs to choose five or six words and write them on a separate slip of paper, leaving out all the vowels (Ss should be familiar with this kind of vocabulary activity from the Lookback pages). Each pair then passes their slip of paper to the pair on their left, who have to fill in the missing vowels.

VOCABULARY FOOD

1A You could start by telling Ss to cover the words and see how many of the food items in the pictures they can name, either working together as a class or in pairs. Then give them a few minutes to match the words and pictures, working alone. In feedback, you could use the picture of fruit to check *banana*, and use the picture of vegetables to check *lettuce*, *pepper* and *tomato*. (NB: These items are also covered in the Photo bank – see below.)

> **Answers:** 2 B 3 E 4 H 5 A 6 F 7 D 8 C 9 G 10 I

B PRONUNCIATION word stress Ss could work in pairs, saying the words to each other, underlining the stressed syllable and counting the syllables. For **weaker classes**, you may want to say the words yourself for Ss to identify the stress. You could point out that six of the words have just one syllable and that one word (*vegetables*) has three syllables. If Ss query the pronunciation of *vegetables*, point out that the second e is 'squashed' between *veg* and *tab* because of the stress pattern (Ooo).

C Play the recording for Ss to check their answers, then once or twice more for them to repeat in chorus and individually. If you checked them earlier, you could also incorporate *banana*, *lettuce*, *tomato* and *pepper* at this stage. Then Ss could 'test' each other in pairs: Student A says a letter and Student B responds with the name of the food.

> **Answers:** 1 pasta (2) 2 steak (1) 3 chicken (2) 4 rice (1)
> 5 fish (1) 6 fruit (1) 7 vegetables (3) 8 eggs (1) 9 cheese (1)
> 10 biscuits (2)

2 You could demonstrate this with a **stronger student**. When Ss have asked each other about all the food, find out from a few pairs which food they both like.

▷ PHOTOBANK p143

Several of the items in the Photo bank exercises appear in the texts in Ex 3. To help Ss process these vocabulary items, they could choose the three items that they like best and tell their partner.

> **Answers:**
> **1A** 1 F 2 E 3 B 4 L 5 G 6 I 7 D 8 K 9 A 10 C
>   11 H 12 J
> **1B** 1 pepper (because it's not a fruit)
>   2 cereal (because it's not a vegetable)
>   3 bread (because it's not a drink/because it's not a liquid)

READING

3A Tell Ss to look at the names and the photos, but not the texts. Ask Ss if they think the people eat good or bad things and why. Give Ss a few minutes to decide which of the foods both people eat every day.

B Tell Ss to read the texts quickly, just to see if they were right about the foods.

> **Answers:** They both eat chicken, rice and lettuce every day.
> (NB: Petra has cheese and steak, but not every day.)

C Before Ss read the texts again, check the following: *a meal* (e.g. breakfast, lunch, dinner), *junk food* (e.g. chips, hot dogs, burgers, donuts), *a strict diet* (eat only certain foods, e.g. to lose weight), *raw* (not cooked), *tinned* (mime opening a tin of food), *toast* (mime making toast), *to snack* (eat something small). Tell Ss to read the texts to find the answers to the questions, then compare answers in pairs.

> **Answers:** 2 P 3 P 4 B 5 BP 6 B 7 P

D You could start by giving an example about yourself, e.g. *My diet is similar to Byron's because I have eggs for breakfast, but I don't eat 6,000 calories a day!* Ss can discuss in pairs or in small groups, then report back to the class.

> **Optional extra activity**
> Highlight the following phrases from the texts for Ss to use when they talk about their diets:
> *I eat / don't eat a lot.*
> *I have / don't have a strict diet.*
> *I eat (number) meals a day.*
> *For (meal) I have the same thing every day.*
> *I eat / don't eat (raw / tinned) food.*
> *I snack / don't snack between meals.*

GRAMMAR ADVERBS OF FREQUENCY

4A You could find the first word in the box with the class (*sometimes* in the Byron Hanson text) then give Ss a few minutes to underline the rest, and check their answers in pairs. Tell Ss to think about the meaning of the words, but not to worry about their exact meaning for the moment.

> **Answers:**
> Byron Hanson text: sometimes, always, never, usually
> Petra Leon text: never, often, not often, usually

B Put the following sentences from the Byron Hanson text on the board:

For lunch I have the same thing every day. I always have fish or steak (sometimes I have both).

Show Ss that *the same thing every day* helps them to guess the meaning of *always*.

Point out where *sometimes* is on the line and ask Ss where to put *always* (next to 100%). Give Ss time to add the other adverbs, working in pairs or alone.

Answers: 80% usually   60% often   10% not often   0% never

C PRONUNCIATION word stress When Ss have underlined the stress, elicit/point out that the stress is on the first syllable for all the adverbs. Also highlight that *usually* has three syllables: Ooo (not four). Play the recording again for Ss to repeat.

Answers: usually   often   sometimes   not often   never

D For **weaker classes**, write the sentences and the rules on the board and go through the rules with the whole class. Otherwise, give Ss a few minutes to discuss the rules in pairs first.

Answers:
1 The adverb goes *after* the verb 'be'.
2 The adverb goes *after* 'don't' and 'doesn't'.
3 The adverb goes *before* other verbs.

▷ **LANGUAGEBANK 5.2** p126–127

The Language bank gives Ss more examples of the adverbs in sentences and highlights the fact that *not usually* is possible as well as *not often*. If you feel that your Ss need more basic practice with the position and meaning of adverbs, Ss could do Ex 5.2A and B in class. Otherwise they could do them for homework.

Answers:
A 2 My mother *usually* phones me on Monday evenings.
   3 He's *often* tired in the mornings.
   4 We *always* have a drink after work on Fridays.
   5 Do you *usually* walk to work?
   6 I'm *not usually* at home in the afternoons.
   7 Classes are *sometimes* on Saturdays.
   8 I *don't often* watch TV.
B B: Er, no, doctor. I *never eat* vegetables and I *don't often eat* fruit.
   A: What about meat and fish?
   B: Well, I *sometimes eat* fish, maybe once or twice a week and I *often eat* chicken. I like steak so I *always eat* steak for lunch and I *usually have* it with chips.

5A Go through the example with the class, then give Ss a few minutes to put the sentences in order and check answers in pairs.

Answers: 2 I never eat sweets.   3 I'm never hungry.
4 I often eat chicken.   5 I'm usually home for dinner.
6 I don't often eat fruit.   7 I sometimes have vegetables for lunch.
8 I always eat steak on Sundays.

B Demonstrate the activity yourself first: tick the sentences that are true for you, and change the others to make them true. Show Ss that they can change the adverb or any other part of the sentence, e.g.

I always have fish on Fridays. OR
I usually have pizza on Fridays. OR
I usually have fish on Mondays.

SPEAKING

6A Write the first sentence from the questionnaire on the board, then ask a student if they have a coffee before breakfast, and depending on how they answer, write the appropriate letter next to the sentence. Give Ss a few minutes to complete the questionnaire individually.

B Ask two Ss to demonstrate the activity, using their own answers to the first item. Remind Ss to try to find two things the same, then give them time to go through all the questions. Monitor carefully and note down examples of good language use and problem areas for praise and correction. When Ss have finished, ask any pairs who found two (or more) things the same to tell the class about them.

WRITING   LINKERS TO SEQUENCE

7A As they read the description, Ss could put a tick next to anything that is the same for them and a cross next to anything different. They can discuss their answers in pairs, e.g. *I get up at six, too, but I don't read emails or listen to the radio.*

B Direct Ss to the example *First …* in the text, then give them a minute or two to find the other three linkers. To help Ss see the need for linkers to show the sequence of events in the text, you could read it without the four linkers and elicit/point out that it sounds as if all the activities happen at the same time.

Answers: 2 then   3 after that   4 finally

C Ss read through the text again to find the linker without a comma after it.

Answers: then

speakout TIP

Direct Ss back to the description and ask them to find and circle the six words. Give them a minute or two to decide which word does not join two ideas. (Answer: *at* – preposition) *At* answers the question *where?* or *when?* Suggest that Ss make a list of linkers in example sentences in their vocabulary books.

8A Ask Ss to write their descriptions on a separate piece of paper, so they can be passed round or displayed around the room. Tell Ss to use at least four adverbs of frequency, as well as the linkers. Circulate and help Ss while they write their descriptions, if necessary.

B The descriptions can either be passed around the class, or displayed for Ss to walk round and read.

Optional extra activity

Instead of *your typical morning*, the description could be of:
your Saturday morning, or *your ideal morning*
your typical/ideal Friday evening

Homework ideas

• Ss write two short paragraphs: one about someone they know who has good eating habits, and one about someone with bad eating habits, e.g. *My best friend's eating habits are very good. He always has a big breakfast, with cereal and fruit. He usually eats a lot of … and … He doesn't often eat … and he never eats …*

• **Workbook:** Ex 1–6, p34–35

WHEN DOES IT OPEN?

Introduction

Ss practise asking for information about hotel services, using sentence stress appropriately. They also practise listening and learn to use two-part exchanges.

> **SUPPLEMENTARY MATERIALS**
> **Resource bank:** p160
> **Ex 5 (optional extra activity):** prepare a set of cards for each pair of Ss (see notes).

Warm up

You can lead into the topic via a discussion about hotels. Put these prompts on the board for Ss to discuss in small groups or as a class: *Do you like big or small hotels?/Do you like old fashioned or modern hotels?/Do you like hotels in the city centre or in the countryside?*
Alternatively, review telling the time. Tell Ss you are going to read some questions. Using the board, demonstrate that they should write the answers in a different order from the questions, so it's not obvious which answer matches which question. Read out the following questions: *What time do you … get up from Monday to Friday?/have lunch from Monday to Friday?/go to work or school?* etc. Then Ss show each other their answers and try to guess which questions they relate to, e.g.
A: (looking at 9.30a.m.) Do you get up at 9.30 at the weekend?
B: No, I don't.
A: Do you go to work at 9.30?
B: Yes, I do!

VOCABULARY   HOTEL SERVICES

1A Direct Ss to the photos. Elicit ideas about what the places are. Give Ss a minute or two to look at the services in the box. Check *gift shop* (a place that sells small things to give as presents) and *guided tour* (a trip round a city, building, etc. with someone who tells people about it). Also check the stress on *café, gift shop, exchange, hairdresser's, guided tour*.

> **Answers: A** a guided tour   **B** a gym   **C** a hairdresser's
> **D** a gift shop

B Ss could match the services and activities in pairs or alone.

> **Answers: 2** a money exchange   **3** a hairdresser's   **4** a gym
> **5** a café   **6** a swimming pool   **7** a gift shop   **8** a guided tour

> **Optional extra activity**
> Student A covers the box in Ex 1A and looks at the activities in Ex 1B. Student B looks at the box in Ex 1A and covers the services in Ex 1B. *A: I want to get a haircut./B: Go to the hairdresser's.*
> A and B swap roles. (NB: We say *go on a guided tour.*)

C Put Ss in pairs and demonstrate using a **strong student**:
S: I think a gym is important because …
T: I don't. I think a gift shop is important because …
Tell Ss to try to agree on two important services to tell the rest of the class at the end.

FUNCTION   ASKING FOR INFORMATION

2A You could play the first part of the recording for Ss to hear the example, then play the rest of the recording for them to write the other three services.

> **Answers: 2** a restaurant (breakfast)   **3** a hairdresser's
> **4** a guided tour

B Tell Ss to read through the woman's notes about opening times and the price of the guided tour. Using the board, demonstrate that Ss should correct the information by crossing out the mistakes and writing the correct answers above. Play the recording again.

> **Answers:** gym: 6a.m.–9p.m. *10p.m.*   closes 12–1
> breakfast: 6.30–9.00 in café *restaurant*
> hairdresser's: 10–6; Tuesdays to 8p.m *9p.m.*   closes Mondays
> guided tour: 9a.m. and 2p.m. *3p.m.* €50 *€15*

3A Before you play the recording again, Ss work in pairs and help each other to complete as many of the sentences as they can.

> **Answers: 2** opens   **3** time   **4** to   **5** Do   **6** every   **7** does
> **8** leaves   **9** cost   **10** It

B **PRONUNCIATION** sentence stress   Remind Ss that we usually stress the words that give the message of the sentence or phrase. You could demonstrate this when you go through the answers by only writing the stressed words on the board and pointing out that the questions and answers can still be understood, e.g.
When – gym – open?   opens – 6a.m. – 10p.m.   time – breakfast? etc.
When Ss repeat the questions and answers, encourage them to copy the falling intonation on the *Wh-* questions. You could help by doing an exaggerated model yourself so that Ss can hear the movement.

> **Answers: 2** It opens from 6a.m. to 10p.m.
> **3** What time is breakfast?   **4** From half past six to nine o'clock.
> **5** Do you have a hairdresser's in the hotel?
> **6** Yes, it opens every day except Monday.
> **7** When does the tour leave?   **8** It leaves at 9a.m. and at 3p.m.
> **9** How much does it cost?   **10** It costs fifteen euros.

> ▷ **LANGUAGEBANK 5.3** p126–127
>
> You could use the tables in the Language bank to give Ss some question and answer practice across the class. *A: When does the café open? B: It opens at nine. C: How much is it? D: It's twenty euros.* Ss could do Ex 5.3 in class, then you could use the completed conversation to give them some speaking practice in pairs before the prompted conversation in Ex 4A (p56).
>
> **Answers:**
> A: Excuse *me?*
> B: Can I help you?
> A: Yes, *what* time is dinner?
> B: From seven *to* half past ten.
> A: And *do* you have a swimming pool?
> B: Yes, it opens every day *except* Sunday.
> A: When *does* it open?
> B: It *opens* at seven in the morning.
> A: When does *it* close?
> B: *It* closes at nine in the evening.

> **Unit 5 Recording 6**
>
> A: Excuse me?
> B: Yes, can I help you?
> A: Yes. I have a reservation for tonight.
> B: And your name?
> A: Shannon.
> B: Ah, yes. Miss Shannon. A single for two nights.
> A: That's right.
> B: I'm sorry. Your room isn't ready.
> A: That's a shame. Am I early? What time is check-in?
> B: Two p.m. usually. Your room is almost ready. Please have a seat.
> A: Thank you. I have one question.
> B: Yes?
> A: When does the gym open?
> B: It opens from six a.m. to ten p.m., except lunchtime. It closes from twelve to one.

A: Thanks. Oh, just one more question. What time is breakfast?
B: From half past six to nine o'clock.
A: And where is it?
B: Breakfast is in the restaurant.
A: Right. Thank you. … The restaurant …?
B: Over there.
A: Right. Oh, I have one more question.
B: Sure.
A: Do you have a hairdresser's in the hotel?
B: Yes, it opens every day except today, Monday.
A: That's too bad.
B: Yes, I'm sorry. But tomorrow is OK.
A: Tomorrow.
B: Yes, from ten to six. Actually, I'm wrong. On Tuesdays, it closes at nine o'clock in the evening.
A: Right. Thank you.
B: You're welcome.

B: Excuse me, madam.
A: Yes?
B: Your room's ready now. Here's your key card. Room 538 on the fifth floor.
A: Thank you.
B: No problem. Enjoy your stay.
A: Oh, but I have one more question.
B: Yes?
A: I want to go on a guided tour of the old town. Do you know a good one?
B: Ah, yes. We do a tour from the hotel.
A: Great. When does the tour leave?
B: It leaves at nine a.m. and at three p.m.
A: How much does it cost?
B: It costs fifteen euros.
A: Right. Thank you. Do you have a map of the city?
B: Yes, here you are.
A: Thank you.
B: Have a nice day.
A: You too.
B: Any more questions I can help you with?
A: No, thank you. Oh, just one …

4A Ss write the full conversation in their notebooks, or for **stronger classes**, Ss could complete it orally, without notes.

Answers:
A: When does the gift shop open?
B: It opens from 10a.m. to 8p.m.
A: Is the swimming pool open all day?
B: Yes, it opens from 6a.m. to 9p.m. But it closes from 12p.m. to 1p.m.
A: How much does the guided tour cost for children?
B: It's free for children.
A: When does it leave?
B: It leaves at 10a.m.

B If Ss have written the full conversation, ask them to use the prompts for practice, rather than reading aloud. You could encourage **stronger Ss** to substitute some of the services in the conversation, e.g. money exchange for gift shop. Monitor the practice and note down examples of good language use as well as any problems for praise and correction afterwards.

LEARN TO USE TWO-PART EXCHANGES

5A Go through the example with the class, then put Ss in pairs to write R or G next to the other sentences. Point out that a guest is a person who stays at a hotel.

Answers: 2 R 3 G 4 R 5 G 6 R

B Look at the first pair of answers with the class and elicit which answer shows that the person is not happy (Answer: a) That's a shame = That's not good. Point out that answer b) is correct if the receptionist says Your room's ready. Give Ss time to choose the

answer for the other sentences. If necessary, demonstrate Here you are by giving something to a student as you say it.

C Play the recording for Ss to check their answers, and again for them to repeat in chorus.

Answers: 2 b) 3 a) 4 b) 5 a) 6 b)

D Point out to Ss that it's useful to learn the answers in these exchanges because they are 'fixed' and can be used without any changes in many situations. Ask two **stronger Ss** to demonstrate the activity, then put Ss in pairs to practise.

speakout TIP

Elicit ideas from the class for the second part of the three exchanges, and give Ss time to write these and the two-part exchanges from Ex 5 in their phrasebooks. You could also ask Ss for the second part of the following exchanges:
1 Coffee? Yes, please. / No, thanks.
2 Here you are. Thank you.
3 Bye. See you.
4 Sorry! That's OK, don't worry. (If you're late, accidentally knock into someone, etc.)

Answers: 1 How are you? Fine, thanks. 2 Nice to meet you. You too.
3 Let's have a break. Good idea.

Optional extra activity

For further practice, prepare a set of nine small cards/slips of paper for each pair of Ss, with the following:
1 How are you? 2 Nice to meet you. 3 Let's have a break.
4 Coffee? 5 Bye. 6 Thank you. 7 Have a nice day.
8 Here you are. 9 Sorry!
Ss in pairs put the cards face down in front of them, then take turns to pick up a card and say the phrase for their partner to respond to.

SPEAKING

6A Focus Ss on the example question then put them in pairs to write the others. Circulate and help, and encourage Ss to practise asking their questions, paying attention to polite intonation.

Suggested questions:
What time does the Café Slavia open? How much does a coffee cost?
What time does the hotel café open?
When does the guided tour leave? How much does it cost?
What time is the opera? Where is it? How much does it cost?

B Move Ss around so they're working with new partners. Direct Bs to p150 and give them time to look through the information. Tell As to start asking their questions and remind them to write the answers in their notebooks. Monitor and note down examples of good language use and any problems for praise and correction in feedback.

C Direct As to the information on p152 and give them time to look through it. Tell Bs to ask their questions and note the answers.

D Students check their partner's notes.

Homework ideas
- Ss think about a hotel they've been to, or research one on the internet, and make some notes about the hotel services: what the hotel has, opening times, costs, etc. In the next lesson, Ss work in small groups, taking turns to tell the group the name of their hotel and answer questions about it. When they've finished, the groups decide which hotel is the best.
- **Workbook:** Ex 1–3, p36

HOW TO FEED YOUR KIDS

Introduction

Ss watch an extract from a BBC programme about children and food. Ss then learn and practise how to talk about food choices and write a forum entry about food and drink to take to a desert island.

> **SUPPLEMENTARY MATERIALS**
> **Ex 1A/B (alternative approach):** bring in some of each of the snacks in the photos.

Warm up

Review food vocabulary and lead in to the topic of snacks. Tell Ss to close their books and write the following on the board: *Two things you like to eat: 1 for breakfast, 2 for lunch, 3 for dinner, 4 in a restaurant, 5 for a snack.* (Remind Ss that a snack is something small to eat between meals.)

Tell Ss to work alone and write their answers in their notebooks. Then put Ss in pairs and tell them to take turns to read out their answers in random order: their partner guesses the meal/situation. You could demonstrate this with a **stronger student**, eg:

A: pizza, chips
B: in a restaurant
A: That's right!

DVD PREVIEW

1A Direct Ss to the photos and elicit that they are all types of snack. Put Ss in pairs to match the photos to the words in the box, or do this with the whole class. Check the pronunciation of *raisins* /reizinz/, *crisps*, *biscuits* /biskits/ and *sweets* /swi:ts/.

> **Answers:** A biscuits   B nuts   C mango   D crisps   E raisins
> F sweets

B Check the meaning of *healthy* (good for you). You could then tell Ss which of the snacks you eat/don't eat, then put them in pairs to discuss the questions. You could also ask the class for some more examples of healthy snacks.

> **Answers:** healthy snacks are: nuts, raisins, mango

Alternative approach

Tell Ss to close their books and use the real snacks instead of the photos. Put the samples on a surface where all the Ss can see them and elicit/give the name of each snack. Check the pronunciation of *crisps*, *raisins* /reizinz/, *sweets* /swi:ts/ and *biscuits* /biskits/. Then pass round samples of the snacks for Ss to taste, and ask them which they like/don't like. Also establish which snacks are good for you/healthy (nuts, raisins, mango). Finish by asking Ss to rank the three healthy and three unhealthy snacks in order of preference from 1–3, and invite a few Ss to share their answers with the class.

2A Before directing Ss to the programme information, check the meaning of *kids* (informal word for *children*), *feed* (mime feeding someone), *habits* (things we do every day – give an example), *experiment* (people do experiments to find answers to questions, e.g. *What happens if you put water in the freezer?*). Then give Ss time to read the questions and establish that they need to tick two answers for each. Direct them to the programme information and give them three or four minutes to answer the questions.

> **Answers:** 1 a), c)   2 a), b)

B Read out the two questions at the end of the programme information and put Ss in pairs or small groups to discuss their answers. Invite two or three Ss to share their answers with the class.

DVD VIEW

3A Before playing the DVD, focus Ss on the two sentences and the three options. Check that Ss understand *like the same* and *like more*. You could give an example and use your voice to show the difference, e.g. *I like biscuits, but I like chocolate more. I like nuts and crisps the same.* Then play the DVD and give Ss time to choose the correct endings.

> **Answers:** 1 c)   2 a)

B Before putting Ss in pairs to underline the correct alternatives, check *whistle* (demonstrate), *crazy* (very, very excited), *together* (all in one place). Give Ss a few minutes to work in pairs on the alternatives, then play the DVD again. After you have checked the answers with the class, you could ask the Ss what they think of the experiment.

> **Answers:** 1 school, children   2 second   3 raisins   4 animals
> 5 together   6 'no'

DVD 5   How to feed your kids

N = Narrator   K = Kids   G = Giles   G1 = Girl 1   W = Woman
B1 = Boy 1   G2 = Girl 2   B2 = Boy 2   B3 = Boy 3

N: What do you think about children and food? Do kids like healthy food? Do they snack too much? Most parents say 'yes.' It's a big problem. So, how can we change kids' snacking habits? In this experiment, you need: one school, twenty children and two snacks –mangoes and raisins. The children like raisins and mangoes the same. And then we say, 'No raisins!' Let's watch the experiment. Now we go to the classroom. We put mangoes and raisins on the table for snack time. This is the experiment: At the first whistle, it's mango time. The children can eat the mangoes but no raisins. After that, at the second whistle, the children can eat the raisins. Remember, the kids like mangoes and raisins the same. The first whistle: It's mango time! But no raisins! Now the second whistle: the raisin whistle.
K: Raisins!
K: I've got a thousand.
K: I've got a thousand and one hundred.
K: I've got a thousand and two hundred.
K: I've got five hundred and one.
N: It's day one and the children want the raisins.
It's day two. And it's mango time.
Watch Giles.
G: No you can't! Don't take the raisins.
N: After that, it's raisin time. Poor Giles.
Day three, day four, day five … Now raisins are the favourite. On day ten, the kids are raisin crazy. They're animals! After ten days, we ask the kids: Which snack do you like more?
G1: I like mango about that much.
W: And raisins?
G1: Um, raisins that much.
B1: The raisins.
G2: Raisins.
B2: Raisins.
B3: Raisins.
W: How much do you like raisins?
N: Then we ask all the children together. Which is your favourite snack?
K: Raisins!
N: So, to change children's snacking habits, don't say no. Say no and children want the snacks more.

speakout desert island food

4A Introduce the idea of a desert island with a simple board sketch and elicit some ideas about life there, e.g. the weather, where to live, things to do, other things on the island such as plants, animals, rivers, etc. Give Ss a few minutes to write their list of food and drink.

B Ss write down the food and drink as they listen to the recording. They could check answers in pairs.

> **Answers:** bananas   apples   cake   pasta (with cheese)
> cereal   milk   English tea

C Give Ss a few moments to look at the key phrases then play the recording again for them to tick the phrases they hear. After you've checked the answers, give Ss some pronunciation practice by modelling the phrases for them to repeat.

> **Answers:**
> What's on your list? ✓
> Number [one ✓/two/three] on my list is … ✓
> I really like …
> It's [good/bad ✓] for you …
> Do you really like …? ✓
> Me too. ✓
> Really? ✓
> What about drinks? ✓
> I don't like [it/fruit/eggs].

Unit 5 Recording 9

A: What's on your list?
B: Well, number one on my list is fruit.
A: Fruit? Why fruit?
B: It's good for you.
A: Do you really like it?
B: I like bananas and apples.
A: Bananas and apples. That's two things.
B: OK, fine. One is bananas and two is apples.
A: And what's number three on your list?
B: Number three is cake. I love chocolate cake.
A: Me too. It's on my list.
B: Maybe it's bad for you, but …
A: Chocolate cake and fruit. That's OK.
B: Yeah, with fruit, it's good.
A: And number four?
B: Pasta with cheese.
A: Mmm … that's two …
B: No, I think it's one. I eat pasta every day. With cheese …
A: OK, pasta and cheese, fine.
B: And number five is cereal.
A: Really? Do you really like cereal?
B: I do, yes.
A: What about drinks?
B: Milk for my cereal.
A: Yes. And what other drink do you have?
B: I have tea. English tea.
A: Of course. Me too.

5A Give Ss a few minutes working alone to review the list they made in Ex 4A and think about how to incorporate some of the key phrases into their talk. Circulate and help. Then put Ss in pairs to talk about their lists, and encourage the listeners to use the appropriate key phrases (*Me too, Really? I like X too.*) to keep the conversation going. At the end direct Ss to the audio script to check how these phrases are used in practice.

B Put Ss in groups of four or five. Monitor the group work closely and make notes of any good language use and problem areas for praise and correction later.

> **Alternative approach**
> Tell Ss that they need to discuss the best five food types and two drinks to take, and to agree on one list between them. Then ask each group to report back to the class and justify the choices on their list.

writeback a forum entry

6A Give Ss a few minutes to read the entry and compare the list to their own, then put them in pairs/small groups to discuss the questions.

B Ss could work in pairs and help each other think of reasons for including the items on their lists. Circulate and help with vocabulary. When Ss have finished writing, they could walk round the classroom and read each other's lists, and tell each other which reason for including an item in the list they thought was the best.

> **Homework ideas**
> Ss write a short paragraph describing a simple dish from their country.
> *(X) is a dish from (region) in my country.*
> *It has (ingredients) in it.*
> *You (cook it in the oven/cook it on the grill/you don't cook it).*
> *You have it for (breakfast/lunch/dinner/a snack).*
> *(It's very good/It's not very good) for you because it has (X) in it.*
> *(I make it/(X) makes it for me/I usually eat it in a restaurant/café).*

LOOKBACK

DAILY ROUTINES

1A Give Ss a minute or two to look at the word webs, then go through the answers with the class.

> **Answers:** 1 get   2 go   3 have

B Go through the example, using two **stronger Ss** to demonstrate. Put Ss in pairs to practise.

Optional extra activity

Put the following groups of verb phrases on the board. Ss work in pairs and think of reasons for the untypical order:

1 have breakfast, 2 get up (you have breakfast in bed on a special day, e.g. Mother's Day)

1 get up, 2 go to work (you get up late and don't have time for breakfast)

1 have breakfast, 2 don't go to work (you work at home, or you're not well)

1 have dinner, 2 go to work (you work at night)

1 make lunch, 2 go to work (you take lunch to work)

1 leave school, 2 start your homework, 3 get home (you do your homework on the bus or train)

PRESENT SIMPLE: QUESTIONS HE/SHE/IT

2A You could run this as a team competition (Ss have their books closed). Write up or display one question at a time and the first team member to 'buzz' and tell you the complete question wins a point for their team. If they make a mistake, the other team can try for a bonus point. You could also give bonus points for good pronunciation.

> **Answers:** 2 Does she like coffee or tea?
> 3 What time does he go to work?   4 What does she have for lunch?
> 5 Does he have a car?   6 When does she get home?
> 7 Does she study at the weekend?   8 Does he phone you every day?

B Demonstrate this by taking the role of B and prompting Ss to ask questions. Point out that Student A will need to change *he* to *she* and vice versa, depending on whether the person is male or female. For **stronger classes**, encourage Ss to think of some more questions of their own, e.g.

What does he/she do in the evening?
When does he/she go to bed?
What does he/she do at the weekend?

FOOD

3A You could run this as a race, with Ss working in pairs. The first pair to write out all the words and bring them to you wins, as long as all the words are spelled correctly.

> **Answers:** 2 chicken   3 cheese   4 pasta   5 biscuits   6 fish
> 7 steak   8 rice   9 vegetables   10 fruit

B Tell Ss not to show their three circles to their partner. Remind them that there are more food words in the Photo bank, p143: they could choose any of these to put in the circles.

C You could demonstrate this by saying a food and inviting Ss to guess whether you like/don't like or don't eat it. You could teach *I'm allergic to it* and/or *It's bad for me* as reasons for not eating something. Put Ss in pairs to take turns to say a food item and to guess. You could ask a few pairs to report back on anything that they have in common.

ADVERBS OF FREQUENCY

4A Ss could start by finding the sentence that is correct. Then remind them that they need to think about the word order, i.e. the position of the adverb, in most of the sentences.

> **Answers:**
> 1 We always speak English together in class.
> 2 correct
> 3 I'm never late for English lessons.
> 4 I don't often watch English videos.
> 5 My English teacher often says 'Good!'
> 6 I never read an online English newspaper.
> 7 I'm not usually tired in English lessons.

B Go through the example, pointing out that Ss can add another sentence to extend/explain their answer.

HOTEL SERVICES

5 You could run this as a race. Give Ss a minute or two in pairs to circle the words. The first pair to finish put their hands up, then spell out each word for the class. If they make a mistake with spelling, another pair can try to spell all the words, and so on.

> **Answers:** 1 gym   2 café   3 gift shop   4 swimming pool
> 5 money exchange   6 guided tour   7 restaurant   8 hairdresser's

Optional extra activity

Ss write four or five sentences about how often they use hotel services when they stay in a hotel, either alone or with their family, partner, etc.

e.g. *I sometimes go to the gym.*
   We often go to the café for lunch.
   My children usually go to the swimming pool.

Ss work in pairs and tell each other their sentences.

ASKING FOR INFORMATION

6A Give Ss a few minutes to complete the questions, working alone.

> **Answers:** 1 does   2 does   3 When, on   4 When

B Point out that Ss decide on the times for themselves.

C Remind Ss about the falling intonation on *Wh-* questions. You may want to give them some repetition practice with the questions before you put them in pairs.

Optional extra activity

Divide Ss in to two groups: hotel receptionists and customers. Tell the hotel receptionists to write their own timetable of hotel services, as in Ex 6A. Tell the customers to write three hotel services that are important to them. Then tell the customers to go and visit at least three hotels and ask about the services. Finally, the customers decide which is the best hotel for them and tell the rest of the class in feedback.

BBC interviews and worksheet

What do you usually do at the weekend?

In this video people describe their weekend activities: what time they get up and what they do. The material enables Ss to consolidate and extend the vocabulary used for talking about routines and also offers authentic usage of adverbs of frequency (focused on in lesson 5.2).

OVERVIEW

6.1 NO TRAINS

VOCABULARY | places
PRONUNCIATION | word stress
LISTENING | listen to a man stuck at a station
GRAMMAR | *there is/are*
PRONUNCIATION | sentence stress
SPEAKING | find differences between places; talk about places in towns
WRITING | start and end emails

6.2 GETTING THERE

VOCABULARY | transport
READING | read some fun facts about transport
GRAMMAR | *a/an, some, a lot of, not any*
PRONUNCIATION | linking
SPEAKING | ask and answer questions about transport

6.3 SINGLE OR RETURN?

VOCABULARY | travel
FUNCTION | buying a ticket
LISTENING | listen to someone buy a bus ticket
LEARN TO | check numbers
PRONUNCIATION | word stress for checking
SPEAKING | buy a ticket for travel

6.4 RUSH HOUR BBC �)) DVD

DVD | watch a BBC programme about rush hour in India
speakout | talk about travel in your country
writeback | write in a travel forum

6.5 LOOKBACK

Communicative revision activities

BBC �)) INTERVIEWS

How do you get to work?

In this video people talk about their journeys to work. The material revises and extends vocabulary around the topics of transport and travel. Ss can also listen to and revise expressing opinions about journeys (*I love/like/hate*, etc.). Use the video at the end of the unit to recap and recycle the key vocabulary and language learnt.

NO TRAINS

Introduction

Students practise listening and talking about places, using *there is/are* and related vocabulary, and with attention to word and sentence stress. They also practise starting and ending an email.

> **SUPPLEMENTARY MATERIALS**
> **Resource bank:** p163
> **Ex 1C (optional extra activity):** prepare a matching activity.
> **Ex 9B (alternative approach):** prepare a gap fill of an email.

Warm up

Focus on the unit theme of *journeys*. Establish that a *journey* is when you go from one place to another, and elicit some ideas from Ss about where and why people go on journeys, e.g. go to work or school/university, go to another city to visit someone, on holiday or on business, etc. Ss could discuss in pairs how often they go on a journey, where they go, and who with. For **stronger classes** you could also direct Ss to the photos on p61 and ask them what they think of the types of journey they can see there.

VOCABULARY PLACES

1A For **stronger classes**, Ss could cover the words and, working in pairs, see how many of the pictures they can name.

> **Culture note**
> Instead of *pharmacy*, Ss may have heard or seen the word *chemist's*, which is common in British English.

> **Answers: A** a hotel **B** a restaurant **D** a café
> **E** a pharmacy **F** a payphone **G** a cash machine
> **H** a newsagent's

B PRONUNCIATION word stress Before you play the recording, give Ss an opportunity to count the number of syllables in each word. They could also predict where the stress is, then listen to check. You may also want to point out that *hotel* is the only word with an unusual stress pattern: all the other nouns have the stress on the first syllable (or first word if they are compound nouns like *internet café* or *cash machine*).

> **Answers:** a <u>news</u>agent's   a ho<u>tel</u>   a <u>ca</u>fé   a <u>res</u>taurant
> a <u>phar</u>macy   a <u>pay</u>phone   a <u>cash</u> machine

C Ss should cover the words in the box in Ex 1A to do this activity.

> **Optional extra activity**
> Prepare an activity like the one below: Student A has a list of places, Student B has a list of activities. Ss practise asking and answering in pairs, then swap roles:
> *Student A: What do people do at a …?*
> *Student B: They …*
>
> | A | B |
> |---|---|
> | snack bar | check emails |
> | payphone | have dinner |
> | pharmacy | buy a newspaper |
> | hotel | get money |
> | restaurant | buy medicine |
> | internet café | make a call |
> | cash machine | have a sandwich |
> | newsagent's | relax |

▷ **PHOTOBANK** p144

Several of the places in the Photo bank should be familiar to Ss from previous units, e.g. *an airport, a cinema, a gym, a school, a supermarket*. Ss could match the names of the places to the photos for homework, or at some stage before Ex 5, so they have the option of using the place names in the practice activity. It would also be useful to highlight the stress on the words of more than one syllable, especially *a factory, a library, a museum, a post office, a theatre*.

Answers:
Places:	1 O	2 H	3 J	4 F	5 B	6 A	7 C	8 N	9 P	10 L
	11 D	12 G	13 K	14 I	15 M	16 E			
Signs:	1 I	2 C	3 D	4 E	5 B	6 J	7 A	8 F	9 H	10 G

LISTENING

2A Give an example of one thing you think is good or bad about train travel. Then put Ss in pairs to discuss their opinions. Use this context to teach *bad weather*, i.e. trains are slow or sometimes stop if the weather is bad. Ss may also try to express ideas such as *crowded, expensive, fast*: you could teach these words if they come up, although they are dealt with systematically in lesson 6.4.

Suggested answers:
good: fast, comfortable, safe
bad: sometimes expensive, noisy, crowded, sometimes slow

B Refer Ss back to Ex 1A and tell them to write the numbers either next to the pictures or next to the words.

Answers: 2 internet café   3 restaurant   4 café   5 cash machine
6 hotel
newsagent's and *pharmacy* are not in the conversations

C Before you play the recording again, give Ss time to look through the alternatives in pairs and encourage them to help each other with unfamiliar words or try to guess their meaning by looking at the other words around them. If they can't guess, they should look in their dictionaries or check with you. Check that everyone understands *dead* (no battery power) vs *broken* and *full* (no free rooms). Play the recording, then Ss check answers in pairs.

Answers: 1 bad   2 dead   3 isn't   4 closed   5 expensive

Unit 6   Recording 2

A: Excuse me …?
B: Yes?
A: Is there a train to York tonight?
B: No, sorry, there aren't any trains tonight. It's the weather. It's very bad.
A: Not any trains? Not one?
B: No, not tonight. Maybe tomorrow. They …
A: Sorry, excuse me.
C: Hello? Pete, where are you?
A: Hi, I'm here in London, in the station, but there aren't any trains and … Megan, Megan…? Oh, no … Excuse me, is there a payphone near here? My phone's dead.
D: Yes, there's a payphone over there.
A: Thanks. Oh, and is there an internet café?
D: Erm … I don't think so. No, there isn't an internet café. Not in the station but there's one in Judd Street.
A: Judd Street. Thanks.
D: You're welcome.

E: Can I help you?
A: Yes. Are there any restaurants in the station?
E: Yes, there are … but … what's the time?
A: Erm … Half past eleven.

E: Ah, they're closed now, but there's a café over there. That's open.
A: And is there a cash machine here?
E: Yes, over there.
A: Right. And hotels?
E: There are two hotels near here. The Charlotte Street Hotel … that's about two hundred and fifty pounds a night.
A: Two hundred and fifty pounds? That's expensive.
E: And there's the Ridgemount, that's about eighty pounds.
A: Where's that?
F: It's here on the map.
A: Great … thanks for your help.
E: No problem.

GRAMMAR   *THERE IS/ARE*

3A Go through the example with the class, and use the classroom to elicit one or two more examples with *there's a*, e.g. *There's a mobile phone on the desk./There's a jacket on the chair.* Elicit/Point out that *'s* is the contracted form of *is*. Then give Ss time to complete the table. They could work in pairs and help each other to do this.

B You may need to pause the recording as Ss check their answers.

Watch out!

Ss may try to say *There isn't any trains* or *There aren't any train*. Tell them that *any* is used with plural nouns (uncountable nouns are not dealt with at this level).

Answers:

	singular	plural
+	There's a payphone over there.	There *are* two hotels near here.
–	There isn't an internet café.	There *aren't* any trains.
?	*Is* there a train to York tonight?	*Are* there any restaurants in the station?
	Yes, there is. No, there *isn't*.	Yes, there are. No, *there* aren't.

C **PRONUNCIATION sentence stress** You could do the first sentence with the class as an example, pointing out that the stress is on the words that carry the important information. Play the recording, pausing if necessary for Ss to underline the stressed words.

Answers:

1 There's a <u>payphone</u> over <u>there</u>.
2 There are <u>two</u> <u>hotels</u> near <u>here</u>.
3 There <u>isn't</u> an <u>internet</u> <u>café</u>.
4 There <u>aren't</u> any <u>trains</u>.
5 Is there a <u>train</u> to <u>York</u> <u>tonight</u>?
6 Are there any <u>restaurants</u> in the <u>station</u>?
7 <u>Yes</u>, there <u>is</u>.
8 <u>Yes</u>, there <u>are</u>.
9 <u>No</u>, there <u>isn't</u>.
10 <u>No</u>, there <u>aren't</u>.

Optional extra activity

Ss find and underline all the examples of *there is/are* (including questions and short answers) in the audio script of the conversations in Ex 2. There are 14 examples.

▷ **LANGUAGEBANK 6.1** p128–129

The Language bank reminds Ss to use *any* in the question form and negative with plural nouns. It also shows them that the question is formed simply by inverting the order of *there* and *is/are*. Ss could do Ex 6.1A in class, then for further practice they could show each other the contents of their own bags/pockets and make sentences following the pattern of the exercise, e.g. *There are car keys, so you have a car. There's a gym membership card, so I think you go to the gym.*

Answers:
A 2 There's a cinema ticket
  3 There a business card (for a bank)/There's a bank business card
  4 There aren't any (car) keys
  5 There's a (wedding) ring
  6 There are glasses
  7 There's a picture/photo of a cat
  8 There aren't any pictures/photos of children
B 2 isn't 3 there's 4 are 5 there 6 are 7 Are 8 aren't
  9 are 10 is 11 there 12 is

4A Tell Ss that the sentences are about an imaginary class, not theirs. Point out that they need to make the sentences positive or negative according to the symbol at the end.

Answers: 2 There's 3 There isn't 4 There are 5 There's
6 There aren't

B Once Ss have ticked the sentences that are true about their class, they could change the others to make them true. In this case they will need either to change the form of *there is/are* or to change other words in the sentence, e.g. *There are six students with black shoes. There's one person with a red jacket.* Pairs could then write three more sentences of their own about their class.

5A Go through the example (Ex 5B) and make sure that A and B know where they're writing their questions about. If you feel it would generate more discussion, you could change the locations, e.g. to the city centre, Student A's office, etc. You could also encourage Ss to add questions about two or three of the places in the Photo bank, p144.

B Put Ss in pairs to practise. Monitor the activity and make notes of good language use and problems, for praise and correction in feedback.

SPEAKING

6 Give Ss time to find their pictures and to think about/write the questions they're going to ask to find the differences. For *weaker classes* you may want to group As and Bs together for this stage, to help each other prepare questions and practise describing their picture. Then put Ss into AB pairs to start the activity. Tell Ss to circle the differences they find, then they can report back to the class afterwards, e.g. *There's a French restaurant in my picture, but in (X's) picture there's a Chinese restaurant.*

Answers:

Student A's picture	Student B's picture
French restaurant	Chinese restaurant
two hotels	one hotel
pharmacy is closed	pharmacy is open
one payphone	two payphones
man and woman	two women

7A You could demonstrate this by drawing a simple map of a street on the board and labelling places, e.g. *a pharmacy*, *a clothes shop*, *a gym*, *a café*, *a bank*. Then give Ss a few minutes to prepare their own maps. Ss could also use their phones to find a street and check what places are on it.

B Demonstrate this by inviting a **stronger student** to come to the board and ask you about one or two of the places on your map. Then tell Ss to walk around the class and ask different people about their maps. Encourage them to recommend or criticise the places, e.g. *I like it because the coffee's good* or *I don't go there because it's expensive*, etc. In feedback you could invite Ss to report back on places they heard about that they want to go to.

WRITING **STARTING AND ENDING AN EMAIL**

8A Tell Ss to read the email quickly and decide who it's to. Suggest that they underline words/phrases that help them decide, e.g. *Hi, mum*, etc. (also the fact that he mentions the company credit card so it's unlikely to be to his manager). Also check that Ss understand where the man is and why (he's in a hotel because the weather's very bad and there aren't any trains).

Answer: someone in his family ('Give my love to mum')

B Tell Ss to copy the table into their notebooks. Ss can help each other in pairs or work alone.

Answers:

	to someone close (a family member, partner, friends)	to your manager
Start	Hello	Dear Jack, Dear Mr Wilson,
End	Take care, See you soon,	Regards,

9A Focus Ss on the list of problems and the example. Put them in pairs to discuss how often they have the problems.

B Once Ss have chosen their two problems, tell them to use the email in Ex 8A as a 'model' to follow, e.g.
Start the email.
What's the bad, or good and bad news?
Where are you? Why?
Give the person a message/your love.
End the email.
Encourage Ss to start by writing a few notes as a first draft, then to write the email itself. While they're doing this, circulate and help with grammar, punctuation and vocabulary.

Alternative approach

Weaker classes may need more support with their emails. You could either prepare a gap fill of an email for Ss to complete with their own ideas, or tell Ss to go through the email in Ex 8 and change some of the information, e.g. *There aren't any planes tonight … I'm in a nice hotel, but the restaurant isn't good.*

C You could put Ss in groups of four to swap and read each other's emails. Then ask a few Ss to report back on the worst situation in their group.

Homework ideas

• Ss write an email to another person, i.e. if they wrote to their friend in class, they write to their manager, and vice versa.
• **Workbook:** Ex 1–5, p37–38

GETTING THERE

Introduction

Ss practise reading and talking about transport and getting around town. They practise using transport vocabulary and *a/an*, *some*, *a lot of*, *not any*, with a focus on natural linking in pronunciation.

> **SUPPLEMENTARY MATERIALS**
> **Resource bank:** p161 and p162
> **Ex 3A** (alternative approach): bring in paper cups and sweets/nuts.

Warm up

Review vocabulary related to places and transport from the previous lesson. Write the following words on slips of paper (one set per group of 5–6 Ss): *a hotel, a pharmacy, a train, an internet café, a café, an airport, a newsagent's, a payphone, a plane, a cash machine, a station* (you may also want to add three or four places from the Photo bank, p144).

In their groups, Ss take turns to pick up a slip of paper and mime, draw or give a verbal clue for the word for the rest of the group to guess. The first person to guess the word keeps the slip of paper and the winner is the student with most slips of paper at the end.

VOCABULARY TRANSPORT

1A You could start by telling Ss to cover the words in the box and see how many of the types of transport they can name, either working together as a class or in pairs. Then give them a few minutes to match the words and pictures, working alone. Check the pronunciation of *underground* Ooo and *motorbike* Ooo.

> **Culture note**
> Synonyms for *underground* are *metro* and *subway*. The London Underground is also known as 'the tube'.

> **Answers:** **B** a taxi **C** a car **D** a bike (more formally, *bicycle*)
> **E** a train **F** a plane **G** the underground **H** a motorbike

B Tell Ss to use *by* with all the types of transport (*by car, by bus*, etc.), but point out that they should say *I walk/I come on foot* if they don't use transport. Give Ss a few minutes to discuss the questions and ask some of the pairs to report back about things they found in common, e.g. *We both usually come to class by bus. We never use the underground.*

READING

2A Focus Ss on the title of the text and the four headings. Establish that they need to read quickly and find six different types of transport to complete the headings. Set a time limit for Ss to complete the headings, then give them a minute or two to check answers in pairs.

> **Teaching tip**
> When Ss are scan reading a text just to find certain pieces of information, ask them to underline the words/phrases in the text. Point out that they may find the actual word they are looking for (e.g. *taxi, train, bus, underground, car* in the first three paragraphs) or a related word (e.g. *road* in the paragraph about cars, or *airport* and *airline* in the paragraph about planes).

> **Answers:** train, bus, underground car plane

B Check *mice* (simple board drawing), *secret* (people don't know about it), *bends* (simple board drawing), *to charge* (ask for money). Go through the example with the class, pointing out that the word *stations* tells us to look in the paragraph about trains. Ss work alone and compare answers in pairs.

> **Answers:** **2** on a plane (with a pay toilet) **3** taxis in Rome
> **4** a golf course in an airport in Thailand
> **5** the London Underground **6** pink taxis in Moscow/Chennai
> **7** the villages in Bhutan (without bus service)
> **8** the Tianmen Mountain Road in China

> **Culture notes**
> **Bhutan** is a small landlocked country in the Himalayas. It has a strong sense of culture and tradition and had no phones until 1960 and no TV until 1999.
> The **London Underground** system began operating in 1863. It has 270 stations and carries about 1.3 billion passengers every year.
> In **Venice** people either travel on foot (it's only an hour from one end of the city to the other) or in water buses and water taxis (and sometimes gondolas).
> The 11-kilometre section of the **Tianmen Mountain Road** rises 1,100 metres and took five years to build.
> The airport in **Thailand** is Bangkok's Don Muang International airport. The golf course is between two runways and golfers are stopped by a red light when a plane is landing.

C Check *surprising* (act out reading something and being surprised: 'Oh really? I didn't know that!'). Go through the example, then put Ss in pairs to discuss the facts and decide which one is not true.

> **Answer:** It's not true that Venice has a secret road system.

GRAMMAR A/AN, SOME, A LOT OF, NOT ANY

3A Focus Ss on the pictures and ask about C and D: *Is it a small number? Is it a large number?* Then give Ss time to match the sentences, working in pairs to help each other.

> **Answers:** **2** A **3** C **4** D

> **Alternative approach**
> Use real objects, e.g. four paper cups and small sweets or nuts to demonstrate the meaning of *a/an*, *some*, *a lot of*, *not any*.
> In the four cups put a sweet, a small number of sweets, a large number of sweets and no sweets. As you do this, ask Ss *How many sweets are in the cup?* and elicit/give the answer, checking the difference between *some* and *a lot of* by asking *Do you know the exact number?* (No.) *Is it a large number? Is it a small number?*
> You could add an element of fun by turning the cups upside down with their contents underneath, then moving them around quickly and asking Ss if they can remember how many sweets are under each cup.
> You can then use Ex 3B to consolidate and give Ss a record of the language.

B Ss can work alone and check answers in pairs.

> **Answers:**
>
> | | | | | |
> |---|-------|-------|----------|-----------------------|
> | + | There | 's | a | train at four o'clock. |
> | | | are | some | buses this afternoon. |
> | | | are | a lot of | cars. |
> | – | There | isn't | an | airport here. |
> | | | aren't| any | cars in the centre. |
> | ? | Is | there | a | bus to the airport? |
> | | Are | there | any | taxis? |

C Play the recording for Ss to check their answers.

D PRONUNCIATION linking Focus Ss on the examples and play the recording once or twice for Ss to listen to the linking. Then play the recording again for Ss to repeat.

speakout TIP

Write *lot⌣of, isn't⌣an, aren't⌣any* on the board and show Ss how the final 't' sound joins the vowel sound after it. Then write *there are a lot* and demonstrate that although the words finish with -*e*, it is the final sound /r/ that joins to the vowel sound after it. Give Ss a minute or two to mark the links in the phrases, then mark them on the board. For more practice, you could give Ss these examples to work on: *What time is it? It's eleven o'clock. It's eight o'clock.* (*What time⌣is⌣it? It's⌣eleven⌣o'clock. It's⌣eight⌣o'clock.*)

Answers: How much⌣is⌣it?   When does⌣it leave?

▷ **LANGUAGEBANK 6.2** p128–129

The Language bank highlights the fact that *no* is possible instead of *not any*, e.g. *there are no buses/there aren't any buses.* For practice of the language in a different context from transport, Ss could do Ex 6.2A and B in class or for homework.

Answers:
A 2 There are some   3 There isn't a   4 There's an
5 There are a lot of   6 There aren't any
B 1 Students don't have a lot of money.
2 A book usually has a lot of pages.
3 Some people don't have a home.
4 Ben has a sister but he doesn't have any brothers.
5 Our school has a lot of students.
6 Some people have a lot of children.

4A Ss could work on this alone or in pairs.

Answers: 2 some   3 any   4 a lot   5 an   6 some   7 any   8 a lot of

B If Ss are from the same town/city, tell them to make the sentences true for a town/city they know, so that in the next stage, their partner won't already know the answers to the questions and the communication will be more realistic. Ss should also make notes so they can give more information about their answers, e.g. *There's an airport, it's fifteen minutes from the city centre. It's very big.*

C Demonstrate this by inviting two or three Ss to ask you questions about a town/city you know. Remind Ss to extend their answers and give more information. You could suggest that Ss ask the questions in random order, so their partner can't predict which answer they need to give and has to listen more carefully.

Optional extra activities

1 Ss write three positive and three negative sentences about their town/city, using *there is/are* and *a/an, some, a lot of, not any*, then they compare their sentences in small groups. If they're from the same town/city, they can agree or disagree with each other's sentences, and if they're from different towns/cities, they can find things in common. (NB: Encourage Ss to include some places from the Photo bank, e.g. *In all our cities there's a good hospital.*)

2 Put Ss in small groups and tell them to write down the names of five towns/cities that they all know. Each student then writes three sentences about one of the towns/cities using *there is/are* and *a/an, some, a lot of, not any*. Encourage Ss to include some places from the Photo bank, e.g. *In this city there are a lot of parks and there's a zoo.* Ss read out their sentences to the group without mentioning the name of the town/city. The other Ss try to guess which one they're describing.

SPEAKING

Culture notes

Sydney's Kingsford Smith airport is the busiest in Australia, and the oldest commercial international airport in the world. It's eight kilometres south of the city centre.

London's Heathrow airport is the busiest of London's five airports and the third busiest in the world. It's used by ninety airlines, travelling to 170 destinations. It's twenty-two kilometres west of the city centre.

Barcelona's El Prat airport is the second largest in Spain after Madrid's Barajas airport. It's twelve kilometres south west of the city centre.

Hong Kong's International airport is on the island of Chek Lap Kok and is one of the world's busiest passenger airports. It replaced the Kai Tak airport (which was in the built-up Kowloon City District) in 1998.

5A Give Ss A time to find their page and give all the Ss a few minutes to look through their information. While they're doing this, draw the table for Sydney on the board. Go through the table, eliciting the questions, e.g. *Is there a train/an underground/an airport bus from the airport? What other information do you have?* Show Ss that they should make a note of their answers in the table. Monitor the pairwork carefully and make notes on good language use and any problem areas for feedback. (NB: You may want to highlight and correct any common errors with the class before Ss move on to Ex 5B, so they can avoid repeating their mistakes.)

B Ss change roles so that Student A is asking the questions and Student B is answering. Monitor and be prepared to give Ss praise for improvements made since the previous stage.

C Tell Ss to look at all their information with their partners and decide on the best way in each case.

Suggested answers: These will depend on Ss' preferences, but in terms of price:
Sydney – the train   Heathrow – the underground
Barcelona – the train   Hong Kong – the airport bus

Homework ideas

• Ss write an email to a friend who is coming to visit their town/city, giving them information about getting to their house from the airport/station. You could give them some phrases to use, e.g.
Hi _____,
I'm sorry but I'm at work/school on (Friday). There's a (train) from the airport, it costs (X), or there's a (taxi).
Have a good trip, see you soon.

• Ss do some research on the internet and find out two facts about each of the following types of transport:
· double decker buses in London
· London taxi cabs
· bicycles in Amsterdam
· gondolas in Venice
You could give prompts for guidance, e.g. *How old? Colour? Who uses them? Why popular?* Ss could also write one 'fact' which is not true. In the next lesson, Ss work in pairs, comparing their findings and deciding which 'fact' is not true.

• **Workbook:** Ex 1–5, p39–40

SINGLE OR RETURN?

Introduction

Ss practise buying a ticket at a bus station, using travel vocabulary. They also practise listening skills and learn to check numbers using word stress.

> **SUPPLEMENTARY MATERIALS**
> **Resource bank:** p164
> **Ex 3 and 7B (optional extra activities):** collect some local bus and train timetables or print them from the internet.

Warm up

Review the transport vocabulary from Ex 1 in lesson 6.2. Put Ss in pairs and tell them to write one positive thing and one negative thing about each of the eight types of transport, without mentioning the name, e.g. *It's cheap. It's sometimes cold (bike).* Put the pairs into groups of four or six. Then they take it in turns to read out their clues and the other Ss try to guess the type of transport.

VOCABULARY TRAVEL

1A Introduce the idea of long journeys, i.e. from city to city, rather than within the city. You could give an example about your own preference then put Ss in pairs to discuss theirs. You could write some prompts on the board to help, e.g. *see/countryside, meet/people, fast, cheap, comfortable, walk around, have/break, read/book, have/meal,* etc. Ask a few pairs to report back to the class on their ideas.

B Tell Ss to cover the words in the box. Direct them to the pictures and ask them what they can see there, e.g. *bus station, people, buses,* etc. Then direct them to the box and ask them to find the items in the pictures, working alone or in pairs. As you go through the answers, check the stress on *passenger* Ooo, *ticket machine* Oo Oo, *return* oO, *monthly pass* Oo O, *platform* Oo. Also check the meaning of *gate* in this context (the place where you go to get your bus).

> **Answers:** a bus station, a passenger, a ticket machine, a gate

C You could first establish with Ss which words are also for travel by plane (*a passenger, a gate, a single ticket, a return ticket*), then elicit which are not for plane travel.

> **Answers:** a ticket machine, a bus station, a monthly pass, a platform

> **Optional extra activity**
> You could go on to ask which words are also for travel by train, i.e. *a passenger, a ticket machine, a single/return ticket, a monthly pass, a platform.*

2A Tell Ss that the list of actions are what you do at the bus station. Establish which is number 1 (c) and put Ss in pairs to order the rest. In feedback, you could ask Ss to repeat the phrases in chorus and individually to familiarise them with the rhythm.

> **Answers:** c) b) f) e) d) a) g) (the order might vary according to how things are done where Ss come from)

B Before Ss start the activity, remind them of the linkers *first, then, after that.* Put them in pairs to describe the sequence of actions. Once they have taken turns to describe each step in the sequence, they could then take turns to remember the whole sequence while their partner checks the order in their Students' Book.

FUNCTION BUYING A TICKET

> **Optional extra activity**
> Tell Ss they're going to buy a ticket for a bus journey and ask them to suggest some places they could go to and which day/time they want to go. Elicit some ideas about what they could say at the ticket office and how the person at the ticket office could answer. Put Ss in pairs to act out the conversation using any ideas/language they have. You could ask a few pairs who do well to act out their conversation for the class. Then when Ss listen to the recording, they can compare what they hear to their performance, and notice useful language which will help them to improve their conversation next time.

3 Give Ss time to read through the questions and all the options in the answers so they understand what they are listening for. Then play the recording.

> **Answers:** 1 b) 2 c) 3 b) 4 a) 5 b)

> **Unit 6 Recording 6**
>
> **A:** A ticket to Amsterdam, please.
> **B:** Single or return?
> **A:** A return, please.
> **B:** Leaving today?
> **A:** Yes.
> **B:** When do you want to come back?
> **A:** Tomorrow afternoon.
> **B:** OK. That's twenty-nine euros.
> **A:** Sorry? How much?
> **B:** Twenty-nine euros.
> **A:** What time's the next bus?
> **B:** There's one at half past two.
> **A:** Right. What time does it arrive in Amsterdam?
> **B:** At quarter past four. Here's your ticket.
> **A:** Thank you. Which gate is it?
> **B:** The bus leaves from gate twenty-four.
> **A:** Sorry? Gate thirty-four?
> **B:** No, gate twenty-four.
> **A:** Thanks a lot.

4A Tell Ss that there is one word missing from each gap and they can use the words around the gap to help them guess what's missing. Check the meaning of *leave*: in this context it means *go.* Also point out that in B's line *there's one at half past two* 'one' means 'a bus' and is used to avoid repeating 'bus'. Ss can help each other in pairs or work alone. Play the recording for Ss to check their answers.

> **Answers:** 1 to 2 Single 3 come 4 much 5 next 6 does 7 Which 8 leaves

B The idea here is that Ss repeat as soon as the voice on the recording starts, rather than waiting for each sentence to finish before they repeat it. The result may sound rather strange at first, as Ss are unlikely to be in chorus, but it encourages them to mimic natural stress and intonation patterns. You may need to try the technique a couple of times with the class for it to be really effective.

C When Ss have practised the conversation once, encourage them to go through it again, this time looking up from the page as they say their lines.

D Elicit some suggestions for a key word or two from the beginning of the conversation, e.g. *return? leaving?* then give Ss a few minutes to choose their ten words and write them in their notebooks. Tell SS to close their Students' Books before they practise the conversation again. Monitor the practice and note down examples of good language use and any problems for praise and correction in feedback.

Optional extra activity

Write the following words on the board:

*No, tomorrow.   on Sunday afternoon   twelve B
quarter past ten   forty   Madrid (x2)   quarter to two*

Ss find the correct place for these words in the conversation in Ex 4A, and practise it again. Then they can substitute their own ideas in the same places.

▷ **LANGUAGEBANK 6.3** p128–129

You could use the tables in the Language bank for Ss to practise making questions and answers, choosing from the alternatives. Ss could do Ex 6.3 in class, then you could use the completed conversation to give them some speaking practice in pairs, especially if they were not very confident with the conversation practice in Ex 4.

Answers:
A: Two *singles* to Glasgow, please.
B: For today?
A: Sorry, no, for *tomorrow*.
B: When *do* you want to go?
A: At about nine o'clock in the morning.
B: OK, that's seven pounds fifty.
A: What time's the bus?
B: There's one at quarter to nine.
A: When does *it* arrive in Glasgow?
B: At half past nine.
A: Which *gate* is it?
B: It leaves *from* number 22.
A: Thanks *a* lot.

LEARN TO CHECK NUMBERS

5A PRONUNCIATION word stress for checking Give Ss a moment or two to read the four lines of conversation before you play the recording.

Answers:
B: The bus leaves from gate twenty-<u>four</u>.
A: Sorry? Gate <u>thir</u>ty-four?
B: No, gate <u>twen</u>ty-four.
A: Thanks a lot.
(NB: It's usual to stress the second part of numbers over twelve, e.g. thir<u>teen</u>, twenty-<u>five</u>, thirty-<u>seven</u>, forty-<u>nine</u>, etc. The first part is only stressed when the speakers are checking the number, as in the last two examples.)

B You may need to let Ss repeat this a couple of times. You could divide the class in half, with one side repeating A's part, and the other B's, then swapping roles and playing the recording again.

Teaching tip

Ss can sometimes struggle to make the stressed syllable 'stand out' enough. To help them with this, demonstrate that they need to speak more loudly and raise the pitch of their voice on that syllable. Use your hand to show the pitch moving up on *twen* and quickly down on *ty-four*.

---

speakout TIP

You could ask Ss whether they use stress like this in their own language(s), and if not, what they would do to check or correct this kind of information.

C Ss could prepare by reading through the conversations silently first and underlining the syllables that need to be stressed in each case. Monitor carefully while they practise the conversations and give some feedback on their use of stress.

6A Ss write the prices, times and numbers in their notebooks. Point out that they can write the prices in any currency they know.

B You could demonstrate this with a **stronger student**. If appropriate to your Ss, you could suggest that they mumble or say the numbers indistinctly as well as fast, so there's a real reason for their partner to check. This will also add an element of fun to the activity.

SPEAKING

7A Give Student B time to find p153 and look through their information. You may also want to give Ss time to prepare and practise their questions before you put them into pairs.

B Monitor the pairwork carefully and note down examples of good language use and any problems for praise and correction in feedback.

Optional extra activity

Take in some local train and bus timetables or print them from the internet. Give half the class the train timetables and the other half the bus timetables. Ss think about where they want to go in the local area, then pair up with someone from the other half of the class and practise buying a ticket.

Homework ideas

- Ss write an email with real instructions for someone travelling to their city or around their city, e.g. *The bus leaves from King's Cross. It's number 73. A single ticket costs £2.50. It leaves at 8.30a.m.*, etc.
- **Workbook:** Ex 1–4, p41

RUSH HOUR

Introduction

Ss watch a BBC extract with people talking about travelling in India in the rush hour. Ss then learn and practise how to do a travel survey, and write a travel forum entry about transport in their town/city.

> **SUPPLEMENTARY MATERIALS**
> **Ex 1A:** bring in/download a large map of India.

Warm up

Tell Ss to close their books and write the title *Rush Hour* on the board. Establish that it's the time (usually twice a day, and longer than an hour) when a lot of traffic is on the roads because people are going to or coming home from work, school, etc. Give Ss the example of rush hour in London: 7.30–10.00a.m. and 4.30–7.00p.m., and write the following questions on the board to discuss:

When is rush hour in your country?
Do you travel in rush hour?
How do you travel?
Is it easy or difficult? Why?

DVD PREVIEW

1A Tell Ss to keep their books closed and show them a map of India, or draw one on the board. Prompt Ss to tell the class what they know about India, i.e. names of cities (e.g. Mumbai, Delhi), food (e.g. curry), drink (e.g. tea) and other well known places, people, etc. (e.g. the Taj Mahal, Mother Teresa, elephants, Bollywood movies).

Go through the first example with the class, then put Ss in pairs to complete the matching activity.

> **Answers:** 1 a), e) 2 d) 3 b) 4 g) 5 c) 6 f) 7 h)

> ### Culture notes
>
> **Daal** is a thick soup or stew made from lentils and spices.
>
> **Naan** is a flat bread which is baked in a hot clay oven.
>
> **Mumbai** is on the west coast of India. It has a population of about 12 million (in the city) and is the wealthiest city in India.
>
> **Delhi** is in northern India and has a population of about 11 million.
>
> **Mother Teresa** (26 August 1910–5 September 1997) was a Catholic nun who was born in Macedonia and lived most of her life in India. She founded the Missionaries of Charity in Kolkata (formerly Calcutta) in 1950. After her death she was beatified by Pope John Paul II and given the title Blessed Teresa of Calcutta.
>
> **Gandhi** (2 October 1869–30 January 1948) was the political leader of India during the Indian independence movement. He led India to independence and he also inspired non-violent movements for civil rights across the world. His birthday, 2nd October, is a national holiday in India and the International Day of Non-Violence.
>
> The **Ganges** is the most sacred river to Hindus. Millions of Indians who live along the river depend on it for their daily needs.
>
> The **Taj Mahal** is a mausoleum (a building with a tomb inside it) in Agra. It was built by Emperor Shah Jahan in memory of his third wife and is regarded as one of the eight wonders of the world.

B Give Ss a minute or two to read the text, then direct them to the photo. Ask Ss what they can see and use the photo to teach *rickshaw* and *tuk-tuk* (a *rickshaw* is pulled by a bicycle, a *tuk-tuk* is a motorised rickshaw). On the board, make a list of the types of transport Ss think people use.

DVD VIEW

2A Ss check the ideas they predicted in Ex 1B.

> **Answer:** People go to work and school by train, bike, rickshaw, motorbike, tuk-tuk and taxi.

B Ss can complete the sentences alone or in pairs. You could check Ss' understanding of the adjectives by asking them for examples of places in their city/country which are popular/expensive/noisy/dangerous/crowded. Also check the pronunciation of the adjectives: *popular* Ooo, *expensive* oOo, *dangerous* Ooo, *crowded* Oo.

> **Answers:** 2 noisy 3 expensive 4 dangerous 5 crowded 6 slow

C Play the DVD again for Ss to underline the adjectives. Point out that more than one adjective may be mentioned for some of the types of transport.

> **Answers:** 1 trains – crowded, popular 2 bikes – slow
> 3 motorbikes – fast, dangerous 4 tuk-tuks – popular, noisy
> 5 taxis – fast, safe, expensive

D Give Ss a few minutes to complete the sentences then play the DVD again.

> **Answers:** 1 train 2 bike 3 motorbikes 4 Tuk-tuks 5 taxi

DVD 6 Rush Hour

N = Narrator   B = Boy   M = Man   W = Woman

N: India, it's a country of millions of different people, colours and sounds. Every morning in India, millions of people travel to work or to school.

B: I get up every morning at five o'clock and go to school by train. I like it because I can see a lot of places and people from the train. There are a lot of people on the train. It's very crowded.

N: The Indian train system is over a hundred years old. It goes to hundreds of places in India, and it's a very popular way to travel. On the roads people and animals walk everywhere. Hundreds of people use bikes and rickshaws.

M: I live in Delhi and I go to work by bike every day. There are a lot of bikes on the road. It's sometimes very slow.

N: A motorbike is a good way to travel around. You often see three or four people from a family on one motorbike.

M: Motorbikes are great, they're fast, but they're often dangerous. There are sometimes bad accidents with lorries and motorbikes.

N: And then there are tuk-tuks. Tuks-tuks are very popular, but they are also very noisy. Finally, taxis go everywhere in the cities.

W: I travel to Mumbai on business a lot. In Mumbai, I usually travel by taxi. It's fast and it's safe, but taxis are expensive.

N: For a visitor, the different types of transport and the millions of people can be too much, but it's all part of the many faces of India.

speakout a travel survey

3A Tell Ss to write the headings *in cities* and *in the countryside* in their notebooks, then put them in pairs to discuss how people travel in the two areas. Remind Ss to use *by* with forms of transport, but to say *on foot* or *I walk* if they don't use transport. Also point out that people often say *I drive* instead of *I go by car*. Circulate and help Ss with any vocabulary they need, e.g. other types of transport: *ferry*, *water taxi*, *van*.

B Tell Ss to complete the table with one- or two-word answers. Play the recording and give them a moment to compare answers in pairs.

Answers:

in a big city	in the countryside
1 by car	1 by car
2 by underground	2 by bus
3 by bus	3 by bike
4 by train	
5 by bike	

C Give Ss a few moments to look at the key phrases. Check that Ss understand *public transport system* (bus and train services for everyone to use). Then play the recording again for Ss to tick the phrases. As you check the answers, you could elicit some different ways of completing the phrases using the prompts in brackets, e.g. *I live in Madrid, but I'm from Cadiz*; *Some people go to work by bike*; *The best way to travel is by train*; *People also go by ferry*; *In my village, I walk everywhere*; *The public transport system isn't very good*.

Answers:
I live in [São Paulo], but I'm from [the countryside]. ✓
There's a good public transport system. ✓
[A lot of ✓/Some] people use [the underground/buses]. ✓
Some people go to work by [bus/bike].
The best way to travel is by [car/underground ✓].
People also go by [bus].
In [my village ✓/the city], I go everywhere by [car/bike ✓].

Unit 6 Recording 9

I live in São Paulo, Brazil, but I'm from the countryside. Brazilian people love their cars, but it's difficult to drive in São Paulo – there are too many cars and it's very, very slow. There's a good public transport system and a lot of people use the underground or buses and the suburban train. More and more people go to work by bike, but I don't. I think bikes are dangerous in the city. The best way to travel in the city centre is by underground, but it's very crowded in the mornings. In the countryside, a lot of people drive, of course, or they use buses. In my village, I go everywhere by bike.

4A Give Ss a few minutes working alone to write some notes about their country. If Ss are from the same town/city, suggest that they talk about a family member or friend who lives somewhere different, i.e. smaller/bigger, where there isn't an underground, etc. Circulate and help, and encourage Ss to practise saying some of their sentences for you to check. Put Ss in pairs to talk about their ideas.

B Put Ss in groups of 4–6 to take turns to talk about travel in their country. Tell the listeners to write one question that they want the speaker to answer when they've finished, e.g. *Why do a lot of people go by bike? Why is the best way to travel by car?* Monitor and note down examples of good language use as well as any problems for praise and correction in feedback.

Alternative approach

Instead of Ss giving a prepared talk, they prepare a series of questions about travel, then walk around and interview two or three other Ss. When they've finished, they sit in groups of 4–5 and report back on their findings. Example questions for the survey:
Where is your city/village?
Is there a good public transport system?
How do people travel to work/school/the shops?
What's the best way to travel? Why?
What other ways do people travel?
Do a lot of people walk?/use the …?/go by …?

writeback a travel forum entry

5A Give Ss a few minutes to read and answer the question.

Answer: He usually goes to work by train but in Kobe he usually walks.

B Tell Ss to underline the things in the text that the writer includes. (The writer doesn't mention cycling.) You could highlight some useful patterns from the text, e.g.
There are (number) trains/buses every hour.
It's about (number) minutes from (X) to (Y).
I have a (weekly/monthly) pass.
A one-day tourist pass is (cost).
I live in/near … so I usually …
It's a good city/village for walkers/cyclists.

C Circulate and help with vocabulary, etc. as Ss write their information.

Homework ideas

Ss review all the new vocabulary items they've studied in this lesson and choose five that they think will be most useful to remember. They write a short paragraph about transport in India that includes all five words.

LOOKBACK

PLACES

1A You could run this as a team competition (Ss have their books closed). Write up or display one phrase at a time and the first team member to 'buzz' and tell you the missing vowels wins a point for their team. If they make a mistake with any vowels, the other team can try for a bonus point.

Answers: **2** restaurant **3** pharmacy **4** newsagent's **5** payphone **6** cash machine **7** hotel **8** café

Alternative approach

To provide more challenge, put Ss in pairs and direct them to the 'places' vocabulary on p62. Tell them to jumble the letters of each word and write them on a piece of paper. They then pass the paper to the next pair, who have to put the letters in order.

B Point out that Ss can't use a thing which is already in the word, e.g. for *cash machine*, they can't write *cash*, but they could write *money*, *euros*, etc. Circulate and help. Possible ideas for Ss who are struggling: pharmacy – *aspirin, medicine*; newsagent's – *magazine, newspaper, pen*; payphone – *credit card, cash, talk*; hotel – *shower, bed*.

C Put Ss into groups of 4–6 to guess the places from each other's clues.

THERE IS/ARE

2A Ss could complete the questions in pairs, or working alone. As you check the answers, you could take the opportunity to give Ss pronunciation practice, modelling the questions with polite intonation for them to repeat.

Answers: **2** Is there **3** Are there **4** Is there **5** Are there **6** Are there

B Tell Ss to match the answers to the questions by using the vocabulary to help them.

Answers: **2** d) **3** e) **4** a) **5** f) **6** b)

C Ss complete the answers alone, then compare answers with a partner. Then they can practise the conversations.

Answers: **a)** there aren't **b)** there are **c)** there is **d)** there is **e)** there aren't, There's/is **f)** there aren't, there's/is

Optional extra activity

In pairs, Ss change the answers that begin with *Yes* to *No* and vice versa, and change the rest of the information in each answer so that it makes sense, e.g. *Is there a guided tour of the city tomorrow? – Yes, there is. It leaves at 9.30a.m.*

Each pair then acts out two or three of their new conversations for the rest of the class.

TRANSPORT

3A You could run this as a race, with Ss working in pairs. The first pair to circle all the words and bring them to you wins.

B Go through the example with the class. You could also demonstrate drawing a picture, and show Ss that it doesn't need to be very sophisticated.

Answers:

Q	P	B	H	I	U	M
B	U	S	F	H	N	O
I	A	S	N	B	D	T
K	P	L	A	N	E	O
E	E	G	J	T	R	R
K	Z	Y	G	Z	G	B
E	O	K	R	E	R	I
T	R	A	E	N	O	K
A	T	R	C	U	U	E
X	T	R	A	I	N	H
I	W	S	R	S	D	K

A/AN, SOME, A LOT OF, NOT ANY

4A Establish that the sentences are referring to the Students' Book. You could go through the mistakes with the whole class.

Answers:
2 Some *pages* have six photos.
3 There's *a* Spanish word on page 6.
4 There aren't *any shoes* on page 32.
5 There *aren't* any clocks on page 45.
6 There's *an* apple on page 54.

B Give Ss enough time to look through the book (later units as well as earlier ones) and find the correct information.

Answers: **1** F Some pages don't have photos. **2** T
3 T ('libro' is Spanish and Italian for 'book')
4 F There are some shoes on page 32.
5 F There are some clocks on page 45. **6** T

C If Ss need some help with ideas for this, you could give them some prompts on the board:
There's a picture of a famous person/place on page …
There are some pictures of food/clothes on page …
The title of lesson (4.2) is …
Circulate and help Ss to write their sentences.

D When Ss have finished this group work, they could report back to the class any true facts about the book that they found surprising.

TRAVEL

5 You could run this as a race. Give Ss a minute or two in pairs to complete the words. The first pair to finish put their hands up, then spell out each word for the class. If they make a mistake with spelling, another pair can try to spell all the words, and so on.

Answers: **1** machine **2** station **3** passengers **4** gate **5** platform **6** single **7** return **8** monthly

BUYING A TICKET

6A Go through the example, pointing out that Ss need to add one or two words to each line. Give Ss a few minutes to complete the sentences, working alone.

Answers: **2** I want to go tomorrow morning.
3 What time's the first bus? **4** What time does it arrive in Lisbon?
5 Which gate is it? **6** Thanks a lot.

B When Ss have practised the conversation once or twice using the prompts, encourage them to look up from the page and try to remember as much of their lines as they can.

C Tell Ss to change the price, times and gate number.

D Remind Ss how to check numbers using the numbers from the original conversation in Ex 6A:
A: *That's €39.*
B: *Sorry? €35?*
A: *No, €39.*

A: *Which gate is it?*
B: *It leaves from gate 34.*
A: *Sorry? 44?*
B: *No, 34.*

CONSOLIDATION 3: UNITS 5–6

Introduction

The aim of the consolidation units is for Ss to revise and practise the grammar, vocabulary and pronunciation from the previous two units in a different context. The context for this consolidation unit is problems.

> **SUPPLEMENTARY MATERIALS**
>
> **Ex 1A:** take in some examples of 'agony aunt' pages from a magazine or website.
>
> **Ex 5A (optional extra activity):** prepare prompts on cards (see notes).

READING AND GRAMMAR

1 Start by brainstorming some examples of problems, e.g. that you might read about in the 'agony aunt' page of a magazine or website (you could take in some examples of these). You could put some categories on the board and ask Ss to think of one or two problems for each category, e.g. *work, family, money, relationships, health*. Then put Ss in pairs to talk about the question. You could encourage them to report back to the class afterwards, using adverbs of frequency, e.g. *I sometimes talk to one or two friends about it; I often think about it alone.*

2 You could suggest that Ss cover the answers while they read the problems and first think about the answer they would give to each person, then match the answers to the problems and see if any of their own ideas were similar.

> **Answers: a)** Rob's problem   **b)** Layla's problem   **c)** Jon's problem

3A Point out that there are two questions for each of the three people in the text in Ex 1, so that Ss can refer back to the content.

> **Answers:**
> 1 b) Does he go out in the evenings?
> 2 a) Does Layla buy the food?
>   b) What does her husband do at home?
> 3 a) Is there a problem with planes?
>   b) When does Rob go on holiday?

B For **stronger classes**, you could ask Ss to cover Ex 2B and write their own answers to the questions first, then they can compare the two versions. Ss could also practise asking and answering the questions in pairs.

> **Answers: 2** – 2 a)   **3** – 3 a)   **4** – 1 a)   **5** – 2 b)   **6** – 1 b)

> **Optional extra activity**
>
> Working in pairs, Ss invent two more problems and write about them on two pieces of paper (two or three sentences each), putting their names at the end of the problem, as in the texts in Ex 1B. Circulate and help while Ss are doing this, then collect in the problems and redistribute them so that all the pairs have two new problems to read about. Ss then write their answers and send them back to the pair who wrote them. Some of the pairs can then read out their problems and the answers they got to the class and say what they think of the answers.

LISTENING AND GRAMMAR

4A You could play the first conversation for Ss to confirm that it's in a café. Then play the rest of the recording.

> **Answers: 2** newsagent's   **3** cash machine   **4** internet café   **5** pharmacy

B Before you play the recording again, give Ss a minute or two to read through the alternatives. Vocabulary to check: *ill* versus *well*.

> **Answers: 1** another coffee   **2** doesn't have, doesn't buy   **3** doesn't have money, She   **4** three, goes to another computer   **5** ill, doesn't buy

Consolidation 3   Recording 1

Conversation 1
A: Excuse me.
B: Yeah.
A: There's a problem with my coffee. It's cold.
B: Oh, sorry. Let me get you another one.
A: Thanks.

Conversation 2
A: Do you have *The New York Times*?
B: Sorry, we don't. We usually have it, but not today.
A: Oh. Well, do you have any other newspapers in English?
B: We have *The Times*.
A: That's a British paper, yeah?
B: That's right.
A: Hmm, no thanks. I really want an American paper.

Conversation 3
A: OK, let's get some money out.
B: What's the problem?
A: It says there isn't any money in the machine.
B: Oh, no.
A: Maybe it's because it's a bank holiday. Look, I have some money. Let's go to Salvatore's café. It isn't expensive.

Conversation 4
A: Excuse me.
B: Is there a problem?
A: Yes, I'm in number three and the computer's broken.
B: Let me see. Ah, yes, there's a problem. Please try number five.

Conversation 5
A: Can I help you?
B: Yes, I'm not very well. I'm very hot and I'm tired all the time. Do you have something to help?
A: These are good. Go home and go to bed.
B: How much are they?
A: Five euros.
B: Five euros. Hmm, no thank you.

SPEAKING

5A Put Ss in pairs and give them a few minutes to choose a conversation and practise it.

B Demonstrate this by playing the first conversation while Ss follow it in the audio script. Ask them to call out 'Stop!' when they want to suggest a keyword: if the rest of the class agrees, write the keyword on the board and continue until you have a list of 6–8 words for the conversation. Tell Ss to choose a different conversation and write keywords. Circulate and help.

C Monitor this practice carefully so you can give Ss feedback on their language use.

6A Go through the example with the class, then give Ss time to choose a place and think of a problem.

Optional extra activity

Give Ss the following prompts on cards to pick up and look at if they need help (either one set of cards for Ss to come and choose from at the front of the class, or one set of cards per pair):

- 1 café
  2 customer, waiter
  3 you have chicken soup, you want vegetable soup
- 1 newsagent's
  2 customer, shop assistant
  3 you want cola; they have it, but it's a big bottle (you want a small bottle)
- 1 pharmacy
  2 customer, assistant
  3 you're ill; you don't have money
- 1 cash machine in a bank
  2 customer, bank assistant
  3 your card is stuck in the machine
- 1 snack bar
  2 customer, waiter
  3 you have a sandwich with white bread, you want brown bread

B Encourage Ss to practise their conversation two or three times, asking you for help with any words/phrases they're not sure of, so that they feel confident to act out their conversation in a group.

C Ss could work in groups of six, or in a smaller class, act out their conversations in front of the whole class. The other Ss guess the place and say why they think it's that place. Make notes of some good examples of language use so you can give Ss praise when they've finished.

SOUNDS: /ð/ AND /θ/

7A Direct Ss to the table and point out that the symbols represent the sounds. Play the recording for Ss to listen to the sounds and the words. You could also show Ss that to make the two sounds, their tongue needs to touch the bottom of their top teeth (demonstrate that if their tongue touches the roof of the mouth instead, the sounds produced will be /s/ and /z/).

B You may want to ask Ss to predict which group the words belong to before they listen. You could pause the recording after each group of words and ask individual Ss to repeat them, rather than Ss repeating in chorus. This will give you more opportunity to correct their pronunciation of the 'target' sounds.

Answers:
/ð/ father, with, these, together
/θ/ monthly, thirsty, think, thirteen

8A Tell Ss they will hear each word twice on the recording, but only one has the correct pronunciation. You could do the first word as an example with the class.

Answers: 1 a) **2** a) **3** b) **4** b) **5** b) **6** a) **7** a) **8** b) **9** a) **10** b)

B Give Ss time to practise saying the sentences several times. This should be kept light-hearted.

C You could set this up as a race and see which pair finishes first. Then Ss can demonstrate saying the sentences fast for the whole class.

Homework ideas

- Ss email three or four other Ss from the class with an invented problem and answer each other's problems. Then they choose the answer they think is best and email that person to tell them.
- **Workbook:** Ex 1–4, p42–43

BBC interviews and worksheet

How do you get to work?
In this video people talk about their journeys to work. The material revises and extends vocabulary around the topics of transport and travel. Ss can also listen to and revise expressing opinions about journeys (*I love/like/hate*, etc.).

OVERVIEW

7.1 WHERE WERE YOU?

LISTENING | listen to people talk about New Year
GRAMMAR | past simple: *was/were*
PRONUNCIATION | weak and strong forms: *was/were*
VOCABULARY | dates
SPEAKING | find out where people were in the past
WRITING | improve your punctuation

7.2 RECORD BREAKERS

VOCABULARY | actions
READING | read about amazing records
GRAMMAR | past simple: regular verbs
PRONUNCIATION | *-ed* endings
SPEAKING | talk about the past

7.3 HOW WAS IT?

FUNCTION | asking for and giving opinions
LISTENING | listen to people give their opinions
VOCABULARY | adjectives
LEARN TO | show feelings
PRONUNCIATION | intonation
SPEAKING | give your opinion

7.4 THE CHILEAN MINERS BBC DVD

DVD | watch a programme about the Chilean miners
speakout | do a quiz
writeback | write a history quiz

7.5 LOOKBACK

Communicative revision activities

BBC INTERVIEWS

Where were you on your last birthday?

In this video people talk about their birthdays, what they usually do on that day and what they did on their last birthday. This material allows Ss to consolidate and recap vocabulary areas including family, dates and places, and the past simple form of *be*. Use the video after lesson 7.2, at the end of the unit or set it for homework.

7 past

WHERE WERE YOU?

Introduction

Students practise listening and talking about where they were at certain times, using dates and *was/were, wasn't/weren't*, with attention to strong and weak forms. They also review punctuation in an email.

SUPPLEMENTARY MATERIALS
Resource bank: p166
Exercise 5A: take in a calendar or a diary, or both, to illustrate *months*.

Warm up

Review phrases with the prepositions *at*, *in* and *on*. Draw three columns on the board and write *at*, *in* and *on* at the top of each. Ask Ss to do the same in their notebooks. Tell Ss you are going to read out some words and they should write each one in the correct column. Read out the following, pausing after each one to give Ss time to write: *home, class, a café, a party, holiday, work, 2015, December, a beach, a boat, Sydney, my friend's house, Saturday, four o'clock, television*. Put Ss in pairs to compare their lists.

Answers:
at: home, a party, work, my friend's house, four o'clock
in: class, a café, 2015, December, Sydney
on: holiday, a beach, a boat, Saturday, television

Ss then take turns to 'test' each other (Student B covers their notebook):
A: work
B: at work
A: Correct!

LISTENING

1A Write the date 31/12 on the board and ask Ss for another way to say that day (New Year/New Year's Eve). Focus Ss on the photo and ask them if they usually celebrate like this at New Year. Check *fireworks*. Then put them in pairs to compare what they do at New Year with the photo. Ask one or two pairs for their answers.

B Give Ss a moment or two to look at the places. Check *sunrise*. You could play Speaker 1 for Ss to check the example.

Answers:
Speaker **2** – at a concert
Speaker **3** – at work
Speaker **4** – on a beach
Speaker **5** – in hospital

C Use the example to establish that the speakers may talk about more than one of the subjects. Play the recording, then tell Ss to compare their answers in pairs. You could also ask them to discuss which speaker's New Year they like best, then ask a few pairs to share their answers with the class.

Answers: **b)** 4 **c)** 1, 3 **d)** 2 **e)** 4 **f)** 1, 5 **g)** 3 **h)** 5

Unit 7 Recording 1

1 I was at home with my parents and my brother and sister. There was a family party, but nothing really special. There were fireworks on TV … but I think I was asleep at midnight. I don't really remember.

2 We were in Miami, Florida, at a concert. The bands were great – the Gipsy Kings and some other local bands. It was great.

3 I was at work in Sydney. I work at a club and of course it was a very big night for us. The money was good. Everybody was happy, crazy. There were fantastic fireworks over the Sydney Opera House.

4 I was on a beach in Fiji with my friends. There was a beautiful sunrise. We were the first people to see the start of the year 2000. And we weren't alone – there were hundreds of people on the beach with us. It was a beautiful morning, very peaceful …

5 I was in hospital. I was born on January 1st, 2000. My mother says there was a party. Maybe it was for the New Year … or was the party for me?

GRAMMAR PAST SIMPLE: WAS/WERE

2A Tell Ss that the sentences come from the recording in Ex 1 and ask them if they're about the present or the past. You could write today's date on the board and elicit *present*, then write two or three past dates, including 31/12/2000 and elicit *past*. You could then go through the sentences on the board with the class, or give Ss a minute or two to work on them alone first.

Answers: 1 was 2 were 3 weren't 4 Was

B Ss could complete the tables in pairs, then check with the rest of the class.

Answers:

I/He/She/It	was *wasn't*	at home. at work. tired.
You/We/They	*were* *weren't*	

Was *Were*	he you	here? in class?
Yes,	he we	*was.* were.
No,	he we	*wasn't.* weren't.

3A Tell Ss to underline one or two words in each sentence. Point out that the main stress is always on the words carrying the important information.

Answers: 1 I was at home. 2 We were tired. 3 She was at work.
4 They were here. 5 He wasn't well. 6 You weren't in class.

B PRONUNCIATION weak and strong forms: *was/were* Play the recording again for Ss to listen to the weak and strong forms. Establish that the negative forms *wasn't/weren't* are stressed.

Teaching tip

To help Ss to say weak forms naturally, ask them to try saying the word/phrase without any vowel sounds, e.g. *was = wz, were = w.*

▷ **LANGUAGEBANK 7.1** p130–131

Give Ss a few minutes to read through the summary of the form of *was/were*. Ss could do Ex 7.1A and B in class, if you feel they need some basic practice of the form, before moving on to the more sophisticated practice in Ex 4 on p74.

Answers:
A 2 isn't, was 3 weren't, 're/are 4 were, aren't
  5 wasn't, 's/is 6 're/are, weren't
B 2 Was the film good? Yes, it was.
  3 Were your brothers and sisters nice to you? Yes, they were.
  4 Were you cold in Scotland? No, I wasn't./No, we weren't.
  5 Were you and Emma at the party? No, we weren't.
  6 Was there a gift shop in the hotel? Yes, there was.

4A Before Ss start the exercise, check *birthday* and *public holiday* (a special day when people don't go to work and shops don't usually open).

Answers: 2 Were 3 Was, was, Were 4 was, were, was

B Establish that a)–d) are the answers to 1–4 in Ex 4A. Check *mountain* and *Thanksgiving*.

Culture note

Thanksgiving is a holiday in the United States and Canada. It is a day of giving thanks for the harvest. It is on the fourth Thursday of November in the United States and the second Monday of October in Canada. It is traditional to serve roast turkey and pumpkin pie at Thanksgiving.

Answers: a) wasn't, were b) weren't, were c) was, wasn't
d) was, were, weren't, were

C You may want to give Ss time to think about/make notes on their answers first. However, discourage them from writing full sentence answers, to avoid reading aloud and keep spontaneity. You could also model the rhythm and intonation of questions 1–4 for Ss to repeat in chorus, before they start asking each other in pairs. Monitor carefully so you can give feedback on Ss' use of language, especially *was/were*, etc. and their intonation in the questions.

speakout TIP

Establish that there's no difference in the meaning of the three questions, but that they all invite the other person to continue speaking, so the conversation can keep going.

VOCABULARY DATES

5A Check *months* by showing Ss a calendar and asking what month you are in now.

Answers: 2 February 3 March 4 April 5 May 6 June 7 July
8 August 9 September 10 October 11 November
12 December

B As Ss listen and check, they could underline the stress on each month with more than one syllable: <u>Ja</u>nuary, <u>Fe</u>bruary, <u>A</u>pril, Ju<u>ly</u>, <u>Au</u>gust, Sep<u>tem</u>ber, Oc<u>to</u>ber, No<u>vem</u>ber, De<u>cem</u>ber.

C Ss should cover Ex 5A while they do this.

6A Write *5th April* and *2nd June* on the board and say them aloud (*the fifth of April, the second of June*), then show Ss these dates on a calendar or in a dairy. Look at the examples with the class, then put Ss in pairs so they can help each other to write the other numbers. Then say the numbers for Ss to repeat, reminding them to touch the bottom of their top teeth with their tongue to pronounce the final -*th* in *fifth, ninth, twentieth, fourth, eighth, fifteenth* and *twelfth*, and the initial *th*- in *third* and *thirty-first*.

Answers: 3 ninth 9th 4 twentieth 20th 5 fourth 4th 6 third 3rd
7 thirty-first 31st 8 eighth 8th 9 first 1st
10 twenty-second 22nd 11 fifteenth 15th 12 twelfth 12th

Optional extra activity

Put Ss in pairs to practise asking and answering:
A: *What's the (fourth) month?*
B: *(April), etc.*

B Give Ss a few moments to read through the dates before you play the recording.

Answers:
15th October – 2
16th April – 5
8th August – 6
21st September – 4
25th March – 3

C Point out to Ss that the number and month are stressed and *the* and *of* are unstressed. You could also show the linking between the number and *of*: *the first␣of December, the fifteenth␣of October.* (NB: Another common way to say dates is *December the first, October the fifteenth.*)

7A Establish that the dates could be birthdays, public holidays, anniversaries, etc. and give Ss a few minutes to think about and write their dates. Circulate and help as necessary. Then Ss dictate their dates to their partners.

B Write a date that is important for you on the board and invite a student to ask you about it, eliciting the question *Why is the … of … important?*

▷ PHOTOBANK p145

Use these phrases to give Ss practise of years and time phrases. For extra practice of the time phrases you could use the actual date and ask Ss to say or write the appropriate days/dates/times for time phrases 1–8.

Answers:
Dates: Years 1 E 2 A 3 H 4 C 5 D 6 G 7 B 8 F
Dates: Time phrases 1 e) 2 c) 3 g) 4 a) 5 h) 6 b)
     7 d) 8 f)

SPEAKING

8A Point out that the order ends with the most recent. Ss can work alone and compare answers with a partner. As you go through the answers, say the phrases for Ss to repeat in chorus.

Answers: e) a) b) d)

B Demonstrate this by inviting different Ss to ask you the five questions. Then put Ss in pairs to practise.

Optional extra activity

Ss change the time phrases in Ex 8A and practise asking and answering with a new partner, e.g.
last (Wednesday)
last (week)
yesterday (morning)
this time last (month)
on (Sunday) afternoon

WRITING PUNCTUATION REVIEW

9A Look at the example with the class and elicit when a comma is used (to show a short pause in a sentence and make it easier to read). Then put Ss in pairs and ask them to match the punctuation marks and explain when they are used.

Answers:
2 full stop b) – at the end of a sentence
3 exclamation mark a) – after a word, phrase or sentence to show emotion, e.g. you're surprised, excited, amused, angry
4 question mark c) – at the end of a question
5 capital letter d) – at the beginning of a sentence and names of people, places and special days

B Give Ss a minute or two to read the email and find the answers.

Answers: Jane is at the Olympic Games (Ss might know or remember that the Games were in London in 2012). Paola is in Italy.

C Ss can work on this in pairs, or work alone and compare answers in pairs when they've finished.

Answers: 1 , (it's a convention to use a comma after 'Hi' or 'Dear' at the beginning of a letter or email, although the next sentence starts with a capital letter) 2 ? 3 . 4 . 5 . 6 ? 7 . or ! (the exclamation mark shows that the person is excited about their news)
8 , 9 . or ! (see note for 7) 10 . or ! (see note for 7) 11 . 12 ,
Capital letters: Paola (line 1), Matt (line 3), Olympic Games (line 5), Italy (line 6), Jane (line 12)

10A Ss could write their email in pairs to help each other with ideas. Tell them to follow the shape of the email in Ex 9B (and to put XXXX instead of the name of the place). Circulate and help as required.

B Either put Ss into groups of six to swap and read their emails, or display the emails round the classroom and give Ss time to walk round and read them.

Homework ideas

* Ss write another email like the one in Ex 9B, from a different place. They can swap emails with their partner in the next lesson and guess the place.
* **Workbook:** Ex 1–5, p45–46

RECORD BREAKERS

Introduction

Ss practise reading about people breaking records. They practise talking about past activities, using vocabulary to describe actions and the past simple of regular verbs. They also learn to pronounce past simple -ed endings accurately.

> **SUPPLEMENTARY MATERIALS**
> **Resource bank:** p165

Warm up

Review verb + noun collocations. Write the following verbs on the board: *go, be, listen to, watch, play*.
Put Ss in pairs and give them two minutes to write down two nouns that go with each verb.

> **Suggested answers:** go: to work, to a party be: a student, at home
> listen to: music, the radio watch: TV, a film play: tennis, football

Go through Ss' answers and add the nouns to the board.

VOCABULARY ACTIONS

1A Give Ss a moment or two to read through the actions, then play the first part of the recording for them to hear the example: *start*. Play the rest of the recording.

> **Answers:** **2** move home **3** stop **4** talk **5** arrive **6** wait
> **7** travel **8** play tennis **9** try **10** walk

B You could demonstrate this by acting out one of the verbs yourself for Ss to guess. Tell Ss to take turns to act out or draw and guess the actions.

READING

2A Put Ss in pairs to look at the photos. In feedback, introduce the verb *sail* for Jeanne Socrates on her boat.

> **Answers:** **1** talk, in a room **2** travel, on a boat
> **3** play tennis, on a tennis court **4** walk, in Africa

B Remind Ss that the title of the lesson is *Record breakers* and establish what happens when someone breaks a record, e.g. someone runs 100m in 10 seconds, then another person runs 100m in 9.58 seconds and breaks the record. Tell Ss to read the headings and imagine what record the person is/people are breaking. Check *match* (like *game*: an organised sports event between two people or teams). Then tell Ss to read the four texts quickly and match the headings to the texts. You could give them a time limit of a minute to encourage them to read just enough to decide on the heading. In feedback, check *audience* (the people who listen to a talk, a concert, etc.).

> **Answers:** **1** Man talks for six days **2** Grandmother sails round world
> **3** Nonstop tennis match **4** Woman walks for eleven years

C Look at the example with the class and give Ss a minute or two to find the relevant information in the text. When they've found all the names, Ss can compare answers in pairs. Check *a trip* (a journey to a place and back); *win* (v) (get the most points in a game) and *winner* (n) (the person who wins); *amazing* (very surprising); *childhood* (the part of your life when you are a child).

> **Answers:** **2** Jeanne Socrates **3** Arvind Mishra
> **4** Carlo (Santelli) **5** Jeanne Socrates (she sailed 'nonstop')
> **6** audience member at Arvind Mishra's talk **7** Carlo and Daniel
> **8** Ffyona Campbell

D Give Ss a few minutes to find and correct the mistakes in the notes. In feedback, ask Ss to read out the correct numbers like this: *it was 139 hours, 42 minutes, not 24 minutes*, etc.

> **Answers:**
> talking: 139 hours, ~~24~~ 42 minutes, ~~59~~ 56 seconds
> sailing: ~~295~~ 259 days
> playing tennis: ~~32~~ 38 hours, ~~12~~ 2 minutes, 9 seconds
> walking: 32,000 ~~metres~~ kilometres

> **Teaching tip**
>
> You can make a text memorable for Ss by asking for a personal response to it if the subject matter lends itself to this, e.g. *Which story did you like best/least? What surprised you? Do you know anyone like this? Which person would you like to meet?*

GRAMMAR PAST SIMPLE: REGULAR VERBS

3A Tell Ss to write the past form next to the verb, as in the example, and to copy the spelling carefully. Give them several minutes to find the past forms, and to check their answers with a partner.

> **Answers:** **2** talked **3** arrived **4** played **5** waited **6** moved
> **7** tried **8** stopped **9** travelled **10** finished **11** wanted
> **12** asked

B Either go through the table on the board with the whole class, or put Ss in pairs to work out the rules. Make sure they understand *vowel, consonant, add, change, double* (demonstrate these with examples on the board).

> **Answers:**
>
> | | spelling | examples |
> | --- | --- | --- |
> | most verbs | add -ed | *started, talked, played, waited, finished, wanted, asked* |
> | verbs ending in -e | add -d | *arrived, moved* |
> | verbs ending in consonant + -y | change to -ied | *tried* |
> | most verbs ending in consonant + vowel + consonant | double the final letter, then add -ed | *stopped, travelled* |

C Point out/Elicit that the verb doesn't have -ed or -d on the end in the negative because *didn't* already tells us it is a past form.

> **Answer:** didn't

4A PRONUNCIATION -ed endings You could model the examples for Ss to repeat, so they can feel and hear the difference between the three endings. Then play the recording.

> **Answers:**
> /t/ talked, stopped, finished, asked
> /d/ arrived, played, moved, tried, travelled
> /ɪd/ started, waited, wanted

B Ss listen to the three groups and repeat after each group.

5A Before Ss start this, check *when he was a boy* (from about 4–12 years old), *cry* (mime crying) and *the whole time* (all the time). Ss work alone then compare answers in pairs.

> **Answers:** **1** lived, moved **2** waited, didn't arrive **3** cooked, liked
> **4** walked, closed **5** asked, didn't understand **6** watched, cried

B You could ask two Ss to demonstrate the activity for the class first. Then when Ss change roles and it's Student A's turn to read out the sentences, suggest that they read them in random order.

Optional extra activity

1 Ss complete the second part of the sentences with their own ideas, e.g. *He lived here when he was a boy, but he didn't like it.*

2 Ss choose one of the people from the 'record breakers' texts and imagine that it's the day after they broke the record. In pairs, they tell each other what they did and ask each other how they feel about it now, and why. Ss then report back to the class about what their partner said.

▷ LANGUAGEBANK 7.2 p130–131

The Language bank reminds Ss that the past simple form is the same for all persons (*I/you/he/she/it/we/they*). It also highlights when the past simple is used, i.e. for past events at a point in time, or over a period of time in the past. Ss could do Ex 7.2A and B in class or for homework.

Answers:
A 2 Last weekend my father played tennis.
3 Last year Francisco worked in a shop.
4 Last night I studied English all night.
5 In 2009 my parents moved to Barcelona.
6 Yesterday the train stopped for half an hour.
B 2 Noriko emailed me yesterday, but she didn't phone.
3 The film didn't start until eight and it finished at eleven.
4 James wanted to see the concert, but he arrived an hour late.
5 I repeated the instructions because the students didn't understand.
6 I tried to phone you last night, but you didn't answer.

SPEAKING

6A Start by telling Ss to write the name of a friend or student where the asterisks are. Give Ss a few minutes to write their sentences in their notebooks. Circulate and help as required.

B/C You could demonstrate this by reading out one false and one true sentence of your own for Ss to guess. Put Ss in groups of four or five to do this. Monitor and note examples of good language use and problems for praise and correction in feedback.

Optional extra activity

To give practice of the verbs in Ex 3A, Ss complete the following sentences to make them true, then compare answers in small groups:

Last week/weekend I arrived late for …
On (day) I asked the teacher about …
Last night I started dinner at … and finished at …
Yesterday I waited for …
Last month/year/summer I travelled to … with …
When I was young I wanted to …
Last year/week I tried to …

Homework ideas

• Ss write their diary for the last week, including at least two sentences about each day, e.g. *On Monday morning I … In the evening I …* Tell them that some verbs are irregular so they should check past forms in their dictionaries.
• **Workbook:** Ex 1–4, p47–48

HOW WAS IT?

Introduction

Ss practise giving opinions, using positive and negative adjectives. They also practise listening and learn to use intonation to show feelings.

> **SUPPLEMENTARY MATERIALS**
> **Resource bank:** p167 and p168

Warm up

Review adjectives to describe feelings. Divide the class into two teams, then bring one member of each team to the front of the class and sit them with their backs to the board. Tell the teams to look at the word you write on the board and help their team member to guess what it is: they can do this by giving verbal clues or by miming. When one of the people with their back to the board calls out the word, they win a point for their team, and the next member from each team comes up to guess the next word, and so on.

Adjectives: *happy, cold, tired, hungry, ill, angry, surprised, unhappy, thirsty, well, scared, bored, interested* (leave out the last two if you feel your Ss will get confused between *bored/boring* and *interested/interesting*).

FUNCTION ASKING FOR AND GIVING OPINIONS

1A Put Ss in pairs to discuss the photos and remind them to use some of the adjectives to describe feelings. Ask a few pairs to share their ideas about the photos.

Answers: A in a restaurant; happy (about the food), hungry
B at a party; happy, excited C at the cinema; surprised, scared, interested

B Tell Ss to write F, P or R next to each number (1–3). Play the recording.

Answers: 1 F 2 R 3 P

C Give Ss a few moments to look through the phrases before you play the recording again. Then Ss can compare answers in pairs before checking with the class.

Answers: 1 d) 2 f) 3 e) 4 c) 5 b) 6 a)

Unit 7 Recording 8

Conversation 1
A: Hey, Emma, let's go!
B: What?
A: Let's go!
B: Why? What's the problem?
A: This film. It's terrible.
B: Really? I think it's all right.
A: Oh, come on. Let's go.
B: No, I want to stay.
C: Ssshhh!
B: Have some popcorn.
A: No, thanks.

Conversation 2
A: How was your steak?
B: Delicious, just right. I really liked it. How was your chicken?
A: Urgh, I didn't like it. It wasn't very good.
B: Oh well, here's the ice cream. Thank you.
A: What do you think of the ice cream?
B: Mmm. It's fantastic!
A: Yes, this is good.

Conversation 3

A: Hi, Emma. How are you?
B: Fine, thanks and you?
A: I'm OK. Um, were you at Warren's party yesterday?
B: Yeah.
A: How was it?
B: It was all right …
A: But …?
B: Mmm. Well, it was boring – there weren't a lot of people there.
A: Ah.
B: So where were you?
A: Ah, well. I went to Adam's party.
B: Adam's party?
A: Yeah.
B: I didn't know about it.
A: Uh, sorry …
B: Oh. How was it?
A: Er … it was very good.

2A You could go through part B of the first question with the class as a further example. Ss work alone or in pairs on the rest of the questions and answers.

> **Answers:**
> 1 **B:** Delicious, just right.
> 2 **A:** How was your chicken? **B:** It wasn't very good.
> 3 **A:** What do you think of the ice cream? **B:** It's fantastic!
> 4 **A:** How was the party? **B:** It was boring.

B Elicit/Remind Ss that we usually stress the words that carry the message of the sentence or phrase. Give them a minute or two in pairs to decide on the stressed words.

> **Answers:**
> 1 **A:** <u>How</u> was your <u>steak</u>? **B:** <u>Delicious</u>, just <u>right</u>.
> 2 **A:** <u>How</u> was your <u>chicken</u>? **B:** It <u>wasn't</u> very <u>good</u>.
> 3 **A:** <u>What</u> do you <u>think</u> of the <u>ice</u> <u>cream</u>? **B:** <u>It's</u> <u>fantastic</u>!
> 4 **A:** <u>How</u> was the <u>party</u>? **B:** It was <u>boring</u>.

C When Ss repeat the questions, encourage them to start with a high pitch (to show interest), and to use the weak form /wəz/ for *was*. To help them to do this, you could start by modelling and asking them to repeat *How – steak? How – chicken? What – think – ice cream? How – party?* then add the rest of the question without changing the rhythm, so the unstressed words are 'squashed in' between the stressed ones.

D Point out that Ss need to stress the adjective in the answer. Monitor the practice, so you can give Ss feedback on their pronunciation afterwards.

▷ LANGUAGEBANK 7.3 p130–131

Ss could do Ex 7.3 in class after Ex 2 or for homework.

> **Answers:**
> **Conversation 1**
> **A:** Hi, Sally. *How* was the film?
> **B:** It was *fantastic/very good*, really great.
> **A:** Who was in it?
> **B:** Tom Hanks.
> **A:** How *was* he?
> **B:** *He* was fantastic.
> **Conversation 2**
> **A:** *What* do you think of the chicken?
> **B:** It's *not* very good – really awful.
> **A:** Oh, I'm sorry.
> **B:** *How's* your steak?
> **A:** *I* think it's OK.
> **B:** And this restaurant is very expensive.
> **A:** Yes, it is!

VOCABULARY ADJECTIVES

3A Go through the examples with the class, checking that Ss understand what the symbols +, – and +/– mean. Then put Ss in pairs to help each other with the meanings of the adjectives. Encourage Ss to discuss the meaning together first, before consulting their dictionaries. As you go through the answers, if Ss ask about the difference between *boring/bored* and *interesting/interested* (*bored* was introduced in unit 2), give them examples to show that *bored/interested* are for feelings, whereas *boring/interesting* describe places and things, e.g. *The Taj Mahal is interesting. The book was boring.*

> **Teaching tip**
>
> Ss can benefit from using an English to English dictionary, even at very low levels. Although it's challenging for them to understand an explanation in English, it will expose them to more English and be more memorable for them.

> **Answers:**
>
> | + | – | +/– |
> |---|---|-----|
> | great delicious interesting | not very good boring awful | not bad |

B Tell Ss to write *VG*, *VB* or *F* next to the appropriate words in the table, and encourage them to help each other. When checking the answers, to avoid Ss making mistakes by saying *very delicious*, etc. you could write on the board:
delicious = very good ✓ ~~very delicious~~
Then check by asking *Is it OK to say 'very delicious'?* (*No.*)

> **Answers:** 1 (VG) fantastic, great, delicious, interesting
> 2 (VB) terrible, awful, not very good 3 (F) delicious

C You may want to give Ss a chance to predict where the stress goes before you play the recording.

> **Answers:** <u>te</u>rrible, fan<u>tas</u>tic, <u>great</u>, de<u>li</u>cious, <u>not</u> very <u>good</u>, <u>bo</u>ring, <u>in</u>teresting (NB: This is usually pronounced with three syllables: Ooo.), <u>aw</u>ful, not <u>bad</u>

D Direct Ss to the example, then give them a minute or two to give their opinions in pairs.

> **Optional extra activity**
>
> Put Ss in pairs and direct them to the photos in these previous lessons: 1.4, 2.2, 3.4, 4.1, 4.4, 6.2, 6.4
> Ss ask each other for their opinions:
> *A: What do you think of the …?*
> *B: I think it's …*

4A You could give Ss some ideas:
person: an actor, a singer, a politician
place: a city, a country, a shop, a café, a street
thing: a sport/game, a type of food, a drink, a book/magazine/newspaper, a type of music

B Demonstrate by saying the name of something yourself and pointing out that Ss should close their books while they're trying to guess (this will be more challenging because they'll have to remember the adjectives). Ss could report back at the end of this activity about something they have in common, e.g. *We both think R&B is great.*

▷ **PHOTOBANK** p145

There are nine more adjectives with their opposites in the Photo bank. Ss could do the exercises at this stage of the lesson, before the speaking practice (Ex 6 and Ex 7) or for homework.

Answers:
A 2 I 3 A 4 F 5 C 6 D 7 G 8 H 9 B
B 1 far – near 2 soft – hard 3 heavy – light 4 dark – light
   5 long – short 6 full – empty 7 expensive – cheap
   8 noisy – quiet 9 fast – slow

LEARN TO **SHOW FEELINGS**

5A Point out that Ss need to listen carefully to the answers to the questions, then play the recording.

Answers: 1 + 2 – 3 + 4 –

B PRONUNCIATION intonation Play the first conversation again and check that Ss can hear that the voice is high. As you check the answers, ask Ss what difference the high or low voice makes to the opinion (i.e. positive versus negative).

Answers: 1 H 2 L 3 H 4 L

speakout TIP

Read the information with the class and demonstrate the difference between the two intonation patterns. You may need to exaggerate the voice movement in order for Ss to hear the difference easily. You could use your hand to show that the positive intonation starts much higher than the negative one.

C Demonstrate by inviting one or two Ss to ask you a question and answering with high or low intonation. In each case, ask Ss whether you sounded positive or negative. Then Ss can give each other feedback on their intonation while they practise this in pairs.

Teaching tip

An effective way of providing Ss with feedback on their intonation is for them to record themselves. You could encourage them to use their mobile phones to record themselves, then play back the recording and comment on each other's intonation.

SPEAKING

6A Start by eliciting some names of films that are showing currently and the names of the main actors in them. Also direct Ss to the example and point out that *go* is an irregular verb and its past form is *went*. Give Ss a few minutes to write out the lines of the conversation in their notebooks or, for **stronger classes**, Ss could work in pairs and say the lines without writing them. To check the answers, you could either elicit the lines and model them for Ss to repeat (if your Ss aren't very confident) or you could give Ss the complete conversation as a key for them to check their answers against.

Answers:
A: Where were you last night?   **B:** I went to the Adele concert.
A: How was it?   **B:** It was fantastic! I loved it.
A: How was Adele?   **B:** She was great.
A: Yes, she's very good.   **B:** And you? Where were you?
A: I went to the cinema to see (*name of film*).   **B:** How was it?
A: It was OK but (*name of actor/actress*) was great.

Culture note

Adele is a British singer and songwriter. Her first two albums were *19* and *21*: the success of *21* earned her many mentions in the *Guinness Book of World Records*. In 2013 she received an Academy Award, a Grammy Award and a Golden Globe Award for her song *Skyfall*, which she wrote and composed for the James Bond film of the same name

B Ss could work with new partners to role-play the conversation. Encourage them to look up from the page as much as possible, so they can concentrate on their intonation, rather than reading the prompts.

C Start by eliciting some names of restaurants and bands/singers, and types of class, e.g. art class. Tell Ss to practise the conversation once with the prompts, changing them as necessary, then to close their books and try to remember as much as they can. Monitor and note down examples of good language use and problem areas for praise and correction afterwards.

7 Ask Ss to walk round the room with a notebook and talk to at least three different people about their weekends. They should make a note of the people's names, where they went and their opinions. In feedback, ask a few Ss to report back on what they found out and what different people had in common. Monitor the activity and note down examples of good language use and problem areas for praise and correction in feedback.

Optional extra activity

Put the following prompts on the board for Ss to talk about:
café: coffee, cake
holiday: hotel, weather
match: referee, crowd
conference: people, hotel (NB: *How* were *the people?*)
cooking class: teacher, food
Encourage Ss to use adjectives from the Photo bank exercises to help them describe their experiences, e.g.
A: Where were you last weekend?
B: I went to a football match.
A: How was it?
B: It was great! The crowd was very noisy!

Homework ideas

• Check that Ss have the email address of at least one other person in the class. Ss write an email to another student in the class telling them about something they did at the weekend and giving their opinion on it. They finish the email by asking about the other student's weekend, and the other student replies.
• **Workbook:** Ex 1–3, p49

THE CHILEAN MINERS

Introduction

Ss watch an extract from a news programme about the rescue of thirty-three miners from a mine in Copiapó, Chile, in 2010. Ss then learn and practise how to discuss the order of events in history and write questions for a history quiz.

> **SUPPLEMENTARY MATERIALS**
>
> **Ex 4B:** bring in material about important events in history for Ss to use to write a quiz.

Warm up

Use the photo to lead in to the topic with the class. Ask Ss who the men are and where they work (miners, a mine). Then put Ss in pairs to discuss:

Is it a good job? Why/Why not?
Is it easy or difficult? Why?
What about a miner's wife and family?

In feedback on the discussion, elicit *dangerous* and *accident* (these words have been introduced in lesson 6.4), then ask if Ss know any examples of accidents in mines.

DVD PREVIEW

1A Look at the example and elicit/point out that *drill* is a noun and a verb. Put Ss in pairs to help each other, and use their dictionaries (preferably English–English) to check the vocabulary if necessary.

As you go through the answers, you could check the meaning and pronunciation of the following words, underlining the stressed syllables and asking questions that test whether Ss understand the meaning:

tunnel – *Where else do you see a tunnel?* (on a road or railway)
microphone – *Which other people use microphones?* (singers, politicians)
surface – touch the surface of your desk
accident – *When do you sometimes see accidents?* (on a road, e.g. two cars, a car and a bike).

> **Answers: B** tunnel   **C** miner   **D** underground   **E** surface
> **F** note   **G** microphone   **H** accident

B Tell Ss the programme is about some miners in Chile: they were in an accident, but people rescued them (mime rescuing someone from a dangerous situation). Focus Ss on the summary and establish that they need to read the programme information and write a number in each of the three gaps in the summary below. For **weaker classes** explain that the numbers answer these questions: *How many miners were in the accident? How many days were they underground before the rescue? How many days did their families wait to know if they were alive?* Ss check answers in pairs.

> **Answers:** 33, 69, 17

DVD VIEW

2A Focus Ss on the three choices and emphasise that they are watching to see who was the last man out. Play the DVD.

> **Answers:** the boss

B Check that Ss understand the words in the box and the following words from the sentences: *healthy* (not ill), *positive* (not sad, confident). Ss complete the sentences in pairs or alone.

> **Answers: 2** worked   **3** families   **4** rescue   **5** travelled   **6** days

C Focus Ss on number 1 and ask *Who is 'they'? The miners? Their families? The workers?* Then put Ss in pairs to discuss the rest of the underlined words. Play the DVD again or direct Ss to the script to check their ideas.

> **Answers: 1** workers, the rescue team   **2** the note   **3** the miners
> **4** the miners' families   **5** the trip from the mine to the surface
> **6** Luis Urzúa, the last man out

Optional extra activity

Ss work in pairs and prepare a role-play between a rescued miner and a news reporter. You could give some prompts for possible questions for the interviewer, e.g.

Tell us about your life in the shelter.
Was it (difficult/boring)? Why?
Tell us about your feelings in the first days/after (four) weeks/when the rescue started.
How do you feel now?

Give Ss time to prepare and practise the role-play, providing help with vocabulary and grammar as required. Then invite a few pairs to act out their role-play for the class.

DVD 7   The Chilean Miners

2010, near Copiapó, Chile. The San José Mine. Thirty-three men. Sixty-nine days. This is their story.

August the fifth, 2010. It was two o'clock in the afternoon. Thirty-three miners were underground, seven hundred metres underground. There was a bad accident in the mine. Were the men dead or alive?

Workers started to drill down. They listened to microphones, but nothing.

August the twenty-second, 2010, day seventeen.

Finally, there was a note. It was from the miners; 'We are well in the shelter, the thirty-three.' The men were safe. The rescue wasn't easy, the drills worked day and night.

The miners worked to keep healthy and positive. The miners' families watched and waited. The world watched with them.

October the twelfth, 2010, day sixty-eight.

The tunnel was finished. The rescue started. It was eighteen minutes from the mine to the surface.

At twenty past eleven at night, the first man arrived to meet his family and friends.

Then, one by one, the miners travelled to the surface.

October the thirteenth, 2010, day sixty-nine.

Twenty-four hours later, the last man arrived. He was the boss, Luis Urzúa. After sixty-nine days, the miners were free.

speakout   do a quiz

3A Start by checking that Ss can say the years on the timeline correctly, i.e. *nineteen sixty-nine, two thousand and seven, twenty eleven,* etc. Also check that Ss are familiar with the four events to some degree. Give Ss time to discuss all four events and mark them on the timeline.

> **Teaching tip**
>
> Ss could record themselves (e.g. on their mobile phones) discussing where to put the events on the timeline so they can later (after Ex 3C) listen and compare what they said with the key phrases. The idea is that when they do the same type of task again (in Ex 3D) their language use will improve. They could record themselves again and compare the two recordings.

Culture notes

Nelson Mandela died at his home in Johannesburg on 5 December 2013.

The **Japanese tsunami** in 2011 killed nearly 16,000 people. Some of the waves were over forty metres high. The earthquake moved the main island of Japan 2.4m east, shifted the earth on its axis by 10–25cm and caused 3 nuclear accidents. It was the most expensive natural disaster in history, with an estimated economic cost of US$235 billion.

Google is an American company best known for its search engine. It was founded by Larry Page and Sergey Brin in 1996.

The **first man on the moon** was Neil Armstrong, on 21 July 1969. As Armstrong stepped onto the surface of the Moon he said, 'One small step for man, one giant leap for mankind.'

B When Ss have listened to the recording, you could find out how many pairs got all four answers right.

Answers: a) Nelson Mandela died 2013   **b)** Google started 1996
c) Japanese tsunami, 2011   **d)** the first man on the moon, 1969

C Give Ss a few moments to read the key phrases. Then play the recording again for Ss to tick the phrases, including the correct options inside the brackets.

Answers:
Which was first? ✓
I think [the Japanese tsunami] was [first /next].
Yes, I agree. ✓
I don't know./I'm not sure. ✓
No, Google was [before ✓/after] the Japanese tsunami. ✓
Which date? ✓
I remember it well. ✓
Let's check the answers. ✓
We were [right ✓/wrong ✓] about [three answers ✓/Google ✓].

Optional extra activity

To give Ss some practice of the key phrases before they start doing the history quiz, make a copy (large enough to display on the board) of the phrases with gaps, e.g.

Which was _____?
I think [the Japanese tsunami] was [first/_____].
Yes, I _____.
I don't _____./I'm not_____.
No, Google was _____/_____ the Japanese tsunami.
Which _____?
I remember it _____.
Let's _____ the answers.
We were [right/_____] about [three answers/Google].

Tell Ss to close their books and elicit the complete phrases from the class, one at a time, prompting the class to repeat the phrase in chorus and/or individually.

D Put Ss in small groups of three or four and direct them to the quiz. Remind them to use the key phrases, both for doing the quiz and for checking their answers. Monitor and note down examples of good language use (especially of the key phrases) and any problem areas for praise and correction afterwards. Invite groups to report back to the class about which dates they got right/wrong.

Unit 7   Recording 11

A: OK, so which was first?
B: I think the first man on the moon.
A: Yes, I agree. But which date – 1969 or 1975?
B: I think it was 1969.
A: OK, let's put that. So, what was next?
B: I think Google started.
A: I'm not sure. Maybe the Japanese tsunami?
B: No, Google was before the Japanese tsunami.
A: OK. Which date?
B: Erm … 1987, I think.
A: Was there internet in 1987?
B: Sure. Well, I think so. Maybe.
A: OK. 1987.
B: And I think the Japanese tsunami was next, in 2011.
A: Not 2007?
B: No, 2011. I remember it well because I was in London at that time.
A: OK, so that's 2011. And Nelson Mandela?
B: He died in 2013, I think.
A: 2013. Right, let's check the answers.
A: OK, we were right about three answers. The first man on the moon was in 1969, the Japanese tsunami was in 2011 and Nelson Mandela died in 2013.
B: But we were wrong about Google?
A: Yes. Google didn't start in 1987. It started in 1996.

writeback   a history quiz

4A You could go through the quiz with the whole class (e.g. divided into two or three teams), or put Ss in pairs to discuss it. Then check the answers at the bottom of the page.

B Direct Ss back to the quiz in Ex 4A and focus on the beginning of the questions, i.e. *When were …? Which … was …? Why was …? What was …?* Elicit some other possibilities, e.g. *Who was …? Where was …?* (NB: Ss can only write questions with *was/were*: try to direct them away from making questions in the past with any other verbs. Ss could research their questions on the internet if there is access in class, or on their phones. Otherwise, you could bring in some material, either printed from the internet, e.g. via a search such as: *important historical events in the 20th century*, or from reference books.)

Ss work on their questions and multiple-choice answers in pairs. Circulate and help as required, especially with the word order in the questions. Ss could also practise asking their questions in the same pairs to build their confidence and check their pronunciation.

C Move Ss around so that they have new partners and give them time to ask each other their questions and check each other's answers.

Homework ideas

Ss choose five famous people from history and write their names at the top of a piece of paper. Then they write a short paragraph (three or four sentences) about each of them, e.g.

He/She was from …
He/She was a …
He/She lived in …
He/She worked/played/travelled/liked/wanted/invented … (one or two sentences about what the person did/was famous for)
His/Her first name was …
He/She died in …

The paragraphs should be in a different order from the names of the people. In the next lesson, Ss exchange their pieces of paper and try to match the people with the paragraphs.

LOOKBACK

PAST SIMPLE: WAS/WERE

1A Tell Ss they need to write the name of another student next to each statement 1–8. Give them a few minutes to write the questions in their notebooks: point out that all the questions should use the positive form of the verb, even when they want a negative answer.

> **Answers:**
> 2 Were you tired this morning?
> 3 Were you in the town/city centre at the weekend?
> 4 Were you here in the last class?
> 5 Were you in a café before class?
> 6 Were you on a train at eight o'clock this morning?
> 7 Were you late for something yesterday?
> 8 Were you ill yesterday?

B Demonstrate how the activity works by inviting three Ss to ask you the first three questions. Answer *No, I wasn't* to 1 and 2 and *Yes, I was* to 3, and ask Ss where they should write your name (i.e. next to number 3, but not 1 or 2). Point out that Ss should write the names of the people they find on the left of the statements in Ex 1A. Put Ss in groups of six or, preferably, ask Ss to stand up and walk around asking their questions: in this way they will talk to more people and have more chance of getting an answer to all their questions. Encourage Ss to give reasons for their answers, e.g.
Were you here in the last class?
No, I wasn't because I was at the dentist.
When Ss have finished, ask some of them to tell the class what they found out.

DATES

2A You could ask a student to come and write the date on the board and ask the rest of the class to check it.

B You could do the first date (for *yesterday*) with the class as an example. Then give Ss a few minutes to write the other dates, working alone.

C Demonstrate this by asking a student to say one of the time phrases, and choose another student to say the appropriate date. Then put Ss in pairs to continue.

D Give Ss time to write their dates, then repeat Ex 2C. For **stronger classes** you could ask Ss to do this orally, without writing their list of dates first.

ACTIONS

3A You could run this as a competition in teams. Write or display the words on the board, one at a time. When a team member guesses a word, they put up their hand or 'buzz' to answer, then they have to both say the word and spell it correctly to win a point.

> **Answers:** 2 talk 3 try 4 arrive 5 stop 6 travel 7 start
> 8 walk 9 move home 10 play tennis

B Look at the example with the class, then give Ss a few minutes to complete the sentences, working alone.

> **Answers:** 2 arrive 3 starts 4 talks 5 walk 6 travel 7 try
> 8 wait 9 play tennis 10 stop

C Demonstrate this by telling Ss one sentence which is true for you and changing another to make it true. For **stronger classes**, tell Ss to change the sentences orally, rather than writing them out in full.

PAST SIMPLE: REGULAR VERBS

4A Start by eliciting the three ways of making the past of regular verbs: add *-ed*, add *-d*, change *-y* to *-ied*. When you go though the answers, check Ss' pronunciation of the past forms, i.e. watched, asked, stopped /t/, waited, studied /ɪd/, phoned, played, tried /d/.

> **Answers:** 2 waited 3 phoned 4 asked 5 played 6 studied
> 7 stopped 8 tried

B You may want to give Ss some repetition practice of *When was the last time you …?* and make sure that they're using the weak form /wəz/. Go through the example or demonstrate the activity yourself, showing Ss that they should explain what happened, as well as saying when. (NB: If Ss haven't done the action, they can answer *never*.)

ADJECTIVES

5A You could run this as a race in pairs. The first pair to finish put their hands up, then read the word and the missing vowels only, e.g. *terrible*: e, i, e. If they make a mistake, another pair can take over, and so on.

> **Answers:** 1 terrible 2 delicious 3 interesting 4 awful
> 5 fantastic 6 boring 7 great 8 all right 9 not very good
> 10 not bad

B Point out that Ss can either agree with each other and use adjectives with a similar meaning (as in the example) or disagree, e.g.
A: The concert was terrible!
B: Oh no, I think it was great!

ASKING FOR AND GIVING OPINIONS

6A Give Ss a few minutes to number the sentences, working alone.

> **Answers:**
> 1 A: Hi, Pete, how was the restaurant last night?
> 2 B: It wasn't very good.
> 3 A: Why not?
> 4 B: Because the food was terrible. And how was the film?
> 5 A: It was great, really good. Hey, what do you think of our new manager?
> 6 B: He's not bad.
> 7 A: Yes, I think he's all right, too.

B Give Ss time to practise the conversation once or twice (swapping roles), then put the following prompts on the board. Ask Ss to close their books and practise the conversation again, using the prompts:
restaurant? not/very good food/terrible
film? great
new manager? not bad all right

> **BBC interviews and worksheet**
> **Where were you on your last birthday?**
> In this video people talk about their birthdays, what they usually do on that day and what they did on their last birthday. This material allows Ss to consolidate and recap vocabulary areas including family, dates and places, and the past simple form of *be*.

OVERVIEW

8.1 STRANGE MEETINGS

READING | read about how people met their friends
GRAMMAR | past simple: irregular verbs
PRONUNCIATION | sounds: irregular past verbs
VOCABULARY | prepositions of place
SPEAKING | talk about first meetings

8.2 A GOOD HOLIDAY?

VOCABULARY | holiday activities
LISTENING | listen to a radio programme about holidays
GRAMMAR | past simple: questions
PRONUNCIATION | linking: *did you?*
SPEAKING | ask and answer about a good holiday
WRITING | use linkers *so* and *because*

8.3 WHERE IS IT?

VOCABULARY | prepositions of place
PRONUNCIATION | word stress: prepositions
FUNCTION | giving directions
LISTENING | listen to someone asking for directions in a supermarket
LEARN TO | use examples
SPEAKING | give directions in a supermarket

8.4 GUIDED TOUR BBC)) DVD

DVD | watch a BBC comedy about tourists in Spain
speakout | tell a bad holiday story
writeback | write a travel review

8.5 LOOKBACK

Communicative revision activities

BBC)) INTERVIEWS

Where did you go on holiday last year?

In this video people talk about the holiday they had last year. They describe holiday activities and say whether they enjoyed themselves. The material could be used as a lively introduction to the unit or, alternatively, at the end of the unit as a means of consolidating the use of the past simple (regular and irregular verbs), lifestyle vocabulary and phrases for expressing opinions.

STRANGE MEETINGS

Introduction

Students practise reading and talking about meeting people for the first time, using past simple irregular verbs (with a focus on sounds that they have in common) and prepositions of place.

> **SUPPLEMENTARY MATERIALS**
> **Resource bank:** p169 and p171
> **Warm up:** prepare sets of cards for a vocabulary review (see notes).

Warm up

Review vocabulary related to places and holidays from previous units and preview from the stories in this lesson. Write the heading *Places and Holidays* on the board, then write the following words randomly underneath it (alternatively make sets of cards with the words on – one set per pair of Ss): *a train, a village, a hospital, a guide, a café, a passport, a bus, a mountain, a bridge, a waitress, scared, money, a town, a desert, hungry, a tunnel*. Put Ss in pairs and tell them to find eight pairs of words. As you check the answers, you could ask Ss to explain why the words are a pair. If Ss have sets of cards, they first match the pairs, then use them to play a memory game: Ss put all the cards face down in front of them, then take turns to turn over two cards. If the cards make a pair, the student who turned them over keeps them, if not he/she turns them back over in the same place. The winner is the student with the most pairs when all the cards have been picked up.

> **Answers:**
> *a train, a bus* (you travel in them)
> *a village, a town* (people live and work in them)
> *a hospital, a café* (places in a town)
> *a guide, a waitress* (jobs)
> *a passport, money* (things you need to travel)
> *a mountain, a desert* (natural places)
> *a bridge, a tunnel* (they carry a road)
> *scared, hungry* (adjectives)

READING

1A Elicit one or two examples for question 1, then put Ss in pairs to think of more examples and discuss question 2.

> **Suggested answers:**
> **1** at a party, at a café, at a friend's house, at school/university/ an evening class, at work, at the gym, on holiday
> **2** in the desert; a rope bridge; a hospital; a café
> They are not usually places where you meet a new friend.

B Then tell Ss to read the stories and number them 1–4, starting with 1 for the most unusual. Set a time limit for this, to encourage Ss to read just to get the gist of the stories and to discourage them from looking up unfamiliar vocabulary. Ss can then discuss their choices in pairs or with the whole class.

C Tell Ss to cover the text before doing this exercise. They could work in pairs and help each other to find and correct the mistakes.

D Ss read the text to confirm the correct information, then check again in pairs. (NB: If individual Ss ask you about any of the irregular past forms in the text while they're reading, tell them it's a verb in the past and encourage them to guess which verb it is. Reassure them that you are going to study these verbs next.)

Answers:
1 The bus was in the ~~mountains~~ (Sahara) desert.
2 Habib ~~was~~ wasn't the bus driver.
3 The bridge was in ~~India~~ Pakistan.
4 Cynthia and Anne were on the bridge for ~~an hour~~ half an hour.
5 Jon was in a ~~train~~ car accident.
6 Jon was in hospital for a ~~month~~ week.
7 Someone took Alison's ~~passport~~ money.
8 The waitress said, 'Do you need ~~money~~ help?'

GRAMMAR PAST SIMPLE: IRREGULAR VERBS

2A You could use the first story to show Ss the difference between regular and irregular verbs. First, ask Ss to underline the examples of *was/were* in the story (there are two examples of *was* and one of *were*), then the regular verbs (*stopped*, *talked*), then to find a past form of a verb in the second line (*had*). Elicit the present form of this verb (*have*). Establish that irregular verbs do not add -ed in the past, but their form changes in different ways. Remind Ss that, like regular verbs, the past form is the same for all persons. Give Ss a few minutes to find the irregular verbs in the rest of the text and compare answers in pairs. Check *become* by using a timeline:

you meet → you talk → you like the person → you become friends

B Play the recording for Ss to check their answers. Encourage Ss to repeat the present and past forms together to help them remember the combination. You could also put Ss in pairs to 'test' each other on the past or present form, e.g.

Student A: *take* Student B: *took*
Student B: *broke* Student A: *break*

Answers: 2 came 3 took 4 thought 5 became 6 broke 7 went 8 had 9 sat 10 said

speakout TIP

Before Ss read the Speakout tip, you could ask them how they can find the past simple form of an irregular verb and establish that any good dictionary will have this information. Give Ss a minute to read the tip and emphasise the importance of keeping good records of past forms in their notebooks, so they can find them easily and try to use them whenever possible. Suggest that they keep a separate section of their notebooks for verbs and their past forms, and/or that they group verbs on different pages according to topic (e.g. travel and holidays, work, friends and family, etc.). Give Ss a few minutes to record the five verbs: *drive – drove*, *eat – ate*, *see – saw*, *give – gave*, *put – put*.

C PRONUNCIATION sounds: irregular past verbs Read through the examples so that Ss can familiarise themselves with each sound. Tell Ss to write four more verbs from Ex 2A and five from the Speakout tip next to the correct sound. Encourage them to work in pairs and say the verbs to each other. Play the recording for Ss to check their answers.

Answers: 1 /e/ went, said, ate 2 /eɪ/ became, gave 3 /ʊ/ put 4 /æ/ sat 5 /əʊ/ drove 6 /ɔː/ saw

D Give Ss a minute or two to find the example in the text (it's in Alison's story). Establish that, as with regular verbs, *didn't* indicates the past, so the main verb stays in its infinitive form.

Optional extra activity

Ask Ss to find three ways of saying *be very good friends* in the text:
be/become friends for life
be/become great friends
be/become (instant) best friends
Ss can make a note of these to use in the speaking practice (Ex 6).

▷ **LANGUAGEBANK 8.1** p132–133

Give Ss a few minutes to look at the summary and examples and the list of common irregular verbs. You could use Ex 8.1A for basic practice in manipulating the positive and negative past forms. Ex 8.1B is another story about an unusual place to meet: when Ss have completed the story and checked their answers, they could work in pairs and take turns to close their books and try to remember as much of the story as they can.

Answers:
A 2 take 3 say 4 thought 5 became 6 sat
B 2 went 3 became 4 saw 5 didn't have 6 had 7 broke 8 gave 9 ate 10 had 11 drove

3A Tell Ss to read the stories quickly and decide which two people from the stories are speaking.

Answers: Habib and Claudia

B Give Ss a few minutes to complete the stories, working alone. As you go through the answers in feedback, check spelling and pronunciation of the past verb forms.

Answers:
1 2 came 3 didn't want 4 asked 5 drove 6 met 7 stayed 8 thought 9 became
2 1 worked 2 saw 3 went 4 said 5 didn't have 6 didn't know 7 sat 8 talked 9 gave

C Put Ss in pairs and focus them on the example, then give them a couple of minutes to change three things in their stories.

D You could demonstrate this by starting to tell story 1 as in the example, and indicate that Ss should say *Stop!* and correct you.

Optional extra activity

Refer Ss to the story in the Language bank Ex 8.1B, about how a man met his wife, Manuela. In pairs, Ss rewrite the story from the point of view of Manuela. Tell them they can invent any extra information they need, e.g. *One Saturday afternoon in 2008 I was on a mountain in Scotland. I lived near the mountain and I often walked there …*

Two or three pairs then read out their stories and see what's similar/different about them.

VOCABULARY PREPOSITIONS OF PLACE

4A You could go through these sentences with the whole class, referring Ss back to the photo for *on a bridge*, and reminding them that we use *in* for towns, cities and countries. You could also explain that we say *at work*, *at school* for places we go to regularly. See more about *at* versus *in* below.

Answers: 1 on 2 in 3 at

B Give Ss time to look carefully at the word webs and help each other decide on the correct preposition. If Ss ask whether it's also possible to say *in Dublin airport*, you could demonstrate, e.g. by drawing a box with sides and a person inside it, that with some places (also *station*, *café*, *restaurant*, *office*) we use *in* if we think of the space as three-dimensional, but we use *at* if we think of the place as a point, like a point on a map.

Answers: 1 at 2 in 3 on

Optional extra activity

Ss look back through the stories in Ex 1 to find other examples of *in* and add them to the word web.

(Answers: *in the desert, in a village, in hospital, in a car accident, in my room, in a café*)

5A Ss work on the sentences alone, then compare answers in pairs.

Answers:
2 I met one of my friends *on* the internet.
3 I went *on* holiday with a friend last year.
4 I wasn't *in* class last week.
5 I was *at* a friend's party on Saturday.
6 I had lunch with a friend *in* the city centre yesterday.

B Demonstrate this by making one of the sentences true for you. Give Ss time to tick and/or change the sentences, then put them in pairs to read out and compare sentences.

▷ PHOTOBANK p146

Use these exercises to give Ss further practice of the prepositions *in*, *on*, *at*, as well as *under* and *over*. Ss could do these for homework.

Answers:
A 1 The cat's *on* the table.
2 There's a man *under* a car.
3 There's a plane *over* the sea.
4 There are two elephants *in* a river.
5 I live *at* number sixty-six.
6 Rome is *on* the River Tiber.
B 1 I live in a flat ~~under~~ *in* Beijing.
2 We flew ~~at~~ *over* the Red Desert …
3 Could you give me my glasses? They're ~~over~~ *on* the sofa …
4 Let's meet ~~in~~ *at* the crossroads …
5 Your keys are ~~in~~ *on* the table …
6 Our house is ~~over~~ *on* the main road …

SPEAKING

6A Give Ss time to prepare their timeline and to make notes about how they met each person (e.g. what they did, what they said, etc.) and why they liked them. Encourage Ss to look back at the stories in Ex 1 and Ex 3 for ideas.

B Put Ss into groups of four to six and invite a **stronger student** in each group to start talking about their timeline. Encourage the listeners to ask questions. Monitor the practice and make notes of good language use and any problem areas for praise and correction afterwards.

(NB: For the next lesson, ask Ss to bring in some photos from their last holiday: these could be photos downloaded from the internet of the place(s) they went to, or their own personal photos. They could also bring a map which shows the location of the place(s) they went to.)

Homework ideas

- Ss write a story for a class competition about how they met a friend (the winning story is the one with the best use of English). Ss should use the stories in Ex 1 and Ex 3 as models and write about five sentences, starting with *In/On …*, *in …*, continuing with what they said/did and ending with a sentence about becoming friends.
- **Workbook:** Ex 1–6, p50–51

A GOOD HOLIDAY?

Introduction

Ss practise listening to people talking about good and bad holidays. They practise talking about holidays (using vocabulary related to holiday activities) and past simple questions. They also learn how to use linking in past simple questions and the linkers *so* and *because* in writing.

SUPPLEMENTARY MATERIALS
Resource bank: p170
Warm up (option 2): bring/download some world maps and maps of the country you are in.
Ex 6B: bring in some photos from your last holiday.

Warm up

Lead in to the topic of holidays (2 options).

1 Write the heading *Holidays* on the board, with three subheadings underneath it: *Places*, *Activities* and *Things*. Put Ss in small groups and tell them they have three minutes to write as many words/phrases as they can think of for each heading. After three minutes, elicit answers to the board, checking any words/phrases that you think will not be familiar to everybody.
Some possible answers (this will depend on your Ss' prior knowledge):
Places: airport, hotel, beach, station
Activities: travel, relax, read a book, swim, ski, go shopping
Things: passport, ticket, dictionary, bag, suitcase

2 Write *Good places for a holiday* on the board. Put Ss in groups and give half the class world maps and half the class maps of the country you're in. Tell them to find good places for a holiday on their map and be prepared to tell the class why they think the places are good. After about five minutes, invite the groups to share their ideas with the class.

VOCABULARY HOLIDAY ACTIVITIES

1A Prompt Ss to ask you the questions. In your answer, include an explanation of when and where you went and why it was/wasn't a good holiday. Then put Ss in pairs to do the same.

B Before Ss start the activity, check *local* Oo (from the place or area) and the pronunciation of *building* (the *u* is not pronounced). Ss can work alone or with a partner on the matching activity. As you go through the answers, you could ask Ss for examples of the local food from their area.

Answers: 2 d) 3 a) 4 b) 5 g) 6 h) 7 e) 8 f)

C Give Ss a minute or two to discuss the pictures.

Answers: see old buildings, go camping

D Demonstrate this with a **strong student**, showing the class that they should take turns to be A and B, so they both get practice in saying the complete phrases. When Ss have finished, check the past forms of all the verbs. Then Ss can repeat the activity, this time adding a pronoun and changing the verb to the past form, e.g.
A: *old buildings.*
B: *I saw them.*

E Give Ss a few moments to read the example, then put them in pairs to ask and answer. Afterwards, ask two or three Ss to report back about their partner.

LISTENING

2A Give Ss a few minutes to read through the list and decide on their order. Tell them to be prepared to justify their choices. Check *sightseeing* (visiting famous/beautiful/interesting places).

B You could demonstrate this by telling Ss which holiday you put first/last and indicating that they should ask you why. Justify your choice. Put Ss in pairs to compare and justify their choices. They could then report back about any choices in common, e.g. *We both put b) a holiday in Surfer's Paradise for number one.*

3A Tell Ss that they'll hear different people talking about the holidays in Ex 2A and that they should just listen for whether each holiday was good or bad.

Answers: a) G **b)** B **c)** B **d)** G **e)** G

B Give Ss time to read through the sentences and check *lose/lost* (mime searching for something in your pockets/bag) and *lunch* vs *dinner* (midday vs evening meal). Also remind Ss that *get to/got to = arrive(d) in*. Ss can work in pairs to help each other remember the correct information before listening again to check.

Answers: 2 television **3** passport **4** food **5** got **6** dinner
7 Chinese **8** spoke

Unit 8 Recording 3

A: Welcome to *Good and Bad*. This week we talk about holidays – good holidays and bad holidays. Our hotline is 123 2222. And here's our first caller. Hello, Ken?
B: Hi.
A: So, tell us about your two holidays.
B: Yeah, well my family went camping in Canada when I was twelve. We had one tent for six people, and we didn't have water or electricity.
A: Oh, right. Did you like it?
B: Yes, I did. It was … fantastic. No TV, no internet … we cooked on a fire and played games.
A: Sounds great. And your other holiday?
B: Last year I went to Australia with my girlfriend, to Surfer's Paradise. I lost my passport on the first day.
A: Sorry to hear that.
B: But the beach at Surfer's Paradise was beautiful. The water was fantastic. We went swimming and just relaxed … but then I ate some bad food … fish … and I became very ill. I was ill for a week.
A: Ow. So that was a bad holiday. But as you say Surfer's Paradise is a beautiful place.
B: Yes, it is.
A: OK, Ken. Thank you for calling. Next caller, Clare? Are you there?
C: Yeah, hello.
A: Hi. Tell us about your holidays.
B: Well, last year we went to France, on a group tour.
A: Oh, where did you go?
B: We went to Paris, but … there was a problem with the plane. We waited for ten hours at the airport. Then they said there weren't any seats on the next plane. Or the next plane.
A: Oh, no! What did you do?
B: We went by train! We had five hours in Paris. We saw some interesting buildings and a museum and then we came home.
A: By plane?
B: No, by train. We had dinner on the train. Expensive sandwiches!
A: So that wasn't very good. How about your other holiday? The good one?
C: Ah yes, it was in China. I was there for two months. I was alone, so I met a lot of local people. They were very nice.
A: Did you speak English with them?
C: No, I didn't. I spoke a little Chinese and they liked that.

A: Great. Thanks, Clare. And next we have Dan. Hi, Dan.
D: Hi.
A: Is your first holiday good or bad?
D: Good – really good. I went to Peru. It was a walking holiday and it was wonderful.
A: Why was that?
D: Well, I went with a friend and we …

Optional extra activity

Tell Ss to read through the audio script and underline A's responses when the caller tells him something good or bad about the holiday. (Answers: Good: *Sounds great. Great.* Bad: *Sorry to hear that. Ow. So that was a bad holiday. Oh, no! So that wasn't very good.*)

Then put Ss in pairs and tell them to take turns to say something good or bad about a holiday. Their partner responds with an appropriate phrase, e.g.
A: I had some fantastic food in …
B: Sounds great.

GRAMMAR PAST SIMPLE: QUESTIONS

4A Play the recording once for Ss to listen to the questions and answers, then again for them to complete the table. Point out that *did* always comes before the pronoun in questions and that in a *Wh-* question, the *Wh-* word comes before *did*.

Answers:

Questions and short answers						
Did	you	like	it?	Yes,	I	did.
		speak	English?	No,		didn't.

Wh- questions				
Where	did	you	go?	
What			do?	

B **PRONUNCIATION linking: *did you?*** Play the recording again and ask Ss how the speaker says *Did you …?* Highlight the way that the final *-d* and initial *y-* merge together and make a 'j' sound, then model this for Ss to repeat. Play the recording again for Ss to repeat the complete questions (paying attention to their intonation) and answers.

▷ LANGUAGEBANK 8.2 p132–133

Give Ss a few minutes to read the Language bank and look at the examples of *Wh-* questions. Highlight that the question form is the same for regular and irregular verbs. You could use Ex 8.2A for some basic question and answer practice with irregular verbs and Ex 8.2B to review *Wh-* question words.

Answers:

A 2 A: Did, meet **B:** didn't, met
  3 A: Did, cry **B:** did, cried
  4 A: Did, see **B:** didn't, saw
  5 A: Did, write **B:** did, wrote
  6 A: Did, have **B:** did, had
B 2 Where did you go?
  3 What did you eat?
  4 What did you drink?
  5 What did you watch?
  6 When/What time did you come home?

5A Point out that Ss may need to add other words apart from *Did you*, then tell them to write the questions in their notebooks.

Answers:
2 Did you have a good time?
3 Did you meet (your) friends last night?
4 Did you speak English yesterday?
5 Did you have breakfast this morning?

B Tell Ss to write the completed answers next to the relevant questions in their notebooks.

Answers:
2 Yes, we did. We had a great time. We stayed in a good hotel.
3 No, I didn't. I stayed at home and watched a film on TV.
4 Yes, I did. I spoke English with my teacher.
5 No, I didn't. I wasn't hungry and I was late.

C Give Ss a few minutes to think about their answers to the questions. Before Ss start asking and answering in pairs, you could put prompts on the board for the questions in Ex 5A and use them to give Ss pronunciation practice, with a focus on intonation and the linking in *Did you …?* e.g. *go / holiday / last year ?*

▷ **PHOTOBANK** p146

Use these exercises to help Ss learn to talk about the weather. Give Ss a few minutes to go through Ex 1A. For Ex 1B, give Ss a few minutes to write their answers to the four questions, then put them in pairs to ask and answer.

Answers:
2 D   3 E   4 C   5 A   6 B

SPEAKING

6A Go through the example, pointing out that the student's note *Italy* tells us the question starts with *Where …?* Give Ss a few minutes to work on the questions alone, then check answers in pairs.

Answers: 2 Did   3 How   4 Where   5 How   6 How   7 What
8 Why

B If Ss have brought in photos from a holiday, they should refer to them while they make notes for this speaking activity, and think about when to incorporate them, e.g. to show who they went with, the weather, what they did. If you brought in maps for the warm up, Ss could use them to show where they went. Refer Ss to the notes in Ex 6A and point out that they only need to write two or three words. Give them time to prepare their notes, working alone, and circulate to give help as required.

C You could demonstrate by inviting Ss to ask you about a good holiday that you had and show them photos as you answer their questions. Then put Ss in groups of four to do the same. Monitor carefully and make notes of good language use and any problem areas for praise and correction afterwards.

WRITING *SO AND BECAUSE*

7A Start by eliciting some ideas from Ss about mistakes people make when they plan/book a holiday, e.g. they go in the summer holidays and the hotel/plane is expensive, etc. Then give Ss a minute or two to match the decision to the mistake. In the meantime, write sentences 1–3 on the board.

Answers: 1 c)   2 a)   3 b)

B Put the sentences on the board. Underline *so* and *because* and establish that *because* answers the question *why*?

C Write the two sentences on the board and go through the answers with the class. Point out that *so = that's why* (it gives the reason).

Answers: 1 because   2 so

D Point out that the first and second part of the sentence have 'changed place'. You could go through the first sentence with the class, then give Ss a minute or two to complete the other two.

Answers:
1 … we went camping.
2 … I thought the city was dangerous.
3 … we were hungry.

8A Ss work on this exercise alone before comparing answers.

Answers:
1 Our plane was at three *so* we got to the airport at two.
2 I didn't book a hotel *because* I didn't have time.
3 We went to New Zealand in July *because* we have school holidays in the summer.
4 There was no mineral water *so* we drank the local water.

B Look at the example with the class and elicit a possible ending, e.g. *so we missed our flight*. If Ss need some help with ideas for situations 2–4, put the following prompts on the board:
2 sleep / car / hotels / full
3 July / winter / New Zealand / weather / cold
4 ill / water / bad

C Tell Ss the bad holiday can be real or invented. They could also use ideas from the radio programme in Ex 3. Elicit ways of starting the email, e.g.
Hi! How are you? I arrived home from my holiday (yesterday) – it was (terrible/awful)!
First, … Big mistake …! Then, …
I'm happy/It's good to be home!
Where did you go on holiday? Email me about it!
Take care/See you soon.

Homework ideas
Workbook: Ex 1–5, p52–53

WHERE IS IT?

Introduction

Ss practise listening to and giving directions and learn to use prepositions of place with accurate word stress. They also learn to use examples to explain word meanings.

> **SUPPLEMENTARY MATERIALS**
> **Resource bank:** p172
> **Ex 7 (optional extra activity):** prepare cards for students A and B (see notes).

Warm up

Review the names of things you can buy in a supermarket. Say *I went to the supermarket and I bought (bread)* then indicate that the nearest student should continue by saying *I went to the supermarket and I bought bread and (cheese)*. They choose another student who has to remember the two things already mentioned and add one more, and so on. If a student can't remember everything, they say *Pass* and choose another student. To make it more challenging, Ss say the items in alphabetical order. (NB: Avoid using *some* because Ss haven't studied uncountable nouns.)

SPEAKING

1 Check *Where did you last buy some food?* (= the last time you bought food, where did you buy it?) Then focus Ss on the photo of the supermarket and elicit some responses from the class to question 1. Put Ss in pairs to discuss the questions.

VOCABULARY PREPOSITIONS OF PLACE

2A Look at the example with the class, then put Ss in pairs to match the other prepositions to the pictures.

B Play the recording for Ss to check their answers. With the class, check the difference between *in front of* and *opposite*: the two things/people are facing each other if they are *opposite*; *near* and *next to*: *next to* is closer than *near*.

> **Answers:** **A** in front of **B** behind **C** next to **D** near
> **E** on the left of **F** on the right of **G** opposite **H** between

C PRONUNCIATION word stress: prepositions Write the six stress patterns in a row on the board and tell Ss to do the same in their notebooks. Tell Ss to write the prepositions under the correct pattern and play the first one on the recording as an example. Then play the recording, pausing if necessary to give Ss time to think and write. Ss check answers in pairs. Play the recording again for Ss to repeat.

> **Answers:**
>
> | O | Oo | oO | Ooo | oOo | ooOo |
> |---|----|----|-----|-----|------|
> | near | next to | behind | opposite | in front of | on the left of |
> | | | between | | | on the right of |

D Ask two Ss to demonstrate the example, then Ss practise in pairs.

Alternative approach

Tell Ss to close their books. Use objects on your desk to show Ss the eight prepositions in Ex 2A. One at a time, position the objects and ask, e.g. *Where's the (key)?* eliciting the preposition from the Ss if possible. Ss then open their books and do Ex 2A.

Put Ss in pairs to practise with their own objects on their desks, e.g. A says *Put your pen on the right of your notebook* and B moves the objects into the correct position. Alternatively, Ss take turns to tell their partner to stand in different places in the classroom, e.g. *Stand near the door/opposite the teacher.*

3A Check *window* and *picture* before Ss read the sentences. They tick the sentences that are true and check with a partner.

B Change one sentence with the class as an example, e.g. *There are some windows opposite the door.* Ss work in pairs on the other sentences. They could also add one or two sentences of their own and read these out to the class.

Optional extra activity

In groups, each student draws a simple picture showing the location of two or three items, e.g. *a cat, a chair, a book.* Then they whisper a sentence describing the picture to the person next to them, etc. until it gets back to the original student – they then see if the sentence that came back to them is the same as in the picture.

FUNCTION GIVING DIRECTIONS

4A Give Ss time to read through the types of food and check *cereal* (e.g. cornflakes) and *snacks* (small amounts of food you eat between meals, at a party, etc.). Play the recording. Point out that while Ss listen, they just need to write the numbers 2 and 3 next to the appropriate food.

> **Answers:** bread – 2   cakes – 3

B Establish that Ss write a letter for a section of the supermarket next to each food. Using the diagram or a simple board drawing, explain that *opposite* is used to describe two sections that are across the aisle from each other. Play the recording again.

> **Answers:** bread e)   cereal d)   cakes a)

Unit 8 Recording 6

Conversation 1
A: Excuse me, where's the fruit?
B: Do you see the vegetables over there?
A: Vegetables? What are they?
B: Vegetables … you know, tomatoes, potatoes, carrots.
A: Oh, vegetables.
B: Yeah. Vegetables.
A: OK … vegetables.
B: The fruit's behind the vegetables.
A: Sorry?
B: You see the vegetables? They're in front of the fruit. Over there.
A: Let me check. The fruit's behind the vegetables.
B: Yes, that's right.
A: Oh, OK. Thanks.
B: No problem.

Conversation 2
A: Excuse me, where's the bread?
B: Er … Do you see the snacks?
A: Snacks? I don't know 'snacks'.
B: Snacks, for example, chocolate, nuts and crisps.
A: Oh, I understand.
B: The bread is on the right of the snacks.
A: Can I check? On the right of the snacks?
B: Yes. Opposite the fruit.
A: Thank you.
B: You're welcome.

Conversation 3
A: Excuse me, where are the cakes?
B: I think they're near the snacks.
A: Near the snacks. Which way?
B: I'm not sure. I know the cereal is opposite the snacks …
A: Cereal? What's that?
B: Cereal. Like Corn Flakes.
A: Er …?
B: Erm, for breakfast. You have it with milk.
A: Oh, OK.
B: Yes, so the cereal is opposite the snacks.

A: OK, and the cakes?
B: I think they're on the right of the cereal.
A: On the right. Thank you.
B: No problem. Or maybe …
A: Thank you!

Optional extra activity

Use the diagram in Ex 4B. Tell Ss to write the names of each type of food in the correct section and to allocate sections b) and c) to meat and fish. Then Ss work in pairs and take turns asking and answering *Where's the …?/Where are the …? It's (behind) the …/They're (next to) the …* For more of a challenge, tell the person answering that they need to give at least two prepositions for each type of food, e.g. *Where's the cereal? It's opposite the drinks and in front of the cakes.*

5A Ss could complete the conversation in pairs or working alone. For **stronger classes**, you could tell Ss to cover the words in the box and try to complete the gaps with their own ideas. (NB: At this level, treat *Let me check* as a fixed phrase that we use to see if we understand.)

Answers: 2 where **3** Do **4** see **5** over **6** of **7** Let **8** behind

B Before putting Ss in pairs, you could model the lines of the conversation for them to repeat in chorus, focusing on stress and polite intonation. When Ss have practised the conversation once or twice reading from the book, encourage them to try to remember as much as they can or to write one or two word prompts for each line. Then they close their books and practise again.

C Before Ss change the names of the food and the prepositions in the conversation, tell them to write the names of each type of food in the correct section on the supermarket diagram, and to allocate sections b) and c) to meat and fish. Give Ss a minute or two to change the conversation, then move them around so they are with new partners. Then they take turns to role-play each other's conversations.

▷ LANGUAGEBANK 8.3 p132–133

Give Ss time to read through the summary, including *Can I check?* as an alternative to *Let me check*. Ss could then do Ex 8.3 and practise the conversation in pairs.

Answers:
A: Excuse me, where ~~is~~ are the sweets?
B: ~~Are~~ Do you see the newspapers over there?
A: Where?
B: Over there, near ~~of~~ the snacks.
A: Oh, yes.
B: Well, the sweets are next *to* the newspapers, on the right.
A: Can I check? They're *on* the left of the newspapers.
B: No, they're on *the* right.
A: Ah, yes. Thanks a lot.
B: No problem.

LEARN TO   USE EXAMPLES

6A Before you play the recording, give Ss time to read the conversations and try to predict the missing words. Play the recording. Ss check answers in pairs.

Answers: 1 What **2** know **3** example **4** that **5** Like

Unit 8 Recording 7

1
A: Vegetables? What are they?
B: Vegetables … you know, tomatoes, potatoes, carrots.
A: Oh, vegetables.

2
B: Do you see the snacks?
A: Snacks? I don't know 'snacks'.
B: Snacks, for example, chocolate, nuts and crisps.
A: Oh, I understand.

3
A: Cereal? What's that?
B: Cereal. Like Corn Flakes, porridge.

speakout TIP

Before Ss read the Speakout tip, ask them to look through the three conversations and find three ways of giving examples. Then they can read the tip to check. You could also play the recording again and pause after the person gives each example for Ss to repeat. Point out that there is a pause after *you know* and *for example*, so Ss intonation should rise on *know* and *example*. After *like* there is no pause.

B Ss could practise the conversations twice, so they take turns to be A and B.

C Demonstrate this with a **strong student** taking the part of A. Check that Ss understand *dairy*.

SPEAKING

7A Give Ss a few minutes to decide where to put the types of food and to think about how to explain where they are in relation to the other sections. (NB: Ensure Ss realise where they're standing – *You are here* – so they use *behind* and *in front of* accurately.)

B Do an example with the class first, showing Ss that they shouldn't show their diagram to their partner. Monitor carefully, making notes of any good language use and any problem areas for praise and correction afterwards.

Optional extra activity

Put Ss in pairs and explain that Student A is new to Student B's city/town (i.e. the city/town where Ss are studying). A wants to buy some things and asks B who explains where to find them, e.g.
A: Excuse me, where's a good place to buy (pens)?
B: OK, go to (name of shop). It's in (name) street, (next to/near) …
Tell Bs that if they don't understand what A wants, they should ask for examples.
Give As the following on a card/slip of paper: *You want to buy crockery (plates, cups, bowls); jewellery (rings, earrings, bracelets); stationery (paper, pens, pencils).*
Then B is the new person in town, with the following on a card/slip of paper: *You want to buy toiletries (soap, toothpaste, deodorant); furniture (tables, chairs, beds); sports equipment (footballs, tennis racquets, skis).*

Homework ideas

- Ss have a friend staying with them who has offered to go to the supermarket for them. They write a note to leave on the kitchen table for their friend, telling them five things they need and where to find them in the supermarket. Check that Ss know *aisle*, e.g. *it's in the second aisle/the biscuits and snacks aisle, near the …*
- **Workbook:** Ex1–3, p54

GUIDED TOUR

Introduction

Ss watch an extract from the BBC comedy show *Little Britain*, about people on holiday in Spain and their rude tour guide. Ss then learn and practise how to tell a story about a bad holiday, and write a travel review.

> **SUPPLEMENTARY MATERIALS**
> **Ex 4C (optional extra activity)**: make a copy of the key phrases to display on the board with the past verb forms removed.

Warm up

Review some common verb + noun collocations. Tell Ss to write each of the following verbs inside a circle, with three 'branches' from each circle, for them to add nouns/phrases: *take, have, stay, go*. Read out the following nouns and phrases, pausing for Ss to write each one next to the correct verb: *a photo, fun, dinner, home, in bed, a guided tour, a good time, at home, a bus/train, out in the evening, in a hotel, on holiday*. Give Ss a few minutes to compare answers in pairs and check their spelling. Check *a guided tour* (a visit to a place with a guide who tells you things about the place).

> **Answers:**
> *take: a photo, a guided tour, a bus/train*
> *have: fun, dinner, a good time*
> *stay: in bed, at home, in a hotel*
> *go: home, out in the evening, on holiday*

DVD PREVIEW

1A Give Ss a few minutes to tick the relevant sentences and tell them to be prepared to justify their answers using *because*, e.g. *On holiday, I always read about the place because I want to see all the important things.*

B Put Ss in pairs and encourage them to ask each other about other things, e.g.

A: *I always relax and do nothing because that's the meaning of 'holiday' for me!*
B: *Same for me! What other things do you do?*
A: *I get up late!*

2 Give Ss a minute or two to read the questions and check that they understand *funny* (demonstrate by laughing), *tour guide* (or *rep*, short for *representative*, which is how Carol describes herself in the extract), *episode* (a TV programme that is part of a series). Then direct Ss to the text. When they've decided if the sentences are true or false, they can compare answers in pairs.

> **Answers:** **1** T: it's a *comedy* **2** F: a man (David Walliams) plays Carol
> **3** F: she's rude **4** T

Culture note

Little Britain is a sketch show which features exaggerated parodies of British people in various situations familiar to the British. A narrator comments on the sketches in a way which suggests that the programme is a guide – for non-British people – to the ways of life of different classes in British society.

Majorca is a very popular tourist destination for the British because of its good weather and cheap prices, and because there are a lot of British people there and British products are readily available – it's like a sunny version of Britain.

DVD VIEW

3A Ss use the text to help them decide which photo is Carol.

B Play the DVD to confirm which photo is Carol.

> **Answer:** photo B

C Give Ss time to read through the phrases before you play the extract again. They can compare answers in pairs and/or with the whole class.

> **Answers:** **a)** 5 **b)** 3 **c)** 6 **e)** 2 **f)** 4 **g)** 7

D Go through the example (you could play the first part of the DVD extract to the close up of the sign that Carol is holding), then put Ss in pairs to discuss the others and correct as necessary. Check *the couple* (the man and woman who speak to Carol) and *throw something off the bus* (mime). As you play the DVD for Ss to check their answers, you could ask them to shout 'Stop!' at the appropriate point and tell you the number of the sentence and whether it's true or false.

> **Answers:** **2** F: Carol doesn't answer **3** T
> **4** F: she says, '… you'll see Spain' **5** F: Carol speaks bad Spanish
> **6** T **7** T **8** F: the bus leaves

E Put Ss in groups to discuss their answers and who found the programme funny, and if so, why (e.g. Carol's face, her voice, her bad pronunciation of Spanish). Ask a few groups to share their opinions with the class.

Optional extra activity

Ss work in groups of three and discuss what the couple from the DVD extract did next (e.g. they walked, they waited for a car to come along the road, they phoned a taxi). Then they prepare a conversation between the couple and the tour company manager, explaining what happened. The manager apologises and offers some kind of compensation. While Ss prepare the conversation, help with vocabulary as necessary. The groups then act out their conversation for the class.

DVD 8 Guided Tour

N = Narrator   C = Carol   H = Husband   W = Wife

N: Spain is very popular for tourists from Britain. Here in Majorca Carol Beer is the friendly tour guide for Sunsearchers Holidays.
H: Sunsearchers. Er, this must be us, dear.
W: Morning.
H: Morning.
C: Hello, my name is Carol. I am your rep. Welcome to Spain. If you look to your left, you'll see Spain. If you look to your right, you'll see Spain. Now I'm here to make sure your holiday is fun, fun, fun. Fun. Any questions or problems, come to me.
H: Excuse me. … Excuse me.
C: Yes, old man?
H: Sorry, sorry, ah, my wife's feeling rather nauseous. Do you think it would be possible just to stop the coach for a moment so she can get out and get some air?
C: Gonzalez, ¿puedes parar el bus?
H: Thank you. Thank you, excuse me. OK, all right.
C: Gonzalez, vamos.
H: OK, yeah? It must be something you had on the plane or …
W: My stomach!
H: Hey, hey, hey, hey! Hey, hey! It's all right.

speakout a bad holiday story

4A You could write on the board: *The man had a bad holiday because …* and tell Ss to think of as many reasons as they can, in pairs. Remind them that they can use *so*, *because* and linkers such as *first*, *then* and *the first day/night*, *the next day/night*. At the end, ask some pairs to tell the class their ideas.

> **Suggested answers:** The man had a bad holiday because … first, he missed the plane. Then it rained, so he stayed in the hotel and he was bored. He didn't sleep because the hotel room was noisy, and the hotel restaurant was expensive. He was happy to go home.

B Tell Ss to look at the pictures while they listen and find the difference. Play the recording.

> **Answer:** Picture **C** – the man didn't watch TV. He read a book.

C Give Ss a few moments to read the key phrases. Check *dirty* (mime looking through a window and not being able to see, then cleaning it). Then play the recording again for Ss to tick the phrases.

> **Answers:**
> I missed my [plane ✓/train/bus].
> I arrived [in Honolulu ✓] one [hour/day ✓/week] late.
> I lost my [passport/money/bags].
> It rained for [the first three days ✓/all week].
> I stayed in [my hotel room ✓/the café] all day.
> The hotel was [noisy ✓/expensive/dirty].
> The food was [bad/expensive ✓].
> I was very happy to go home. ✓

> **Optional extra activity**
> To give Ss some practice of the key phrases before they make their own version of the story, either make a copy (large enough to display on the board) of the phrases with the past verb forms removed, or write the phrases on the board, e.g.
> I _____ my (plane/train/bus).
> I _____ one (hour/day/week) late.
> I _____ my (passport/money/bags).
> It _____ for the first (three days/week), etc.
> Tell Ss to close their books and elicit the complete phrases from the class, one at a time, prompting the class to repeat the phrase in chorus and/or individually.

5A Elicit one or two examples from the class of how they could change the story, e.g. *First, I missed my train, so I waited for six hours in the station and took another train*, etc. You could also encourage Ss to use different adjectives to describe the hotel and the food (e.g. hotel: *crowded*, *old*; food: *boring*, *cold*). When Ss have decided on the changes, they should practise telling the story until they can remember it with the pictures in front of them, but without looking at the key phrases (tell them to cover the key phrases when they're ready).

B Move each student along one place in the class, so they're working with a new partner. Encourage them to sound interested while they're listening to their partner's story, e.g. by saying *Oh no! Really? That's awful!* etc. When both Ss have told their story, they should note down the differences, then two or three pairs report back to the class. Monitor the practice closely and be prepared to give praise for good language use and deal with any problem areas afterwards.

> **Unit 8** Recording 8
>
> This is my bad holiday story. Last year I went to Hawaii on holiday. First, I missed my plane, so I took another plane. I arrived in Honolulu one day late. The weather was very bad, and it rained for the first three days. I stayed in my hotel room and read a book. The hotel was noisy because my room was next to the road. There was a restaurant, but the food was expensive, and it wasn't very good. I was there for two weeks, and I was very happy to go home.

writeback a travel review

6A Establish that a review tells you good and bad things about something (e.g. *a restaurant*, *a hotel*, *a book*, *a film*) and ask Ss where they can find travel reviews (in a magazine, on the internet). Tell Ss to read the review and write *P* or *N* in the margin next to the positive and negative things they find. Give them a minute or two to compare answers in pairs.

> **Answers:**
> 3 positive things: the journey, the hotel, the restaurant
> 2 negative things: the hotel room, the weather

B For ***weaker classes***, go through the sections of the Edinburgh review, highlighting useful phrases:
Last … we went to …
I went with …
We took a … to …
It was a … journey
We stayed at the …, in/near …
It was/wasn't …
The people were/weren't …
Our favourite … was …
It's a good idea to …
Also remind Ss to use a variety of adjectives to describe their experience:
hotel: cheap/expensive, lovely/terrible
hotel room: small/big, noisy/quiet, clean/dirty
people: friendly/not very friendly
food: delicious/fantastic/not very good/awful
If Ss can't think of a place to review, they could start by working in pairs and brainstorming ideas. Circulate and help with vocabulary while Ss write their reviews.

C Either put Ss in groups of four to read each other's reviews, or display the reviews round the class so that Ss can walk round and read them. Ss can then vote on the best place to visit either in their group or with the whole class.

> **Homework ideas**
> Ss either write a final draft of the travel review they wrote in class, making improvements, corrections, etc., or they write another travel review.

LOOKBACK

PAST SIMPLE: IRREGULAR VERBS

1A Go through the example with the class, then give Ss time to complete the sentences and compare answers in pairs.

Answers:
2 Two students came to class late for this lesson.
3 I thought English was difficult, but now I think it's easy.
4 I went home by train last night.
5 I didn't sit here last lesson.
6 I didn't have breakfast at home.
7 I saw the teacher in a supermarket yesterday.

B Demonstrate how Ss can change any part of the sentence, e.g.
I met <u>my sister</u> in a café yesterday.
I met a friend <u>at the gym</u> yesterday.
I met a friend in a café <u>on Saturday</u>.
I <u>didn't meet</u> a friend in a café yesterday.

C You could encourage Student A to read their sentences in random order, so Student B has to listen carefully to find their equivalent sentence. For **stronger classes**, Ss could also report back on what they found in common, e.g. *We both met a friend in a café on Saturday.* (NB: If the answer is negative, Ss can simply say: *We didn't meet a friend in a café*, or you could introduce the phrase: *Neither of us (met a friend in a café yesterday).*)

PREPOSITIONS OF PLACE

2A Tell Ss to circle all the examples of *in*, *on* or *at* as they complete the sentences.

Answers: 1 home, work   2 car, bike   3 holiday, Rome
4 class, street

B Go through the example with the class and point out that Ss can write any sentences they want but they must start with the words in bold and the sentences must contain two prepositions: *in*, *on* or *at*.

C Ss read out their sentences to each other and comment on anything that is similar/different, e.g. *Really? Me too. Really? I'm surprised.*

HOLIDAY ACTIVITIES

3A You could run this as a competition in teams. Write or display the words on the board, one at a time. When a team member guesses a word, they put up their hand to answer and say the missing vowels only. They win a point for each correct vowel and continue until they make a mistake (and another team can continue) or finish the phrase.

Alternative approach
Run the activity as a team game, but for each phrase just write the correct number of dashes on the board. Teams guess one missing letter at a time, winning a point for each correct letter and losing a point if the letter isn't in the phrase.

Answers: 2 speak English   3 see old buildings
4 drink the local water   5 eat the local food   6 become ill
7 have a good time   8 meet the local people

B Put Ss in pairs or small groups to discuss the questions. Ss could also think of other activities that they do on each of the three holidays, e.g. *relax and do nothing, take a guided tour, take lots of photos, go shopping, go out in the evening, go to museums and galleries, play games, cook on a fire.*

PAST SIMPLE: QUESTIONS

4A Start by eliciting how to make questions in the past simple, i.e. *Did* + subject + verb/*Wh-* + *did* + subject + verb. Ss work alone, then compare answers in pairs.

Answers: 2 What did you *do*?   3 Did you *meet* any friends?
4 Where did you *go*?   5 a) Did you buy anything? (correct)
b) What *did* you buy?
6 a) *Did you* see a film at the cinema or on TV? b) What *was* it?

B Before Ss start asking and answering, remind them how to make short answers in the past, i.e. *Yes* + subject + *did*/*No* + subject + *didn't*. When Ss have finished, they could ask other Ss in the class about their partners, e.g. *Maria, did Sonja have a good weekend? Yes, she did.* etc.

Optional extra activity
Review the weather vocabulary from the Photo bank.
Write the following on six slips of paper and give them to six Ss:
It was windy./It was hot and sunny./It was cold./It was cloudy./It rained./It snowed.
Ss mime their weather for the rest of the class who try to guess the answer.
Then put Ss in pairs to ask each other the following questions (point out that *last* means *the last time*):
When was it last hot and sunny?   When was it last cold?
When was it last cloudy?   When was it last windy?
When did it last rain?   When did it last snow?

PREPOSITIONS

5A You could run this as a race in pairs or as a competition in teams. To win points, Ss need to say the word and spell it correctly.

Answers: 1 right   2 between   3 next   4 left   5 behind
6 opposite   7 near   8 front

B When Ss have found the mistakes, they write three sentences to describe where the things are in the picture.

Answers: In the picture:
2 The tree is between the shop and the <u>road</u>.
5 The man is behind the <u>shop</u>.
6 The woman is <u>in front of</u> the <u>house</u>.
7 The <u>shop</u> is near the car. OR The house is near the <u>road</u>.

GIVING DIRECTIONS

6 Give Ss a few minutes to put the words in the correct places in the sentences, working alone.

Answers:
A: Excuse me, where *are* the cakes?
B: Do you see the fruit over *there*?
A: Where?
B: Over there, *near* the magazines.
A: Yes, I see it.
B: Well, the cakes are *next* to the fruit. On the left.
A: Let me check that. They're on the left *of* the fruit.
B: Right.
A: On *the* right?
B: No, you were right. On the *left*.
A: I see. Thank you.
B: *No* problem.

CONSOLIDATION 4: UNITS 7–8

Introduction

The aim of the consolidation units is for Ss to revise and practise the grammar, vocabulary and pronunciation from the previous two units in a different context. The context for this consolidation unit is a murder mystery story.

READING AND GRAMMAR

Warm up

Use the pictures (tell Ss to cover the rest of the page) to check the following vocabulary: *a hotel, play tennis, listen to the radio, a cleaner, a body/a dead person, kill someone*. Then put Ss in pairs and tell them to think of a story that connects all these things. Give them a few minutes to make notes (reminding them to use the past to tell the story), then put the pairs together into groups of four to tell each other their stories. Invite one pair from each group to tell the rest of the class their story.

1A Give Ss a minute to skim the article and find the answer to the question.

> **Answer:** Someone killed him./He died.

Optional extra activity

Write/Display the following questions on the board for Ss to answer as they read the text again:
1 Where is the hotel? (Edinburgh.)
2 What did Rose Green do? (She found the body.)
3 Was Jim Black rich? (Yes, very rich.)
4 Did he die in the hotel? (No, behind it.)
5 When did he die? (Between ten o'clock and midnight.)
6 Who's Carla? (Jim's wife.)
7 Who's Mike Brown? (Jim's business partner.)

B Establish that the police *interview* Mike and Carla and take their *statements*. Elicit some examples of questions they might ask (e.g. *Where were you between … and …?*) then give Ss a few minutes to complete the questions, working alone.

> **Answers:**
> 2 Did you see Jim yesterday afternoon?
> 3 Did you have dinner with Jim and Carla?
> 4 What time did you go to your room?
> 5 Where were you between ten o'clock and midnight?

C Check that Ss understand *witness* (someone who sees a crime or, as in this case, says what they know about a crime). Tell Ss to find the answers to the questions in the statement and answer them as if they are Mike.

> **Answers:** 1 Yes, we were. 2 Yes, I did. 3 Yes, I did.
> 4 At ten o'clock. 5 In my room.

Optional extra activity

Ss role-play the interview between a police officer and Mike Brown. They could add one or two extra questions of their own, e.g. *Did you talk to Jim at dinner? What time did you go to bed?*

2A Give Ss a few minutes to complete the statement, working alone.

> **Answers:** 2 were 3 weren't 4 didn't like 5 played 6 walked
> 7 went 8 wrote 9 came 10 didn't talk 11 met 12 had
> 13 wanted 14 was

B Give Ss time to find the differences on their own.

> **Answers:**
> 1 **Mike:** Jim Black was a good friend.
>   **Carla:** They weren't friends. Mike didn't like Jim.
> 2 **Mike:** At half past three, we went to our rooms in the hotel.
>   **Carla:** Jim came back at six.
> They also both say that the other person killed Jim.

C Ss could discuss what reasons each person possibly had for killing Jim, and who they think did it at this stage. Possible reasons: Carla wanted his money; Carla thought he had another woman; Mike wanted his part of the business; Jim discovered that Mike took money from the business and Mike wanted to 'silence' him; Mike and Carla were in love and killed Jim together.

LISTENING AND GRAMMAR

3A Draw a clock face on the board and briefly review how to tell the time: *o'clock, quarter past, half past, quarter to*, also *ten to/ten past*. Give Ss time to read through the information in the table before you play the recording. Ss can compare answers in pairs.

> **Answers:** 1 b) 3.30 2 10.00 3 10.00–11.00 4 a) 10.00
> 4 b) 10.15 5 10.30

B Before you play the recording again, give Ss a minute or two to read through the statements. As you check the answers, elicit any differences between what these witnesses said and Mike and Carla's statements, e.g. *Carla said she danced with Jim from 10.00 to 11.00, but the waiter says she danced with one of the men from 9.30 to 10.00, before Mike left the restaurant; the guest says the radio was on in Jim and Carla's room at the time Carla said she danced with Jim.*

> **Answers:** 2 T 3 F 4 F 5 T

C Ss could discuss this as a class. The most likely answer is that it was Carla, in a man's clothes.

Consolidation 4 Recording 1

1
My name's Sara. I'm the receptionist in the hotel. Mr Black and Mr Brown went out yesterday afternoon at a quarter to two. They came back together … at about half past three, and they went to their rooms.

2
My name's Alan. I'm a waiter in the hotel restaurant. I was in the restaurant last night. There were two men and a woman in the restaurant all evening. One man and the woman danced for about half an hour – from half past nine to ten o'clock. They all left at ten o'clock.

3
I'm a guest in the hotel. My room is on the right of Mr and Mrs Black's room. Their radio was on last night from about ten to eleven. It was very noisy!

4
I'm the night receptionist. Mr Black went out at ten o'clock. He said he wanted to take a walk. Then at a quarter past ten, another man went out. I didn't see him very well. Maybe it was Mr Brown. I don't know.

5
My name's Mary White. I'm a guest in the hotel. I came back from the town at about half past ten. I saw a woman in front of the hotel. She had men's clothes: a man's jacket, a man's trousers and a man's hat. I was surprised, you know. A woman in a man's clothes. Was there a party or something?

SPEAKING

4A The idea of this role-play is that Students A and B provide an alibi for each other by saying they were together somewhere else at the time of a robbery. The 'police' try to find differences between their stories, to prove that they were the robbers.

Put Ss into groups of at least four: the two suspects (students A and B) and at least two police officers (there could be up to six police officers, i.e. groups of up to eight).

Direct Ss A and B to p149 and tell them to read the information and start preparing their answers. If possible, they should go out of the room to prepare their story, but if this isn't practical, divide the classroom and ask all the As and Bs to move to one side so the other people in their group (the police officers) can't hear them.

At the same time, the police officers read the information and put the four questions in order.

Answers:
1. What time did you arrive at the restaurant?
2. What was the restaurant's name?
3. What did you eat?
4. How much did it cost?

B You could give the police some prompts to help them to write further questions: *what/drink? a lot/other people/restaurant? waiter/waitress? time/leave? do/next?* In the meantime, check that Ss A and B are preparing their story and emphasise that it must be exactly the same because the police will question them separately. Prompt them with ideas about other things the police might ask about.

C Divide each group of police officers in half: they question Student A and Student B at the same time, then swap, so that both groups of police officers have questioned both suspects.

D The police officers work together to compare A's and B's answers, and decide if they are the robbers. Ask the police from the different groups to report back to the class about their decisions, and see which robbers got away with it!

SOUNDS: /ʌ/ AND /ʊ/

5A Direct Ss to the pictures and point out that the symbols represent the sounds. Play the recording for Ss to listen to the sounds and the words. You could also show Ss that to make /ʊ/ their mouth is rounded with lips pushed forward, then for /ʌ/ their jaw needs to drop.

B You may want to ask Ss to predict which group the words belong to before they listen. You could pause the recording after each group of words and ask individual Ss to repeat them, rather than Ss repeating in chorus. This will give you more opportunity to correct their pronunciation of the 'target' sounds.

Answers:
/ʌ/ month, country, hungry, colour
/ʊ/ good, cook, look, full

6A/B Look at the example with the class, then put Ss in pairs to work out the answers. Alternatively, you could put Ss in teams and run this as a competition, writing/reading out one section at a time (Ss close their books).

Answers:
brother, husband, son
bus
Russia
Sunday, Monday
one
football
good book
push, pull
July
sugar

Homework ideas

- Ss write Carla's confession: why she killed Jim and how she did it.
- Ss write an email from Sara, the receptionist at the hotel, to a friend or family member, telling them about the events of the past two days, i.e. the dead businessman, the police interviews, etc.
- **Workbook:** Ex 1–6, p55–56

BBC interviews and worksheet

Where did you go on holiday last year?

In this video people talk about the holiday they had last year. They describe holiday activities and say whether they enjoyed themselves. The material consolidates the use of the past simple (regular and irregular verbs), lifestyle vocabulary and phrases for expressing opinions.

9 shopping

OVERVIEW

BBC ◗ INTERVIEWS

Do you like shopping?

In this video people talk about whether they like shopping and shopping mistakes they have made. The material enables Ss to revise structures and vocabulary related to expressing opinions and shopping or spending money. Use the video as an introduction to the unit or at the end of the unit to revise the language learnt.

A WASTE OF MONEY

Introduction

Ss practise listening to people talking about shopping mistakes. They practise talking about shopping and things that are a waste of money, using object pronouns and vocabulary related to money. They also practise using linking with object pronouns and learn how to write listings to sell things online.

> **SUPPLEMENTARY MATERIALS**
> **Resource bank:** p173 and p175
> **Ex 1A (alternative approach):** prepare a handout with statements about shopping (see notes).
> **Ex 6C:** take in photos of objects for Ss to write captions.

Warm up

Tell Ss to close their books and write the title *A waste of money* on the board. Illustrate the meaning of the phrase by telling an anecdote, e.g. *This morning I bought a coffee on my way to school, but I didn't have time to drink it and now it's cold and I don't like it. It was a waste of money.*

Write the following statements on the board (or ask Ss to think of their own examples):

CDs Flowers Holidays Newspapers Birthday cards	*are a waste of money.*

Put Ss in pairs and tell them to choose two statements and think of reasons why they're true, e.g. *Newspapers are a waste of money because people see the news on TV and read the news on the internet.* Then invite a few pairs to tell the class their ideas.

VOCABULARY   MONEY

1A You could start by telling Ss whether you like shopping and explain why/why not. Then put Ss in pairs to discuss, and invite one or two Ss to report back to the class about their partners' opinions afterwards.

> **Alternative approach**
> Prepare a handout with the following sentences and ask Ss to circle the options to make the statements true for them:
> 1 I go shopping *once/twice/three times a week/month/year.*
> 2 I *often/don't often* go shopping *at the weekend/after work or school.*
> 3 I usually go shopping *with my friend(s)/with my (mother)/on my own.*
> 4 I like shopping for *clothes/shoes/gifts/books/things for the house/(other).*
> 5 I prefer *small shops/big shops/markets.*
> Ss then compare and justify their answers in pairs.

B Tell Ss to focus on the sentences with the verbs in bold at the moment, and that they'll have time to answer the questions in Ex 1C.

> **Answers:** 1 buy 2 sell 3 pay 4 cost 5 get

C Put Ss in pairs and tell As to close their books and answer Bs as they read out the questions, then swap roles. In this way Ss will need to listen to each other, rather than simply reading the questions in their Students' Books. Ask a few pairs to tell the class how many of their answers were the same.

2A Give Ss time to write the past forms working alone using their dictionaries.

> **Answers:** 1 bought 2 sold 3 paid 4 cost (point out that there are a few irregular verbs like this, that have the same form in the past) 5 gave 6 got

Teaching tip

A good English–English dictionary will have a list of irregular verbs at the front or back. Encourage Ss to check the past form of any new verb to see if it is regular or irregular.

B You may want to ask Ss to just listen the first time you play the recording, to familiarise themselves with the sentences, then play the recording again for them to repeat. Make sure Ss repeat the infinitive, the past form and the example sentence.

C Demonstrate this with one or two Ss first. You could tell *stronger Ss* to respond with a short example sentence (similar to the ones on the recording) rather than just the past form.

▷ PHOTOBANK p146

To practise more about the language of money, get Ss to complete Ex 1A alone and discuss Ex 1B in pairs.

> **Answers:**
> 1 E 2 A 3 D 4 G 5 C 6 F 7 H 8 B

LISTENING

3A Direct Ss to the pictures and see if they can name any of the objects without looking at the words in the box. Then give them a minute or two to match the words from the box and check answers in pairs.

> **Answers:** A a hat B a lamp C a tent D an exercise bike
> E drums

B Ss could discuss this in pairs or together as a class. Encourage Ss to justify their opinions, i.e. why they think the object is good to have or a waste of money.

C Before you play the recording, check *break – broke* (mime breaking something) and *fix* (regular verb). Also give an example of a shopping mistake, i.e. something you bought that you didn't use/ like. Tell Ss to write the letter of the picture next to speakers 1–5.

> **Answers:** 1 C 2 D 3 A 4 E 5 B

Optional extra activity

Ss listen again for more detail. Write the following sentences on the board and tell Ss to listen to the recording and correct the sentences:
1 He never used the tent. *(He used the tent once.)*
2 His wife used the bike three times. *(He used the bike three times.)*
3 Her boyfriend liked the hat. *(Her friend liked the hat./ Her boyfriend didn't like the hat.)*
4 The little boy never plays the drums. *(The little boy plays the drums all day.)*
5 The lamp wasn't expensive. *(The lamp cost a lot of money.)*

D Start by showing Ss the meaning of *too big/small* and *the wrong size/colour*. You could do this with simple board drawings (e.g. a person with a very small hat and a very big coat) or by borrowing one or two items from Ss, e.g. a jacket that's too small for you, a watch that's too big, a tie/scarf (for *the wrong colour*). Go through the example with the class, then give Ss time to choose a mistake and prepare what they're going to say about it. (NB: If a student doesn't have an example of a shopping mistake, tell them to invent one. Put Ss in groups of 4–5 to talk about their mistakes.)

Unit 9 Recording 3

1   A shopping mistake? Um … well, my boyfriend wanted to go camping, so I bought him a tent. It was a good tent. I paid seventy pounds for it. Anyway, he put it up in the garden – once, I think. Imagine that, just one time! He never used it again. It was a waste of money. The truth is he really likes hotels!

2   I don't really know … Oh yeah, last year my wife bought me an exercise bike. I thought it was a good idea, too, but you know, I think I used it three times. It was hard work! A real waste of money!

3   Shopping mistakes? Oh, that's easy. Clothes. I often buy clothes and then when I get them home I don't like them. For example, last month I went shopping with a friend and I bought a hat. It cost a hundred euros. My friend said it looked beautiful. My boyfriend said it was terrible … so I sold it … on the internet. I got fifty euros for it. It was a real waste of money.

4   A shopping mistake? Oh yes, all the time. For example, I got my sister's little boy some drums. For his birthday. I thought it was a good idea. He loves those drums. He plays them all day. So he's happy … but my sister isn't happy. Now she doesn't talk to me! I phoned her yesterday, but she didn't answer.

5   A shopping mistake. Erm … oh yeah, my mother gave us a lamp. We didn't like it, but I know it cost her a lot of money. Then after a week I broke it. I tried to fix it, but it was impossible. Whoops!

GRAMMAR   OBJECT PRONOUNS

4A Give Ss a minute or two to complete the sentences, working alone. For *stronger classes*, you could tell Ss to cover the box and try to complete as many sentences as they can from what they know already. You may also want to point out at this stage that pronouns are words that go in place of nouns, e.g. *it* is in the place of *exercise bike* in sentence 1.

> **Answers:** 1 it 2 him 3 her 4 them 5 us

B You could draw the table on the board and write the answers in the second column as you elicit them from the class or ask Ss up to the board to write them. Ask Ss which pronouns have the same form as subject and object pronouns (*you, it*).

> **Answers:** object pronoun: him, her, it, us, them

C Refer Ss back to the sentences in Ex 4A to help them with the rule. For *weaker classes*, write sentence 4 on the board: *He loves those drums. He plays them every day.* Use the example to highlight the position of *He* (before *loves*) and *them* (after *plays*).

> **Answers:** Use a subject pronoun *before a* verb. Use an object pronoun *after a* verb.

D **PRONUNCIATION connected speech: linking** Give Ss time to read the examples and note which sounds are linked or dropped (the final consonant sound in the first word links to the initial vowel sound in the next. Initial 'h' sounds are dropped). You could also say the examples without the linking (i.e. pronouncing the 'h' in *him/her*) to show Ss that it sounds unnatural.

> **LANGUAGEBANK 9.1** p134–135

Give Ss a few minutes to read the summary of object pronouns in the Language bank. If you have a mixed level class, you could give Ex 9.1A to the **weaker Ss** and Ex 9.1B to the **stronger Ss** and give them a key to check their answers.

Answers:
A 2 Give it to ~~him~~ *her*.
3 Deena lived with ~~we~~ *us* for three years.
4 Come and dance with ~~I~~ *me*.
5 correct
6 I don't like ~~these~~ *them*.
7 correct
8 I played with ~~he~~ *him* yesterday.
9 Diana's in my class. I like ~~she~~ *her* a lot.
10 The exit is over there, in front of ~~your~~ *you*.
B 2 B: I didn't like *it*.
3 B: Oh no! I put *them* in my other coat.
4 B: Sorry, I sent you a text. Did you get *it*?
5 B: He phoned *me* this morning from home. He isn't well.
6 B: No, I asked *her* but she didn't want to go.
7 B: A taxi met *us* at the airport.
8 B: Wait a minute, class. Did I give *you* your homework?

5A Ss can complete the sentences alone or in pairs.

Answers: 2 them 3 it 4 me 5 you 6 us 7 her 8 him

B Go through the example with the class, or you could do a different one about you. Point out that Ss can change any of the information in the answer, but not the question. In numbers 7 and 8 they can also change the name of the student.

C Ss should read their sentences aloud to their partner, rather than simply showing them the sentences in their notebooks.

WRITING LISTINGS

6A Focus Ss on the listings and ask them where they would see them (online, for selling things, e.g. on *Ebay*). Put Ss in pairs and give them a minute or two to read the four headings (not the texts) and discuss which thing costs the most.

Answers: the Honda 500T motorbike

B Go through the example on the board, erasing *the boots* (x2) and writing *them* and *They* instead. Ss rewrite the captions alone, then check their answers in pairs.

Answers:
2 DVD of Beyoncé live at Roseland: I saw Beyoncé at the Roseland concert in New York City in 2011. *She* was fantastic – I really like *her* – and the DVD is great too, but I never watch *it* because I don't have a DVD player.
3 For sale: Honda 500T: I bought my Honda 500T in 2004. *It* is a beautiful motorbike but I don't use *it* much now.
4 A signed photo of Brad Pitt: I met Brad Pitt in Sydney last year. *He* gave me two photos and I want to sell one of *them*.

C You could bring in some photos of objects to help Ss with ideas, e.g. a sofa, a handbag, an iPod, a jacket, a boat, a child's dress. Give Ss a framework for their captions, i.e.
• a short heading describing the object
• when/where/how you got it
• why you want to sell it.
Monitor Ss as they write the captions and provide any vocabulary they need, and/or help them to make corrections.

D Ss either read each other's listings in groups or display them round the class for other Ss to walk round and read. You could tell Ss to choose one object that they want to buy, then, in feedback, they tell the class about it and why they want to buy it.

SPEAKING

7A Give Ss a few minutes to write their answers, while you circulate and help. Encourage them to give some information to support their answer, as in the example in Ex 7B.

B Put Ss in pairs and go through the example. Point out that Student A should use the sentence stem *Tell me …* to prompt their partner to talk about one of the things, then ask them another question to find out more.

Optional extra activity

Ss choose one of the examples from Ex 7A then walk round the class asking all the other Ss about it (*Tell me …*), and making a note of their answers. Afterwards they summarise what they found out and tell the class, e.g. *Seven people really want to buy a new computer and five people want to buy clothes.*

Homework ideas
• Ss write two more listings for photos of objects for sale.
• **Workbook:** Ex 1–5, p58–59.

THE RIGHT GIFT

Introduction

Ss practise reading and talking about giving gifts. They also practise talking about likes and dislikes, using *like, love, hate +*
-ing (with a focus on sentence stress) and vocabulary related to activities.

SUPPLEMENTARY MATERIALS

Resource bank: p174

Ex 1 (alternative approach): prepare a handout with alternatives for Ss to tick (see notes).

Warm up

Tell Ss to close their books. Write the following words on the board and put Ss in pairs to talk about what they have in common: *a book, jewellery, flowers, wine, a scarf, chocolates, a watch, a pen.* Then direct Ss to the title of the text on p98 and tell them (if they haven't already guessed) that this is what the words have in common: they can all be gifts. Mime to show the meaning of verbs that are commonly used with *gift*, i.e. *give, get* (*receive*), *wrap, open/unwrap.*

READING

1 You could start by giving Ss one example of when you personally give gifts, and one example of who you give gifts to. Then put Ss in pairs to discuss the questions. After a minute or two, ask a few pairs to share their answers with the class.

Alternative approach

Give Ss the following on a handout or display it on the board. Tick the alternatives which are true for you:

1 I give gifts to people …   on their birthdays.
                                on special festivals.
                                in business situations.
                                other (give example).

2 I buy gifts for …   my family.
                       a lot of my friends.
                       people at work or school.
                       other (give example).

When Ss have ticked the alternatives, they can compare and discuss their answers in pairs.

2A Before directing Ss to the text, check the following vocabulary: *lucky/unlucky* (good/bad things will happen to you), *death* (the end of someone's life), *funeral* (a ceremony for a person who has died). Encourage Ss to put ticks on the text in the margin next to the things that are the same in their country. Ss can discuss their answers in pairs and with the whole class.

B Make sure Ss cover the text and try to remember the names of the countries together.

C Ss read and check their answers to Ex 2B.

Answers: **2** China **3** China and Japan **4** the UK **5** Thailand
6 Russia **7** Mexico **8** India and Tibet

D You may want Ss to do the Photo bank exercise (matching names of gifts to photos) before they start this discussion. You could also demonstrate the activity by completing each sentence with your own examples.

GRAMMAR *LIKE, LOVE, HATE + -ING*

3A You could say the four sentences for the class, showing with your facial expression and intonation that *love* and *hate* are stronger than *like* and *don't like*. Draw the line on the board and ask Ss to help you complete it with the verbs.

Answers: **2** like **3** don't like **4** hate

B Give Ss a minute or two to look at the rules. You could check their understanding by asking them to choose the correct sentence from each pair below:
I like give gifts. I like giving gifts.
She loves dogs. She loves dog.

Answers: **1** plural **2** verb + *-ing*

▷ **LANGUAGEBANK 9.2** p134–135

You could provide a challenge for **stronger Ss** here by asking them to work out the spelling rules for *-ing* forms before they look at the Language bank. Write the following examples on the board and ask Ss what (if anything) is added or taken away before *-ing*: *using, giving; buying, opening; getting, wrapping.* Ex 9.2A gives more practice in spelling *-ing* forms, and Ss could practise the conversations in Ex 9.2B in pairs, after they've completed them.

Answers:
A **2** chatting **3** working **4** writing **5** saying **6** having
    7 starting **8** stopping **9** cooking **10** emailing
B **1** A: Do you like doing sport?
       B: Well, I like swimming but I don't like running.
       A: Do you like playing tennis?
       B: Yes, I do.
    2 A: Sam doesn't like speaking on the phone.
       B: Does he like writing emails?
       A: No, he doesn't but he loves meeting people online.
       B: And does he like playing computer games?
       A: Yes, he does.

C **PRONUNCIATION sentence stress** The six sentences on the recording are from the table in Ex 3B. You could ask Ss to copy them into their notebooks before they listen and underline the stressed words. Give Ss time to check answers in pairs, then play the recording again for them to repeat.

Answers:
I <u>love</u> <u>flowers</u>.
We <u>like</u> going <u>shopping</u>.
He <u>doesn't</u> <u>like</u> <u>flying</u>.
She <u>hates</u> <u>chocolates</u>.
Do you <u>like</u> <u>peaches</u>?
Does he <u>like</u> getting <u>gifts</u>?

4A Give Ss a few minutes to complete the sentences, working alone or in pairs.

Answers: **2** watching **3** having **4** reading **5** going **6** living
7 getting up **8** wrapping

B Use the first two sentences to demonstrate this, ticking or changing them as appropriate for you. Ss work alone to change the sentences.

C Ask Ss to be prepared to tell the class about the two things in common, e.g. *We both like … but we don't like …*

VOCABULARY ACTIVITIES

5A Tell Ss to pay attention to the spelling as they write the *-ing* forms and remind them about the rules in the Language bank (p134).

> **Answers:** **2** relaxing **3** cooking **4** swimming **5** camping **6** playing **7** taking **8** going **9** chatting **10** going

Optional extra activity

In pairs, Ss take turns to mime the activities in Ex 5A for their partner to guess. You could demonstrate by miming one of the activities yourself.

B Check that Ss understand the options here by eliciting an example for each one, e.g. outside – running; inside – playing computer games; with someone – going to the theatre; in special clothes – swimming; with a machine – taking photos. Encourage Ss to find as many examples as they can for each option, then share their ideas with the whole class.

> **Suggested answers:**
> outside: 1, 5, 10 are likely; also possibly 2, 3, 4, 7, 8
> inside: 3, 6, 8, 9 are likely; also possibly 2, 4, 7
> with someone: 8, 9 are likely; also possibly 1, 2, 3, 4, 5, 6, 7, 10
> in special clothes: 4 is likely; also possibly 1, 8, 10
> with a machine: 3, 6, 7, 9

C Invite Ss to ask you about two or three of the activities, so you can provide a model of different answers, e.g. *Yes, I do. No, not really. Yes, I love it. No, I hate it. It depends.* Put Ss in pairs or small groups to ask and answer.

Optional extra activity

In pairs, Ss think of at least one more activity for each category in Ex 5B. You could give them some verb prompts on the board to help, e.g. *do, go, eat, wash, listen, clean, write, learn.*
Possible ideas: *doing sport, going to the shops, eating in restaurants, washing the car, listening to music, cleaning the house, writing emails, learning English.*
Then Ss take turns to say one of their activities and their partner guesses how they feel about it, e.g.
A: *Washing the car*
B: *You hate it.*
A: *No, actually, I like it!*

speakout TIP

Give Ss a few minutes to read through the examples of short answers and write them in their phrasebooks. Check their understanding of *It depends* (sometimes I do, sometimes I don't). Then model the short answers for Ss to repeat, focusing on natural intonation. Ss could then practise asking *Do you like …?* and answering with short answers in open pairs, i.e. across the class, e.g.
A: *Marie, do you like camping?*
M: *It depends. Pietro, do you like cooking?*
P: *Yes, sometimes.*

▷ PHOTOBANK p147

The Photo bank contains eight more everyday activities and an opportunity for Ss to discuss them in pairs.

> **Answers:**
> **A 1** D **2** C **3** F **4** B **5** A **6** E **7** G **8** H

SPEAKING

6A Remind Ss about the 'activity gifts' mentioned in the text in Ex 2A and elicit some ideas for activities that would be good gifts. Write these on the board, then focus Ss on the list of activities on the webpage and give them a minute or two to see how many are the same as their ideas. Then tell Ss to find photos of the activities. Check *one-to-one* (a private lesson), *beauty spa* (a place where people have different beauty treatments).

> **Answers:** driving a Formula-1 car, beauty spa, sushi-making, hot-air balloon trip

B Check *sweets* (simple board picture), *eating out* (eating in cafés and restaurants), *plays* (you see them at the theatre), then put Ss in pairs to ask and answer, and record their partner's answers.

C Give Ss a few minutes to decide on the best activity and to make a few notes about why they chose it, then to tell their partners, e.g. *I chose salsa lessons for you, because you love dancing and you like doing exercise.*

D Give Ss a minute or two to think about what to say, then invite Ss to tell the class about their activity gifts, starting with **stronger Ss**.

Optional extra activities

1 Ss imagine that they went and did the activity, and now they are going to tell the class about it and why they liked/didn't like it. You could demonstrate this by doing an invented example of your own, e.g.
My activity gift was a …
It was a good idea because …
I enjoyed the activity and I was/learnt/saw/had/spent/relaxed …
Give Ss a few minutes to make notes before they tell the class about their 'experience'.

2 Ss decide which activity gifts they would give to three other people, e.g. friends or family members, then share their ideas in small groups of 3–4.

Homework ideas

- Ss write an email to a friend or family member telling them about an activity gift that they've bought for them. You could give Ss a framework for this, e.g. *Dear (Anna), Happy (birthday)! I hope you have a (great) day! I bought you an activity for your (birthday), it's (a hot-air balloon trip). I chose this because I know you love (flying) and you like (adventure). To book the (trip), phone (4456 3246). The trips are every day at (3p.m.). Choose the best day for you. I hope you enjoy it! Love*
- **Workbook:** Ex 1–5, p60–61

I'D LIKE A …

Introduction

Ss practise listening to and making requests, with a focus on polite intonation. They also practise using names of shopping departments and learn to use hesitation phrases.

SUPPLEMENTARY MATERIALS
Resource bank: p176

Warm up

Check Ss understand the idea of a department store (they could name some famous department stores). Put them in pairs to discuss the advantages and disadvantages of shopping in department stores, as opposed to smaller, specialty shops, or shopping online.

VOCABULARY   SHOPPING DEPARTMENTS

1A Start by eliciting the names of the items from Ss and checking their pronunciation:
A – *armchair* Oo, B – *ring*, C – *toy car* OO, D – *TV* oO, E – *luggage* Oo, F – *perfume* Oo. Put Ss in pairs to talk about the best shops for these things in their town/city (if they're studying away from home, they could tell each other about places they've found so far in the town/city where they're staying).

B Ss work on this in pairs, writing the department name next to the the letter of the item.

Answers: **A** Furniture & Lighting   **B** Jewellery & Watches   **C** Toys   **D** Home Entertainment   **E** Travel & Luggage   **F** Beauty

C You could give Ss a minute or two to think about which syllables are stressed before you play the recording. Ss will hear the departments starting with the third floor and going down.

Answers: <u>Fur</u>niture and <u>Light</u>ing   <u>Bed</u> and <u>Bath</u>   <u>Trav</u>el and <u>Lugg</u>age   <u>Sky</u> Restaurant   <u>Child</u>ren's <u>clothes</u> and <u>Shoes</u>   <u>Toys</u>   Com<u>pu</u>ters and <u>Phones</u>   <u>Home</u> entertainment   <u>Sports</u>   <u>Wom</u>en's <u>clothes</u> and <u>Shoes</u>   <u>Star</u> café   <u>Beau</u>ty   <u>Jew</u>ellery and <u>Watch</u>es   <u>Mens</u>wear and <u>Shoes</u>

Optional extra activity

Ss work in pairs and take turns. Student B closes his/her book and Student A asks where certain departments are: Student B tries to remember, e.g.
A: *Where's the (Menswear and Shoes) department?*
B: *I think it's on the (ground) floor.*
A: *Yes, that's right!*

2A Start by eliciting two things for Furniture and Lighting (e.g. *lamp, sofa, bed*). Put Ss in pairs to think of things for five other departments. Circulate and help with vocabulary and pronunciation.

Suggested answers: Bed & Bath: sheets, a bedcover, towels
Travel & Luggage: a bag, a laptop bag, a lock
Sky Restaurant: coffee, tea, a salad, a meal, breakfast, lunch
Children's clothes and Shoes: a dress, a jacket, a hat, trousers
Toys: a doll, a ball, a board game, a doll's house
Computers & Phones: a laptop, a smart phone, a memory stick
Home entertainment: a DVD player, speakers, a screen
Sports: a tennis/badminton racquet, a football/tennis/golf ball, skis
Women's clothes & Shoes: a dress, a jacket, trousers, jeans
Star café: coffee, tea, biscuits, a cake, a sandwich
Beauty: make-up, face cream, a lipstick, body cream
Jewellery & Watches: earrings, a bracelet, a necklace, a watch
Menswear & Shoes: trousers, a shirt, a tie, a jacket, boots

B Go through the example, then put Ss in pairs to practise.

FUNCTION   MAKING REQUESTS

3A Tell Ss they're going to hear some conversations that a woman called Lisa has while she's in a department store. Give Ss time to read through the options in questions 1–3, then play the recording.

Answers: **1** b)   **2** a)   **3** a)

Unit 9   Recording 6

A: Hi, Tom. It's Lisa.
B: Oh hi, Lisa. How are you?
A: Fine, thanks. Listen, what do you want for your birthday?
B: Oh, I don't know. Let me think … I don't know.
A: I'm in Bridge's Department Store, so it's a good time to tell me …
B: Um … well, maybe something from the World Cup.
A: For example?
B: Er …
A: Well, would you like a football shirt, or …?
B: Um … no. Oh, I know! I'd like a DVD.
A: A DVD of what?
B: Well, can you get me a DVD of the World Cup?
A: OK.
B: Great. Thanks.
A: No problem. Bye.
B: Bye.

A: Excuse me, can you help me? Where's the Sports Department?
C: It's over there. Behind the Toy Department.
A: Thanks.

D: Can I help you?
A: Yes, I'd like a football DVD, but there aren't any DVDs here.
D: No, the sports DVDs are in Home Entertainment. In the DVD section.
A: Where's that?
D: It's opposite Computers and Phones. Over there.
A: Thanks.

E: Can I help you?
A: Yeah, I want a DVD of the World Cup, but there are two different DVDs here. Which one is best, do you think?
E: Er … let me see … this one has all the important matches.
A: Can I see it? Oh, yes. How much is it?
E: It's twenty euros.
A: OK, can I have this one, please?
E: Yes, you pay over there.
A: Oh, right. Thanks.
E: You're welcome.

B Focus Ss on the sentences and give them a minute or two to predict the missing word in each one. Then play the recording for them to check and compare answers in pairs.

Answers: **1** like   **2** get   **3** Can   **4** 'd   **5** I   **6** have

C Give Ss a minute or two to discuss their ideas in pairs. As you go through the answers, check:

• *I'd like a DVD* means 'now', whereas *I like DVDs* means 'in general'.
• if you ask *Would you like this DVD?* you are offering it to the person, whereas *Do you like this DVD?* is asking for an opinion.
• the difference between *Can I …?* (I want to do it) and *Can you …?* (I'm asking you to do it). Both are requests, and need an answer, e.g. *Yes/OK/Of course/No, sorry*.

Answers:
1 *I'd like = Can I have*
2 *Can I = I want to do something*
3 *Can you = Please do something for me*

Optional extra activity

For practice of requests using *Can I/Can you*, write the following on the board:

Can I	turn on the lights,	please?
Can you	sit down,	
	stand up,	
	open the door,	
	go out,	
	look at your book,	
	change places with (name),	
	open/close the window,	

Ask Ss at random round the class to make requests to you, then either you or the student does the action, e.g.

St: *Can I turn on the lights, please?*
T: *Yes, of course.*
St turns on lights.
St: *Can you turn on the lights, please?*
T: *Yes, of course.*
T turns on lights.
Ss then work in pairs, making and responding to requests.

▷ LANGUAGEBANK 9.3 p134–135

Give Ss time to read through the summary, and check that they understand the difference between *Would you like* and *Do you want* (both are used to make an offer).
Would you like is more polite. *What would you like?* (open choice) and *Which one would you like?* (limited choice).
You could use Ex 9.3 for conversation practice in pairs. (NB: Point out that *Can I help you?* is a common way for a shop assistant to start a conversation, and *Can I have …?* is another way to make a request.)

Answers: 2 'd   3 like   4 have   5 I   6 I'd   7 Would   8 thanks

---

4A Tell Ss to write the four conversations in their notebooks. They can then practise the conversations, remembering to look up from the page as much as possible, so they're not reading aloud.

Optional extra activity

Working in pairs, Ss expand the four conversations by adding at least two lines to each one, e.g.

A: *Can I help you?*
B: *Yes, I'd like one of those cakes, please.*
A: *Would you like cream?*
B: *No, thank you.*
A: *OK, that's 4 euros, please.*

Ss then practise the conversations and choose one to act out for the class. Ask each pair to act out their conversation and encourage the class to comment on the similarities and differences.

Answers:
1 **A:** Can I help you?
  B: Yes, I'd like one of those cakes, please.
2 **A:** Can you take a photo of us, please?
  B: Sure, can you stand over there?
3 **A:** Can we have two of these T-shirts, please?
  B: Yes, which colours would you like?
4 **A:** I'd like a cappuccino, please.
  B: Would you like chocolate on it?

B PRONUNCIATION intonation Tell Ss they will hear each sentence twice: once it is polite, and once it is not polite. Play the recording.

Answers: 1 a) NP b) P   2 a) P b) NP   3 a) P b) NP   4 a) NP b) P

C Play the first sentence and elicit or demonstrate (e.g. by using your hands) that there is more movement (or 'music') in the voice when someone is being polite, and there is a fall-rise movement at the end of the sentence. Play all four sentences for Ss to repeat.

D You could do an example, asking a **stronger student** to be Student A and the rest of the class to respond as Student B. Then put Ss in pairs to take turns.

LEARN TO   USE HESITATION PHRASES

5A Elicit/Point out that when you don't have an immediate answer for someone, it's better to say something, however small, than to stay silent. Give Ss a minute or two to underline the phrases.

Answers: 2 Let me think.   3 Um …   4 well …   5 Er …
6 let me see

speakout TIP

Put Ss in pairs to think of hesitation phrases/sounds in their language(s). If Ss are from different countries, they can demonstrate them for their partner/the class.

B Ss work in pairs to do this. After each question, pause the recording long enough for both Ss in the pair to answer.

Unit 9   Recording 10

1   What's your favourite fruit?
2   Where were you last Saturday afternoon?
3   Do you want a new car?
4   What did you study in the last lesson?

C Give Ss time to find their questions, then tell them to take turns asking and answering, using hesitation phrases. Monitor the activity and be prepared to give feedback afterwards on good use of hesitation phrases.

SPEAKING

6A Tell Ss to complete the conversation orally, so that the hesitation sounds more natural. You could write the complete conversation on the board for Ss to check, then erase it before they start practising.

Suggested answers:
A: What would you like for your birthday?
B: Let me think … I'd like a new pen.
A: What colour would you like?
B: Um … Can you get me a black one?

B Ss take turns to be A and B, using the prompts.

C While Ss work on this you could elicit/give some ideas for possible presents and options, e.g.

bag – colour   wallet – colour   shirt – size (small/medium/large)
DVD – type of film (comedy/drama/romance)
book – type of book (cookery/biography/novel)

D Monitor the practice closely so you can give feedback on Ss' use of phrases for making requests (including polite intonation) and for hesitation. (NB: Ask Ss to bring in a favourite or very useful possession (or a photo of it) for the next lesson.)

Homework ideas

- Ss write a description of a well-known department store in their town/city, saying where it is, how old it is, how many floors there are, if there's a café or restaurant, what their favourite department is and why, etc.
- **Workbook:** Ex 1–4, p64

THE BORROWING SHOP

Introduction

Ss watch a BBC programme about a borrowing shop in Berlin. Ss then learn and practise how to talk and write about a favourite or very useful possession.

SUPPLEMENTARY MATERIALS

Ex 1: be prepared to answer the three questions about borrowing.
Ex 4B: be prepared to answer questions about a favourite possession.

Warm up

Ask Ss to think of something they have that they use every day, something they rarely use, and something they never use. Put the following prompts on the board:

I use my … every day because …
I rarely use my … because …
I never use my … because …

You could start by giving examples about your own possessions, then give Ss a few minutes to make notes. Put Ss in small groups to tell each other about their things and see what they have in common. Then ask the groups to discuss what they could do with the things they rarely or never use. After a few minutes ask the groups to share their ideas.

(NB: You may want to put some examples of things on the board to help Ss with ideas: *car, bike, radio, calculator, tent, phone, watch, coffee maker, bread maker, skis, laptop, sewing machine, glasses, tennis racquet, camera*, etc.).

DVD PREVIEW

1 Invite Ss to ask you the three questions first, as examples. Then put Ss in pairs to ask each other the questions. Ask a few pairs to report back to the class.

2A Put Ss in pairs. They could start by deciding which items are not in the photos (this should be familiar vocabulary), then help each other to work out the meaning of the other items. In feedback, check the stress on the compound nouns: *ice skates, a coffee maker, a baby carrier, a bike helmet, a power tool.*

Answers: A a baby carrier **B** a bike helmet **C** ice skates **D** a power tool **E** a mixer **F** a coffee maker

B Start by discussing *a book* as an example with the class. You could point out that some people think it's OK to borrow a book from a library, but not from a friend. Others think it's OK to borrow a book from a friend, while other people prefer to buy a book to keep. Then ask Ss who they agree with. Give Ss a few minutes to make the two lists in their notebooks, then put them in pairs to compare lists.

C Tell Ss to read through the four questions first, then find the answers in the text. Check *original* (first).

Answers: 1 a suitcase, plates and cups, toys **2** Leila, in Berlin **3** You borrow things, you don't buy them. **4** over (= *more than*) 400

DVD VIEW

3A Refer Ss back to their list of things that are 'OK to borrow'. Tell them to watch and listen for those things on the DVD. Play the DVD, then put Ss in pairs to discuss which of their things are in the shop.

B Put Ss in pairs and give them time to read through the sentences and try to correct them before you play the DVD again. Check *member* (someone who belongs to a group, club, etc.).

Answers:
1 F: Customers *borrow* things from the shop.
2 T
3 F: When a member borrows something, the shop puts their name in *a notebook*.
4 T
5 F: The people in the shop want to *see borrowing shops* in other cities.

C Give Ss a few minutes to read through the sentences alone. Check *stuff* (an informal word = things), *fee* (= money you pay to use something) and *genius* (= very clever). Put Ss in pairs to decide on the correct alternatives then play the DVD again. Check answers with the class.

Answers: 1 Stuff **2** of their own, fee **3** seat **4** in return **5** genius

D Put Ss in small groups to discuss the question. If they think it's a good idea for their town, you could also ask them to discuss:
What thing would you take to the shop for your membership fee?
What would you like to borrow from the shop?

Optional extra activity

Ss role-play a conversation at a borrowing shop, taking turns to be the assistant and 'borrower', e.g.
A: *Can I help you?*
B: *Yes, I'd like to borrow … Do you have any?*
A: *Yes, … there's one/there are some over there.*
B: *OK. Can I borrow this one/these?*
A: *Sure. What's your name?*
B: *(name)*
A: *Right, and how long do you want to borrow it/them?*
B: *Er … a week, I think.*
A: *OK, that's fine.*

DVD 9 The Borrowing Shop

N = Narrator   M = Malke   W1 = Woman 1   W2 = Woman 2

M: I've got a car coffee machine, baby carrier, ice skates, plates and cups, power tools … Stuff like this.
N: This shop in Berlin is different from other shops. Here you don't buy things. You borrow them. And it doesn't cost you any money. You only need to be a member.
How do you become a member? That's free too. You bring one item to the shop, something that other members can borrow. Then you are a member.
M: So each member has to bring an item of their own to the shop, and that's their membership fee.
W1: Today I would like to have a helmet for my child because I'm getting a children's seat for the bike.
N: When you're a member, you come in and borrow something. They write it down in a notebook, and you say how long you want to borrow it. You can borrow for one day, or one week, or more.
W1: It's a great idea because I have so many things at home that I don't need, and I would love to bring them and get something that I need in return.
W2: I probably make a cake once a year. It's coming and just getting a mixer for the day. It's genius. I would love to see this in places like Chicago.
N: The people in the shop want to see borrowing shops in other cities around the world. So next time you need a power tool, or a cart or a bike, you can borrow one – for free.

speakout a favourite possession

4A Start by brainstorming some examples of favourite or very useful possessions with Ss, e.g. *a ring, a watch, a pen, a book, a phone, a laptop, an iPod (or other electronic gadget), a power tool (or other tool), a coffee machine (or other kitchen appliance), a doll, a teddy bear, a bag, a fishing rod, golf clubs, certain shoes or clothes.* Provide vocabulary as Ss need it and make a list on the board. Give Ss a few minutes to answer the questions alone. You could also suggest what to include in *Other information,* e.g. size, colour, material and adjectives to describe it.

B You could start by inviting different Ss to ask you the questions about a favourite possession of yours.

C You may need to play the recording twice for Ss to answer all the questions. Give them time to compare answers before listening a second time.

> **Answers:**
> Possession: camera
> Where did you get it? New York.
> Where is it now? In his bag.
> What do you do with it? He takes pictures of friends, places and himself.
> Why do you like it? It's easy to use, it takes good pictures.
> Other information: He puts his pictures on his website. His camera is his travel partner.

D Give Ss time to read the key phrases, then play the recording again.

> **Answers:**
> One of my favourite [things/possessions ✓] is …
> My most useful [thing/possession] is …
> It's [very small ✓/big/red …].
> I keep it [in my bag ✓/pocket/at home].
> I bought it [last year ✓/in New York … ✓].
> [My brother/wife/best friend …] gave it to me …
> for [my birthday/Christmas …]
> I like it because it's [easy to use ✓/useful/beautiful].
> I use it [all the time/a lot].

> **Unit 9** Recording 11
>
> One of my favourite possessions is my camera. It's very small, and I keep it in my bag. I bought it last year in New York. I like it because it's easy to use and it takes very good photos. I take photos of my friends, and of places and of me. I have a lot of photos of me in different places. I put them on my website. I travel a lot, and I usually travel alone, but my camera is my travel partner.

> **Optional extra activity**
>
> Put Ss in pairs to think of different examples to put in the brackets in the key phrases, then invite the pairs to share their ideas with the class and compile them on the board.
> Suggested ideas:
> *It's (black/silver/metal).*
> *I keep it (in a drawer/in a box/in my car).*
> *I bought it (ten years ago/a long time ago/in a market/on holiday).*
> *(My mother/boyfriend/daughter) gave it to me …*
> *(for Valentine's Day/when I left university/for good luck in my exams).*
> *I like it because it's (fun/cute/lucky/easy to carry).*
> *I use it every day.*

5A First, give Ss time alone to prepare what they want to say about the possession: encourage them to make notes rather than writing full sentences and provide help as required. If Ss have brought their possession or a photo of it to class, they can think about how they will use it in their presentation. If they don't have the possession or a photo of it with them, they could draw a simple sketch of it. Then move Ss around so they're working with new partners, and give them time to tell each other about their possessions. Encourage the partners to give feedback, i.e. what was interesting, surprising and also anything they didn't understand. Ss can then adjust what they say about the possession before they move into groups in the next stage.

B Put Ss in groups of four or five. Tell Ss that while each person is talking about their possession, the listeners should write one question about the possession to ask the person when they've finished. When all the Ss have finished, each person in the group decides which possession is the most interesting/unusual/useful and tells the rest of the class about it. Monitor the speaking activities carefully and make notes of good language use and any problem areas for praise and correction at the end.

writeback a useful possession

6A Direct Ss back to the questions in Ex 4A and tell them to tick each question that is answered in the text.

> **Answers:**
> Where did you get it?
> What do you do with it?
> Why do you like it?
> Other information: (it's twenty years old) (it's a fantastic little bike)
> It doesn't answer: Where is it now? (it could be in the street or in the garden)

B Remind Ss to use the example description as a model. You could suggest that they write about a different possession from the one they talked about in Ex 5, then when they've finished, collect in the descriptions and redistribute them. Ss then read out the description they've received, and the rest of the class has to guess whose possession it is.

> **Homework ideas**
>
> Ss write about another favourite possession or about someone else's (e.g. a best friend or family member) favourite possession.

LOOKBACK

MONEY

SUPPLEMENTARY MATERIALS
Ex 4B (optional extra activity): prepare matching exercise for
Ss A and B (see notes).

1A You could run this as a competition in teams. Write or display the words on the board, one at a time. When a team member guesses a word, they put up their hand to answer and spell the verb. They win a point if the spelling is correct, and a point if they can give the correct past form of the verb.

> **Answers:** 2 give   3 sell   4 cost   5 get   6 pay

B Give Ss a minute or two to complete the sentences, working alone.

> **Answers:** 2 costs   3 pays   4 give   5 get   6 sell

C Ss decide whether they agree with the sentence, or change it so they agree with it, e.g. *Food costs too much in my country.* ✓
I agree because I paid (X amount) for (bread) yesterday. or
Food doesn't cost too much in my country.

OBJECT PRONOUNS

2A You may want to review subject and object pronouns first. You could put Ss in pairs to 'test' each other (e.g. *A: he – B: him*, etc.) Tell Ss to pay attention to whether the pronoun is singular or plural as they match the sentences to the nouns.

> **Answers:** 2 d)   3 c)   4 e)   5 b)   6 a)

B Look at the example with the class and establish that Ss need to write their own alternatives for a)–f). Ss work alone on this. Circulate and help with ideas and with vocabulary if required.

C Before you put Ss in pairs, demonstrate the activity with a student. Encourage Ss to respond with *Really?* and a follow-up question (*Why …? Where …? How often …?*) if the answer is surprising, e.g.
A: My parents.
B: They often phone you.
A: Yes!
B: Really? Why?
A: They're away on holiday for two months.

LIKE, LOVE, HATE + -ING

3A Tell Ss to write the questions in their notebooks.

> **Answers:** 2 What do you like reading?
> 3 What TV programme do you like watching?
> 4 Who do you like phoning?   5 What do you like eating for dinner?
> 6 Do you like flying?   7 What sport do you like doing?
> 8 What music do you like listening to?

B Tell Ss to ask each other the questions in random order. Ss could report back to the class on things they have in common, and any answers that were surprising.

Optional extra activity
Ss change one thing about each of the questions (see ideas below) then find a new partner and ask their questions.
1 and **2** cook / sing   **3** films   **4** text / meet for coffee
5 lunch / a snack   **6** drive / cycle   **7** watch   **8** dance

ACTIVITIES

4A You could run this as a competition in teams. Write or display the words on the board, one at a time. When a team member guesses a word, they put up their hand to answer and say the missing vowels only. They win a point for each correct vowel and continue until they make a mistake or finish the phrase.

> **Answers:** 1 camping   2 cooking   3 going for long walks
> 4 chatting online   5 running   6 going to the theatre
> 7 playing computer games   8 relaxing   9 taking photos
> 10 swimming

B Tell Ss to think of an object (or place) for five of the activities in Ex 4A before they start asking and answering. Help with vocabulary as required. Go through the example and invite one or two Ss to ask you the questions about an activity.

Optional extra activity
If Ss need extra support with places and objects, tell Student A to answer questions about activities 1–5, and Student B activities 6–10. Then give A and B the following matching exercises on slips of paper:
A Match each place and object to an activity 1–5:
  place: *in the park; in the kitchen; in a campsite; on the beach; in an internet café*
  object: *trainers; a computer; a sleeping bag; a cookbook; a map*
B Match each place and object to an activity 6–10:
  place: *on the sofa; in the city; on the train; in a pool; at a wedding*
  object: *a camera; an iPod; a ticket; a towel; a good book*

SHOPPING DEPARTMENTS

5A You could run this as a race in pairs or as a competition in teams. To win points, Ss need to spell the word correctly.

> **Answers:** 1 Jewellery & Watches   2 Computers & Phones
> 3 Furniture & Lighting   4 Travel & Luggage
> 5 Home Entertainment   6 Bed & Bath   7 Menswear & Shoes
> 8 Beauty   9 Children's clothes & Shoes   10 Toys

B Give Ss a few minutes to discuss this. Ss who don't like shopping in department stores could tell their partners about good websites they've found for some of the categories (furniture, luggage, etc.).

MAKING REQUESTS

6A Give Ss a few minutes to correct the mistakes, working alone.

> **Answers:** **B:** Yes, *I* would *like* this pen.   **A:** OK. Is *it* he a present?
> **B:** Er … yes. Can *you* I wrap it for me?
> **A:** Of course. Which wrapping paper *would* you would like, red or green?
> **A:** *Who* Where is the gift for?   **B:** For *me* I. Today is my birthday!

B Encourage Ss to look up from the page as much as possible, and cover the conversation when they feel confident with it.

C Demonstrate how to change parts of the conversation, e.g.
I would like this T-shirt.

D Ss take turns and practise both parts in the conversation. Ask a few pairs to act out their conversations for the class.

BBC interviews and worksheet
Do you like shopping?
In this video people talk about whether they like shopping and shopping mistakes they have made. The material enables Ss to revise structures and vocabulary related to expressing opinions and shopping or spending money.

OVERVIEW

10.1 A NEW JOB

VOCABULARY | collocations
READING | read about jobs
LISTENING | listen to job interviews
GRAMMAR | *can/can't*
PRONUNCIATION | strong and weak forms: *can/can't*
SPEAKING | discuss the best job for you

10.2 TIME FOR A CHANGE

VOCABULARY | life changes
LISTENING | listen to street interviews about people's goals
GRAMMAR | *be going to*
PRONUNCIATION | weak form: *going to*
SPEAKING | talk about plans
WRITING | check your writing

10.3 HELLO AND GOODBYE

FUNCTION | starting and ending conversations
LISTENING | listen to how people start and end conversations
PRONUNCIATION | sentence stress
LEARN TO | use two-part exchanges
VOCABULARY | saying goodbye
SPEAKING | starting and ending conversations

10.4 MIRANDA BBC)) DVD

DVD | watch a BBC programme about someone trying something new
speakout | talk about when you tried something new
writeback | write an interview

10.5 LOOKBACK

Communicative revision activities

BBC)) INTERVIEWS

What did you want to be?

In this video people talk about their jobs and whether they like them or not. Ss can recap and extend their knowledge of vocabulary on the topic of jobs/work and leisure activities. They can also practice listening to and revise structures with the past simple. Use the video after lesson 10.1 or at the end of the unit.

A NEW JOB

Introduction

Ss practise reading and talking about job adverts and listening to job interviews. They also practise talking about ability, using *can/can't* (with attention to the pronunciation of strong and weak forms) and related collocations.

> **SUPPLEMENTARY MATERIALS**
> **Resource bank:** p177 and p179
> **Ex 2A:** bring in a driving licence for vocabulary checking.
> **Ex 4D (optional extra activity):** prepare a handout with extracts from the recording in Ex 3, with gaps for Ss to complete (see notes).

Warm up

Review names of jobs. Put Ss in pairs and give each pair a blank piece of paper. Tell them to think of five jobs, check their spelling in a dictionary, and write them with the letters jumbled on the paper. Each pair then passes the paper to the next pair, who try to guess the jobs and order the letters correctly, then pass the paper back for the writers to check. Bring the class together and make a list on the board of all the jobs Ss thought of. Check that Ss understand all the jobs by asking what the person does, where they work, etc.

VOCABULARY   COLLOCATIONS

1A You could start by telling Ss to cover the word webs and look at the verbs in the box. Elicit one or two examples of a noun or phrase that goes with each verb, e.g. *cook pasta*, *ride a bike*, *speak English*, etc. Then direct Ss to the example and put them in pairs to complete the other word webs.

> **Answers:** **2** play   **3** speak   **4** read   **5** remember   **6** make
> **7** use   **8** ride

B Demonstrate the activity with a **strong student** taking the part of Student B. Point out that Student B should try to remember the words without looking at the word webs. Ss take turns to be Student A and Student B.

READING

2A Before Ss look at the text, write the four jobs on the board and elicit some ideas about what the people do in their jobs. Check the following vocabulary: *need* (it is important/necessary), *memory* (if you remember things well, you have a good memory), *driving licence* (show an example), *sales department* (the department that sells things), *manage* (have control of), *busy* (have a lot to do), *team* (group of people). Then give Ss a few minutes to read the adverts and discuss in pairs which one is best for them. Ask a few pairs to tell the class which job(s) they chose and why.

B You could go through sentence 1a) as an example with the class. Ss work alone or in pairs.

> **Answers:**
> **1** a) You need to speak ~~three~~ *two* languages.
> **1** b) You *don't* need a car. *You need to drive./You need a driving licence.*
> **2** a) You sell computers to ~~local~~ *international* businesses.
> **2** b) correct
> **3** a) You *don't* need to live in the city. *You need to know the city well.*
> **3** b) You *don't* work in the kitchen every day. *You sometimes work in the kitchen.*
> **4** a) You work ~~alone~~ *with a team/with other people* in the shop.
> **4** b) correct

3A Tell Ss to write the numbers 1–3 in their notebooks and write the name of the job next to each number as they listen, as well as Y for *the person gets the job*, N for *the person doesn't get the job* and ? for *we don't know*. Ss could also underline key words/phrases in the job adverts to help them decide which job the person wants.

Answers:
1 pizza delivery person (No, he doesn't get the job.)
2 airport sales assistant (Yes, he gets the job.)
3 tour guide (We don't know if she gets the job.)

B Give Ss a minute or two to discuss this question with a partner before they listen again to check their ideas.

Answers:
1 He knows the city, he can work alone and also likes people. He's OK with cleaning and cooking, but he has an accident on the motorbike.
2 He can work fast and says he can get up early, but he was late on the day of the interview.
3 She speaks three languages and she has a driving licence, but she doesn't remember the interviewer's name.

Unit 10 Recording 1

Conversation 1
A: So, Greg. Thanks for coming in.
B: No problem.
A: Right, I have some questions for you.
B: OK.
A: Er … first of all, can you ride a motorbike?
B: Yes, um … yes, I can. Of course.
A: That's good. And do you know the city well? Can you find a place fast?
B: Yes, I can. No problem.
A: And in this job you sometimes work alone …
B: That's not a problem.
A: … but you meet a lot of people.
B: I like people.
A: OK, good. Oh, and we sometimes get very busy and we need help in the kitchen – cleaning or cooking. Is that OK?
B: Yeah, no problem. I worked in a café last year and I made sandwiches … and pizzas.
A: Great! Can you start tomorrow?
B: Sure. Wow, I got the job?
A: Yes, congratulations! Come and look at the motorbike.
B: Oh, it's big.
A: Yeah, here you go. Try it.
B: Oh, er, OK. It's a bit difficult to ride. But I'm sure I can learn.
A: Be careful!
B: Aaah!
A: Oh, no! Greg, are you OK? Next interview, I think.

Conversation 2
A: So, you think this is the job for you.
B: Yeah, yeah, I do.
A: OK, are you good with people?
B: Yes, I am.
C: And can you work fast? The shop is very busy with lots of people waiting for their planes.
B: I like that. Busy is good.
C: Mmm. And what about the hours? The job starts at five o'clock in the morning some days. Can you get up early?
B: Yes, I can. No problem.
A: Mmm. But this interview was for nine o'clock and you were late. You arrived at half past nine.
B: Erm, well. My train was late.
A: Mmm. Well, okay, we'd like to try you … for a month.
B: That's great!

Conversation 3
A: So, what languages can you speak?
B: English, Japanese, Russian.
A: Great. And can you drive?
B: Yes.
A: OK. And can you remember facts and information?
B: Yes, I can. I have a very good memory.
A: So, can you remember my name?
B: Er … Did you say your name? Erm … Sorry, I can't remember.
A: Oh, dear … OK, let's try some other questions.

GRAMMAR CAN/CAN'T

4A First, demonstrate the meaning of *can/can't* by acting out two examples, e.g. draw something badly on the board, then write the sentence *I can/can't draw* and ask Ss which alternative is correct. Then say something fairly complicated in English and write *I can/can't speak English* for Ss to choose the correct alternative. Then give Ss two minutes to complete the tables.

Answers:

Can	you	ride a motorbike? make pizzas?
Yes, No,	I	can. can't.

| + | I/You/He/She/We/They | can | speak English. |
| − | | can't | drive. |

Watch out!

Ss may think they need to use *to* with the verb, e.g. *I can to sing*. You could put the following sentences on the board and ask the class which are correct:
I can to sing.   I can sing.
Can you dance?   Can you to dance?

B You could write the rule on the board and elicit the correct answer.

Answer: your ability

C **PRONUNCIATION strong and weak forms:** *can/can't* Play the recording at least twice for Ss to listen to the difference between the strong and weak forms. Then ask them where the stress is in each sentence. Point out that in the positive statement (1) and the question (2), the stress is on the main verb, *cook*, so *can* is not stressed, but in the short answers (3 and 4) the stress is on *can* or *can't*.

Teaching tip

If Ss have difficulty producing the weak form of *can*, tell them to try saying /kn/: *I can cook*.
        /kn/
Also show them the stress pattern: O o O
                                    I can cook.

D Remind Ss of the three sounds written in phonemic script in Ex 4C. Play the recording and pause after the first sentence to check the example with the class. Then tell Ss to write the numbers 2–6 next to the appropriate sound and play the rest of the recording. When Ss have checked their answers, they could practise repeating the sentences.

Answers: a) 1, 3, 4 b) 2 c) 5, 6

▷ **LANGUAGEBANK 10.1** p136–137

Direct Ss to the note about using *very well*, *well*, *quite well*, and *not very well* after *can*. You could give Ss Ex 10.1A for homework and use Ex 10.1B in class. When Ss have completed the conversation, they could practise it in pairs, then two or three pairs act it out for the class as dramatically as possible.

Answers:
A 2 can you speak   3 can ride   4 can't remember   5 can take
6 Can you read   7 can never understand   8 can't see
B B: Let me try. Yes, I *can*.
A: *Can* you walk on it?
B: I don't know. Oh, no, I *can't*.
A: OK, just sit down and relax.
B: I *can't* relax! Where's my mobile?
A: I *can't* see it. You *can* use my mobile.
B: It's no good. I *can't* get a phone signal here. *Can* you go and get help?

Optional extra activity

Prepare a handout for Ss with the following extracts from the recording about job interviews in Ex 3. Put Ss in pairs to help each other complete the conversations with the missing verbs (seven in total), then refer them to the audio script to check, or play the recording again. Ss could also practise the conversations with their partners.

1 A: Er … first of all, can you _____ a motorbike?
B: Yes, um … yes, I can. Of course.
A: That's good. And do you know the city well? Can you _____ a place, fast?
B: Yes, I can. No problem.
2 A: OK, are you good with people?
B: Yes, I am.
C: And can you _____ fast? The shop is very busy with lots of people waiting for their planes.
B: I like that. Busy is good.
C: Mmm. And what about the hours? The job starts at five o'clock in the morning some days. Can you _____ early?
B: Yes, I can. No problem.
3 A: So, what languages can you _____?
B: English, Japanese, Russian.
A: Great. And can you _____?
B: Yes.
A: OK. And can you _____ facts and information?
B: Yes, I can. I have a very good memory.

5A Go through the example with the class, then put Ss in pairs and give them a few minutes to correct the questions.

Answers: 2 Can she use a power tool?   3 Can Barbara ride a horse?
4 Can you dance?   5 correct   6 Can George read Chinese?

B When Ss have completed the answers and checked their work, they could practise asking and answering in pairs. **Stronger Ss** can cover the answers and try to remember them.

Answers: 2 she can   3 she can't   4 I can, I can
5 we can't, we can speak   6 he can, he can't

Optional extra activity

In pairs, Ss ask each other the questions in Ex 5A about themselves *Can you …?* or about other Ss in the class *Can (Maria/Alex) …?* and answer using the pattern in Ex 5B:
Yes, ___ ___ and ___ ___ ___, too. or *No, ___ ___, but ___ ___ ___.*

▷ **PHOTOBANK** p147

Ss match the photos to sentences with *can/can't* and ability verbs.

Answers:
1 I   2 G   3 D   4 H   5 F   6 C   7 E   8 B   9 A   10 J

Optional extra activity

Ss work in groups of three or four. Student A thinks of a job and the others guess what it is by asking up to ten questions with *Can you …?* and a verb from Ex 1A. Student A guesses which job they're referring to and answers *Yes* or *No*, e.g.
Student B: *Can you play the guitar?*
Student A: *No, I'm not a musician.*
Student C: *Can you ride a motorbike?*
Student A: *No, I'm not a delivery person.*
Student D: *Can you drive a taxi?*
Student A: *Yes, I'm a taxi driver.*

SPEAKING

6A Direct Ss to the questionnaire and give them a minute or two to write a number for each activity.

B Put Ss in pairs to ask and answer the questions and note a number for their partner's answer next to each question. Elicit how to give positive answers as well as the negative one in the example, e.g. *Can you dance? Yes, I can dance quite well/very well.* Monitor the pair work carefully and make notes of good language use and problem areas for feedback later.

C Tell Ss to look at the sections where their partner got ten points or more. Then Ss refer to the key and tell each other which job(s) is/are good for them. You could encourage Ss to think of other jobs for their partners that are not mentioned in the key.

D Go through the example with the class, then give Ss a few minutes to talk about the questions in pairs. Bring the class together and invite Ss to report back on whether the questionnaire was right about them or not.

Homework ideas
• Ss write a job advert, following the examples in Ex 2. You could give them a framework, e.g.
Title
Can you _____?
Do you _____?
Are you _____?
We are _____.
We need a _____.
Contact us at (email address).
• **Workbook:** Ex 1–4, p63–64

TIME FOR A CHANGE

Introduction

Ss practise listening to people talking about their goals. They practise talking about their plans and goals for the future, using *be going to* (with attention to the pronunciation of weak forms) and vocabulary related to life changes. They also learn how to check their written work.

> **SUPPLEMENTARY MATERIALS**
> Resource bank: p178

Warm up

Write the following on the board and tell Ss that these are important things in life: *work, money, family, health, love, home, education, friends*. Then ask Ss to choose the three things that they think are most important and put them in order from 1–3 (1 = most important). Put Ss in pairs to compare answers, then invite pairs to share their top three with the class.

VOCABULARY LIFE CHANGES

1A Elicit an example from the class first, then put Ss in pairs. Possible examples: people often want to change their job, the city or country where they live, their house, their car, their school, their hair (colour or style), the way they spend their free time, etc.

B Tell Ss to cover the text and focus on the photos. Elicit from the class what the person wants to do in the future in each case and establish that these things are *goals*. Then tell Ss to uncover the text and identify the goals in the photos.

> **Answers:** save money, lose weight, get organised, get fit, stop smoking, work less and relax more, spend time with family or friends

C You could tell Ss about one of the things on the list that you want to do, then put them in pairs to ask each other. Ask a few pairs to tell the class what they want to do.

> **Optional extra activity**
>
> Ss work in pairs. Student A gives a clue about one of the goals in Ex 1B and Student B guesses which one it is. Then Student B gives a clue, and so on, e.g.
> *A: You don't eat cakes and sweets.*
> *B: Lose weight!*
> *A: Correct!*

LISTENING

2A Set the scene of someone stopping people in the street to ask them questions (you could act this out with one or two Ss). Check that Ss understand what they have to do by looking at the example and asking what Tom's goal is from Ex 1B (Top ten goals). Point out that some people may have more than one goal and then play the recording.

> **Answers:** **2** Fiona 10 **3** Liam 3, 4 **4** Rudi 2 **5** Alex 9, 3

B Give Ss time to read the sentences before they listen again. They may already be able to decide if some of the sentences are true or false, then check when they listen again.

> **Answers:** **1** F **2** T **3** F **4** F **5** F **6** T **7** T **8** T

C Give Ss a few minutes to discuss the question, then invite a few individuals to report back to the class.

Unit 10 Recording 4

Conversation 1
A: Hi, do you have a minute?
B: Yeah, sure.
A: What's your name?
B: Tom.
A: OK, Tom. Can you look at this list? It's people's top ten goals in life.
B: Oh, OK.
A: So, do you have a goal for this year?
B: A goal? Yes, I want to learn something new. My girlfriend can cook really well, but she doesn't like cooking. So I'm going to learn to cook.
A: That's interesting. Any special type of cooking?
B: Yeah, Japanese food. I lived in Japan and I love Japanese food.
A: I see, well …

Conversation 2
A: So, Fiona, do you have a goal for this year?
C: I'm going to change jobs.
A: That's a big change!
C: Yeah, well, I work in an office, and I don't like it. I'd like to work outside.
A: Great.
C: My friend Sheila is going to help me.
A: Well, good luck with that.
C: Thanks!

Conversation 3
A: Liam, do you have a goal for this year?
D: Yes, I do.
A: So, what are you going to do?
D: Well, I work with computers, sometimes twelve hours a day, and I often take work home. It isn't good …
A: Right.
D: … so this year I'm going to spend more time with my friends and I'm not going take work home.
A: Great.

Conversation 4
A: Rudi, what are your goals?
E: Er… I'm going to get fit. I never do sport. I can't play tennis or anything, but I'm going to start exercising. Something easy. Take a walk every day.
A: Sounds good.

Conversation 5
A: What's your goal this year, Alex?
F: I have two goals really.
A: Oh, and what are they?
F: One is to save more money. The other is to see my friends more.
A: That's great. And what are your plans? With your friends?
F: Well … hmm … maybe go shopping together.
A: Go shopping? Then you aren't going to save money!
F: Yeah, but I'm not going to stop shopping!

GRAMMAR BE GOING TO

3A You could either put the four sentences on the board and go through the two questions with the whole class, or put Ss in pairs to discuss them first. You may also want to check the idea that *be going to* is for plans, by asking a question such as *Is this my idea/ opinion about the future, or my plan (something I decided before)?*

> **Answers:** **1** they are all about the future **2** + a, b; – c, d

B You could draw the table on the board and write the answers into the gaps as you elicit them from the class. You could also elicit/point out that the form is *be* + *going to* + infinitive.

> **Answers:**
>
> | I'm
You're
She's | | change jobs.
work less. |
> |---|---|---|
> | | going *to* | get fit.
be there. |
> | He isn't
We aren't | | come. |

Watch out!

Ss may leave out *be*, e.g. *I going to change jobs.* You could write one or two examples without *be* on the board and ask Ss if they're correct in order to raise their awareness of the potential omission. Monitor the practice activities carefully for mistakes like this.

C You could invite two Ss to come up and write the two questions on the board.

Answers:
1 What are you going to do?
2 Where is she going to work?

D PRONUNCIATION weak form: *going to* When Ss have listened to the sentences, ask them if they could hear *to* in *going to change*, etc. Point out that, although it is there, it isn't stressed, so it's a very small sound.

Teaching tip

If Ss have difficulty producing the weak sound /ə/ in /tə/, tell them to try just saying /t/. There will naturally be a small 'explosion' of air after the consonant, which will sound like a schwa /ə/.

▷ LANGUAGEBANK 10.2 p136–137

You could use Ex 10.2A for a listening correction activity. Ss close their books and you read out one sentence at a time. Ss put up their hands and either tell you the correct version of the sentence or say it's correct. Ss could do Ex 10.2B in pairs, then practise the conversation together.

Answers:
A 2 I ~~are~~ 'm going to stay at home tomorrow.
 3 Is Charlotte going *to* be a writer?
 4 correct
 5 Antonio's going to leave work at five.
 6 Are you going *to* pay?
 7 Kiera and Sam ~~is~~ are going to drive to Chicago.
 8 correct
B 2 to 3 not 4 he 5 Are 6 buy 7 is 8 going

4A Ss can complete the sentences alone or in pairs.

Answers:
2 I'm not going to do the homework tonight.
3 I'm not going to write any emails tomorrow.
4 Tomorrow afternoon, I'm going to relax.
5 On Friday, my friends and I are going to see a film.

B Show Ss how to change the example sentence, e.g. *After class, I'm going to have a sandwich.* or *After class, I'm going to meet a friend.* Tell Ss not to change the day/time (*after class, tonight, tomorrow,* etc.). Give them a few minutes to work on the sentences alone.

C Go through the example, then elicit the question Ss need to ask for numbers 2–4: *What are you going to do tonight/tomorrow/tomorrow afternoon/on Friday?* Also point out that they need to ask *What about you?* to find out their partner's answer. Tell them to make a note of their partner's answers, as they'll need to remember them for the next stage.

D Look at the example with the class and remind Ss they need to use *he's/she's going to …* to talk about their partner. Put Ss in groups of four or five to tell each other about their plans.

SPEAKING

5A Start by putting the following verb prompts on the board to help Ss with ideas: *get, learn, change, spend, stop, work, meet, see, go to, visit.* You could demonstrate this by drawing your own boxes with future goals on the board and explaining them to the class. Ss could put their future goals on a separate piece of paper to give themselves more space to write or draw simple pictures representing the goals (this will also be easier for Ss to carry round with them if necessary in the next stage).

B This could be done in groups, or Ss could stand up and walk round the class talking to different people. Monitor the activity closely and make notes of good language use and problem areas for praise and correction later.

WRITING CHECKING YOUR WORK

6A First, check that Ss understand *punctuation*, by writing punctuation marks on the board and eliciting their names (capital letter, apostrophe, question mark). Ss can work alone, then compare their answers in pairs before checking with the whole class.

Answer: Hi Elif, Thanks for your email. Here's the information about my plans. I'm going **to** be in Istanbul for three days. Can we **to** meet? My hotel is the FiveStar in Topsu Street. I'**m** going to visit the Blue Mosque on Sunday and I'd like to look around the markets. Can we have lunch together one day? ~~Are~~ **Is** Saturday good for you? Email me or text~~ed~~ me.

speakout TIP

To help Ss to think of other things to check in their writing, put the following on the board to show mistakes with spelling, word order and vocabulary, and elicit corrections, e.g.
tomorow, munth
We can meet?
I'm going not to have lunch.
say two languages
pass time with friends

B You could tell Ss to imagine they're visiting a different city, and think of the places they'd like to see there. For **weaker classes**, tell Ss to follow the email in Ex 6A, changing the place names and days.

C Ss swap emails and check them for mistakes. You could suggest that they use a code, e.g. *P* (punctuation), *V* (verbs), *S* (spelling), *WO* (word order), *VO* (vocabulary) and write the letters in the margin, on the same line as the mistake. Then they give the email back and correct their own mistakes.

D You could give Ss some ideas about what to include here, e.g.
Dear _____,
Nice to hear from you. I hope you enjoy your visit to _____. Yes, _____ is good for me. Let's meet at (name of café/restaurant) at (time).
See you then,
_____

Homework ideas
Workbook: Ex 1–6, p65–66

HELLO AND GOODBYE

Introduction

Ss practise listening to and using phrases for starting and ending conversations, paying attention to sentence stress. They also learn to use two-part exchanges.

> **SUPPLEMENTARY MATERIALS**
> **Resource bank:** p180
> **Ex 2A (alternative approach):** prepare cut up copies of the conversations in Ex 2A for each pair of Ss.
> **Ex 6B (optional extra activity):** prepare a prompt on a slip of paper for each student (see notes).

Warm up

Write the following question on the board: *When and where do you say 'Hello' and 'Goodbye'?*

Put Ss in pairs and tell them to think of as many times and places as they can in two minutes. Then invite the pairs to share their answers with the class.

Suggested answers: *in a shop, at the beginning of a lesson, at work, on the phone, when guests arrive, when you have arranged to meet someone, when you meet for the first time, e.g. in a new job, at a party.*

FUNCTION **STARTING AND ENDING CONVERSATIONS**

1A For the first question: if Ss are from the same country, they can brainstorm as many ways as possible of saying hello and goodbye. If Ss are from different countries, they can teach each other how to say hello and goodbye in their language.

For the second question: go through the example, then Ss can discuss when they start conversations with strangers, and what they say. Suggested answers: *at a social event, in a new job, in a queue (e.g. for the bus), in a department store (asking where things are).*

B *Stronger Ss* could note down any key words or phrases that help them to decide if the people are friends or strangers, e.g. *How are you? Nice to meet you.*

Answers: 1 F   2 S   3 S

C Give Ss a minute or two to read through the options before playing the recording again. Check: *get off a train/bus* (mime, also compare with *get on*), *bank card* vs *business card* (one is to pay for things, one has your contact details on it).

Answers: 1 b)   2 a)   3 c)

2A Ss could work in pairs to complete the conversations. Give them time to check their answers in the audio script or, if you think it would benefit Ss to hear the complete conversations, play the recording again.

Answers: 2 time   3 have   4 meet   5 think   6 around   7 friend
8 talk

> **Alternative approach**
> Prepare copies (one per pair of Ss) of the completed conversations from Ex 2A and cut them up into separate lines. In pairs, Ss first separate the three conversations, then put them in order. They then listen to the recording to check, moving the lines around, if necessary, as they listen.

B Go through the examples with the class and point out that they need to find three more examples of each. You could tell Ss to underline the phrases and/or write them in their notebooks.

> **Answers:**
> **1** Excuse me, do you have the time?
> What do you think of the music?
> Are you from around here?
> **2** I hope we meet again.
> I'm sorry, I can see an old friend over there.
> Nice to talk to you.

C **PRONUNCIATION sentence stress** You could remind Ss that the stress is usually on the words that carry the message of the sentence, and give them an opportunity to predict where the stress will be before they listen to the recording. When Ss listen again and repeat the phrases, tell them to say the stressed words a little louder than the others, to help them with the rhythm.

> **Answers:**
> **1** <u>What</u> do you <u>think</u> of the <u>music</u>?
> **2** Are you from <u>around</u> <u>here</u>?
> **3** Is <u>that</u> the <u>time</u>?
> **4** <u>Nice</u> to <u>talk</u> to you.

> ▷ **LANGUAGEBANK 10.3** p136–137
>
> Give Ss time to read through the summary of phrases for starting and ending conversations. You could use Ex 10.3A for conversation practice in pairs.
>
> **Answers:**
> **2** This is a nice place.   **3** What do you think of the music?
> **4** I can see an old friend over there.   **5** Nice to talk to you.
> **6** I hope we meet again.   **7** Is that the time?
> **8** I have a meeting in ten minutes.

Unit 10 **Recording 6**

Conversation 1
A: Hi, Duncan.
B: Hi, how are you?
A: Good thanks. Hey, this is a great place.
B: Yes, it's really good. I often come here.
A: … well, that was delicious. Let's have coffee.
B: OK … wait, is that the time? I'm sorry, I have a lesson at two. Here's some money for lunch.
A: No, that's all right. Keep in touch!
B: See you in two weeks, after the holidays, yeah?
A: Oh yes, that's right. See you then …

Conversation 2
A: Excuse me, do you have the time?
B: Yes, it's half past four.
A: Thanks. So … erm … where are you going?
B: Me? I'm going to …
… so you're from Madrid. That's interesting.
A: Yes, well, I come from Córdoba. I moved to Madrid when I was ten.
B: I see … Oh, look, this is my station.
A: Look, here's my card.
B: And here's mine.
A: Very nice to meet you.
B: Nice to meet you, too.
A: I hope we meet again.
B: I hope so, too.
A: Goodbye.
B: Bye!

Conversation 3
A: What do you think of the music?
B: It's not bad.
A: Hi, I'm Doug.
B: Oh, hello. I'm Jo.
A: So, are you from around here?
B: No, I'm not actually. I'm from …
A: … yes, and I was in China the next year. I speak Chinese, you know.
B: Oh, really?
A: And I speak four other languages. French, German, Spanish …
B: I'm sorry, I can see an old friend over there. Nice to talk to you.
A: Oh … and you.
B: See you later.
A: See you soon.

3A Working in pairs or alone, Ss write the complete conversations in their notebooks.

> **Answers:**
> **Conversation 1**
> A: This is a good party.
> B: Yes, it is. What do you think of the food?
> A: It's good.
> B: I'm (your name).
> A: Hi, I'm (your name).
> B: Are you from around here?
> A: Yes, I live in (place).
> **Conversation 2**
> A: Is that the time?
> B: Yes, it's eleven o'clock. I have a business meeting tomorrow at eight.
> A: And my train leaves at quarter past eleven.
> B: Nice to talk to you.
> A: Yes, I hope we meet again.

B Ss should use the prompts for practice, rather than reading the full conversation from their notebooks. Once Ss are feeling confident with the conversation, you could suggest that they cover their side of the prompts, so they can only see their partner's prompts, and practise again. Ss could also change some of the words in the prompts, e.g. *food (music), good (great/terrible), business meeting (class/appointment), eight (ten), train (bus), quarter past eleven (half past eleven)*. Monitor the activity closely and be prepared to give Ss feedback afterwards, particularly on their pronunciation.

LEARN TO USE TWO-PART EXCHANGES

4A Elicit some ideas for number 1 from the class as an example, then put Ss in pairs to discuss the rest. Point out that in this case *respond naturally* means *without having to think about what to say*, or *saying something that people always say in this kind of situation*.

B Ss may need to listen more than once to write the responses accurately.

> **Answers:** **1 B:** Yes, it's really good. **2 B:** You too.
> **3 B:** I hope so, too. **4 B:** Here's mine.

speakout TIP

Ask Ss how these two-part exchanges can help their speaking (because Ss can learn them and use them from memory, without having to think about what to say/how to say it). Put Ss in pairs to discuss alternative responses. Check their answers, then give Ss a minute or two to practise the conversations in Ex 4A twice, so they use the alternatives.
1 Yes, it's great/good/nice/not bad/OK.
2 Nice to talk to you, too./And you.
3 Me too./I hope so, too.
4 Thank you./Thanks./And here's mine./Here's mine.

C Encourage Ss to cover the conversations in Ex 4A and just practise from the prompts.

VOCABULARY SAYING GOODBYE

5A Ss can work in pairs and try to help each other complete the phrases before checking in the audio script. Point out that the only phrase that is not fixed is 2 (*in a few weeks/in an hour/in two months*, etc.), and that *see you soon* and *see you later* are used interchangeably, despite the apparent difference in meaning.

> **Answers:** 1 see you soon 2 see you in two weeks 3 keep in touch
> 4 bye 5 see you later

B Ss can do this in pairs, or walking round the class talking to different people. The idea is <u>not</u> to repeat A's phrase but to vary the way of saying goodbye.

SPEAKING

6A Give Ss a few minutes to prepare what they are going to say/ask about the music, food, their plans for the weekend, what they did last weekend, etc.

B If possible, set up the room to suggest a party rather than a classroom, e.g. move some furniture, play some music. You could demonstrate walking up to a student and saying *Hi (X), what do you think of …?* and wait for the student to respond, then gesture for the rest of the class to start talking. If you play music, you could pause it every minute or so, as a 'cue' for Ss to move on to talk to someone else. Monitor and make notes of good language use and any problem areas for praise and correction later.

> **Optional extra activity**
> Set up a situation in which the Ss are at a party where they don't know anybody else (e.g. at a conference, or in the first week at university). Prepare prompts like the following on slips of paper and give one to each student:
> *You don't like parties. You're bored.*
> *You're very hungry because you didn't eat breakfast or lunch today.*
> *You don't have any friends, so try to make friends with people at the party.*
> *You like talking about your pet fish.*
> *You were late for the party because of traffic. Tell everyone you meet about it.*
> *You're very unhappy because you broke up with your boyfriend/girlfriend.*
> *You are very interested in computers.*
> *The music's very loud and you can't hear what people say.*
> *You like talking about the weather.*
> Tell Ss they should use their prompt in the way they talk/act at the party, but they shouldn't repeat exactly what it says to other Ss. Collect the prompts.
> When the 'party' has finished, display all the prompts on the board and ask Ss to identify the person who had each one.

> **Homework ideas**
> • Ss imagine they are one of the people in conversation 2 or 3 from Ex 1. They write an email to a friend telling them about meeting someone new: where they met, what they talked about, what they thought of the other person, etc.
> • **Workbook:** Ex1–3, p67

MIRANDA

Introduction

Ss watch an extract from the BBC comedy series *Miranda*, which shows the main character trying to change her life. Ss then learn and practise how to talk about a time when they learnt something new and write a magazine interview.

> **SUPPLEMENTARY MATERIALS**
>
> **Warm up:** prepare sets of cards with collocations (see notes).
>
> **Ex 2D (optional extra activity):** prepare a handout with sentences about the DVD extract for Ss to choose the correct alternatives (see notes).
>
> **Ex 3A:** bring in/download pictures of ideas for new things to learn.
>
> **Ex 3B:** be prepared to answer questions about a time when you tried to learn something new.

Warm up

Review collocations from lessons 10.1 and 10.2. Prepare one set of cards per pair with the following collocations: *stop smoking, get fit, change jobs, play an instrument, ride a bike, get organised, make a coffee, drive a bus, lose weight, save money, spend time with friends, learn something new.*

Ss put the cards in a pile face down in front of them and take turns to pick a card. The person with the card says the part of the collocation after the verb and their partner has to remember the correct verb and say the full collocation, e.g.

A: *time with friends*
B: *spend time with friends*
A: *Correct!*

DVD PREVIEW

1A Ss could start by covering the prompts and trying to think of one thing for each situation, then tell the class their ideas. When Ss look at the prompts, you may want to check: *the wrong clothes* (give an example, e.g. jeans for a wedding), *feel stupid* (you could mime this), *too expensive* (you can't pay for it). Give Ss a few minutes to decide which problems go with each situation.

> **Suggested answers:**
>
> learn something new: all the prompts apart from *It's too expensive*
>
> change jobs: all the prompts apart from *The teacher doesn't like you, It's too expensive*
>
> go to a new place: *You have the wrong clothes, You don't know the people, It's too expensive*
>
> spend time with friends: *You're bored, You have the wrong clothes*
>
> try to get fit: all the prompts apart from *You don't know the people*

B Before Ss read the information, check: *the star* (the most important person), *thirty-something* (between 31 and 39). Once Ss have checked their answers in pairs, they could think of a possible problem with each of the things Miranda does to become the 'New Me', then share their ideas with the class. Possible problems:

- the French class: she's bored, she makes mistakes, the teacher doesn't like her
- the new job: she has the wrong clothes, she's bored, she doesn't understand what to do
- the diet club: she feels stupid, she doesn't know the people, it's too expensive
- the Japanese restaurant: it's too expensive, she doesn't understand what to do

> **Answers:**
> 1 Miranda wants to change her life.
> 2 She: learns something new, starts a new job, goes to a new place, spends time with friends.

DVD VIEW

2A Give Ss time to read through the problems and places before they watch the extract. Check *get stuck* (mime walking along and your foot getting stuck in a hole), *pies and sweets* (simple board drawing). You could play the extract without sound the first time: Ss can match the problems and places without hearing what Miranda says.

> **Answers:** 1 a), d) 2 c) 3 b), f) 4 a), e)

B Ss try to remember/predict which phrases Miranda said.

C When Ss have checked their answers, you could also ask them who says the other phrases.

b) – her friend at the French class

f), g) – the teacher at the diet club

> **Answers:** c) d) h) i) j)

D Give Ss a minute or two to predict the order of the sentences, then play that part of the DVD again for them to check.

> **Answers:** d) a) c) b) e)

Optional extra activities

1 Comprehension activity, using the past simple. Write or display the following on the board, or put them on a handout for Ss:

  a) The French teacher was Miranda's *friend/teacher* at school.
  b) Miranda wanted to leave before he *saw/smiled* at her.
  c) Miranda felt *nervous/hot* when she arrived at her new job.
  d) At the diet club the *meat/fruit* and vegetables were on the right.
  e) At the restaurant Miranda's *bag/necklace* got stuck.
  f) She offered another customer *soy sauce/tea.*

  (Answers: a) teacher b) saw c) nervous d) fruit e) necklace f) soy sauce)

2 Role-play activity. In pairs, Ss choose one of the following situations and role-play the conversation between the two people:

- Miranda and her flatmate, telling her about the things she tried and what happened.
- The French teacher and his wife/girlfriend, telling her about Miranda.
- The woman working at the sushi restaurant telling her friend about Miranda.
- Another student from the diet club, telling a friend about what happened.

Invite Ss to act out their conversations for the class.

DVD 10   Miranda

Miranda tries a French class

M= Miranda   S= Stevie   MC = Mr Clayton

M: I don't like school. It's freaking me out. Don't run in the corridor, pull your skirt down.
What is this?
S: Oh wow! He's lovely! Cute smile.
M: Oh, it's him! Stevie, that's Mr Clayton, my old French teacher.
S: No way.
M: Right, I'm going to go before he can see me.
I'm stuck in the chair.
Stevie … I'm stuck in the chair!
S: It's about to start.
MC: Bonjour la classe.
Miranda?
M: Good evening. Bonsoir.

Miranda tries a new job

M= Miranda

M: OK, I can do this … deep breath.
Oh … oh.
Hi, morning … just got a very hot leg!
Yo!

Miranda tries a diet club

M= Miranda   W = Woman   G = Group

W: Gather. Gather please. That's it. Gather please. So, which section, to the left or the right, looks the most delicious?
G: To the left.
W: No, try again.
G: To the left.
M: I think we're always going to say to the left, to the left … tell you for why, it's got pies on it.
W: Look, I am just trying to help you help yourself.
M: Say what?
W: Help yourself.
M: Thank you very much. It looks lovely.
W: No, not to the buffet! Sit down!

Miranda tries a new Japanese restaurant

M= Miranda   W = Woman

M: No, I'm stuck. My trinity necklace.
W: Cindy's on the floor.
M: My trinity necklace.
M: I'm stuck. Actually sorry, sorry. OK …
W: Just un, just undo it at the back.
M: I can't. There's too much down the hole. So sorry, sorry. sorry. Hello, afternoon. I've unhooked, I've unhooked, sorry about this, sorry, sorry. Sorry about this. Can I? I mean whilst I'm here, OK. Hello again. Right, where were we?
W: Leaving.
M: Quick!

speakout something new

3A Start by brainstorming some examples of new things people learn. You could bring in/download pictures to represent some of the following and display them on the board to help Ss with ideas: a sport (e.g. sailing, skiing), a game (e.g. cards, chess), riding a horse/a bike, playing a musical instrument, dancing, painting/drawing, making clothes/jewellery/pottery, photography, cooking (e.g. Italian/Indian/Chinese food), learning another language. Give Ss time to make notes, working alone.

B You could start by inviting different Ss to ask you the questions about a time you tried to learn something new.

C You may need to play the recording twice for Ss to answer all the questions fully. Give them time to compare answers before listening a second time.

> **Answers:**
> 1 She started to learn guitar three years ago because she can sing and she likes music.
> 2 Alone (at first) but she wasn't very good.
> 3 She had a teacher. He was good.
> 4 The teacher gave her homework. She learnt to play well after four months. She still plays.

D Give Ss time to read the key phrases, then play the recording again.

> **Answers:**
> I wanted to learn [to play guitar ✓/to cook] because …
> I went to a class.
> I tried to learn it [alone ✓/with a friend].
> I was/wasn't ✓ [very] good at it.
> The teacher was [great ✓/good/not very good].
> After [four ✓/ six] months I [played guitar ✓/did it] really well.
> I still [do it/play ✓] every day.

> **Optional extra activity**
> Remind Ss about some of the prompts in Ex 1A by asking them to complete the following sentence stems with some of the prompts:
> *I went to a class but (the teacher didn't like me/I made mistakes).*
> *I tried to learn it alone but (I didn't understand what to do/I wasn't good at it).*
> Ss could also change the prompts to the positive:
> *The teacher was great because (I didn't feel stupid/I wasn't bored/I made mistakes but it was OK).*

4A First, give Ss time alone to prepare what they want to say: direct them back to their answers to the questions in Ex 3A and tell them to use the key phrases and their own ideas to expand the answers into a story. When they practise telling their story to their partner, encourage the partners to give feedback, e.g. suggest some other information they could include, or explain something more clearly.

B Put Ss in groups of four or five. Tell Ss that while each person is talking about their experience, the listeners should make notes and write one question about what the person tried to learn to ask them when they've finished. Point out that Ss will need this information about each other for Ex 5B and for their homework. Monitor Ss as they tell their stories and make notes of good language use and any problem areas for praise and correction at the end.

> **Unit 10 Recording 9**
>
> Three years ago I bought a guitar. I wanted to learn to play guitar because I can sing and I like music. I tried to learn it alone. I had a book and I practised every day. I learnt some songs, and I played guitar and sang the songs. I was happy, but then my boyfriend said I wasn't very good at it. He said I needed a teacher. So I found a teacher, and studied guitar with him. The teacher was great but it was very different because he gave me homework every week. After four months I played guitar really well. I still play every day.

writeback an interview

5A Give Ss time to read the interview, then discuss the questions in pairs.

> **Answers:**
> 1 To use *Twitter*. Because his or her friends use *Twitter*.
> Answers to **2** and **3** will vary.

B Ss should use the notes they made while they were listening to other Ss in Ex 4B. Point out that they should also extend the interview beyond the last line of the example interview in Ex 5A, i.e. they should include questions and answers about how the person learnt (*Did you have a teacher?*) and how successful they were (*Were you good at it? Do you still do it now?*). You could then invite some individuals to read out their interview with a new partner (not the student in the interview) and ask the rest of the class to guess who it was.

> **Homework ideas**
> Ss write an interview with another student from their group in Ex 4B.

LOOKBACK

COLLOCATIONS

1A You could run this as a race. The first pair to write in the correct verbs and bring them up to show you wins the race.

> **Answers:**
> **2** I ~~read~~ chess every weekend.   *play*
> **3** It's easy to ~~ride~~ maps.   *read*
> **4** I ~~play~~ two languages.   *speak*
> **5** I ~~cook~~ all my clothes.   *make*
> **6** I don't ~~remember~~ Powerpoint in my job.   *use*
> **7** I would like to ~~make~~ a horse.   *ride*
> **8** It's easy to ~~use~~ phone numbers.   *remember*

B You could either elicit the words/phrases from the class as a whole, or put Ss in pairs and give them a time limit.

> **Suggested answers:**
> play: football, the guitar, computer games
> read: music, words in Arabic
> speak: Spanish, Japanese
> make: a pizza, a coffee, a sandwich
> use: a computer, a coffee machine
> ride: a bicycle, a motorbike
> remember: information, English words, birthdays

C Ss could also use the verbs they thought of in Ex 1B to change the sentences and make them true, e.g. *I often cook pasta. I play football every weekend.*

CAN/CAN'T

2A Tell Ss to write the questions in their notebooks. You could say the questions for Ss to repeat, making sure that they stress the noun and the main verb, e.g.
What <u>languages</u> can you <u>speak</u>?

> **Answers:**
> What computer programs can you use?
> What sports can you play?
> What food can you cook?
> What important dates can you remember?

B Tell Ss to ask each other the questions in random order, so they can't predict which question is next and have to listen to each other. Ss could report back to the class on things they have in common, and any of their partner's answers that they thought were surprising.

> **Alternative approach**
> Tell Ss to include one answer which is not true. Their partner then has to guess which answer it is, but they only have two chances to guess. Ss win a point if their partner doesn't guess correctly.

LIFE CHANGES

3A Ss could do this alone or you could run it as a race in pairs.

> **Answers:** **2** change jobs   **3** save money   **4** learn something new
> **5** spend more time with friends   **6** work less and relax more
> **7** help others   **8** stop smoking   **9** lose weight   **10** get fit

B You could suggest that Ss put the life changes in order from *easy → difficult* before they start discussing. For **stronger classes**, tell them to justify their answers, e.g. *It's easy to learn something new if you want to do it.*

BE GOING TO

4A Tell Ss that the man wrote a list when he decided to do the things earlier. Elicit other places to write plans, e.g. in a diary, in the calendar, on your computer or in your phone. Put Ss in pairs to write the sentences and help each other with the correct verbs.

> **Answers:**
> He's going to meet Sue and Jenny at the café.
> He's going to get fit at the gym.
> He's going to get 200 euros at the cash machine.
> He's going to get/buy a newspaper at the newsagent's.
> He's going to buy/get aspirin at the pharmacy.

> **Optional extra activity**
> Tell Ss to close their books and write the following prompts on the board:
> *shampoo   bread and coffee   do a class   125 euros*
> *Tim and Mike   a magazine*
> Ss write the man's plans, remembering the places that he's going to go to and matching the prompts to them, e.g.
> *He's going to buy shampoo at the pharmacy.*

B You could demonstrate this by writing four places for yourself. You may also want to brainstorm some names of places with the class, e.g. *the library, the doctor's, the dentist's, the swimming pool, the cinema, (name) school, the garage*, etc.

C Demonstrate the activity with a student taking the part of B.

STARTING AND ENDING CONVERSATIONS

5A Give Ss a few minutes to complete the conversation, working alone.

> **Answers:**
> A: Hi!
> B: Oh, hi. How *are* you?
> A: Good, thanks. This is a *nice* café.
> B: Yes, I sometimes come here for lunch.
> A: Really? What *do* you think of the food?
> B: Er … it's good. Wait, is *that* the time?
> A: No, that clock's wrong. It's two o'clock.
> B: Oh no, my train leaves in five *minutes*!
> A: No problem. There's a train every half hour.
> B: Sorry, I can see an old friend over *there*.
> A: Oh, OK. *Nice* to talk to you.
> B: You too. See *you* soon …

B Encourage Ss to look up from the page as much as possible, and cover the conversation when they feel confident with it.

C Demonstrate how to change the parts in bold, e.g.
A: **Very well**, thanks. This is a nice **restaurant**.
B: Yes, I sometimes come here for **dinner**.

D Ss can either change partners or stand up and walk around the class, practising the conversation with different people, and changing it as they go along. Monitor this speaking practice and be prepared to give feedback on Ss' language use.

SAYING GOODBYE

6 You could run this as a competition in teams. To win points, Ss need to spell the corrected word correctly.

> **Answers:** **1** See you later.   **2** Bye.   **3** See you ~~one~~ *next* week.
> **4** Keep ~~on~~ *in* touch.   **5** See *you* soon.

CONSOLIDATION 5: UNITS 9–10

Introduction

The aim of the consolidation units is for Ss to revise and practise the grammar, vocabulary and pronunciation from the previous two units in a different context. The context for this consolidation unit is Ss' progress in English so far and plans for improving their English in the future.

> **SUPPLEMENTARY MATERIALS**
> **Ex 4A:** prepare strips of paper with ideas to help Ss (see notes).

Warm up

Tell Ss to close their books and write the title *What can you do in English?* on the board. Also write the following verb prompts and put Ss in pairs to think about what they can do: *talk about, describe, ask, answer, pronounce, tell, write.* Invite Ss to share their ideas with the rest of the class.

> **Suggested answers:**
> talk about (e.g. my job, travel), describe (e.g. a place, a possession), ask (e.g. someone's name and address, about someone's opinions), answer (e.g. about my likes and dislikes, about my family, about my plans), pronounce (e.g. the alphabet in English), tell (e.g. a story), write (e.g. an email to a friend, a quiz)

READING AND GRAMMAR

1A Before Ss start the questionnaire, check the following vocabulary: *count* (demonstrate), *order* (demonstrate), *routines* (things you do every day/week), *sound* (demonstrate *sound happy, sound sad*). Check that Ss understand when to put a tick (✓), a question mark (?) or a cross (✗) if they think they can't do it.

B Go through the example, then suggest a few different answers that Ss could give to their partner, depending on how confident they feel:
Yes, definitely.
Yes, but I need more practice.
I'm not really confident about that yet.
Not really.

Give Ss time to ask and answer all the questions: they could ask some of the questions in random order, so their partners can't predict which question is next and have to listen more carefully. Ss could report back to the class about things they can both do, e.g. *We can both order food and drink in a café.* (NB: The position of *can* comes before *both.*)

C First, check that Ss understand *improve* (make better). Give them a few minutes to think about the skills and complete the sentences, working alone.

D Once again, Ss can see what they have in common.

2A To give Ss a simple reading task while they read the text, ask them which three things from the box in Ex 1C the student writes about (Answer: reading, listening, pronunciation). Ss then work alone to substitute the pronouns and compare answers with a partner.

> **Answers:** **2** her **3** me **4** she **5** us **6** they **7** We **8** them **9** them **10** my **11** him **12** their

B Give Ss a few minutes to discuss the questions in pairs, then invite them to share their ideas with the class.

> **Suggested answers:**
> **2** The most important words in each sentence are stressed by the speaker, so this helps you to follow the overall meaning of the text.
> **3** You can imitate the person's pronunciation and try to match the speed, rhythm and tone, so you sound more natural.

LISTENING AND GRAMMAR

3A Tell Ss that the people are talking about areas of English they want to work on/improve, then play the recording.

> **Answers:** **2** Speaking **3** Listening **4** Grammar **5** Writing

B You could ask Ss to work in pairs and discuss which alternative they think is best, before they listen again and check the speakers' answers.

> **Answers:** **1** seven **2** write **3** coffee break **4** at the same time **5** write **6** day

C You could discuss this question with the class as a whole, and ask Ss to justify their answers.

> **Consolidation 5 Recording 1**
>
> **1**
> I want to learn a lot of vocabulary, so I'm going to learn seven new words every day. I like reading, so I'm going to look at the BBC news website and write down new words.
>
> **2**
> Speaking is a problem for me. In the coffee break, I'm not going to speak in my language. I'm going to speak in English. All the time!
>
> **3**
> I can't understand English very well, so I'm going to practise listening. I'm going to listen to my CD and read the audio scripts at the same time.
>
> **4**
> My grammar is bad. Very bad! I'm going to look on the internet and do some extra grammar practice.
>
> **5**
> I want to improve my writing, so I'm going to write a diary every night, in English. I'm going to write about my day.

SPEAKING

4A As well as directing Ss to Ex 3A for ideas, you could put the following prompts on strips of paper and pass them round the class for Ss to use if they match Ss' goals and appeal to them as a good idea:

- Read and write to an internet forum about something you are interested in.
- Have a speaking partner in the class and speak English for ten minutes every day.
- Use the *speakout* CD to practise sounds.
- Watch the *speakout* interviews at home and read the audio script at the same time.
- Write new words in a vocabulary book.
- Read an easy English book.

B Put Ss in groups of four or five to tell each other their plans. Monitor the activity and invite any student who has particularly good ideas to tell the whole class about them at the end.

5 Direct Ss to p117 and give them a minute or two to look at the game and the instructions. Then check the instructions by asking Ss about squares 1 and 2, e.g.

T: *What do I do for number 1?*
Ss: *You talk about your town/city or country for thirty seconds.*
T: *And for number 2?*
Ss: *You say and spell three transport words.*

(NB: Tell Ss that they should use a watch or timer function on a mobile phone to time the speaker for thirty seconds. Put Ss into groups of three or four to play the game.)

If you don't have any dice, tell each group to tear a small piece of paper into six pieces and write a number from 1–6 on each one. Then they can put the pieces of paper in an envelope or small bag and each person can pick a number when it's their turn. Ss can use a coin or other small object as their counter. Monitor the groups carefully and make notes of good language use and any problem areas for praise and correction later.

SOUNDS: /ɑː/ AND /ɜː/

6A Direct Ss to the pictures and point out that the symbols represent the sounds. Play the recording for Ss to listen to the sounds and the words. You could also show Ss that to make /ɑː/ their mouth is open (as if they're at the dentist's), and that for /ɜː/ the sound is like someone's reaction when they hear about something that sounds horrible to eat (e.g. spaghetti with chocolate).

B You may want to ask Ss in pairs to predict which group the words belong to before they listen. You could pause the recording after each group of words, and ask individual Ss to repeat them, rather than Ss repeating in chorus. This will give you more opportunity to correct their pronunciation of the 'target' sounds.

Answers:
/ɑː/ last, party, guitarist, can't, dance
/ɜː/ first, learn, girlfriend, work, circle

7A/B Look at the example with the class, then put Ss in pairs to work out the answers. Alternatively, you could put Ss in teams and run this as a competition, writing/reading out one clue at a time, e.g. *a yellow fruit with /ɑː/ that begins with a 'b'* (Ss close their books).

Answers:

	/ɑː/
a country	Argentina
a yellow fruit	banana
the 3rd month	March
a form of *be*	are
not near, but …	far
morning, … , evening	afternoon
the opposite of *soft*	hard
	/ɜː/
Berlin is there	Germany
a colour	purple
a type of clothes	shirt
a day	Thursday
a form of *be*	were
Give me water, I'm …	thirsty
a number	thirteen/thirty

Homework ideas

- Ss write an email to a friend telling them about their plans for improving their English.
- Ss start a diary in English.
- Ss look at some websites in English and report back to another student, or to the class if there is another lesson after this one.
- **Workbook:** Ex 1– 4, p68–69

BBC interviews and worksheet

What did you want to be?

In this video people talk about their jobs and whether they like them or not. Ss can recap and extend their knowledge of vocabulary on the topic of jobs/work and leisure activities. They can also practice listening to and revise structures with the past simple.

PAGE	UNIT	PHOTOCOPIABLE	LANGUAGE POINT	TIME
141	1	Famous historical figures	**Grammar: *What's your ...? Are you ...?*** • practise *be: I/you* • practise speaking skills by asking and answering questions about people	20–30
142	1	Where's it from?	**Vocabulary: countries and common words** • practise countries and words for common objects	25–30
143	1	How do you spell it?	**Vocabulary: classroom objects** • review classroom objects • practise letters of the alphabet	30
144	1	Identity card	**Functional language: giving personal information** • practise giving personal information • practise speaking skills by asking and answering questions about people	30
145	2	A family business	**Grammar: *she/he/they; his/her/their*** • practise subject pronouns and possessive adjectives in the third person	25–30
146	2	Hotel rooms	**Vocabulary: numbers and family** • practise numbers • practise words for members of the family • review questions with *Where is ...?*	25–30
147	2	Are you happy?	**Vocabulary: feelings** • practise adjectives for feelings • review numbers • review letters of the alphabet	25–30
148	2	Let's go!	**Functional language: making suggestions** • practise making suggestions and responding to suggestions • review adjectives for feelings	25–30
149	3	Lost property	**Grammar: *that is/those are; possessive 's; because*** • practise *that/those* • practise vocabulary for objects • practise the possessive *'s* • practise using *because* to explain a situation	25–30
150	3	Mystery objects	**Grammar: *What's this? What are these?*** • practise *this/these* • practise vocabulary for objects • review *be*	25–30
151	3	Clothing styles	**Vocabulary: clothes** • practise vocabulary for items of clothing • review the possessive *'s* • practise speaking skills by giving opinions	30–40
152	3	Café Royale	**Functional language: ordering in a café** • practise ordering in a café by putting a conversation in order • review vocabulary for food • practise speaking skills by acting out a scene in a café	30–35
153	4	Similarities and differences	**Grammar: present simple: *he/she/it*** • practise the present simple third person singular to make comparisons between two people • practise verb phrases	20–25
154	4	Things in common	**Vocabulary: verb phrases; *me too*** • practise verb phrases by making sentences in a matching game • practise using *me too* to show agreement	20
155	4	Find someone who	**Vocabulary: time phrases** • practise time phrases • practise using prepositions to form time phrases • practise speaking skills by asking and answering about habits	30
156	4	Times around the world	**Functional language: telling the time** • practise saying the time • practise asking and answering about the time	30
157	5	Game board	**Grammar: adverbs of frequency** • practise adverbs of frequency to talk about habits in the context of a board game • review verb phrases	25–30
158	5	Noisy neighbours	**Vocabulary: daily routines** • practise vocabulary for daily routines • review telling the time	25–30
159	5	Crossword	**Vocabulary: food** • practise vocabulary for food in the context of a crossword • practise asking and answering questions to elicit crossword clues	25–30
160	5	Be my guest	**Functional language: asking for information** • practise asking for information • practise vocabulary for hotel services	30

RESOURCE BANK

Index of photocopiables

PAGE	UNIT	PHOTOCOPIABLE	LANGUAGE POINT	TIME
161	6	Sunny Spain	**Grammar: *a/some*; *Is there a …?/Are there any …?*** • practise *a/some* • practise the question form *Is there a …?/Are there any …?* • practise short answers • review vocabulary for objects	30
162	6	Spot the difference	**Grammar: *there is/are*; *a/an, some, a lot of, not any*** • practise *a/an, some/a lot of/not any* • practise *there is/are* • review vocabulary for shops and services	25–30
163	6	Give us a clue	**Vocabulary: places** • practise vocabulary for places in the context of a crossword • practise asking and answering questions to elicit crossword clues	30
164	6	Paris in the spring	**Functional language: completing travel timetable information** • practise asking and answering about travel information • review vocabulary for transport • review telling the time	30
165	7	Did you know?	**Grammar: past simple regular verbs** • practise the past simple of regular verbs • practise dates	20
166	7	Where were you?	**Grammar: past simple *was/were*** • practise the past simple *was/were* in the context of a board game • practise dates • review time phrases	30
167	7	Great fun	**Vocabulary: adjectives and common collocations** • practise adjectives and common collocations with nouns	30
168	7	How was it?	**Functional language: giving opinions** • practise asking and answering about opinions • review verb phrases	25–30
169	8	Alibi	**Grammar: past simple** • review vocabulary for transport • practise using the past simple of regular and irregular verbs	25–30
170	8	Firsts	**Grammar: past simple questions and answers (irregular verbs)** • practise the past simple question and answer form of irregular verbs in the context of a questionnaire • review verb phrases	20–25
171	8	Missing objects	**Vocabulary: prepositions of place** • practise prepositions of place • review vocabulary for objects	20–25
172	8	Village life	**Functional language: giving directions** • practise asking for and giving directions • review vocabulary for places	20–25
173	9	Opinions	**Grammar: subject/object pronouns** • practise subject and object pronouns • practise expressing likes and dislikes • review vocabulary for objects, activities and food	25–30
174	9	Do you like …?	**Grammar: *love, like, hate* + *-ing*/noun** • practise asking about and expressing likes and dislikes • review vocabulary for activities and animals and verb phrases	25
175	9	Money, money, money!	**Vocabulary: money** • practise vocabulary for money • practise speaking skills by asking and answering a questionnaire	25
176	9	What would you like?	**Functional language: making offers and requests** • practise making offers and requests • review vocabulary for places, objects and adjectives for feelings	30
177	10	Rules	**Grammar: *can/can't*** • practise *can* and *can't* • review vocabulary for places and verb phrases	30–40
178	10	Good intentions	**Grammar: *be going to*** • practise talking about future plans with *going to* • review verb phrases and question words	25–30
179	10	Collocations	**Vocabulary: collocations** • practise verb phrases • practise asking and answering about abilities	25–30
180	10	See you later, alligator!	**Functional language: starting and ending conversations** • review holding conversations in different settings	25–30

Grammar: *What's your …? Are you …?*

You're French. You're a footballer and an actor. Your name is Eric Cantona.	You're Jamaican. You're a singer. Your name is Bob Marley.	You're Spanish. You're an artist. Your name is Picasso.
You're German. You're a scientist. Your name is Einstein.	You're Argentinian. You're a footballer. Your name is Maradona.	You're British. You're a spy. Your name is James Bond.
You're Austrian. You're a doctor. Your name is Sigmund Freud.	You're Italian. You're an artist and an inventor. Your name is Leonardo da Vinci.	You're English. You're a writer. Your name is Shakespeare.
You're Italian. You're a musician. Your name is Vivaldi.	You're American. You're an actress. Your name is Marilyn Monroe.	You're American. You're a singer. Your name is Elvis.

Are you … ?

Einstein

Vivaldi

Maradona

Marilyn Monroe

Shakespeare

Bob Marley

James Bond

Leonardo da Vinci

Sigmund Freud

Elvis

Picasso

Eric Cantona

NATIONALITY	JOB	NAME

CAR	BUS	HAT	CHEESE
CLOCK	SPAGHETTI	FLAG	COFFEE
FLOWERS	PASSPORT	DANCER	SUSHI
GERMANY	GREAT BRITAIN	MEXICO	FRANCE
SWITZERLAND	ITALY	CANADA	BRAZIL
THE NETHERLANDS	CHINA	SPAIN	JAPAN

Worksheet A

1 Complete the words and match them to the pictures.

1 a c _ _ i _   Picture _____
2 a _ e _   Picture _____
3 a n _ _ _ _ b _ _ _ _   Picture _____
4 a p _ _ _ c _ _ _   Picture _____
5 a d _ _ _ r   Picture _____
6 a w _ _ _ k _ o o _   Picture _____

2 Ask your partner for the missing words.

Picture B _____   Picture F _____
Picture C _____   Picture I _____
Picture D _____   Picture L _____

Worksheet B

1 Complete the words and match them to the pictures.

1 a _ _ a b _ _ _   Picture _____
2 a l _ _ _ t _ _ _   Picture _____
3 the b _ _ _ r _ _   Picture _____
4 a _ _ a _ _   Picture _____
5 a s _ _ _ d _ _ _ _ _ 's b _ _ _ k   Picture _____
6 a n _ _ t _ _ c _ _ b _ _ _ _ d   Picture _____

2 Ask your partner for the missing words.

Picture A _____   Picture H _____
Picture E _____   Picture J _____
Picture G _____   Picture K _____

STUDENT REGISTRATION FORM

Name: _Ana Garcia_

Email address: _agarcia21@mail.es_

Country: _Spain_

Occupation: _Student_

Mobile phone number: _0657 453 210_

STUDENT REGISTRATION FORM

Name: _Thiago Alves_

Email address: _talves@mail.com_

Country: _Brazil_

Occupation: _Doctor_

Mobile phone number: _0786 4351112_

STUDENT REGISTRATION FORM

Name: _Jessica Pirelli_

Email address: _pirelli@email.com_

Country: _Italy_

Occupation: _Teacher_

Mobile phone number: _0781 953612_

STUDENT REGISTRATION FORM

Name: _Akemi Fukuda_

Email address: _afukada@mail.jp_

Country: _Japan_

Occupation: _Teacher_

Mobile phone number: _090 456 383 82_

Ask questions to complete the forms.

STUDENT REGISTRATION FORM

Name: _____

Email address: _____

Country: _____

Occupation: _____

Mobile phone number: _____

STUDENT REGISTRATION FORM

Name: _____

Email address: _____

Country: _____

Occupation: _____

Mobile phone number: _____

STUDENT REGISTRATION FORM

Name: _____

Email address: _____

Country: _____

Occupation: _____

Mobile phone number: _____

1 Carolyn is the mother. She's the cook. She's in the kitchen.

2 Her husband is Matthew. He's the manager. He's in the office.

3 Rosanna is their daughter. She's the porter. She's at the entrance.

4 Orlando is their son. He's the waiter. He's in the hotel restaurant.

5 Petra is his wife. She's the waitress. She's in the hotel restaurant.

6 Lionel is her brother. He's the barman. He's in the bar.

7 Paula is her sister. She's the gardener. She's in the garden.

8 Her parents are Scott and Danielle. They're on holiday! They're in the swimming pool.

Worksheet A

1 Look at the hotel plan. Find out which rooms these people are in.

Where is the mother?

The mother _____.
The brother _____.
The husband _____.
The daughter _____.
The children _____.

	The son			The parents
Room 52	Room 99		Room 84	Room 73

HOTEL COLORADO

The wife		The father		The sister	
Room 33	Room 100	Room 19	Room 13	Room 28	Room 67

2 Tell your partner which rooms the family members are in.

The father is in room nineteen.

Worksheet B

1 Look at the hotel plan. Tell your partner which rooms the family members are in.

The mother is in room fifty-two.

The mother			The brother	
Room 52	Room 99		Room 84	Room 73

HOTEL COLORADO

	The husband		The daughter		The children
Room 33	Room 100	Room 19	Room 13	Room 28	Room 67

2 Find out which rooms these people are in.

Where is the father?

The father _____.
The sister _____.
The wife _____.
The son _____.
The parents _____.

Worksheet A

1 Put the letters in the correct order to make feelings. Where is the stress?
Match the word to the picture.

phayp _____   iretd _____   sihtryt _____   dbroe _____

2 Ask your partner for other words: *What's picture …? How do spell it?*

Worksheet B

1 Put the letters in the correct order to make feelings. Where is the stress?
Match the word to the picture.

lcdo _____   ghrnuy _____   tho _____   nagyr _____

2 Ask your partner for other words: *What's picture …? How do spell it?*

Me too!	Let's eat a pizza.	Good idea!
Me too!	Let's go inside.	Yeah! OK!
Are you?	Yes, let's have a break.	OK.
Let's go to a café.	Good idea! Let's have a soft drink.	Oooh! Yes, please!
Let's go!	Where?	Let's go to the cinema.
Me too!	Let's drink some cold water!	Good idea!

Grammar: *that is/those are*; **possessive *'s***; *because*

1 Find the following objects in the picture. Write the number.
   Are the objects singular (S) or plural (P)?

gloves __4__ __P__   newspaper _____ _____   computer _____ _____
bag _____ _____   tie _____ _____   diary _____ _____
shoes _____ _____   passport _____ _____   camera _____ _____
trainers _____ _____   keys _____ _____   German–English dictionary _____ _____

2 Masaka, Anya and Pedro are at Frankfurt Airport lost property office. These are their objects.
   Turn over the cards to match the objects to the person.

Masaki is from Japan.	Masaki is a footballer.	Masaki is on holiday.	Masaki is in The Mirage Hotel.
Anya is German.	Anya is an English student.	Anya lives in Frankfurt. Frankfurt is a very cold city.	Anya is a student at Frankfurt University.
Pedro is from Marbella in Spain.	Pedro is a computer engineer.	Pedro writes a diary.	Pedro is on business.

Grammar: *What's this? What are these?*

Worksheet A

Add the vowels to complete the objects. Then ask and answer about the other objects:
What's this? It's a … What are these? They're …

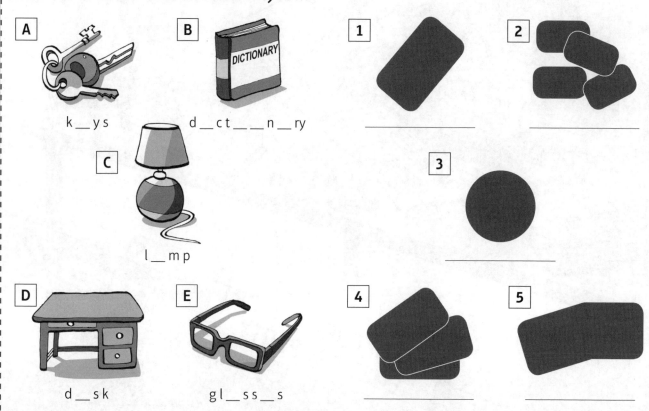

A k _ _ y s

B d _ _ c t _ _ _ n _ ry

C l _ _ m p

D d _ _ s k

E gl _ _ s s _ _ s

1 _____

2 _____

3 _____

4 _____

5 _____

Worksheet B

Add the vowels to complete the objects. Then ask and answer about the other objects:
What's this? It's a … What are these? They're …

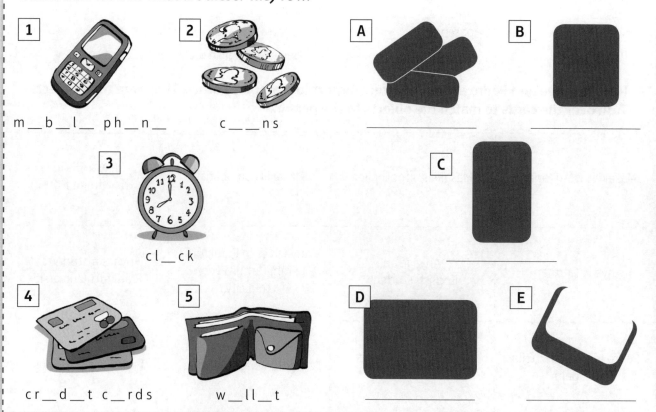

1 m _ _ b _ l _ _ ph _ n _

2 c _ _ _ n s

3 cl _ _ c k

4 cr _ _ d _ _ t c _ _ r d s

5 w _ _ l l _ _ t

A _____

B _____

C _____

D _____

E _____

1 Work in pairs. Find nine items of clothing.

t-shirtshoesshirtcoathattieglovesskirtglasses

2 Look at the pictures. Work in pairs. Match the clothes to one of the people.

Anna   Tina   Chris   Dan

3 Work in groups. Are your answers the same?

1 Put the sentences from the conversation in order.

a) W: Here you are. An egg sandwich and a white coffee. _____

b) C: Yes, an egg sandwich, please. _____

c) C: Brown bread, please. _____

d) W: Anything to drink? _____

e) W: That's ten euros, please. _____

f) W: Can I help you? __1__

g) W: Thank you! _____

h) C: Yes, a white coffee, please. _____

i) C: How much is that? _____

j) C: Here you are. _____

k) W: White or brown bread? _____

2 Practise the conversation with a partner.

3 Work in pairs. One of you is the waiter and the other is the customer. Use the menu to order.

Café Royale

Price list

Black coffee 3.00 €
White coffee 3.60 €
Sparkling water 1.60 €
Still water 1.10 €
Cola 1.75 €

* * * *

Chicken sandwich (brown) 6.70 €
Chicken sandwich (white) 6.40 €
Cheese sandwich (brown) 6.60 €
Cheese sandwich (white) 6.40 €
Egg sandwich (brown) 5.50 €
Egg sandwich (white) 5.20 €

* * * *

Chocolate cake 4.50 €
Carrot cake 4.30 €

Worksheet A

Use the picture to talk about Victoria. Mark the similarities with Judy with a ✓ and the differences with a ✗.

She lives in a house. ✗

Worksheet B

Use the picture to talk about Judy. Mark the similarities with Victoria with a ✓ and the differences with a ✗.

She lives in a flat. ✗

FRIDAY

Worksheet A

1 Complete the questions with the correct preposition: *at/in/on/every*.

	YOU	NAME
What do you do _____ the mornings before work?		
Where do you go _____ Saturday night?		
What do you do _____ the weekend?		
Do you go to the cinema _____ week?		
Do you do your English homework _____ night?		
Do you watch television _____ evening?		
Do you meet your friends _____ Saturdays and Sundays?		

2 Answer the questions for you.

3 Ask the other students. Find another student who has the same answer as you.

Worksheet B

1 Complete the questions with the correct preposition: *at/in/on/every*.

	YOU	NAME
What do you do _____ the evenings after work?		
Where do you go _____ Friday nights?		
Do you play sport _____ the weekend?		
Do you go to English classes _____ week?		
Do you use the computer _____ night?		
Do you drink coffee _____ day?		
Do you work _____ Saturdays?		

2 Answer the questions for you.

3 Ask the other students. Find another student who has the same answer as you.

Worksheet A

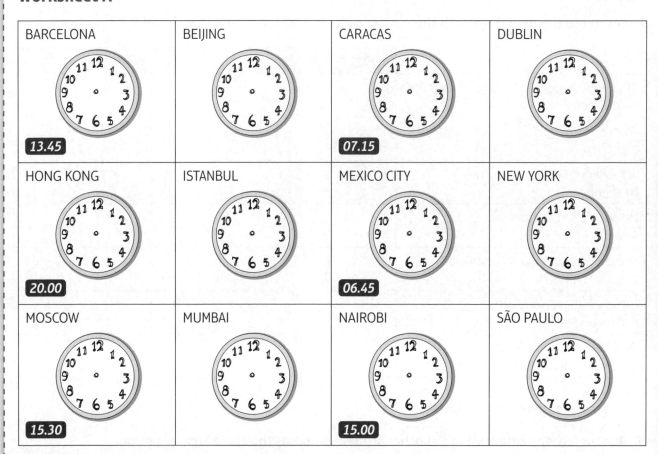

BARCELONA	BEIJING	CARACAS	DUBLIN
13.45		07.15	

HONG KONG	ISTANBUL	MEXICO CITY	NEW YORK
20.00		06.45	

MOSCOW	MUMBAI	NAIROBI	SÃO PAULO
15.30		15.00	

Worksheet B

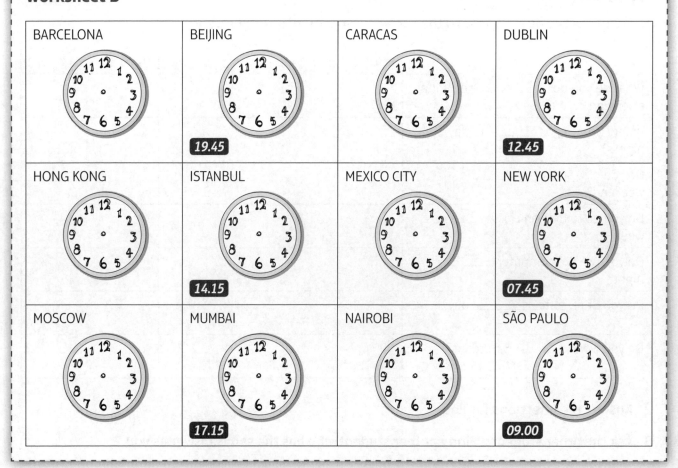

BARCELONA	BEIJING	CARACAS	DUBLIN
	19.45		12.45

HONG KONG	ISTANBUL	MEXICO CITY	NEW YORK
	14.15		07.45

MOSCOW	MUMBAI	NAIROBI	SÃO PAULO
	17.15		09.00

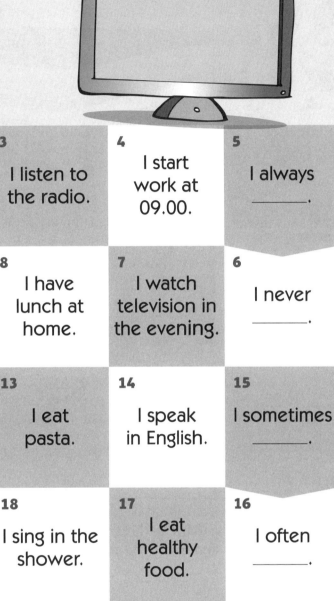

1	2	3	4	5
START	I have breakfast.	I listen to the radio.	I start work at 09.00.	I always _____ .

10	9	8	7	6
I get up late on Sundays.	I have dinner in a restaurant.	I have lunch at home.	I watch television in the evening.	I never _____ .

11	12	13	14	15
I eat fish on Fridays.	I go to bed before midnight.	I eat pasta.	I speak in English.	I sometimes _____ .

20	19	18	17	16
I walk to work.	I do my homework.	I sing in the shower.	I eat healthy food.	I often _____ .

21	22	23	24	25
I'm late for classes.	I go to the cinema.	I drink coffee.	I don't _____ often.	**FINISH**

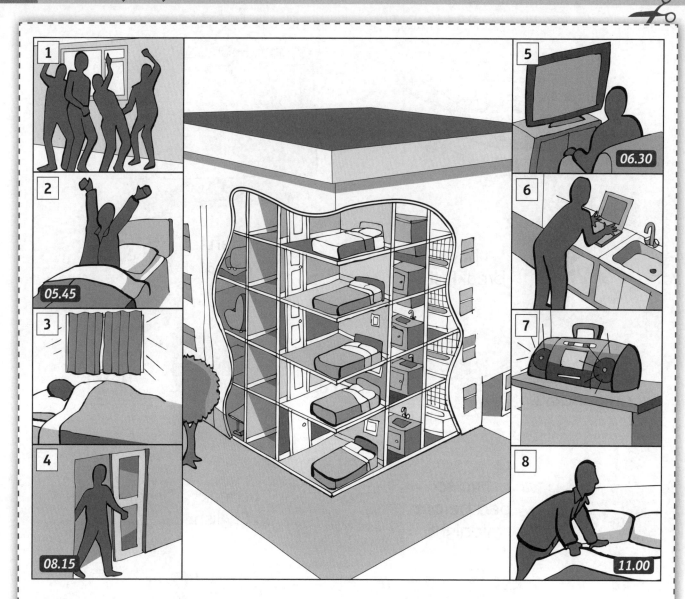

There are four people who live in these flats: Ned, Matilda, Robert and Anya.
Listen to your partner and match the activities and the flat to the person.

A

His name is Ned.

He lives on the second floor.

He plays very loud music every night.

He has parties every Saturday.

B

Her name is Matilda.

She lives on the ground floor.

She gets up at 05.45 in the morning.

She watches the news on television at 06.30 in the morning.

C

His name is Robert.

He lives on the third floor.

He goes to work at 08.15 in the morning.

He goes to bed at 11.00.

D

Her name is Anya.

She lives on the first floor.

She works at home.

She doesn't get up early.

Worksheet A

Find the answers to the clues you have.
Then ask your partner for the other clues.

Across

2 People eat a lot of this in Italy. (5)

5 _____ (8)

7 A green vegetable which you don't cook. (7)

8 _____ (7)

9 This is a kind of meat. (5)

10 _____ (6)

Down

1 _____ (5)

2 People eat a lot of this in Italy. (5)

3 _____ (4)

4 Americans call these *cookies*. (8)

6 _____ (6)

9 Healthy vegetables, served cold. (5)

Worksheet B

Find the answers to the clues you have.
Then ask your partner for the other clues.

Across

2 _____ (5)

5 Make this with bread and ham or cheese. (8)

7 _____ (7)

8 White meat. (7)

9 _____ (5)

10 Some people eat this for breakfast with milk. (6)

Down

1 It is usually white or brown. (5)

2 _____ (5)

3 This food lives in the sea. (4)

4 _____ (8)

6 The French eat a lot of this. (6)

9 _____ (5)

Worksheet A

Complete your hotel information sheet.

Name: _____
Restaurant: YES/NO
Breakfast times: _____
Lunch times: _____
Dinner times: _____
Gym: YES/NO
Opening hours: _____
Exchange: _____
Times: _____
Hairdresser: YES/NO
Times: _____
Guided tour: YES/NO
Price: _____

Ask questions to complete the information about your partner's hotel.

Name: _____
Restaurant: YES/NO
Breakfast times: _____
Lunch times: _____
Dinner times: _____
Gym: YES/NO
Opening hours: _____
Exchange: _____
Times: _____
Hairdresser: YES/NO
Times: _____
Guided tour: YES/NO
Price: _____

Worksheet B

Complete your hotel information sheet.

Name: _____
Restaurant: YES/NO
Breakfast times: _____
Lunch times: _____
Dinner times: _____
Gym: YES/NO
Opening hours: _____
Exchange: _____
Times: _____
Hairdresser: YES/NO
Times: _____
Guided tour: YES/NO
Price: _____

Ask questions to complete the information about your partner's hotel.

Name: _____
Restaurant: YES/NO
Breakfast times: _____
Lunch times: _____
Dinner times: _____
Gym: YES/NO
Opening hours: _____
Exchange: _____
Times: _____
Hairdresser: YES/NO
Times: _____
Guided tour: YES/NO
Price: _____

1 Petra goes on holiday to Spain. Match the pictures 1–12 with the words below.

passport _____   sunglasses _____

sunhats _____   magazines _____

Spanish–English dictionary _____   laptop _____

book _____   mobile phone _____

credit cards _____   pen _____

swimsuit _____   clothes _____

2 Choose eight items that Petra takes on holiday. Write them in the correct column.

a ...

_____
_____
_____
_____

some ...

_____
_____
_____
_____

3 Ask students about the eight items they chose.

Is there a passport? Yes, there is./No, there isn't.
Are there any clothes? Yes, there are./ No, there aren't.

Worksheet A

Find ten differences.

Worksheet B

Find ten differences.

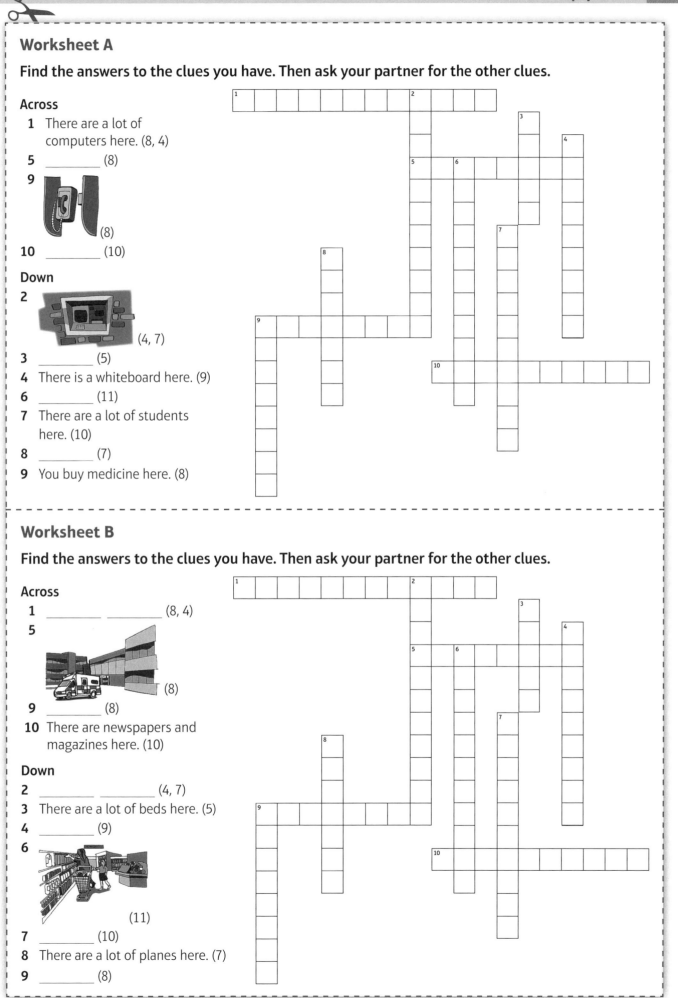

Worksheet A

Find the answers to the clues you have. Then ask your partner for the other clues.

Across

1 There are a lot of computers here. (8, 4)

5 _____ (8)

9 (8)

10 _____ (10)

Down

2 (4, 7)

3 _____ (5)

4 There is a whiteboard here. (9)

6 _____ (11)

7 There are a lot of students here. (10)

8 _____ (7)

9 You buy medicine here. (8)

Worksheet B

Find the answers to the clues you have. Then ask your partner for the other clues.

Across

1 _____ _____ (8, 4)

5 (8)

9 _____ (8)

10 There are newspapers and magazines here. (10)

Down

2 _____ _____ (4, 7)

3 There are a lot of beds here. (5)

4 _____ (9)

6 (11)

7 _____ (10)

8 There are a lot of planes here. (7)

9 _____ (8)

Worksheet A

1 You want to travel to Paris. Ask your partner to complete the missing travel information.

TRANSPORT	LEAVE FROM	TIME	ARRIVE AT	TIME	PRICE
PLANE	London Heathrow	19.40	Paris-Orly	21.50	€139 single
TRAIN					
COACH	London Victoria	21.30	Paris Gallieni	07.30	€48
TRAIN AND FERRY					

2 Decide which way you want to travel.

Worksheet B

1 You want to travel to Paris. Ask your partner to complete the missing travel information.

TRANSPORT	LEAVE FROM	TIME	ARRIVE AT	TIME	PRICE
PLANE					
TRAIN	London St Pancras	10.25	Paris Gare du Nord	13.45	€99.50
COACH					
TRAIN AND FERRY	London Charing Cross	13.10	Paris Gare du Nord	23.20	€75

2 Decide which way you want to travel.

Worksheet A

1 Find the past simple of these verbs. Complete the sentences with the correct verb.

| dance | play | wait | start | talk | stop | cry | walk |

D	A	N	C	E	D	A	Q	R	D	S
S	O	E	B	P	P	C	R	I	E	T
T	Z	W	X	T	L	B	H	W	W	A
O	D	A	T	A	A	W	V	J	A	R
P	N	I	T	L	Y	B	Z	D	L	T
P	Y	T	F	K	E	E	H	T	K	E
E	G	E	I	E	D	K	U	I	E	D
D	Z	D	C	D	C	R	I	E	D	S

1 Lyn O'Bryne from England __ __ __ __ __ __ seven years to find her lost dog in 2001.
2 Some people __ __ __ __ __ __ __ using the internet in 1995.
3 The film director Alfred Hitchcock __ __ __ __ __ __ for one second when he received an Oscar in _____.
4 People __ __ __ __ __ __ __ smoking in bars and restaurants in Ireland in _____.
5 People __ __ __ __ __ __ for 55 hours at a party in India in July 2004.
6 Spain and The Netherlands __ __ __ __ __ __ in the 2010 World Cup Final.
7 The actress Halle Berry __ __ __ __ __ when she received an Oscar in _____.
8 Neil Armstrong first __ __ __ __ __ __ on the moon on July 20th _____.

2 Put the dates into the sentences above. Read your sentences to B to check. Were you correct?

| 1969 | 2001 | 1940 | 2004 |

Worksheet B

1 Find the past simple of these verbs. Complete the sentences with the correct verb.

| dance | play | wait | start | talk | stop | cry | walk |

D	A	N	C	E	D	A	Q	R	D	S
S	O	E	B	P	P	C	R	I	E	T
T	Z	W	X	T	L	B	H	W	W	A
O	D	A	T	A	A	W	V	J	A	R
P	N	I	T	L	Y	B	Z	D	L	T
P	Y	T	F	K	E	E	H	T	K	E
E	G	E	I	E	D	K	U	I	E	D
D	Z	D	C	D	C	R	I	E	D	S

1 Lyn O'Bryne from England __ __ __ __ __ __ seven years to find her lost dog in _____.
2 Some people __ __ __ __ __ __ __ using the internet in _____.
3 The film director Alfred Hitchcock __ __ __ __ __ __ for one second when he received an Oscar in 1940.
4 People __ __ __ __ __ __ __ smoking in bars and restaurants in Ireland in 2004.
5 People __ __ __ __ __ __ for 55 hours at a party in India in July _____.
6 Spain and The Netherlands __ __ __ __ __ __ in the _____ World Cup Final.
7 The actress Halle Berry __ __ __ __ __ when she received an Oscar in 2001.
8 Neil Armstrong first __ __ __ __ __ __ on the moon on July 20th 1969.

2 Put the dates into the sentences above. Read your sentences to A to check. Were you correct?

| 2010 | 2004 | 2001 | 1995 |

Where were you?

1 START

2 yesterday morning

3 at the weekend

4 at 8 o'clock this morning

5 FREE QUESTION

16 on February 14th

17 two years ago

18 MISS A TURN

19 last summer

6 on Christmas Day

15 GO BACK ONE

24 at 20.45 on Saturday evening

25 FINISH

20 GO FORWARD TWO

7 on New Year's Day

14 in August last year

23 three hours ago

22 on December 31st 1999

21 on Monday

8 on your last birthday

13 this time last week

12 at lunchtime yesterday

11 last night

10 MISS A TURN

9 last Sunday

difficult	exam	easy	exam
delicious	food	terrible	food
noisy	bar	quiet	bar
interesting	book	boring	book
lovely	dress	horrible	dress
sad	film	happy	film

Worksheet A

1 How was your last meal in a restaurant?

a It was delicious.
b It was all right.
c It was awful.

2 How was the last programme you watched on television?

a It was interesting.
b It was OK.
c It was boring.

3 How was your last English homework?

a It was easy.
b It was all right.
c It was difficult.

4 How was your last holiday?

a It was fantastic.
b It was OK.
c It was terrible.

5 How was your last birthday present?

a It was lovely.
b It was all right.
c It was horrible.

6 How was the last restaurant you went to?

a It was very quiet.
b It was OK.
c It was very noisy.

Count the number of a, b and c answers.

Mostly as: You are a 'glass half-full' person. You have a positive outlook on life. Or maybe you are just very lucky! But don't be afraid to say when you don't like something!

Mostly bs: You are neither a 'glass half-full' nor a 'glass half-empty' person. You have a neutral outlook on your life but don't be afraid to say what you like and don't like!

Mostly cs: You are a 'glass half-empty' person. You have a slightly negative outlook on life. Or maybe you are just unlucky! But don't be afraid to say when you like something!

Worksheet B

1 How was your lunch yesterday?

a It was delicious.
b It was all right.
c It was awful.

2 How was the last film you watched in the cinema?

a It was interesting.
b It was OK.
c It was boring.

3 How was your last English exam?

a It was easy.
b It was all right.
c It was difficult.

4 How was your last weekend?

a It was fantastic.
b It was OK.
c It was terrible.

5 How was your last present?

a It was lovely.
b It was all right.
c It was horrible.

6 How was the last party you went to?

a It was very quiet.
b It was OK.
c It was very noisy.

Count the number of a, b and c answers.

Mostly as: You are a 'glass half-full' person. You have a positive outlook on life. Or maybe you are just very lucky! But don't be afraid to say when you don't like something!

Mostly bs: You are neither a 'glass half-full' nor a 'glass half-empty' person. You have a neutral outlook on your life but don't be afraid to say what you like and don't like!

Mostly cs: You are a 'glass half-empty' person. You have a slightly negative outlook on life. Or maybe you are just unlucky! But don't be afraid to say when you like something!

1   Last Saturday evening between 7p.m. and 11p.m. somebody robbed a bank in
    Piccadilly Circus in London. The police think Jacques robbed the bank.
    Below are his tickets and receipts. Complete the list of transport he used.

2   Complete the police report about what Jacques did on Friday and Saturday with
    the past simple of the verbs in the box.

| take (x3)   go   have   travel   arrive (x2)   stay   rent   pay   drive   buy |

Jacques _____ a taxi from his house in Toulouse to the airport at three o'clock on
Friday afternoon. He _____ by plane to Paris. In Paris he _____ a train to Calais.
Then he _____ from Calais to Dover by ferry. He _____ in Dover at half past
eleven at night and he _____ in a small hotel. The next morning he _____ a car
and _____ to London. When he _____ in London he _____ lunch in an Italian
restaurant. At half past seven he _____ some flowers. He _____ the underground
to Piccadilly Circus at a quarter to eight. At half past ten he _____ for dinner for
two in a French restaurant by credit card.

3   What do you think? Did Jacques rob the bank?

Worksheet A

Ask your partner about the first time he/she …	When did you first …?	Where did you first …?	:)
went on holiday.			
had dinner in a restaurant.			
went camping.			
spoke English.			
saw a film in the cinema.			

Worksheet B

Ask your partner about the first time he/she …	When did you first …?	Where did you first …?	:)
rode a bicycle.			
went to school.			
made a meal for other people.			
went to another country.			
met an English-speaking person.			

Worksheet A

1 Ask your partner about the objects in the box. Draw them on the picture.

keys   glasses   jacket   dictionary   bag

2 Compare pictures with your partner. Are they the same?

Worksheet B

1 Ask your partner about the objects in the box. Draw them on the picture.

laptop   jeans   bike   magazine   trainers

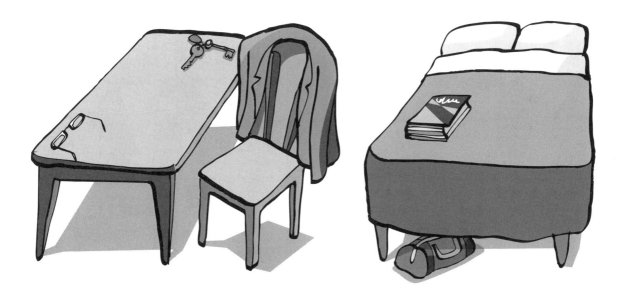

2 Compare pictures with your partner. Are they the same?

Functional language: giving directions

Worksheet A

Match the conversations to the people in the picture. Then write the question or answer.

____	______________________________	There is a swimming pool next to the school.
____	______________________________	Yes, the payphone is opposite the bakery.
____	Excuse me. Where's the pharmacy?	______________________________
____	Where is the bus stop?	______________________________

Worksheet B

Match the conversations to the people in the picture. Then write the question or answer.

____	Where is the swimming pool?	______________________________
____	Is there a payphone?	______________________________
____	______________________________	It's between the restaurant and the bakery.
____	______________________________	The bus stop is in front of the school.

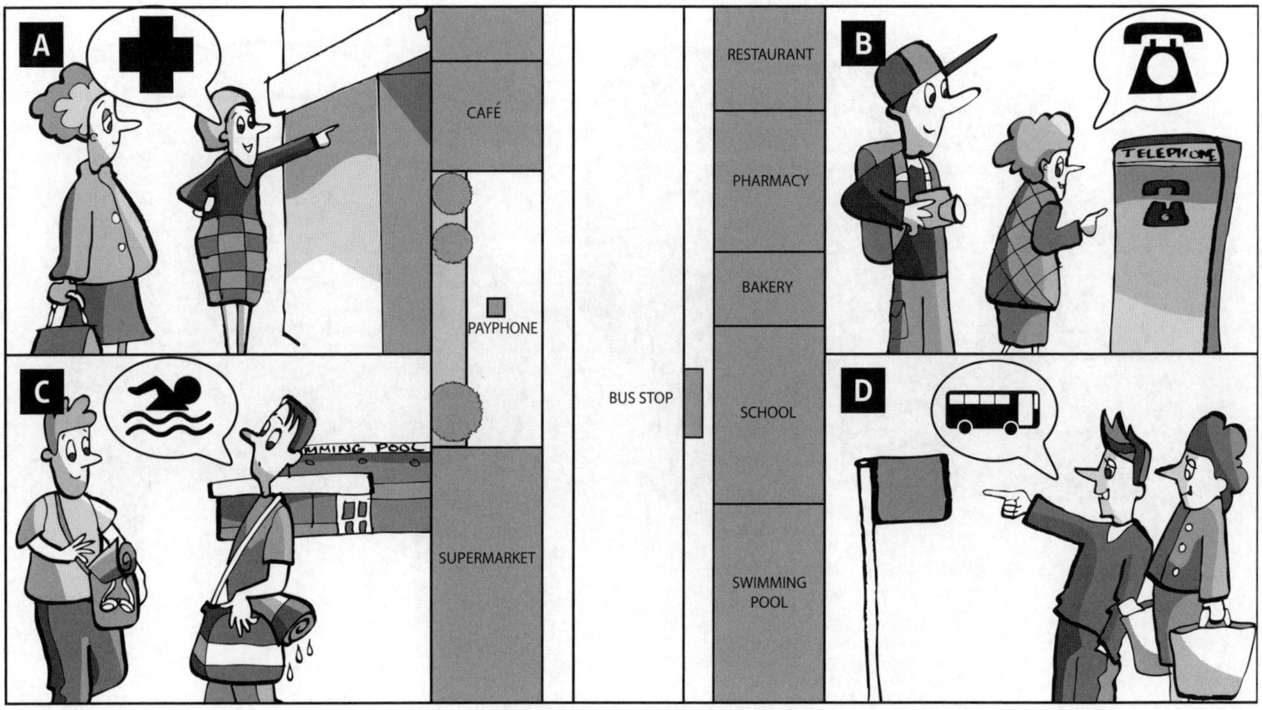

1 Write an example of a person or thing you love or dislike for each category.

1 a film _____
2 a vegetable _____
3 a singer _____
4 a book _____
5 a sport _____
6 an activity _____
7 a city _____
8 an animal _____
9 a sportsperson _____
10 a type of food _____
11 an actor _____
12 a type of music _____

2 Ask your partner: What do you think of …?

Useful language

I like I love I hate I don't really like I don't like	him/her/it/ them.	I think it's I think she's I think he's I think they're	(really/very) good. fantastic. OK/all right. (really/very) bad. terrible.

1 Complete a sentence with *like/love/don't like/hate* so that it is true for you.
Pass the worksheet to your left.

	NAME
I _____ running.	_____
I _____ buying presents.	_____
I _____ camping.	_____
I _____ chatting online.	_____
I _____ dogs.	_____
I _____ late night parties.	_____

2 Complete a sentence with a noun or gerund so that it is true for you.
Pass the worksheet to your left.

	NAME
I love _____.	_____
I like _____.	_____
I don't like _____.	_____
I hate _____.	_____
I like _____ a lot.	_____
I don't really like _____.	_____

Money and you

1

It's near the end of the month. You don't have any money left.
You see a pair of shoes you really like.

   a You buy them with your credit card.

   b You don't buy them. You don't like spending money you don't have.

2

You buy a pair of expensive trousers in July.
In October, you try them on. They're too small.

   a You hope to lose some kilos.

   b You try to sell them on the internet.

3

You buy two tickets for a concert. Your friend wants to pay you later.
A month later your friend still owes you the money.

   a You don't like talking about money. You don't ask your friend for the money.

   b You phone and email your friend regularly to remind him/her to pay you.

4

A friend gives you a jumper for your birthday, but you don't like it.

   a You put it in your wardrobe, but never wear it.

   b You give it to another person for his/her birthday.

5

You buy a beautiful watch in the sales. It cost £300. Normally it costs £600.
You never wear it. You decide to sell it because you need a new computer.
The computer costs £550.

   a You sell it for £300. You don't like asking for more than what it cost you.

   b You sell it for £600. That's what it costs in the shops now.

6

It's May and you need a new television because your old television doesn't work.

   a You buy it now. You hate waiting and you love watching television.

   b You wait until the sales in July.

Mostly as

You probably spend too much money every month. You want things instantly and you hate waiting, but sometimes it's a good idea to be patient and only spend what you have.

Mostly bs

You are very careful with money. You probably never spend more than what you have. Remember sometimes it's good to spend some money and enjoy yourself.

Worksheet A

Would you like something to eat?	Which colour would you like?
Can I help you?	What would the teacher like for her birthday?
Excuse me. Where's the children's clothes section?	The sports department is on the second floor.
Coffee, please. Black coffee.	Let me think. Yes! I'd like the sushi, please.
Yes, of course. Which would you prefer? A banana or an apple?	No, thanks. I think it's a waste of money.

Worksheet B

No, thanks. I'm not hungry.	I'd like the green one, please.
Yes, please. I'd like to buy a camera.	I don't know. Maybe a CD. She loves classical music.
It's on the third floor.	I'd like to buy a football.
Would you like some tea or coffee?	What would you like to eat?
Can I have some fruit, please?	Would you like some wrapping paper for the present?

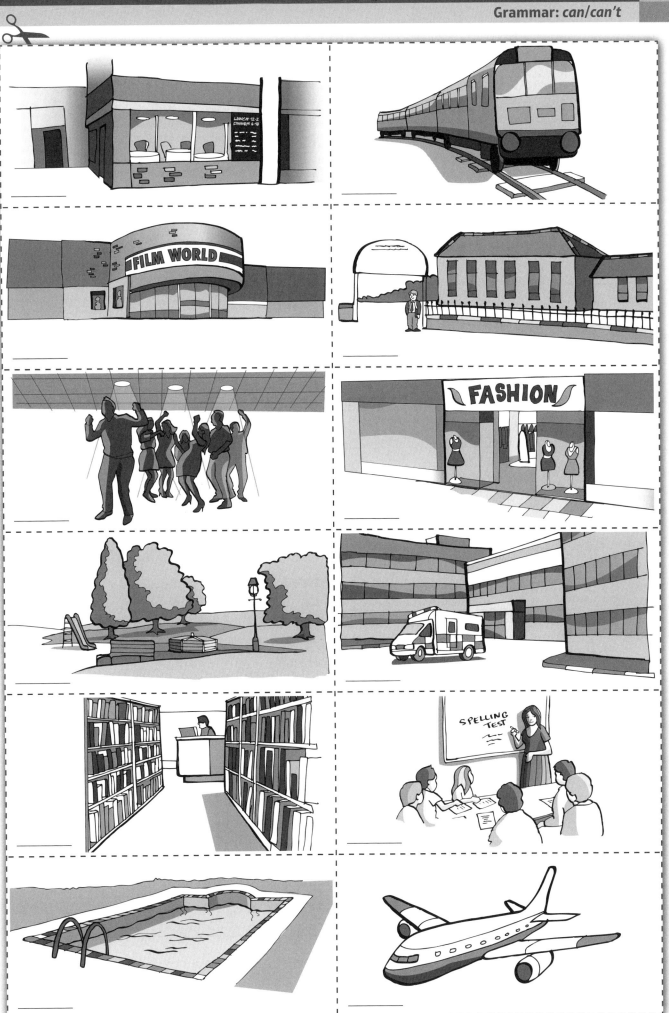

Grammar: *be going to*

I'm going to ...	My answer ✓ = YES X = NO	Ask your partner: What about you? If your partner answers YES, ask the follow-up question.
... save money.	_____	_____ Why? _____
... get fit.	_____	_____ How? _____
... cook tonight.	_____	_____ What? _____
... do sport this weekend.	_____	_____ What? _____
... clean the house.	_____	_____ When? _____
... study English this evening.	_____	_____ How long? _____
... get more organised.	_____	_____ How? _____
... learn something new.	_____	_____ What? _____
... give somebody a present.	_____	_____ What? _____
... study English when this course finishes.	_____	_____ Where? _____
I'm going to _____?	_____	_____ _____? _____

1 Cross out the incorrect phrase in column 2.

CAN YOU SAY … ?		✓ = YES ✗ = NO
play	tennis football chess ~~swimming~~	
ride	a bicycle a horse a car a motorbike	
speak	French three languages in English for 20 minutes your teacher	
cook	ice cream pasta Japanese food vegetables	
make	tea your homework sushi jewellery	
read	music Chinese words maps a phone call	
use	a smartphone a power tool Powerpoint a photo	

2 Use the correct verb phrases to ask your partner about his/her abilities. Mark his/her answers: ✓or ✗ in the table.

Can you play tennis? Yes, I can. = ✓   No, I can't. = ✗

Functional language: starting and ending conversations

A

AT A PARTY

Start a conversation with someone you have just met. Talk about the food, music and so on.

Useful language:

What do you think of …?

A

ON A TRAIN

Start a conversation with the person in front of you. Talk about the destination, where they are from and so on.

Useful language:

Excuse me! Where are you going?

A

IN A RESTAURANT

Start a conversation with the person you are having dinner with. He/She is a business colleague. Talk about the food, work and so on.

Useful language:

What do you think of …?

A

ON THE STREET

You see your neighbour's daughter on the street. Stop and talk to her about school, hobbies and so on.

Useful language:

Hello! How are you?

What do you do at …?

A

IN THE UNIVERSITY CAFÉ

You are a teacher with a new student from one of your classes. Talk about the university, plans for the future and so on.

Useful language:

Do you like …?

A

IN A TRAVEL AGENCY

You are in a busy travel agency. Talk to another customer about travelling, holiday plans and so on.

Useful language:

Where are you going on holiday?

B

Answer your partner's questions. When you leave say:

Nice to meet you.

or

Is that the time? Bye!

B

Answer your partner's questions. When you leave say:

Keep in touch.

or

I have a class now. Bye!

B

Answer your partner's questions. When you leave say:

See you soon!

or

Oh look! This is my station.

B

Answer your partner's questions. When you leave say:

I hope we meet again!

or

I have to go now. Bye!

B

Answer your partner's questions. When you leave say:

Nice to talk to you!

or

I can see a friend over there.

B

Answer your partner's questions. When you leave say:

See you later!

or

Oh, no! I'm late! Goodbye!

UNIT 1

FAMOUS HISTORICAL FIGURES

Materials: One role card per student and one worksheet per student

Distribute the worksheets and the role cards. Tell Ss to complete the first row of the table with their information, but not to show it to anyone else. Explain that they are at a party with each of the famous people on their worksheet. (You could play low background music.) Elicit the following questions and write them on the board using another example, e.g. Brad Pitt. *What's your nationality? What's your job? Are you Brad Pitt?* Explain to Ss that they have to complete the information on the sheet by asking similar questions.

If you have fewer than twelve Ss, do one or two role cards as examples with the class. Give extra role cards to **fast finishers**. It is not necessary for Ss to find all the people. If you have a smaller class or less time, Ss could be told to find a limited number, e.g. six.

As an extension, Ss work in pairs and try to remember who each student is, their job and nationality.

WHERE'S IT FROM?

Materials: One worksheet per group of three, cut up and backed onto card. Separate the cards into objects and countries. (Optional: one colour for picture cards and one colour for map cards.)

Put Ss into groups of three. Give a set of cards to each group and tell them to match the object to the country. Check answers as a class.

Explain that Ss are going to play a memory game. Ss turn the cards face down. The map cards go on one side and the object cards go on the other side of a flat surface. Taking turns, they turn one of the map cards and one of the object cards. If the cards match, they say *The _____ is from _____.* They keep the pair and they have another go. If the cards don't match, they say *The _____ isn't from _____.* They turn the cards face down and it is the next student's turn. Ss play until all the cards have been matched. The winner is the student with the most cards.

As an extension, Ss have five minutes to write down as many combinations as they can remember. They get two points for each correct answer.

> **Suggested answers:**
> car – Germany; bus – Great Britain; hat – Mexico; cheese – France; clock – Switzerland; spaghetti – Italy; flag – Canada; coffee – Brazil; flowers – The Netherlands; passport – China; dancer – Spain; sushi – Japan

HOW DO YOU SPELL IT?

Materials: One copy of worksheet A and worksheet B per pair of students

Put Ss into two groups, A and B. Distribute the worksheets and ask the groups to complete the words, and match them to the pictures. Go round and help with spelling and pronunciation, and check answers carefully as Ss finish.

Put Ss into AB pairs and tell them to ask each other for the names of the silhouette objects in their picture. Model the language they'll need to do this first (e.g. *What's picture E? It's a chair. How do you spell it? C-H-A-I-R*). Go round and check spelling and pronunciation. Check answers as a class.

> **Answers:**
> **Student A**
> **1** a chair, Picture E   **2** a pen, Picture K   **3** a notebook, Picture G
> **4** a pencil, Picture H   **5** a door, Picture A   **6** a workbook, Picture J
> **Student B**
> **1** a table, Picture D   **2** a laptop, Picture F   **3** the board, Picture C
> **4** a bag, Picture I   **5** a student's book, Picture L
> **6** a noticeboard, Picture B

IDENTITY CARD

Materials: One role card and one worksheet per student

Put Ss into groups of four. Distribute one role card and one worksheet to each student. Tell Ss they are the student on the role card and they have just enrolled at a language school. They have to complete the registration forms for the other students. Focus on the blank forms and elicit the questions necessary to complete them. Write the questions on the board: *What's your name? How do you spell it? What's your email address?* (Check Ss know how to say @ (at), and . (dot).) *What's your country? What's your job/occupation? What's your phone number?* Write your details on the board as if they appeared on the registration form. Demonstrate the questions with a student. Ss complete the forms in groups. Check answers as a class.

> **Answers:** As shown on completed registration forms.

UNIT 2

A FAMILY BUSINESS

Materials: One copy of the illustration per group and one role card per student

Put Ss into groups of eight. Give each student a worksheet of the hotel picture and a role card. Tell Ss they have to identify the people in the picture by exchanging information. Tell Ss to do this in numerical order. Do the first one as an example. Read the information about Carolyn and check Ss are able to identify her correctly. Check the spelling of Carolyn and feed in: *How do you spell that?* and write the question on the board. Ss continue in groups until they have labelled all the people in the picture. Get feedback.

As an extension, ask Ss to turn over their role cards and exchange information about the people in the picture in pairs or groups. Do the first one as an example. Prompt Ss by writing these questions on the board: *What's his/her job? Where is he/she?*

> **Answers:** **A** Rosanna   **B** Matthew   **C** Carolyn   **D** Paula   **E** Petra
> **F** Orlando   **G** Danielle   **H** Scott   **I** Lionel

TEACHER'S NOTES

HOTEL ROOMS

Materials: One copy of worksheet A and worksheet B per pair of students

Put Ss into AB pairs and distribute the worksheets. Focus Ss on the examples. Tell them to exchange information with their partner to fill in the hotel plan and complete the sentences. Monitor the Ss. Check answers as a class. Vary feedback by asking: *Who is in room …?* and *Where is …?*

As an extension, Ss ask each other the following questions. They record their partner's answers. Feedback as a class.

1 *What's your telephone number?*
2 *What's the number of your house/flat?*
3 *How many students are there in your class?*
4 *How many children are there in your family?*

> **Answers:** Room 52 the mother; Room 99 the son; Room 84 the brother; Room 73 the parents; Room 33 the wife; Room 100 the husband; Room 19 the father; Room 13 the daughter; Room 28 the sister; Room 67 the children

ARE YOU HAPPY?

Materials: One copy of worksheet A and worksheet B per pair of students

Put Ss in groups A and B. Distribute the worksheets and ask them to unjumble the words in pairs AA and BB. Do the first one in A and in B as examples. Write the words on the board. Model the pronunciation and elicit the stress. Ss mark the stress and pronounce the rest of the words. Monitor and check. Ss then match the words to the pictures.

Put Ss in AB pairs and tell them to ask each other for the names of the remaining adjectives. Model the language they'll need to do this first, e.g. *What's picture 1? happy*, etc. *How do you spell it? H-a-p-p-y.* Check answers as a class and encourage correct pronunciation. Drill the more difficult words.

As an extension, Ss take it in turns to mime a feeling for their partner to guess.

> **Answers:**
> **Student A: 1** happy   **3** bored   **4** thirsty   **7** tired
> **Student B: 2** cold   **5** hot   **6** angry   **8** hungry

LET'S GO!

Materials: One set of cards per group of three or four

Put Ss in groups of three or four. Give each group a set of cards. The face cards are in a pile face down. The response cards can either be divided among the Ss or put face up on a flat surface. Ss take it in turns to turn over a face card and leave it on the table face up. The others find correct responses and put them with the face card. There are three responses for each face card, but they must be in the correct order. Some responses are possible in more than one dialogue. Monitor. The first team to complete all six dialogues wins.

Put Ss into pairs. Ss then practise the dialogues. Write an example on the board and drill it, paying particular attention to intonation.

Tip: Ss can look at the card to read it, but should look at the other speaker when they speak.

> **Possible answers:**
> I'm hungry. / Me too! / Let's eat a pizza! / Good idea!
> I'm cold. / Me too! / Let's go inside. / Yeah! OK!
> I'm tired. / Are you? / Yes, let's have a break. / OK.
> I'm thirsty. / Let's go to a café. / Good idea! Let's have a soft drink. / Oooh! Yes, please!
> I'm bored. / Let's go! / Where? / Let's go to the cinema.
> I'm hot. / Me too! / Let's drink some cold water! / Good idea!

UNIT 3

LOST PROPERTY

Materials: One copy of the worksheet per student and one set of cards per group of students

Distribute the worksheets. Tell Ss to work in pairs to match the vocabulary to the pictures and decide if the words are singular (S) or plural (P). Put Ss into groups of three or four with a set of cards. They take it in turns to turn over one card at a time and match the person to an object. Do an example on the board and elicit: *that* – singular and *those* – plural. Feed in *because*. Write on the board:

That passport is *Pedro's* because *he's Spanish.*
  OBJECT   WHOSE   REASON
Those keys are *Masaki's* because *he's in The Mirage Hotel.*
  OBJECT   WHOSE   REASON

Check answers as a class.

> **Answers:**
> 1 bag 7 S; shoes 1 P; trainers 2 P; newspaper 11 S; tie 6 S; passport 3 S; keys 12 P; computer 5 S; diary 8 S; camera 9 S; German–English dictionary 10 S
> 2 Students' own answers.

MYSTERY OBJECTS

Materials: One copy of worksheet A and worksheet B per pair of students

Distribute the worksheets. Put Ss into AA and BB pairs to complete their words with the correct vowels. Monitor and check. Then put Ss into AB pairs and tell them to ask and answer about the silhouettes using *What's this? It's a …* and *What are these? They're …* Ss first say the corresponding letter (A–E) or number (1–5) and then ask the correct question. Model an example with a student. Feed in *How do you spell that?* Check answers as a class.

> **Answers:**
> **Student A: A** keys   **B** dictionary   **C** lamp   **D** desk   **E** glasses
> **Student B: 1** mobile phone   **2** coins   **3** clock   **4** credit cards   **5** wallet

CLOTHING STYLES

Materials: One copy of the worksheet per pair of students

Distribute the worksheets. Ss work in pairs to find the nine items of clothing. Check answers and put the words on the board. Check for correct pronunciation.

Point to the pictures of the clothes and ask: *What's this? What are these?* Write the questions on the board and establish that *this* is singular and *these* is plural. After asking a few times, teacher to student, the Ss could ask each other in open pairs around the class. Look at the pictures of the people. In pairs, Ss match the people to the clothes. Do an example with the class and write on the board *I think this is* (person's) (clothes). *I think these are* (person's) (clothes). Put Ss into groups to compare answers then check as a class. With **stronger classes**, ask for further explanations, e.g. *I think these are Anna's gloves because she likes sports.*

Answers:
1 t-shirt; shoes; shirt; coat; hat; tie; gloves; skirt; glasses
2 Students' own answers.

CAFÉ ROYALE

Materials: One copy of the worksheet per student

Distribute the worksheets. Focus on the photo to set the context (ordering in a café). Elicit *waiter (W)* and *customer (C)*. Tell Ss to put the conversation in order. The first line is done as an example. Get feedback. Chorus drill the conversation.

Set up the classroom as far as possible to look like a self-service café. Ss should stand up facing each other as if at a counter. Ask Ss to practise the conversation, ensuring that they first look at the line, but then look at their partner when they speak. Ss should be encouraged to accompany the dialogue with appropriate gestures and mime. Gradually, as they become more familiar with the script, the customer for example, can cover their part and respond to the waiter and vice versa, until they are independent of the script. Then ask Ss to order just using the menu. Monitor throughout and help with pronunciation. You could invite a few pairs to perform their dialogue for the class.

Answers: 1 f) 2 b) 3 k) 4 c) 5 d) 6 h) 7 a) 8 i) 9 e)
10 j) 11 g)

UNIT 4

SIMILARITIES AND DIFFERENCES

Materials: One copy of worksheet A and worksheet B per pair of students

Revise the verb phrases used (see Answers). Use mime and drawing to elicit the verb phrases.

Put Ss into AB pairs. Distribute the worksheets. Explain that Victoria and Judy are best friends, but that they are similar in some ways and different in other ways. Tell Ss to describe the person in their picture to their partner. Do an example with a student: *Victoria wears glasses.* Student: *Judy wears glasses.* With **stronger classes** you could elicit *too.* Ss have to find five similarities and five differences. Check answers as a class and focus on the third person singular *s* on verbs in the affirmative and the use of the auxiliary *doesn't.*

Answers:
Similarities: has/wears glasses; drives a car; doesn't smoke; works in an office; has two children
Differences: Victoria lives in a house, Judy lives in a flat. Victoria plays the piano, Judy plays the guitar. Victoria plays golf, Judy plays basketball. Victoria eats Japanese food, Judy eats Italian food. Victoria drinks coffee, Judy doesn't drink coffee.

THINGS IN COMMON

Materials: Two sets of cards per group of students

Review the verb phrases before starting the game (see Answers). Show Ss each card and elicit and drill the verb phrase.

Put Ss into groups of four. Divide the cards equally between each student. Ss take it in turns to say a phrase about each of their cards. The person with the same card says *Me too!* and both Ss discard that card. The winner is the person who discards all their cards first. Demonstrate how the game works by doing a few examples with the Ss. Select a card and say, e.g. *I like cats.* The student with the same card says *Me too!* Put the cards together and repeat with another card. Return the cards to the Ss before starting the game. Monitor closely.

At the end of the game, ask who was first to finish in each group. Get feedback by asking Ss in each group to act out some of the two-line conversations in pairs.

Answers:
like: cats, fish and chips
play: tennis, golf
drive: a taxi, a bus
have: two brothers, a mobile phone
work: in a hospital, in a hotel
go: shopping on Fridays, to the theatre
live: in the mountains
study: at school

FIND SOMEONE WHO

Materials: One copy of worksheet A and worksheet B per pair of students

Put Ss into AA and BB pairs to complete the questions. Check answers as a class. Even though the questions are different on worksheets A and B, the preposition for each time phrase is in the same order, so just ask for the time phrase and not the whole question.

Ss answer the questions for themselves with short phrases. Do one question from A and one from B as an example. Monitor closely and when the Ss have completed their answers, tell Ss to mingle and ask the other Ss their questions. For each question they must find someone who has the same answer as them. Then they write that person's name. Do one or two examples as a class to illustrate. Get feedback. Ask a few Ss who had similar answers to them.

Answers: in; on; at; every; at/every; every; on

TEACHER'S NOTES

TIMES AROUND THE WORLD

Materials: One copy of worksheet A and worksheet B per pair of students

Put Ss into AB pairs and distribute the worksheets. Make sure Ss can't see each other's worksheet. Tell Ss to complete their worksheet by asking each other questions and drawing the hands to display the time on their blank clocks. Elicit the question and answer for the first two clocks on each worksheet and write them on the board: *What time is it in* (the city)? *It's* (time) *in* (city).

> **Answers:** Barcelona: 13.45; Beijing 19.45; Caracas 07.15; Dublin 12.45; Hong Kong 20.00; Istanbul 14.15; Mexico City 06.45; New York 07.45; Moscow 15.30; Mumbai 17.15; Nairobi 15.00; São Paulo 09.00

UNIT 5

GAME BOARD

Materials: One copy of the board and one coin per group, and one counter per student

Put Ss into groups and distribute the board. Ss toss a coin to move: heads moves one space and tails moves two spaces. Ss have to repeat the sentence they land on with an adverb of frequency in the correct place so that it is true for them. In every fifth sentence, Ss have to add the correct verb so that the sentence is true for them. Do one or two examples on the board to demonstrate what Ss have to do. For every correct sentence, the student gets another turn. Monitor closely. The first student to finish is the winner.

Get feedback to some of the sentences. You could ask Ss if anything their partners said surprised them.

NOISY NEIGHBOURS

Materials: One copy of the worksheet per student and one role card per pair of students

Draw a block of flats on the board and pre-teach *live on the ground/first/second/third floor*. Explain to Ss that they are going to match four neighbours to their flats and the activities they do there.

Put Ss into pairs. Give each student the worksheet and give each pair of Ss one role card. Ss match the person on their role card to the activities and flats on the worksheets. Monitor and check they are matching correctly.

Remove the role cards and put Ss into groups ABCD. Tell Ss to exchange the information about the person who was on their card with the other three Ss. Ss must match the neighbour to the flat and activities.

Check answers as a class.

> **Answers: A** 1, 7, second floor **B** 2, 5, ground floor **C** 4, 8, third floor **D** 3, 6, first floor

CROSSWORD

Materials: One copy of worksheet A and worksheet B per pair of students

Put Ss into AA and BB pairs and distribute the crosswords. Ss complete their crossword using the clues provided. Monitor and check.

Put Ss into AB pairs. (**Weaker Ss** could be in groups AABB so As and Bs can find answers in pairs.) Elicit the question and write on the board: *What's* (number) *across/down?* Drill the question.

Ss A and B take it in turns to read the clue. Their partner has 30 seconds to guess the answer (**stronger Ss** could try to give extra information to guide their partner before providing the answer). Check answers as a class.

As an extension, Ss read out the words and their partner has to provide the definition.

> **Answers:**
> **Across: 2** pasta/pizza **5** sandwich **7** lettuce **8** chicken **9** steak **10** cereal
> **Down: 1** bread **2** pizza/pasta **3** fish **4** biscuits **6** cheese **9** salad

BE MY GUEST

Materials: One copy of worksheet A and worksheet B per pair of students

Put Ss into AA and BB pairs. Ss design a hotel brochure by completing the information for their hotel. Then they prepare the questions to find out information about another hotel. Monitor closely and make sure Ss form the questions correctly. With **weaker classes**, model a few example questions.

Put Ss into AB pairs to complete the form. Demonstrate the activity by doing a few examples with Ss, e.g. *Do you have a restaurant in the hotel? Yes, I do./No, I don't.* Remind Ss to use expressions like *Great! Oh good! Lovely!* Get feedback. Ask Ss which hotel they prefer and why.

UNIT 6

SUNNY SPAIN

Materials: One worksheet per student

Distribute the worksheets. Explain to Ss that they are helping Petra select items to take on holiday to Spain. Ss work in groups to label the pictures. Check answers with the class. Then Ss decide which eight items Petra takes on holiday and write the list under *a/some*. Elicit whether each item takes *a* or *some* so Ss can check their lists.

Put Ss into pairs. Ss have to ask questions to find similarities and differences in what Petra takes on holiday. Elicit the questions and short answers and write them on the board. Model and drill: *Is there a (passport)? Yes, there is./No, there isn't. Are there any (sunhats)? Yes, there are./No, there aren't.* Ss find out how many similarities there are between their suitcase and their partner's suitcase. Elicit some answers from different pairs and give whole class feedback on errors/good language used.

> **Answers: 1** mobile phone **2** book **3** clothes **4** sunhats **5** sunglasses **6** passport **7** credit cards **8** pen **9** swimsuit **10** magazines **11** dictionary **12** laptop
> **a:** mobile phone; book; passport; pen; swimsuit; dictionary; laptop
> **some:** clothes; sunhats; sunglasses; credit cards; magazines

SPOT THE DIFFERENCE

Materials: One copy of worksheet A and worksheet B per pair of students

Review *There is/are, a/an, some, a lot of, not any* using objects around the classroom. With a **weaker class**, introduce the topic of airports and review the vocabulary of what you can find in airports (people, shops, airplanes, etc.).

Put Ss into pairs and distribute the A and B worksheets so each pair has one of each. Tell Ss to find the ten differences between their picture and their partner's picture. Ss take turns to describe their picture. They mark their differences on their picture. Check answers and write them on the board.

Tip: You could add a competitive element here by setting a time limit and awarding points for the correct answers. The pair with the most correct answers wins!

As an extension, **stronger Ss** could exchange information using the question form.

> **Answers:**
> **Picture A**
> There is a newsagent's. There are some payphones. There is a snack bar. There are a lot of people.
> **Picture B**
> There is a pharmacy. There is an internet café. There is a cash machine. There are a lot of airplanes. There is a restaurant. There is a bus.

GIVE US A CLUE

Materials: One copy of crossword A and crossword B per pair of students

Put Ss into AA and BB pairs and distribute the crosswords. Ss complete their answers using the clues provided. Monitor and check.

Put Ss into AB pairs. (**Weaker Ss** could be in groups AABB so As and Bs can find answer in pairs.) Elicit the question and write on the board: *What's (number) across/down?* Drill the question.

Ss A and B take it in turns to read the clue and give their partner up to 30 seconds to guess the word(s). For the clues which are pictures, Ss make their own definition or use mine or drawing. Check answers as a class.

> **Answers:**
> **Across: 1** internet café **5** hospital **9** payphone **10** newsagent's
> **Down: 2** cash machine **3** hotel **4** classroom **6** supermarket
> **7** university **8** airport **9** pharmacy

PARIS IN THE SPRING

Materials: One copy of worksheet A and worksheet B per pair of students

Put Ss into AA and BB pairs and distribute the worksheets. Tell Ss they want to travel to Paris but they need more information about how to get there. If necessary, review *train, ferry, plane*. Write *TRAIN, Where from?* and *Time?* on the board. Elicit the questions: *Where does the train leave from? What time does the train leave?* Ask As to work together to prepare the questions they need and Bs to do the same. Focus on the two questions above and elicit the answers from Ss: *It leaves from London. It leaves at 19.40.* If necessary, review all the questions: *Where does it arrive? What time does it arrive? How much does it cost?*

Put Ss into AB pairs. Ss ask each other the questions to complete the timetable. Elicit answers from different pairs and give whole class feedback on errors/good language used.

UNIT 7

DID YOU KNOW?

Materials: One copy of worksheet A and worksheet B per pair of students

Put Ss into AA and BB pairs. Distribute the worksheets. Ss find the past form of the verbs in the wordsearch and complete the sentences with the correct verb in the past simple. Check answers as a class, with Ss only saying the correct verb for each clue NOT the whole sentence. Ss then choose the missing date for their sentences. Ss change into AB pairs. They read their full sentences to each other to check if the date was correct. Check answers as a class.

> **Answers:**
>
> | D | A | N | C | E | D | A | Q | R | D | S |
> |---|---|---|---|---|---|---|---|---|---|---|
> | S | O | E | B | P | P | C | R | I | E | T |
> | T | Z | W | X | T | L | B | H | W | W | A |
> | O | D | A | T | A | A | W | V | J | A | R |
> | P | N | I | T | L | Y | B | Z | D | L | T |
> | P | Y | T | F | K | E | E | H | T | K | E |
> | E | G | E | I | E | D | K | U | I | E | D |
> | D | Z | D | C | D | C | R | I | E | D | S |
>
> **1** waited **2** started **3** talked **4** stopped **5** danced **6** played
> **7** cried **8** walked

WHERE WERE YOU?

Materials: One copy of the board and one coin per group, and one counter per student

Put Ss into groups and distribute the board. Ss toss a coin to move: heads moves one space and tails moves two spaces. When a student lands on a square, another student in the group has to ask him/her the question: *Where were you …?* The student answers: *I was …* It's a good idea to write: *I don't remember.* on the board. Invite Ss to ask you one or two questions first to model the task. On a free question the Ss in the group can ask about any time they want. If a student answers *I can't/don't remember*, they return to the square they were on before. The first student to finish is the winner. Invite Ss from different groups to tell the class about Ss in their group, e.g. *At 8 o'clock this morning Anna was at home.*

GREAT FUN

Materials: One set of cards per group of students

Put Ss into groups of three or four. Distribute the cards. First, Ss sort the cards into adjectives and nouns. Check answers as a class. Then Ss match the nouns and adjectives. Tell Ss that each noun has two adjective collocations that are opposites. Sometimes there is more than one possible combination, but each adjective must have a suitable collocation, so for example, *delicious* can only go with *food*. Check answers as a class. Ensure Ss have the correct adjective collocations (see Answers). (If Ss give a different answer which collocates correctly, e.g. *boring film*, tell them that it is a correct answer but not the answer for this activity). Check pronunciation.

Turn cards face down in a grid. Ss play pelmanism. Each student takes it in turn to turn over two cards and tries to find the correct collocation. The student must say the words on the card out loud. If the two words do not collocate, they must be turned face down and left in exactly the same place. When a student gets a match, he/she keeps the cards and has another go until he/she gets a mismatch. The winner is the student with the most cards at the end. Ask Ss in each group who won.

As an extension, ask Ss to form sentences using the collocations.

> **Answers:** difficult/easy exam; delicious/terrible food; noisy/quiet bar; interesting/boring book; lovely/horrible dress; sad/happy film

HOW WAS IT?

Materials: One copy of worksheet A and worksheet B per pair of students

Put Ss into AB pairs and distribute the worksheets. Ss interview each other and note their partner's answers. (Questions are very similar but not identical to give stronger motivation for listening. The three optional answers are the same.) Ss then count how many as, bs and cs their partner has. Remind Ss that the quiz is for fun and they shouldn't take the results seriously.

Invite Ss to tell the class if they were mostly a, b, or c and if they agree with the conclusion.

UNIT 8

ALIBI

Materials: One worksheet per student

Distribute the worksheets. Read the blurb about the robbery. Explain *alibi*. Ss work in pairs to find the means of transport. Check answers as a class.

Focus on the verbs. With **weaker classes** ask Ss to put the verbs in the past simple before they complete the story. Encourage Ss to work in pairs or groups to do task. Check answers as a class.

Ask Ss to speculate on whether Jacques robbed the bank or not. There is no definite answer, but probably not – he was probably having a romantic dinner with his girlfriend, hence the flowers and the bill in the restaurant for two people.

As an extension, Ss could reconstruct the story in groups using the tickets, receipts and map.

> **Answers:**
> 1 taxi, plane, train, ferry, car, underground
> 2 Jacques *took* a taxi from his house in Toulouse to the airport at three o'clock on Friday afternoon. He *went/travelled* by plane to Paris. In Paris he *took* a train to Calais. Then he *went/travelled* from Calais to Dover by ferry. He *arrived* in Dover at half past eleven at night and he *stayed* in a small hotel. The next morning he *rented* a car and *drove* to London. When he *arrived* in London he *had* lunch in an Italian restaurant. At half past seven he *bought* some flowers. He *took* the underground to Piccadilly Circus at a quarter to eight. At half past ten he *paid* for dinner for two in a French restaurant by credit card.

FIRSTS

Materials: One copy of worksheet A and worksheet B per pair of students

Put Ss into AB pairs and distribute the worksheets. Elicit a few example questions. With **weaker classes**, you could put Ss into groups A and B to prepare the questions. Monitor closely. Elicit some answers from different pairs and give whole class feedback on errors/good language used.

As an extension, group pairs and get Ss to present their partner to the group.

MISSING OBJECTS

Materials: One copy of worksheet A and worksheet B per pair of students

Put Ss into AB pairs and distribute the worksheets. Ss should sit face-to-face. Elicit the questions: *Where is …?* and *Where are …?* using objects around the classroom. Ss cover their eyes while you put the objects in a different place. Ss ask about the missing objects and elicit the prepositions of place. In **weaker classes** you could get groups of A and B to review the location of the objects in their picture.

Ss ask their partner about the objects in the box above their picture. Based on their partner's answer, they draw the object in the correct place on their picture. Afterwards they compare pictures. Elicit some answers from different pairs.

As an extension, Ss can turn over their sheets and see how much they remember about the location of the objects.

> **Possible answers:**
> A The glasses are on the left of the table. The keys are on the right of the table. The jacket is on the chair. The dictionary is on the bed. The bag is under the bed.
> B The laptop is on the table. The jeans are on the floor next to/ near the chair. The bike is between the chair and the bed. The magazine is on the bed. The trainers are under the bed.

VILLAGE LIFE

Materials: One copy of worksheet A and worksheet B per pair of students and one copy of the picture per pair of students

Put Ss into AA and BB pairs and distribute the worksheets and pictures. Tell them to match their sentences to scenes A–D in the picture. Do an example to demonstrate the activity. Monitor and check. Then direct Ss to the map and ask them to complete the conversations by writing the questions or answers. Do an example. Accept any answers that are grammatically correct. Monitor and check while Ss are completing the conversations.

Change Ss into AB pairs. Ss read the printed original versions to each other so they can check if their questions and responses are the same as the original. Note other versions may also be correct.

Get feedback. Ss act out the conversations, first looking at the text, but saying the sentences while looking at their partner. As they become more confident they can practise without looking at the text.

> **Possible answers:**
> C Where is the swimming pool? There is a swimming pool next to the school.
> B Is there a payphone? Yes, the payphone is opposite the bakery.
> A Excuse me. Where's the pharmacy? It's between the restaurant and the bakery.
> D Where is the bus stop? The bus stop is in front of the school.

UNIT 9

OPINIONS

Materials: One worksheet per student

Distribute the worksheets. Review the categories and ensure Ss understand the vocabulary. Elicit a few examples of films they like or dislike. Tell Ss to think of one example for each category. Monitor and check.

Present and drill the question *What do you think of …?* Practise the pronunciation, paying attention to linking and weak forms. Ss ask you two or three questions first. Answer the questions with reference to the Useful language box: *I like it. I think it's really good.*

Put Ss into AB pairs to ask each other their opinions. Feedback with the whole class and ask Ss to tell you some of the opinions their partners expressed.

DO YOU LIKE …?

Materials: One worksheet per student

Put Ss into groups of six. Distribute the worksheets. Tell Ss to complete a sentence in each section so that two sentences are true for them. Tell them not to write their name at this stage. Don't let anybody see what they have written. When they have written their answer they pass the paper to the left and complete the next sentences and so on until all the sentences have been completed. Monitor for correct spelling of the verb + *-ing* form and ensure the nouns are without the definite article.

Redistribute the completed sheets and tell Ss to ask *yes/no* questions to find who wrote each statement. When they find a person who fits the sentence, they write their name. Remind Ss of the structure: *Do you like …?* and the short answers: *No, not at all*; *No, not really*; *Yes, I do*; *Yes, sometimes*; *Yes, a lot.*

MONEY, MONEY, MONEY!

Materials: One worksheet per student

Put Ss into pairs and distribute the worksheets. Pre-teach *You don't have any money left*. Ss read the situations and record each other's answers. When Ss have finished, they count how many as or bs their partner got and read the key at the bottom of the page.

Ask a few Ss if they or their partner spend too much or too little and/or if they agree with the key. Remind Ss not to take the quiz too seriously!

WHAT WOULD YOU LIKE?

Materials: One set of cards per pair of students

First, demonstrate the language by making an offer, e.g. *Would you like my pen?* and eliciting a response. Write the offer and response on the board. Put Ss into AB pairs and distribute the cards (cards A to Ss A and cards B to Ss B). Tell Ss that five of their cards are offers or requests and five of them are responses. Ss separate the cards into offers or requests and answers before they start the task. Monitor and check (in **weaker classes** put Ss into AA and BB pairs to sort the cards). A must not see B's cards and B must not see A's cards. Ss take it in turns to say an offer or request and their partner has to respond with the correct answer. When they find a fit, they put the two cards together face up. When all the cards have been paired off, check answers as a class.

As an extension, Ss can play a game of pelmanism. Ss place the cards face down in a column. In pairs, they take it in turns to turn over one card at a time and try to find a match. If they guess

correctly, they have another turn until they have a mismatch. If the two cards don't match, they must be left in exactly the same place face down. This activity can be used before or instead of the above activity or at a later date.

Answers:
Would you like something to eat? No, thanks. I'm not hungry.
Which colour would you like? I'd like the green one, please.
Can I help you? Yes, please. I'd like to buy a camera.
What would the teacher like for her birthday? I don't know. Maybe a CD. She loves classical music.
Excuse me. Where's the children's clothes section? It's on the third floor.
I'd like to buy a football. The sports department is on the second floor.
Would you like some tea or coffee? Coffee, please. Black coffee.
What would you like to eat? Let me think. Yes! I'd like the sushi, please.
Can I have some fruit, please? Yes, of course. Which would you prefer? A banana or an apple?
Would you like some wrapping paper for the present? No, thanks. I think it's a waste of money.

UNIT 10

RULES

Materials: One set of cards per group of students

Put Ss into groups of three and distribute the cards. Ss write the words to identify the places. Do the first one (a restaurant) as an example. Check answers as a class.

Review the verbs which could be used for each picture, e.g. restaurant: *eat, have lunch/dinner*. Model a sentence for one of the pictures, e.g. *You can have dinner here. You can't play a game here.* Write on the board *You can … here. You can't … here.* Get Ss to place the cards face down on the table. Ss take it in turns to take a card and make two sentences (make sure the other Ss don't see the card). For example: *You can swim here. You can't run here.* The Ss in the group have to guess the place. The person who guesses correctly wins the card. The person with the most cards is the winner.

Ask different groups who won and give whole class feedback on errors/good language used.

Answers: a restaurant, a cinema, a disco, a park, a library, a swimming pool, a train, a school, a clothes shop, a hospital, an English class, a plane

GOOD INTENTIONS

Materials: One worksheet per student

Write on the board: *We are going to talk about our intentions.* Highlight *be going to* and ask if it refers to present, future or past actions. Distribute the worksheets. Check Ss remember the vocabulary. Ss complete the second column so that it is true for them. Give an example of a positive and negative response to show that they use a tick for *yes* and a cross for *no*. Ss write their own last question.

Put Ss into pairs. They take turns to exchange information and make a short note of their partner's answer. If their partner answers *yes*, they ask the follow-up question. Do an example before they start the activity.

Elicit some answers from different pairs. Model the third person singular for *be going to* and write it on the board. Put Ss into groups of four and ask them to share three or four of their partner's answers with their group.

As an extension, get Ss to find common answers in their group and report them to the class using *My friends and I are going to …*

COLLOCATIONS

Materials: One worksheet per student

Put Ss into pairs and distribute the worksheets. Tell Ss that three of the phrases in each group are correct and one is incorrect. Go through the example. Ss cross out the incorrect collocations. Check answers as a class.

Tell Ss to ask each other about their abilities and to record their partner's answers with a tick for *yes* and a cross for *no*. Model the question and short answers on the board using the first question as an example. Get Ss to ask you two or three of the questions. Ss continue in pairs. Monitor and encourage Ss to use: *Yes, I can. No, I can't.*

Elicit some answers from different pairs and give whole class feedback on errors/good language used. Highlight that the third person singular form doesn't use *s*. Then Ss work with a new partner and share three or four of the most interesting answers with their new partner.

As an extension, invite Ss to tell the class what their partner and they have in common *We can both swim*. Highlight the position of *both* after *can*.

SEE YOU LATER, ALLIGATOR!

Materials: One role card per student

You could put the title of the activity *See you later, alligator!* on the board and ask Ss if it is saying *hello* or *goodbye*. Model the phrase to elicit why we say *alligator* (because it rhymes with *later* and it is amusing). If the word *alligator* is unfamiliar, you could show a picture of one.

Ask Ss to stand in two lines facing each other. Give each student a role card. Those with card A start a conversation according to the information on the card with the person opposite them. The Ss with card B have to respond. Model with a student. Clap your hands after about one minute (depending on how the Ss are getting on, it could be longer or shorter). The student with card B has to choose one of the responses as a way of saying *Goodbye*. Sometimes either response will be appropriate and sometimes only one of them. The Ss then exchange cards with their partner. The student at the end of one of the lines comes to the front of that line so that Ss change partners.

The process can be continued until the Ss are back facing their first partner, until all the cards have been used by each student, or at your discretion.

Invite Ss to say which conversation they had was the most interesting or amusing.

Pearson Education Limited
Edinburgh Gate
Harlow
Essex CM20 2JE
England
and Associated Companies throughout the world.

www.pearsonelt.com

First published 2016
Second impression 2016
ISBN: 978-1-292-12017-1
Printed in Slovakia by Neografia
Illustrated by Eric@kja-artists

Acknowledgements
The publisher would like to thank the following for their kind permission to reproduce
their photographs:

(Key: b-bottom; c-centre; l-left; r-right; t-top)

123RF.com: 174 (woman and dog); **Digital Vision:** 173t; **Pearson Education Ltd:**
Gareth Boden 152; **Shutterstock.com:** Andresr 174b, Deklofenak 173c, Dotshock
173bl, Iakov Filimonov 174t, Maridav 174 (man running), Pressmaster 173br

All other images © Pearson Education

Every effort has been made to trace the copyright holders and we apologise
in advance for any unintentional omissions. We would be pleased to insert the
appropriate acknowledgement in any subsequent edition of this publication.